SAI BABA OF SHIRDI
a Unique Saint

SAI BABA OF SHIRDI
A Unique Saint

By
M. V. KAMATH
and
V. B. KHER

JAICO PUBLISHING HOUSE
Mumbai • Delhi • Bangalore
Kolkata • Hyderabad • Chennai

SAI BABA OF SHIRDI
ISBN 81-7224-030-9

First Jaico Impression : 1991
Second Jaico Impression : 1991
Tenth Jaico Impression : 1998
Eleventh Jaico Impression : 1999
Twelfth Revised Edition : 2000
Thirteenth Jaico Impression : 2001
Fourteenth Jaico Impression : 2002

Published by:
Jaico Publishing House
121, Mahatma Gandhi Road
Mumbai - 400 023.

Printed by:
Snehesh Printers,
320-A, Shah & Nahar Ind. Estate A-1,
Dhanraj Mills Compound, Sitaram Jadhav Marg,
Lower Parel, Mumbai - 400 013.

The lives of men like Sai Baba are the very proof of the truth that the Master blesses the seed which he sows in us, and time does the rest, in accordance with the pupil's worthiness of His Grace. Not all the seeds fall on stony ground. Some give a rich harvest. Therein lies hope for the future of erring mankind.

Adapted from 'In Days of Great Peace'
—*by Mouni Sadhu*

THE WORDS OF SAI BABA

An attempt is made here to recount in brief some of Baba's sayings and advice to his devotees and whoever listened to him:

God is and there is nothing higher than Him. He is Perfect, Infinite and Eternal. He is omnipresent, omnipotent and omniscient. He is the Creator, Sustainer and Destroyer. Surrender voluntarily and totally to His will. Not a blade of grass moves without His will. Trust in Him and do the right. Let the inner light (enlightened conscience) guide all your actions.

Perform your duty conscientiously and with detachment regarding yourself not as the doer but only as an instrument in His hands.

Surrender the fruit of action to Him so that action will not harm or bind you. Let your love and compassion flow to all creatures of God. Do not engage in controversy. Words (of others) cannot harm you. Bear with others patiently. Accept your lot cheerfully without comparing yourself with others. Do not speak ill of others. Do not give tit for tat for each is answerable for his own actions.

Do not remain idle but engage yourself in some useful activity. Read the sacred texts. Be moderate in your food and recreation.
Know that God Is.
Do not believe that God is not.
God is Omnipresent.
God's Name is eternal.
This universe is all a *leela* of God.
God is the Lord and the Master. There is no other Truth.
His ways are unique, inscrutable and mysterious.
There is no one higher than God. How He will protect and sustain is known only to Him.
He is the Protector of the Poor.
He is very compassionate. We falter in our faith in Him and lack sufficient patience.

Herculean effort is necessary for the attainment of God.
Who says He is out of reach? He is there in the tabernacle of our heart, nearer to us than the fingernail to the finger.
Without unflinching faith and patience, you will not see Him.
One who has both these will undoubtedly find Him.
It needs insight to recognise God.
His will be done. He will show the way and all your heart's desires will be fulfilled.
Be content with your lot.
Light dispels darkness.
Do good and God will bless you. Do evil and you will displease Him.

I am everywhere and in all places and the whole world is with Me.
I move everywhere and anywhere.
I pervade the universe. I am both the visible and the invisible.
I am unborn, eternal and everlasting.
Do good and offer it to God and He will bless you.
God protects the righteous.
Those who sow nettles expect me to give them corn. How can I do so?
I am God's slave.
Even the learned are confused. Then what of us? Listen and be silent.
One who has received His Grace is silent, but he who falls from grace talks too much. His Grace must be earned by merit.

Even though my children be thousands of miles away, I call them to me. I am happy when they come. I enjoy their company and thrive on it. I have to care for my children night and day because I am accountable to God for them.

The *udi* will be most useful for my devotees. Preserve it carefully. My men will throng to Shirdi like ants. Fear not. I am always with you. Men may come and men may go. What do we have to do with it? How does it concern us?

My blessings will go with him who is firm in his faith and strong in his devotion, wherever he may be. I take care of my men, generation after generation, birth after birth.

I do not babble or whisper any *mantra* in the ear. Our traditions are different.

I have to go thousands of miles to take care of men.
All are equal in my eyes. Men of all sorts, good and bad, come to my *durbar*. I have to care for them equally.

All kinds of people, good, bad, wicked, vicious come to my court. Why indulge in gossip about them?
I am merciful to all.
I am not beholden to anyone except God.
People inhabit villages and towns. I live in the jungle.
People have a roof over their head. I have none.
I have single-horse carriage (the vital breath, *praana*) but it carries ten to twelve men (organs).
I will slay the four bodies (the gross body, the subtle body, the causal body and the *mahakaran*).

Remember my words even when I am no more. My bones will assure you from my *samadhi*. It will communicate with you. It will respond to him who surrenders to it.

Do not think I am dead and gone. You will hear me from my *samadhi* and I shall guide you.
Do not engage in controversy. For every ten words you hear, speak only one word, if that is necessary.
You need neither praise nor blame others.
If you injure others' feelings, I suffer.
I feel disgusted when you quarrel with others.
Remove the fangs of the serpent before he can harm you. Let us see to what length he goes.
He who lays hands on the devotee of God will suffer for it.
Members in a family are bound to have differences. But do not quarrel.
One who means well, will do well.
If you do good, good will follow.
Great is the reward of virtue. The vicious suffer.
If wealth is used judiciously, it will be beneficial.
Wholesome food will bring good health. A man of restraint is better than a man of indulgence.
Do not covet others' wealth.

Are we born merely for sensual pleasures? The mind is tricky for it ensnares us in temptation. Restrain it to attain peace.

See how selfish people are. When it suits them, they leave their companion. So attach yourself to one who will never forsake you. (There is no such companion except the *sadguru*. Love the creation but keep company with the *sadguru* for his companionship will conduce to your welfare).

Once you entrust yourself to the hands of the *sadguru*, you do not have to worry.
I never forsake any one who relies on me.
One has to accept the *guru* wholeheartedly and not mechanically.
Why grieve for the loss of a son? Everyone has to die one day. In this mortal world, death is inevitable.
Whatever may happen, one should remain steadfast and watch everything with detachment.
One who is enlightened will not make a noise about it.
You cannot escape what is pre-ordained. You may face it with a groan or a smile. Only that choice is yours.
Earth will return to earth, and the soul will fly away.
Practice before you preach.

It is *rinanubandh* (ties of previous birth) which brings human beings, birds and animals to each other. Therefore, do not shoo away anyone, even the meekest.

Be hospitable to anyone who comes to you. Give water to the thirsty, bread to the hungry, clothing to the naked and shelter to the homeless and God will bless you.

Whatever you give me will come back to you redoubled. If you sow then only can you reap.

Who can really satisfy the desires of another? For the more you give, the more the desires grow. It is only the Lord and the Master who can give that which is everlasting.

Who can compare with all his munificence to what the Almighty alone can give? The Lord Himself waits anxiously for the devotees to partake of the treasure that He offers, but instead people come to me asking for worldly things. When I try to tell them this, nobody pays attention to what I say or listens to me. The coffers are overflowing with treasure, but no one will make the effort to pick up the treasure.

I have now grown weary of peoples' request for wealth, wife, child. No one wants the treasure that I have. I will wait awhile and one day quietly leave.

Prof. Narke states in *Devotees' Experiences of Sai Baba:*

A saint should not be judged by the character of those that gather around him. Prostitutes, women-hunters, avaricious people and sinners of all sorts came to him (Sai Baba) with a view mostly to gain material advantage. But when they failed to improve themselves and, on the other hand, fell into evil ways, he let them suffer. His justice was severe. He said: "You have to sever your own child from the umbilical cord when it falls athwart the womb."

CONTENTS

FOREWORD

I am overwhelmed by the request to contribute a Foreword to this book on the life of the saint, Sai Baba of Shirdi. The word 'Foreword' is hardly appropriate for what I intend to say. The book is a complete account of the life of piety and miracles of a well-known saint and what I say is not likely to add to the information already contained in it.

In Urdu books, sometimes the words *pesh lafz* (literally a foreword) is used but sometimes the expression *sukhanhai-guftani* (usually some words to say) is used. I am writing this 'foreword' in the latter sense. It is difficult to add anything to the account given by the two authors. It is a complete picture of a life of piety, full of miracles and devotion, written with inspiration and care. I for one had not the good fortune to meet the saint but I often get the *prasad* through devotees who visit Shirdi.

There can be no doubt that saints possess enormous spiritual powers which they receive from the Almighty. Our Holy Book, the Quran, mentions *aulia* (holy men) and charges us to 'fear' (respect) them. I have had some experiences as in Nagpur we had the well-known saint Tajuddin Baba whose *maqbara* was got constructed by the Nizam through my father. He sent me a half-smoked *bidi* through one of his disciples who lived in the jungles of Mornala near Chhindwara. I was then 10 years old and I was told by the messenger that would be my pen and I would rideanelephant. This incident is described in full by me in my memoirs *My Own Boswell*. From that day I have never looked back and have gone from strength to strength. Another saint, Meher Baba, who kept silence for many years, also blessed me. Once, in Delhi, I presided over a meeting where devotees expressed their devotion to him. He was not present and it seems that a tape of the proceedings was sent to him. I had spoken and, as was his practice, he wrote a message of one line. It read: "You will remember me on my birthday." I could not understand it till his birthday came on the 25th of February and I was sworn in as the Chief Justice of India. I remembered his message and him. Often on the 25th of February, I remember him and I am reminded of him on that day in some way or the other.

My father was City Magistrate in Nagpur and Tajuddin Baba was lodged in the Mental Hospital as he used to throw stones at the vast crowds which pestered him. Raja Bhosle then gave him shelter in his palace.

Once, my father in the company of one Azam Shah, went to Shakardara where he was residing in a hut. My father related that he was seated with his eyes shut in a *maraqba* (contemplation of God). He gave my father and Raja Azam Shah two pieces of chappati lying there. My father ate it but Azam Shah threw his piece behind his own back. Tajuddin Baba did not see this as his back was towards them, but he said: "You do not eat the bread given by a faquir. Now you won't be able to eat your own bread." From that day he had to be force-fed every day at every meal! No wonder the Quran said: "Be afraid."

In Delhi there is a *maqbara* of Hazrat Nijamuddin (R.A.). There is another of Hazrat Chisti at Agra and of Gharib Nawaz Mohiuddin at Ajmer. At the last place I prayed that I might stand first in the examination and I did. I had never stood first before that time.

I hope the readers of this biography will read it with devotion and belief and the respect due to it. They will cover themselves with divine grace. I commend it to them and thank the authors for the privilege of giving me a chance to pay this homage.

Before I leave this, I may recount an incident connected with the saint. As a Judge of the Supreme Court, I tried the case of a Muslim butcher who made an appearance as the saint whom he resembled and collected money from the public. He would appear in an alcove dressed like him and the people would prostrate and give money. He was caught and received jail punishment. When his case came before me, a plea was made that the sentence should be reduced. I said of all the people a Muslim butcher should do this was outrageous and I was sorry that the Whipping Act had been repealed as the proper punishment was not jail but whipping!

Bombay
16 May 1991

M. Hidayatullah
(Former Chief Justice &
Vice President of India)

ABOUT THE AUTHORS

M. V. Kamath, who retired as the Editor of the Illustrated Weekly of India in 1981, is a senior and prolific columnist. Starting his career in journalism in 1946 as a reporter in the Free Press Journal, he soon became the editor of Free Press Bulletin and Bharat Jyoti. He has been the correspondent at the United Nations for the Press Trust of India and for the Times of India in Bonn, Paris and Washington D.C. He has covered every important international gathering between 1953 and 1978. Kamath was the President of Bombay Union of Journalists in 1953 and also a founder member of the Foreign Correspondents' Association, Washington D.C. An author of over twenty books on a variety of subjects, his literary works include among others, *Makings of A Millionaire*, Jaico Book of Baby Names*, The Philosophy of Death And Dying, The Pursuit of Excellence, Professional Journalism, B. G. Kher— The Gentleman Premier,* etc.

V. B. Kher is a retired personnel executive. A keen student of Gandhism, he has edited for Navjivan Trust, Ahmedabad, seven collections of Mahatma Gandhi's writings in fifteen volumes including a collection of Gandhi's search for the Supreme in three volumes. He was a trustee of Shri Sai Baba Sansthan of Shirdi from 1984 to 1989 and also the Chairman of its sub-committee for publications. His research papers and articles on Sai Baba have been published in Shri Sai Leela and other periodicals and journals.

*Published by Jaico

The present samadhi and marble idol of Sai Baba in his famous sitting posture with his right leg over the left, in the Samadhi mandir at Shirdi.

The original Shri Sai Baba's Samadhi as it looked then around 1920.

Reproduction of a photograph taken of Sai Baba against his wishes.

This photograph is Shri Sai Baba's Kuladaivat
Mandir–Hanuman of Panchbavadi Pathri.

Hanuman idol in the mandir
of Panchbavadi Pathri.

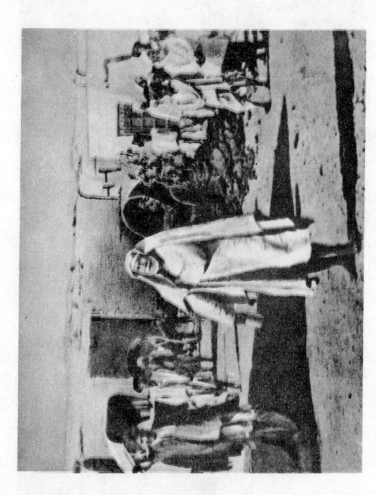

Although Sai Baba, could have got a feast everyday from the villagers, he still preferred 'bhiksha' or begging. He is seen here in the market place with his begging bowl.

This photograph taken somewhere around 1912 shows Sai Baba on his evening round. To his left is Gopalrao Buti and Nanasaheb Numonkar is on his right.

The birth place of Sai Baba of Pathri.

Chand Patil's mud house at Dhup village, now in ruins.

Marble idol of Sai Baba proposed to be installed at Sai Baba Mandir in Dhup Village.

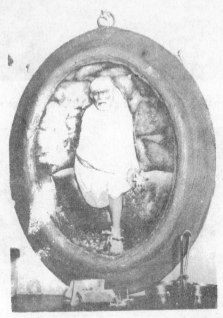

This image of Sai Baba was unexpectedly delivered at the residence of G.R. Dabholkar, author of Shri Sai Satcharit during Holi festival in 1917 in accordance with Dabholkar's dream.

Open ground on the banks of Yelganga river at Dhup Village where Sai Baba camped.

Swami Sai Sharan Anand —one of the most faithful and true disciples of Sai Baba.

"Bane Mia", the fakir of Aurangabad (see pg. 291)

A view of the Sai Shrine at Pathri.

The Sanctum Sanctorum.

The Bronze Moorti of Sai Baba.

A tunnel with old arches and connecting passages discovered below the sanctum sanctorum at Sai Mandir, Pathri while digging.

Dhyan-Mandir in the basement of Sai Mandir, Pathri.

Marble Padukas of Shri Sai Samarth.

Mr. & Mrs. K.V. Ramani lighting the lamp at the inauguration of Pathri Sai Shrine.

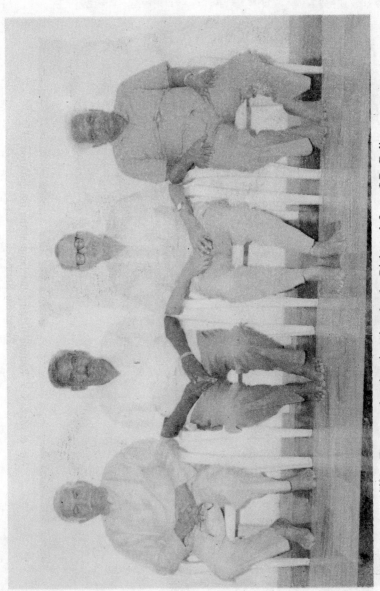

Trustees who played a pivotal role. Right to left are S.R. Dali, V. B. Kher, D.V. Chandhari and S.S. Dhanu.

ADDENDUM

Since the publication of the fifth impression of our biography of Sai Baba of Shirdi, further evidence has come into our possession which lends weight to the proposition put forward therein that Sai Baba was born at Pathri in Marathwada. In the opening paragraph of the foreword contributed by Hari Sitaram Dikshit, the foremost devotee of Sai Baba, to *Shri Sai-Sat-Charita* (Marathi) by Govind Raghunath Dabholkar, it is stated that once a gentleman from Pathri had come to Shirdi for Sai Baba's darshan. Then Sai Baba had enquired with him about some leading citizens of Pathri by name, whom Sai Baba had obviously known. Dinkarrao Chaudhari of Pathri had earlier spoken to Vishwas Kher about the descendant of Sai Baba in Pathri whom he had personally seen and about whom his father Vasudeorao had told him. In April 1993 when Kher visited Pathri, Dinkarrao Chaudhari gave him the further information that Sai Baba had enquired about the well-being of his grandfather Shamrao (Vasudeorao's father) and his younger brother Balerao by name with that visitor. Shamrao Chaudhari and his younger brother Balerao were contemporaries of Sai Baba. The above piece of information had been given to Dinkarrao by his father Vasudeorao.

It is now known that the Bhusaris of Pathri were Shukla Yajurvedi Brahmins of the Madhyandin branch and their *gotra* was Kaushik. *Ramraksha Stotra* was revealed by way of initiation to Kaushik Rishi in his dream. The *kuladaivat* of Bhusaris was Hanuman. Fourteen days before his *mahasamadhi*, Sai Baba had got two *parayanas* of Rama Vijay done in his presence. One of the chief festivals of Shirdi is held on Rama Navami day since 1911.

Mention may be made here of an interesting development which took place recently. At a function held on Thursday, October 13, 1994 — Vijaya Dashmi day — *bhoomi-pujan* at the site of Sai Baba's birth place in Pathri, which Kher had purchased in June 1978 from Prof. R. M. Bhusari in the name of Shri Sai Smarak Samiti, was performed by the President of Pathri Nagar Parishad and a temple is now under construction.

INTRODUCTION

My biography of Mr. Bal Gangadhar Kher, first Chief Minister of the old composite state of Bombay, was hardly out when Mr. Kher's son, Vishwas, a devotee of Sai Baba, asked me to do a biography of Baba as well.

I told him that I was incompetent to do so for two reasons: One, I was not a plighted devotee of Baba and anything that I might write might give offence to his thousands of devotees and I had no intention of hurting them in any way. Two, I had no means of doing the necessary research and I had no intention of doing a poor job, at least as I saw it. So why take on an assignment that was fraught with misunderstandings? Vishwas Kher has been working on Sai Baba's life himself for many years and he said I could leave the research part to him. As for any judgement that I might make on Baba and his work, he said he would trust my *bona fides.* So I undertook the job.

Vishwas Kher did all the translation from Marathi and Gujarati sources, that are not available to the English reader. I have closely followed his translation without sitting on judgement on the statements made. My aim has been, as far as is humanly possible, to present Sai Baba as his devotees and admirers saw him. The credulous are welcome to be critical of the body of this work, but I am satisfied that I have been faithful to the material available to me.

Having completed the assignment, I wonder at the phenomenon called Sai Baba. In all of India's history, there has never been another like him. He is not a conventional saint. He wrote no critique of the Gita or the Upanishads or any other holy work. He made no pretensions to scholarship. He performed 'miracles' but in no manner of means to impress anyone, devotee or otherwise. He built no institution, wrote no tome, initiated no disciple to take over from him. Sai Baba in every way remains unique. I am not qualified to interpret him or assess him. Nor was it my intention to do so in writing this book. Plainly, I wrote it because I was asked to and because Vishwas Kher had faith in me. I wrote it also because

Sai Baba intrigued me. I wanted to understand the phenomenon of Shirdi. For that, indeed, is what he is: a phenomenon.
Many of the things that he said and did must be viewed in the
context of his times. While he is relevant for all times, he could
only speak and function in the context of his work theatre—
Shirdi—and the ethos of his period, the second half of the
nineteenth century. The same thing, of course, can be said
about Christ or the Buddha or Mohammad.

This, obviously, is not the first book written about Sai Baba.
There are several, some of them either badly written or poorly
presented. Baba's devotees will no doubt fall back on them. I
present   this work with great hesitation. The sceptics will
express their reservations, the true devotees may question my
credentials. They have the right to do so. But I dedicate this to
Sai Baba himself to whom I am thankful for grace received. In a
true sense this is a joint work. We claim no credit; only the
imperfections are our own.

M. V. KAMATH

CHAPTER 1

THE ETERNAL *SAKSHI*

If you take a taxi in Bombay, very often the chances are that you would notice on the dash board of the vehicle the framed picture of an elderly man, a white kerchief tied tightly round his head, sitting with his right leg over the left, barefoot and with a quizzical look in his eyes.

The left hand is resting gently on the ankle of the right foot, its thumb, fore-finger and middle finger wide open. It is the picture of man at peace with himself. He is wearing a cloak that obviously has seen better days. The right sleeve is torn at the shoulder but was obviously treated as a matter of no consequence. The man has large ears, a somewhat flat nose and thick lips. A cropped beard gives him the appearance of a holy man. Which he is, if you bother to ask the cabbie about him. His name? Sai Baba.

Some taxis display a picture of Christ. Some others of Ganesha, the Remover of All Obstacles. But Sai Baba probably appeals to more than most, though this is only a theory. What is unquestioned is the fact that those who believe in Sai Baba believe in him with passionate intensity.

About him a devotee wrote:
Thou art eternal, how shall I praise you,
Thou art eternal, how shall I bow to you,
Numerous voices have got exhausted in
Their attempt to sing praises of you.
Therefore, I only salute you with eight-fold
Prostrations, Shri Sainatha.

And another wrote:
I, your servant,
Uninstructed and ignorant
Know nothing,
But to call you.

The world outside has probably heard very little about this man who was born some time between 1838 A.D. and 1842 A.D.— nobody knows exactly when—and passed away on 15 October 1918 on the auspicious day of Vijayadashami. To say that he 'passed away' would not be exactly correct. It would be more accurate to say that on that day he took his *Mahasamadhi* and attained *Nirvana.*

Like the Buddha, he lived to a ripe old age. So wondrous was his life that legends have grown round him. He wrought miracles. He was the friend of his devotees then as he remains friend of his devotees now. The extent of peoples' faith in him is best expressed in a foreword written by Dr. P. M. Mody, retired Principal, Shamaldas College, Bhavnagar, to a book by Swami Sai Sharan Anand. "Baba's help," wrote Dr. Mody, "comes to him who merely seeks His help sincerely. Though there cannot be degrees of sincerity, yet Baba's response to the devotee's call for help is as eager, as ardent and as urgent as the devotee's call itself. Once a man is Baba's devotee, He looks after him, life after life, till he qualifies himself for Eternal Peace under His care."

The statement is unqualified. It has no ifs and buts. The key word is sincerity in belief. Surrender yourself to Sai Baba and He will never let you down is a belief in devotees so deep-rooted that it admits of no argument. He lived in a small village called Shirdi most of his life and Shirdi is as closely associated with Him as Ayodhya is with Shri Ram or Mathura with Shri Krishna or Jerusalem with Christ. Or the Prophet Mohammad with Mecca. People from all walks of life came to see him at his humble abode. Shirdi is a somewhat bustling place today, given, alas, to commercialism, but at the turn of the century and even earlier it was no more than a cluster of houses. To visit Sai Baba when he was alive was a kind of pilgrimage under-taken with determination and commitment—and, what is more, devotion. Sai Baba had no formal education. What kind of 'education' could he possibly have had between 1838 and 1858? There were, of course, temple *pathashalas* and Muslim institutions where Persian, Arabic and Urdu would have been taught, but that is hardly taken into account by those who look up to Him as "knowledge incarnate", "the joyful Brahman, the giver of highest happiness, free from dualities, ether-like, known by the four *Maha Vakyas,* the sole, the pure and the permanent".

Sai Baba did not put down anything in writing. His sayings, of course, have been recorded by his many followers. He was a saint, but a unique one as most saints anyway are. But his uniqueness lies in the fact that he does not follow any of the patterns set by saints in Maharashtra like Nivritti, Jnandev, Sopan, Muktabai, Eknath, Namdeo and Tukaram or by the *dasas* of Karnataka who were to be collectively known as the *dasa koota.* There has never been anyone like Sai Baba either before Him or after. This, in some ways, is a measure of the Man.

It is doubtful whether during his long life, he ever wanted truly to teach. One of his devotees, Mani Sahukar has written: "Sai Baba often hinted that he had not come to teach, but to awaken. He sought to bring about this awakening through the impact of his love. Through centuries men have read volumes of philosophy, but so long as there is no integration between thought and practice, *sadhakas* do not grow in spiritual Grace. Sai Baba, therefore, simplified his teachings, so that *bhaktas* may get down to the sheer practice of spiritual *sadhana".*

Any comparison between Sai Baba and any philosopher, prophet or saint can only be odious and none should even be attempted. But he spoke with the total assurance of one who had no doubts about his powers. He could say, like Christ: "Come unto me!". Indeed, the assurances that he gave to his devotees include that plain, commanding statement. As reported by his devotees they are:

★ Know that my Spirit is immortal. Know this for yourself.
★ My eye is ever on those who love me.
★ Whatever you do, wherever you may be, ever bear this in mind that I am always aware of everything you do.
★ If one meditates on me, repeats my name, and sings about my deeds—he is transformed and his karma is destroyed. I stay by his side always.
★ In whatever faith men worship me, even so do I render to them.

★ If one perpetually thinks of me, and makes me his sole refuge, I become his debtor and will give my life to save him.

★ I am the bond slave of my devotee. I love devotion. He who withdraws his heart from the world and loves me is my true lover and he merges in *Me* like a river in the sea.

★ If you make me the sole object of your thoughts and aims, you will gain *paramatma*.

★ Look up to me and I will look after you. Not vain is my promise that I shall ever lighten your burden.

★ Trust in the *sadguru* fully. This is the only *sadhana*. *Sadguru* is all the gods.

★ Repeat my name. Seek refuge in me. But to know who I am, practise *sravana* and *manana*.

★ Though I be no more in flesh and blood, I shall ever protect my devotees. I shall be with you the moment you think of me.

Sai Baba could say, with the total assurance of one who knew he was an *avatar,* that He was God, he was Mahalaxmi, that he was Vithoba of Pandharpur, that he was Ganapaty, Remover of all Obstacles, Dattatreya, Laxmi Narayana and Maruti. He would say: "Why go for Ganga elsewhere? Hold your palm at my feet—here flows the Ganga".

Those who knew him, who saw him in flesh and blood, who watched him day and night, felt his power of love in their very bones. He would tell his devotees: "I am not the body or the senses. I am the eternal *sakshi* (Witness).

Sai Baba did not mince his words. He was categorical. It was left to his devotees to accept him or reject him. They accepted him. He was their last refuge and shelter, their strength and their very staff of life. Had he not told them: "If you cast your burden on me, I will bear it!" "If you seek my help and guidance I will immediately give it to you". "There shall be no want in the house of my devotee". Once he said, cryptically: "I give people what they want, in the hope that they will begin to want what *I* want to give them!". The implication is that he knew what was good for his devotees. But would *they* know that?

But it was not to his devotees alone that he was the source of succour. There is the strange story recounted by a Londoner,

Arthur Osborne, born in London, educated at Christ Church, Oxford who lived in India for several years and was deeply interested in spirituality and has written a small book entitled *The Incredible Sai Baba.*

In Calcutta, where Osborne lived for four years, he had an old lady as his neighbour, a Miss Dutton. Miss Dutton had been a nun in her younger days but had been given absolution of her vows by the Pope because she found that she could not, in all honesty, accept the rigours of a convent. While her application for release from her vows was pending, she was much too pre-occupied with her internal conflicts to give much thought to her future. It was only when she was about to leave the convent that it dawned on her how hopeless her future was. She was practically penniless. She was well over middle age, without a profession and with scarcely any near relative. The nearest to a relative was a nephew living in far-away Calcutta. The situation was daunting.

One day, while sitting in her cell immersed in the deepest gloom, she suddenly felt the presence of a man in front of her. He was tall, barefoot and looked like a holy man. Miss Dutton's surprise could well be imagined. There was no way any man could have got entry into her cell. In any event he did not look like any holy man in the West. As she told Osborne, he looked at her with compassion and told her: "Do not worry so much. Everything will be all right when you go to Calcutta." Then, Miss Dutton reported, the holy man said: "Now won't you give me a gift?" Miss Dutton told him she had no money with her. "Oh yes, you have," said the holy man, "you have thirty-five rupees in a box in the cupboard up there!" Miss Dutton had completely forgotten about that little treasure, but taken aback by the holy man's prescience, she went to the cupboard, took out the money but, when she turned round, the holy man was nowhere to be seen! He had disappeared as unaccountably as he had come!

She never mentioned this incident to anybody. She left the convent and went to stay with her nephew who turned out to be a kind and loving nephew indeed. Her worries about her future had been taken care of.

Osborne wondered who this holy man—Miss Dutton had called him a *fakir*—could be, but felt instinctively that may be it was Sai Baba. To test out his hunch, he told Miss Dutton: "I will show you a picture of the *fakir*". He went back to his apartment and fetched the picture of Sai Baba to show to Miss Dutton. She took one good look at the picture and exclaimed with unfeigned surprise: "Yes, that is he! He had even the same white kerchief on his head!"

The point, writes Osborne is that Miss Dutton had never heard of Sai Baba before!

2

At this point, it may be worthwhile to give a chronology of events in the life of Sai Baba, so that the reader may follow the course of the saint's life chronologically.

★ He was born between the years 1838 A.D. to 1842 A.D. at a place called Pathri, in Marathwada, in the Nizam's Dominion.

★ He left home at the tender age of eight in the company of a Sufi fakir between 1846 to 1850 A.D.

★ He came to Paithan—Aurangabad terrain and wandered all over Marathwada and may be elsewhere from the age of eight to the age of twenty five to thirty.

★ He stayed in Aurangabad and instructed a *fakir* by the name of Bade Baba, *alias* Fakir Baba *alias* Fakir Peer Mohammad Yasinmia for twelve years.

★ He first came to Shirdi between 1868 to 1872 A.D. with Chand Patil of Dhupkhed, who came for the marriage of his sister with Hamid, the son of Aminbhai of Shirdi. He then stayed as a guest of Aminbhai. After a few days, Sai Baba and Chand Patil left for Aurangabad. Two months later, however, Sai Baba returned alone to Shirdi.

★ When Sai Baba arrived in Shirdi, he was a young man between 25 and 30 years, tempered by the discipline of *tapas* and austerity.

★ On his arrival in Shirdi, Sai Baba toyed with the idea of taking up his residence in Rahata (west of Shirdi) and enquired of Chandrabhan Seth, who had business interests in

Marathwada for a suitable place. Seth offered him Pawar-wada, owned by the Sand family but Sai Baba finally decided in favour of Shirdi for his abode.

★ At Shirdi, he initially stayed on the outskirts of the village in Babul forest for about 2½ years, then under a neem tree for four to five years and finally shifted to the dilapidated masjid. During this period he had no proper food. He received the sustenance he needed from Bayajabai, mother of one Tatya Kote Patil and the wife of one Narayan Teli.

★ When Sai Baba came to Shirdi there were two *sadhus* already in residence in the village: One was Devidas who had come to Shirdi twelve years earlier as a lad of ten or eleven years and had put up in the local Maruti Temple and the other was Janakidas Gosavi of the Mahanubhava Sect.

★ Gangagir Bua of Puntambe, a well-known holy person of the Vaishnava Sect would often visit Shirdi. He told Nanasaheb Dengle of Nimgaon (a village east of Shirdi) that Sai Baba is a *chintamani* (a gem from *swarga* supposed to yield its possessor everything wanted). On hearing that, it is said, Nanasaheb Dengle went to the babul forest and bowed at Sai Baba's feet.

★ Sai Baba would go for alms every morning and stand before the houses of Bayajabai Kote Patil, Patilbua Gondkar, Nandram Savairam, Appaji Kote and Narayan Teli, who would dutifully give him food.

★ Bidkar Maharaj, a disciple of Akkalkot Swami met Sai Baba in 1873.

★ By 1878 Mhalsapati, Appa Kulkarni, Jagle and Nanasaheb Dengle of Nimgaon accepted Sai Baba as their mentor and *sadguru*. Nanasaheb Dengle knew many government officials as he moved in government circles.

★ By 1878-79 Sai Baba was getting recognition. Chidambar Keshav Gadgil, Mamlatdar, was the first important government official to consider Sai Baba as a *jnani* and call on him.

★ Madhavrao Deshpande, who was for some time a teacher in the primary school at Shirdi also accepted Sai Baba as his *sadguru* around 1881.

★ Anandnath Maharaj, a disciple of Akkalkot Swami went to see Sai Baba in 1885. He told the villagers that Sai Baba was a genuine diamond lying on a dung heap!

★ In 1885 Sai Baba went into a trance for three whole days.

★ The villagers considered Sai Baba as a mad fakir, but for all that they would go to him with trifling health problems like fever or a stomach ache in the belief that he could cure them. At first Baba would give them some indigenous remedies, but later started giving them *udi* from his *dhuni*.

★ Abdul, servitor of *fakir* Aminuddin of Nanded came to Shirdi in 1889. Around 1890 Sai Baba went to stay at Rahata with Javar Ali for some time.

★ In 1890 Shankarrao Raghunath Deshpande, *alias* Nanasaheb Nimonkar (Inamdar of Nimon) first met Sai Baba at the Maruti Temple at Rahata. A year later, Narayan Govind, *alias* Nanasaheb Chandorkar, personal assistant to the Collector of Ahmednagar, first met Sai Baba.

★ Ganpat Dattatreya Sahasrabuddhe, *alias* Das Gunu, met Sai Baba, in 1892. That same year Sai Baba wrought the miracle of lighting lamps, in the masjid where he was staying, with water instead of oil.

★ In 1894 Muslims, led by one Kazi of Sangamner, opposed the worship of Sai Baba in the mosque.

★ It was decided to hold the Annual Urs Fair in Shirdi from 1896-97 on Ram Navami Day.

★ In 1904 Rao Bahadur Hari Vinayak Sathe, Deputy Collector, widowed in 1900 went to Shirdi to take Sai Baba's advice whether he should remarry as advised by his friends. He erected the first *wada* in 1908 known as Sathewada, where devotees could stay in Shirdi.

★ Sai Baba performs one more miracle in 1904. It is known as the Jamner Incident when Ramgirbua *alias* Bapugir went at the instance of Sai Baba with his *arati* and *udi* for the smooth and safe delivery of Nanasaheb Chandorkar's daughter Minatai Ganesh Kuvalekar and Sai Baba drove the tonga dressed in the garb of a Garhwali Rajput from Jalgaon to Jamner where both the driver and the tonga suddenly vanished!

★ Balasaheb Bhate, Mamledar of Kopargaon (1904-1909) an atheist, went out of curiosity to see Sai Baba, became his devotee, prematurely retired from service and settled in Shirdi.

★ Congregational worship of Sai Baba commenced in 1909.

★ Bade Baba, *alias* Fakir Baba *alias* Fakir Peer Mohammad Yasinmia whom Sai Baba had instructed for twelve years came to stay in Shirdi in 1909.

★ Sai Baba who used to speak in simple, direct language began to speak in parables and symbology from 1910 as the number of his visitors began to grow in volume.

★ Hari Sitaram Dikshit, a prominent solicitor and M.L.C. first met Sai Baba in 1909.

★ The foundation of Dikshitwada was laid on 10 February, 1910. The construction was completed in April 1911.

★ From 10 February 1910 onwards, *Shej arati* (night arati) of Sai Baba every alternate day was started.

★ Govind Raghunath *alias* Annasaheb Dabholkar, author of *Shri Sai Satcharita* first met Sai Baba in 1910.

★ Ganesh Shrikrishna *alias* Dadasaheb Khaparde, Member, Central Legislative Assembly and author of *Shirdi Diary* first visited Shirdi on 5th December, 1910.

★ Vaman Prangovind Patel, later known as Swami Sai Sharan Anand first met Sai Baba on 11th December, 1911.

★ Lokamanya Bal Gangadhar Tilak visited Shirdi on 19th May, 1917 to see Sai Baba.

★ Sai Baba entered into *mahasamaadhi* on 15th October, 1918.

If we presume that Sai Baba was born in 1838 then, in 1918 when he passed away, he was eighty years old. It was a long life by any standards and there is hardly anyone around who might have seen him in flesh and blood. But the power of his name persists. The number of his devotees keeps increasing. Shirdi has become a place of pilgrimage much as Bethlehem or Jerusalem, Banaras or Rameshwar. His devotees come from all castes, creeds, religions and communities. All of them share one thing in common: faith in Sai Baba. Some will staunchly attest to the Sai Baba's blessings. They go to Shirdi seeking his help or to give their thanks for what they had earlier received or just to pray. It is one of the most remarkable phenomenon of our times.

3

"The birth and parentage of Sai Baba are wrapped in mystery. We have not come across a single person who has any direct knowledge of them." This is according to B.V. Narasimha Swamiji, founder-President of the All India Sai Samaj, who is the author of a four volume biography of Sai Baba, first written in 1955, some 37 years after the passing away of the saint.

Twenty one years after the Swamiji admitted to ignorance of Sai Baba's place of birth and parentage, an article appeared in the January 1976 issue of *Shri Sai Leela* by Vishwas B. Kher who claimed to have done some research on the subject, and has objectively looked into all the statements made about Sai Baba's ancestry.

Sai Baba himself discouraged questions on his parentage and if asked, mostly gave mystifying answers. On one occasion he said that his father was *Purusha* and his mother, *Maya* or *Prakriti* and that, in consequence, he came into the world (of phenomena) as the *dehi* (body). At another time he said that his *Mama* (uncle) had brought him to Shirdi from Aurangabad. On yet another occasion, quoted by Narasimha Swamiji, he revealed very late in his life to Mhalsapati that his parents were brahmins of Pathri, in the Nizam's Dominion. Mhalsapati was well-known in his time as a person of unimpeachable integrity and truthfulness.

There have been nevertheless, voices of dissent. S.B. Dhumal, an ardent devotee of Sai Baba and a leading lawyer of Nasik, in reply to a question put to him by a District Magistrate, an Englishman, has been quoted as saying: "Sai Baba is neither a Hindu nor a Muslim but above both." H.S. Dikshit, a solicitor and yet another selfless devotee of Sai Baba has said in his foreword to *Shri Sai Satcharita:* "There is no reliable information as to where he (Sai Baba) was born or who were his parents. But it can be stated authoritatively that he must have had links with the Nizam's State...In his conversation there were often references to places like Sailu, Jalna, Manavat, Pathri, Parbhani, Aurangabad, Bhir and Bedar. Once a visitor from Pathri came to Shirdi for Sai Baba's *darshan*. Sai Baba gathering information about conditions in Pathri, enquired with him about many leading citizens of Pathri. This suggests that he had special knowledge of Pathri,but *it cannot be stated with certainty* that he was born in Pathri.It cannot be said also definitely whether Sai Baba was a brahmin or Muslim by birth.''

An interesting story is recounted by Arthur Osborne in this regard, that doesn't throw much light on Sai Baba's ancestry even though it confirms his determined refusal not to reveal it, or to treat it of no consequence.

A thief had been arrested with stolen jewellery and brought before the magistrate's court in the neighbouring town of Dhulia. It would have been a simple case, had not the thief brought forward the embarrassing plea that the jewels found in his possession had been given to him by Sai Baba and that with equal nonchalance he distributed them on the same day. In this particular case, however, it was known for sure that the jewellery with the thief was stolen property. The only approach open to prove this beyond a shadow of doubt was to issue a summons on Sai Baba to attend the magistrate's court. So, in due course, the summons was sent.

"Baba, here's a summons for you," said the police constable charged with delivering the summons, hesitatingly and timidly.

Sai Baba looked at him and then roared: "Take that rag of paper and chuck it in the fire, one of you!"

One of them did.

Naturally such flouting of authority was not a matter to be overlooked and a warrant had to be issued for his arrest.

The same unhappy constable now came forward and said: "They've sent a warrant this time, Baba. Will you please come to Dhulia with me?"

With a torrent of oaths, Baba ordered him to throw the warrant into the latrine. Some of the more influential devotees gathered together to talk over what could be done. They drew up a petition to the effect that one who was worshipped by a vast following ought not to be summoned to a law court and praying that a commissioner should be sent to Shirdi instead to take down Baba's evidence. This was conceded and one Nana Joshi, a first class magistrate was despatched.

12

"What is your name?" he began, as the procedure dictated.
"They call me Sai Baba," replied Baba.
"Your father's name?"
"Also Sai Baba".
"Your Guru's name?"
"Venkusa".
"Creed or religion?"
"Kabir".
"Caste or community?"
"Parvardigar"
"Age?"
"Lakhs of years."

It would have been hilarious were it not for the fact that Sai Baba was entirely serious. Sai Baba was not his given name. Nobody knew it. By giving his father's name also as Sai Baba, Baba was implying that he was no longer conditioned by human parentage. Kabir was a great poet-saint of the late 15th and early 16th century who had both Hindu and Muslim followers. By naming him as his Guru Sai Baba was implying that he stood above formal religions as well. "Parvardigar" denotes the Highest Divinity. It is recognised that one who has attained that state is above the four castes. As for his age to be counted in lakhs of years Baba was clearly telling his interlocutor that he was beyond the limitations of time as well.

The Magistrate then switched on to another tack.
"Will you solemnly affirm that what you are going to say is the truth and nothing but the truth?"
"The truth," Baba briefly affirmed.
"Do you know the accused?"
"Yes, I know him."

That at least sounded satisfactory but only until Sai Baba added: "I know every one!"
"He says that he is your devotee and has stayed with you. Is that so?"
"Yes, all are with me. All are mine."

That was an affirmation of the universality of the Divine Man but hardly of any use as evidence.
"Did you give him some jewels as alleged by him?"

"Yes, I gave them to him."

But before the Magistrate could take that down, Sai Baba added: "Who gives what? And to whom?"

"If you gave him the jewels how did you get possession of them?"

"Everything is mine."

The magistrate now lost his patience. He was asking mundane questions and he was getting metaphysical answers.

"Baba," he said in exasperation, "this is a serious charge of theft. The man says that you delivered the jewels to him."

Baba, too, lost his patience. "What is all this about? What the devil have I to do with it?" And he strode away.

Luckily for all concerned the question of getting more evidence from Sai Baba did not arise because it was discovered that the accused had not been to Shirdi at all at the time of the theft.

But Sai Baba had not been asked to sign any document. He never signed any document. He had no name! People called him Sai Baba. It was not his given name. It was as if he had no past. He only lived in the present.

In many ways Sai Baba was like the Sufis of old and the coversation he had with the Magistrate reminded many of the *dervish* (Sufi mendicant) who fell into the river Tigris. Seeing that he could not swim, a man on the brink called out: "Shall I summon someone to help you?"
"No" said the *dervish.*
"Then do you wish to be drowned?"
"No".
"What, then, do you wish?"

The *dervish* replied: "God's will be done! What have I to do with wishing?" But to come back to the research of Vishwas B. Kher. Kher mentions several stories concerning Sai Baba's origins but lays no claim to certitude. One relates to Vaman Prangovind Patel, born in 1889 and passed away in 1982 who, in his later years became a *sanyasi* and assumed the name of

Swami Sai Sharan Anand. Swami Sai Sharan Anand was emphatic that Sai Baba was a brahmin and that the latter would get annoyed if someone disputed the fact. In 1912, the Swami, in his pre-sanyas days had gone to Shirdi wondering whether he should have brought his father then suffering from dropsy with him to get a cure at Sai Baba's hands.

When Sai Baba saw the Swami the first question that he asked was: "Why didn't you bring your father along with you?"

Sai Baba had read the Swami's mind.

But a thought racing in the Swami's mind was whether his father would come to see some one who looked more like a Muslim fakir. Again, the Swami has recorded, Sai Baba read his mind and quickly asked: "Am I not a brahmin?"

So far as Swami Sai Sharan Anand was concerned, that clinched the argument. Kher has recorded another story.

The story goes that there was a Yajurvedi Deshastha brahmin in Pathri who had three sons. Sai Baba was the eldest. When Sai Baba was five years old, a Fakir came to the brahmin and said to him: "Give me my own." The brahmin replied: "Everything I have is yours." Thereupon the Fakir asked for the eldest son and took him away. He reappeared after four years and with the consent of the brahmin again took away the boy for three more years. The point to this is that from the age of twelve to eighteen nothing is known of Sai Baba. He was seen under the neem tree at Shirdi when he was 19. Kher himself decided on his own to check out several stories and went to Pathri some time in 1975 to conduct inquiries. Pathri which was in early medieval times known as Parthapur (named after Partha or Arjuna, the hero of the Mahabharat and the third of the Pandavas) is situated 80 to 85 miles southeast of Devagiri (Daulatabad) and about 2 miles south-west from the confluence of Vidarbha (Mangala) and Godavari rivers. It was once a part of the Vidarbha Kingdom which was ruled by the Yadavas of Devagiri and was a seat of mathematical learning. As Pathri was a part of the Yadava kingdom, its history is also part of the history of Devagiri or Daulatabad. Its Kulkarni *vatan* was held by a family which rose to great eminence in the days of the

Bahmanis. But now let Kher who went to Pathri with his wife, tell his story.

"Pathri is about 10 miles from Manwat Road railway station on the Manmad-Secunderabad Line. When we (Mr and Mrs Kher) decided in the summer of 1975 to camp at Pathri for a few days to get authentic information about Sai Baba's early life, Manwat had come into prominence because of a series of murders which showed diabolical planning. By June we had established links with a family at Pathri who were to be our hosts.

"Our host was none other than Shri Dinkarrao Vasudeo Chaudhuri, a scion of the famous Chaudhuri family of Pathri, with a long history behind him. Shri Dinkarrao is a progressive farmer and a lawyer. He was a perfect host. He regarded us and our mission as his own and rendered us all assistance.

"There are a number of branches of Chaudhari family at Pathri, but most of them live in the fortress which dates back to about the 14th century. Shri Dinkarrao has now constructed a house just outside the fortress, where he lives. It was our abode during our stay in Pathri. On 21 June, in the evening, when we sat in the open verandah overlooking the fortress, in an informal conversation, Dinkarrao made a point which caught my attention. He said that years ago, his late father Vasudevrao had pointed to one Bhau Bhusari in Pathri and remarked at the sad plight of the family descendant of Sai Baba! The next day some Muslim clients of Dinkarrao had come for consultation and they had stated that according to their information, Sai Baba was born in a brahmin family of Pathri, but was taken away by a Wali when a child and what happened later was not known.

"This also furnished another clue. So we promptly commenced with the task of making a complete list of all brahmin families of Pathri. Brahmins of Pathri are all Deshastha brahmins, either Rigvedi or Yajurvedi. There are no brahmins of any other sect or sub-caste.

"This list was made while we made the rounds of Pathri going from door to door, interviewing all old residents, brahmins or otherwise. In discussions, it came to light that the family deity (kula devata) of most of the brahmin families in Pathri is either goddess Renuka of Mahur or Yogeshwari of Ambejogai. There was only one exception. That is Bhusari family. Their family deity is Hanuman of Kumbharbavadi, on the outskirts of Pathri. So our minds began working frantically. We recalled the great devotion and respect Sai Baba had for Ram and Hanuman and wondered whether our search had at last borne fruit. With alacrity we made our way to Vaishnav Galli, where we examined with reverence the ruins of the Bhusari house (House No 4-438-61) for it is no longer standing and proceeded silently to pay our respects to Hanuman of Panchbaavadi. There is also a 'Lendi' river skirting Pathri and we were reminded of 'Lendi Baug' at Shirdi.

"The association between the two is obvious. Similarity between the Marathi spoken by Sai Baba and the language spoken in Marathwada generally, was also noticeable. We were most impressed by the fact that the language spoken by all the stratas of society, from the lowest to the highest, is uniform and there is no difference even in the speech of the elite.

"The population of Pathri is about 10,000. In its appearance, Pathri is as it must have been centuries back. Progress has hardly touched it. Only during the last few years electricity has been brought to its doorstep, and link established with the other parts through the State Transport Service. But otherwise life is placid, as it must have been in the olden days.

"My mind was carried back to the time when Sai Baba was born. No exact date or year of his birth is known. For that matter, there are also differences of opinion about the time of his arrival in Shirdi....

"Can we then say with reasonable certainty that Sai Baba was born in the Bhusari family? Excepting the information given by a prominent citizen of Pathri to his son on the subject, is there any circumstantial evidence? To collect this, if possible, I decided to pursue the matter further.

"I opened correspondence with Prof. Raghunath Maharudra Bhusari who owns the house of Bhusaris at Pathri. He was professor of Marathi at Osmania University and later Principal of a government college, from which post he retired sixteen years ago and settled down in Hyderabad.

"He was born in Pathri and went to Parbhani, a district town, for further education. After matriculating, he moved to Hyderabad from where he graduated in Arts, standing third in the University. This won him a scholarship for M.A. at the Calcutta University, which he completed successfully. Prof. Bhusari states that Konerdada was their first known ancestor. No information is available about the next two generations, but the family tree of three later generations is known which goes thus:

Parashuram

Raghupati   Dada   Haribhau   Ambadas   Balwant

Maharudra   Parashurambapu

Raghunath   Bhau

Prof. Bhusari further states that he had learnt from his grand-mother, when he was a child that Haribhau, Ambadas and Balwant had all left Pathri for good. While Haribhau might have gone in search of God, the latter two had gone to seek their fortune. In the next generation, Parashurambapu had also taken *sanyas* at Manjartha (in Bhir district), which is situated at the confluence of Godavari and Sindhufena. His son Bhau who was not much educated, and died in poverty, was the person about whose condition Shri Vasudevrao Chaudhuri had an occasion to speak to his son Dinkarrao. This is sufficient evidence to confirm that the Bhusari family has produced persons of higher urges and impulses. Could it not be that Shri Haribhau Bhusari was Sai Baba? I wonder! "The theory evinced above is probable. I discussed it jointly with an experienced lawyer and a reputed historian and both of them agreed that it could be so. I do not wish to add anything further....."

18

Some time after Mr. Kher wrote this article, the Bhusari house property at Pathri was bought by a committee of local people who formed themselves into "Shri Sai Smarak Mandir Samiti" and erected a shade where *arati* of Shri Sai Baba is performed every Thursday.

4

Sai Baba's devotees are divided on the issue of whether he was born a Hindu or a Muslim. It was noted during Baba's life time that his ears were pierced, a common Hindu custom, but not prevalent among Muslims. It has been said that he was not circumcised, again a sure indication that he could not have been born to a Muslim family. But Baba dressed like a *fakir* and lived in an old tumble-down mosque which was strangely enough called by him as Dwarkamai. Baba also kept a sacred fire going in the mosque and devotees were allowed to worship him with fanfare, including blowing of conches and ringing of bells. Then again, in the courtyard outside the mosque was a *tulsi brindaban.* Ram Navami was celebrated in the courtyard in which Sai Baba joyfully participated. At the same time he had no objection to the local Muslims taking out a sandal procession on the same day.

He was unorthodox in his food habits and is said to have partaken meat and fish in the company of fellow *fakirs.* The name of Allah Malik was constantly on the tip of his tongue. Yet he appeared in the garb of Rama, Krishna, Ganesh, Shiva, Hanuman or the guru of the devotee concerned.

What, then, did it make him; a Hindu or a Muslim?

He had, apparently, intimate knowledge of the Gita as his exposition to Nanasaheb Chandorkar demonstrated. But he also recited the first chapter of Koran in the company of Muslims. He was known to be fluent in many languages, but none knew how and when he acquired such mastery.

Doubts about his knowledge were expelled after his celebrated exposition of the Gita to Nanasaheb Chandorkar became known.

The story is recounted by Arthur Osborne who does not, however, identify Nanasaheb Chandorkar but writes about "a devotee" who was busy massaging Baba's legs and feet while chanting to himself in a soft undertone. What was he muttering, Baba wanted to know.

"A sanskrit verse," said the devotee, not suspecting that Sai Baba could know the scriptures.

"Sanskrit verse? What verse?" Baba demanded.

"Oh," said the devotee, "it is something from the Gita."

"Say it to me aloud."

So the devotee started reciting the verse from the Gita, Chapter IV:34 that says: "Know that by means of prostration, enquiry and service, the *jnanis* (the enlightened) who have realized the Truth will teach you *jnana* (knowledge)."

"Do you understand this, Nana?" Baba asked him.

"Yes."

"Then tell me what it means."

Nana gave a free rendering in Marathi, but Sai Baba was not satisfied.

He told Nana: "I don't want a paraphrase. I want the strict grammatical meaning, with case, mood and tense."

Nana gave a literal translation, wondering the while whether Baba knew anything of Sanskrit grammar. He found out, soon enough.

"In *tatviddhi,* what does *tat* stand for?" Baba asked him.

"Jnana (knowledge)," replied Nana.

"What knowledge? Knowledge of what?"

"The knowledge referred to in the previous stanza."

"What does *pranipat* mean?"

"Prostration."

"And *pat*?"

"The same."

"If they meant the same, would Vyasa have added two unnecessary syllables?"

"I don't see any difference between them," Nana admitted.

Baba left that for a while and passed on to the next point.

"What does *prasna* mean?"

"Asking questions."

"And *pariprasna?*"

"The same."

"Then if they both mean the same was Vyasa off his head to use the longer."

"I don't see any difference," ruefully admitted Nana.

Now Baba went on another tack.

"Next point. What does *seva* mean?"

"Service, such as I am doing now in massaging your feet."

"Nothing more?"

"I don't see what more it can mean."

Baba said, "We'll leave that, too. Next point. Krishna tells Arjuna to get *jnana* from *jnanis.* Wasn't Krishna himself a *jnani?*"

"Yes."

"Then why does he send Arjuna to others instead of giving him *jnana* himself?"

"I don't know," said Nana, by now thoroughly befuddled.

"Wasn't Arjuna a *jiva* (being) and therefore an emanation of *chaitanya* (universal consciousness)," Baba persisted in asking.

"Yes."

"Then how can Knowledge be given to what is already an emanation of Consciousness or Knowledge?"

That again stumped Nana.

Sai Baba thereafter proceeded to interpret the verse to mean that it is not *jnana* but *ajnana* (non-knowledge or ignorance) that the Guru gives—an entirely new interpretation, of a verse that, to Nana, had thitherto seemed pretty clear and straight forward.

So Nana said: "Baba, would you mind explaining this to me still more?"

Baba did so. He said: "The verse tells us how a disciple is to approach his Guru in order to attain Realization. He must completely surrender body, mind, soul and possessions to the guru. That is the prostration referred to in the verse. The enquiry must be a constant quest for Truth, not questions asked out of mere curiosity or for any wrong motive such as to trap the guru. The motive must be pure desire for spiritual progress and realization. Then the service is not mere physical service such as massaging. For it to be effective there must be no idea that you are free to give or withhold service; you must feel that your body no longer belongs to you since you have surrendered it to the guru and it exists only to do him service."

Then followed what can only be described as a Socratic dialogue between Baba and Nana on the nature of a guru's ignorance.

"Isn't Brahma pure knowledge or being?"

"Yes."

"And everything else non-being or ignorance (non-knowledge)?"

"Yes."

"Don't the scriptures declare that Brahma is beyond the range of speech or mind?"

"Yes."

"Then the speech of the guru is not Brahma or knowledge?"

"No."

"Then you admit that what the guru says is not Knowledge but ignorance?"

"It seems so."

"Then the guru's instruction is simply a piece of ignorance used to remove the disciple's ignorance, just as we use a thorn to remove another thorn from the foot, shall we say?"

"I suppose so."

"The disciple is a *jiva* (being) whose essential nature is Knowledge, isn't he?"

"Yes."

"Then there is obviously no need to give him Knowledge but simply to remove the veil of ignorance that hides the existent Knowledge. This, of course, is not to be done at one stroke since the disciple is immersed in age-old ignorance and needs repeated instruction, perhaps through life after life. And what is the nature of this instruction through speech about what is beyond speech? Isn't it like removing a cover? Ignorance conceals the pre-existent Knowledge just as water plants cover over the surface of a pond. Clear away the plants and you have the water. You don't have to create it; it is already there. Or take another example: a cataract grows on the eye and prevents a man from seeing. Remove the cataract and he sees. Ignorance is the cataract. The universe is the efflorescence of the indescribable Maya, which is ignorance; yet ignorance is needed to illuminate and dissolve this ignorance."

Baba continued in the same vein.

"Divine Knowledge is to be realized, not taught. Prostration, enquiry and service are the methods by which to obtain the Grace of the Guru. It is an illusion to suppose that phenomena are real. That is the screen of ignorance which hides Knowledge. Tear it off and Brahma or Knowledge will shine forth.

"Ignorance is the seed of *samsara* (birth and death). Put the medicine of the guru's grace on the eye and the screen of Maya lifts, leaving only *jnana. Jnana* is not something to be attained, it is eternal and self-existent. On the other hand, ignorance has a cause and an end. The root of it is the idea that the devotee is a separate being from God. Remove this and what remains is *jnana.*"

And finally, Baba added:

"Now the question why Krishna referred Arjuna to other gurus instead of giving him *jnana* himself. Did Krishna consider other *jnanis* separate from himself or their teaching different from his? No. So their teaching is his and there is no difference." Sai Baba then told Nana to bring the Bhagavad Gita and read a chapter before him each day and he would expound it. He did so—and no record was kept.

Osborne, in his short biography of Baba having stated all this adds:

"A book whose vigour and profundity one can imagine from the above fragment simply evaporated and was never written down. Even this, however, is enough to show that when Sai Baba did talk theory it was the purest *Advaita* (non-dualism), that is the very essence of spiritual teaching."

Samuel Johnson had a Boswell. Mahatma Gandhi had a Mahadev Desai. Ramakrishna Paramahamsa had a Mahendra Nath Gupta. Sai Baba was recorded very seldom, but when he was, he comes through as a man with a razor-sharp mind that puts a Socrates in the shade.

23

5

Two questions arise. One is Baba's deep and profound insight into intricate issues of philosophy. Was this a result of a long and arduous apprenticeship to a guru or was Baba a born *jnani,* an aspect of divinity that needs no tutoring? The other is: how come he could be at home both in Vedic and Islamic scriptures?

If the answer is that Sai Baba is no ordinary mortal but is Godhead Himself, we need go no further. The question of his having a guru at a very young age does not arise. We can also dismiss stories about his being born in a brahmin family and being given to a wandering *fakir* by a father who sounds rather heartless. Even for that time and period it sounds rather farfetched that a fakir could go to a brahmin family and imperiously demand the gift of the eldest son by saying, in effect: "Give me what is mine."

The extremist among Sai Baba's devotees hold, more in faith than with solid evidence, that he was self-born, a modern *swayambhu* from which follows that he needed no instruction whether from a vedic teacher or from a mullah.

Faith knows no reason and the point need not be belaboured. Faith transcends reason but then, within the limited jurisdiction of reason, faith has to reckon with it. The belief, in theory, that he was born of no woman and was self-created conflicts with common sense, let alone reason. An *avatar* does not necessarily have to be self-born. Both Shri Krishna and Shri Rama had parents, despite the fact that they are admitted into the pantheon of the ten *avatars.* Apart from that, Sai Baba himself is once said to have spoken thus:

"My mother was greatly rejoicing that she had got a son—me. I was, for my part, wondering at her conduct. When did she beget me? Was I begotten at all? Have I not been already in existence? Why is she rejoicing over this?"

In a manner of speaking, Baba was talking in spiritual terms, in terms of pure *advaita. The soul was indestructible—na hanyate na hanyamaane*—there might be a body that envelops him,

but his soul was unborn, eternal. That being so, where was the
question of being born? How can something that is eternal be
born? But for all that Baba was admitting that he had a mother,
that he was born to her and therefore, taking him at his own
words, Baba was not self-born but was mortal like the rest of us.

There is not much controversy about the birth place of Sai
Baba. However about Sai Baba's guru there are two important
theories that have been forwarded. One is by Das Ganu
Maharaj, and the other by Swami Sai Sharan Anand.

It is the proposition of Das Ganu Maharaj that Shri Gopalrao
Deshmukh of Sailu near Pathri was the guru of Sai Baba. But
who is Gopalrao Deshmukh?

Gopalrao obtained the *jahagir* of Jintur Paragana in the
Nizam's state. He has been described as a man of "humble
disposition," kind and merciful. He is also reported to have had
the power to cure diseases and possessed the eight *maha-
siddhis.**

Understandably, people flocked to him to have his *darshan*. In
course of time, Sailu, near Pathri where Gopalrao lived became

---

* There are twenty three *siddhis* in all which have been graded into three
classes: Great, Medium and Small. The great *siddhis* are eight in number and
are very difficult to acquire. Only he who is established in the Self, who has lost
all consciousness of his body and of the sense of 'I' and 'mine', such a one can
acquire them. The Medium *siddhis* are ten in number and a seeker with divine
qualities and who is pure at heart gets them. The small *siddhis* are five and he
whose heart is purified through devotion or yoga can acquire them.

The Great *siddhis* are as follows:
1. *Anima:* the reduction of one's form to an atom, assuming the subtle and
   invisible state.
2. *Mahima* or *garima:* to make the body weighty or heavy.
3. *Laghima:* to make the body excessively light and beyond what is natural.
4. *Prapti:* to acquire objects of sense pertaining to the respective organs.
5. *Praakaashya:* to see and know invisible things in the other worlds.
6. *Ishitaa:* to stimulate bodies and creatures; to have control over natural
   forces.
7. *Vashitaa:* to have supremacy over the senses.
8. *Yatkaamastadavasyati:* literally, the power to obtain joys in the three
   worlds effortlessly, by mere willing. However, this power leads to the state
   of the highest bliss through ending of all desires.

a place of pilgrimage like Pandharpur or Dwarka. There are legends about Gopalrao. Once, it is said, he went to Ahmedabad to visit the *dargah* (mausoleum) of Suvagshah. As he approached it, the tomb "perspired with joy" and burst into speech. Gopalrao heard it say: *"Salaam alekum!* Oh, you great sage Ramanand, in your present birth truly you have not forgotten me, even though you have changed your form and appear before me as a *Deshmukh* in the Moglai (Nizam's Dominion). From the town of Manwat, ten miles from Sailu, your former disciple, Kabir, will come to you as a child of a fakir." The caretaker of the mausoleum who also heard the words was dumbstruck and wondered wherefrom the voice came.

As prophesied, the wife of the *fakir* of Manwat came to Sailu to see Gopalrao. She was an oldish woman in her fifties and was clad in rags. She wore green bangles on her wrists and carried on her back a boy of five who, Gopalrao guessed, was Kabir in his previous birth. The poor woman was stopped at the gate by the guards who would not allow her to enter the courtyard. So gently putting the boy down she sent a prayer to Gopalrao with folded hands. "Oh virtuous one, you are the protector of the weak and my sole refuge. It is over a month since my husband

---

The Medium *siddhis* are:

1. *Anoormimattvam:* The six modifications of being *(oormis)*, namely, hunger, thirst, grief or sorrow *(soka)*, infatuation (stupefaction), delusion/ confusion of mind *(moha)*, old age and death do not disagree with and affect injuriously, the body.
2. *Doorshravan:* to hear, sitting at one place, speech from however distant a place.
3. *Doordarshan:* to see, sitting at one place, events and things in all the three worlds.
4. *Manojava:* the body travels at the speed of mind to any place one desires.
5. *Kaamaroopa:* to assume at once any form one desires.
6. *Parakaayapravesh:* to enter into another's body, dead or alive, temporarily leaving one's own body.
7. *Swachchandamrutyu:* to die at one's own will, death having no control over one.
8. *Sahakridanudarshanam:* to see the sports of gods in heaven and have capacity and prowess to participate in it.
9. *Yathaasamkalpa samsiddhi:* to attain whatever is desired.
10. *Ajnaapratihataagatih:* whereby one's command and movement have no obstruction.

departed telling me before his death to go to you for shelter.''

The prayer reached Gopalrao's ears and he came out. He warmly welcomed the woman and her child, saying that long he had been waiting for them. The boy immediately recognised his master in a previous birth and sought refuge in him. Both the woman and her child were provided shelter by Gopalrao. As the days passed, the master grew more and more fond of the boy, arousing the jealousy and envy of Gopalrao's household who planned to harm him. When the boy was twelve, his mother died. One day, at dusk, both the master and his disciple disappeared into the dense forest nearby and did not return home for four months to the anxiety and fear of the household. Gopalrao was no ordinary citizen. He was the *deshmukh* and his long absence was a matter of concern even to the government. Some thought that the boy's dead mother may have cast a spell over Gopalrao for ''how else could one account for the fascination of a saintly brahmin for a Muslim boy?'' Some among the household resolved to enter the forest in search of their master. After some search they found him in a clearance, fast asleep. The boy was sitting by his side. One of the group hurled a brick at the boy but it missed him and hit the master on his head. Actually, goes the legend, the brick did not hit the master but was suspended in mid-air because of his *siddhi* power. The brick stayed in the air for an hour but its force had to terminate somewhere and so Gopalrao offered his head as the target to save the boy and was consequently grievously injured.

Gopalrao quickly bandaged his bleeding wound but the person who had hurled the brick fell down dead. The brick itself was gifted by Gopalrao to the boy who, in later life, came to be

---

The small *siddhis* are:
1. *Trikaalajnatvam:* the knowledge of the past, present and future.
2. *Advandvam:* to be beyond the control of the duality of pleasure-pain, cold-heat, soft-very hard.
3. *Parachittaadyabhijnataa:* to tell about another's dream or to know his mind.
4. *Pratishtambah:* to stop the effect of fire, wind, water, weapon, poison and the sun.
5. *Aparaajayah:* not being defeated by anybody; being victorious everywhere.

known as Sai Baba, with the instruction that when in turn the brick broke it would be a sign that Sai Baba's own time was up.

Meanwhile, at the sight of the bleeding head-wound suffered by Gopalrao, the boy burst into tears and craved the forgiveness of his master. But Gopalrao told him: "Do not regret. My time has come. I have only a very few days left before I pass on. But, today I wish to transfer all my powers to you. Go to the cowherd out there and get me the milk of a black cow. There is not a moment to lose."

The boy hurried to the cowherd and asked for milk from a black cow. But the only cow in the herd which was black was barren and could yield no milk. When this was reported back to Gopalrao he personally went over and touched the cow's udders whereupon milk freely flowed! The master gathered three seers of creamy milk and handed it over to the boy. He then removed the piece of cloth covering his head and tied it round the boy's head, saying: "I have given you my entire wealth. The three seers of milk given to you are *karma*, *bhakti* and *jnana*. I have sanctified the milk, hence drink up all of it and you will get *jnana*".

The boy bowed to his master and did as he was told. At that instant his vision appeared as if imbued with God.

The master now caressed the boy and said: "Remember that you were Kabir in your former birth and I was Ramananda. For your sake I had given up the ascetic life in this birth. I tell you now, remain celibate, be of tranquil mind and regard God and the world as One. Make your abode in one place and raise those who surrender to you. My mission is over. I will proceed to Sailu and enter *mahasamadhi*".

Gopalrao told the men who had come to the forest with evil intent, not to hide their faces from him. He also told them that he had transferred all his *siddhi* powers to the boy and as proof thereof, he ordered the boy to revive the dead man. The boy thereupon bowed to his master, took the dust off his feet and applied it to the dead man's forehead. Immediately he came to life!

Stunned by this, the men carried Gopalrao and his disciple to Sailu in a procession. Next day the master assembled all his disciples and addressing them said: "Today I will abandon my earthly life and at that place a peepul tree will rise. If you dig a little near the tree, you will find a purple, four-armed idol of Venkatesha. Raise a temple on that spot." He then read aloud the eighteen chapters of the Gita and asked all assembled to utter the name of Narayana. Then he gave the loin cloth he had to the boy for making a *kafni* and signalled to him to leave at once. Thrice he repeated the name of God and left his physical frame.

The story then goes on to tell how, in a forest, the boy chanced to meet a Muslim, Chandbhai by name who had come in search of his lost mare and helped him find it. Whereupon, Chandbhai invited the boy to his home and after some days left with him for Shirdi to attend a marriage.

In this story, Sai Baba's guru is Gopalrao Keshavrao Deshmukh alias Babasaheb Subhedar.

The story, however, is too fanciful to be believed. It is generally known that Baba had some link with Sailu. Sailu, incidentally, is a big town in Parbhani district and is on the Manmad-Secunderabad railway line. It is only one station before Manwat Road, the distance between the two being nine miles. Pathri and Sailu are separated by a distance of 15 miles and a motorable road now connects the two. Half a mile away from Sailu station is a Venkatesh Mandir with a tall *gopuram* over the *sanctum sanctorum*. The *samadhi* of Gopalrao Keshavrao Deshmukh stands just behind the temple which has an idol of Vishnu (Venkatesh) about 0.91 metre high. The temple was built around 1808. That was a good thirty years before Sai Baba was born.

The theory propagated by Das Ganu and championed by B.V. Narasimhaswami has even found a place in the official record. The Gazetteer of India, Maharashtra State, Parbhani district while describing the *samadhi* of Gopalrao states that the people believe him to be the guru of Sai Baba.

But how reliable is Das Ganu? He rarely saw Sai Baba. And

even when he was in Shirdi, Baba would not allow him to stay long with him. On his own admission Das Ganu got from Baba very few autobiographical details. Das Ganu, it is true, visited Sailu around the turn of the century (1901) when he was a havildar in the Police Department, to make enquiries. He does not name the persons he contacted in Sailu and how he gathered details. He has not specified any villagers as having told him anything in particular nor did Das Ganu establish any contacts with such of Gopalrao's disciples or descendants who might have been living around that time. And many of the assertions made by Das Ganu have been challenged by people who knew him.

Another fact has been unearthed. Gopalrao, according to one of his sixth generation descendants, Laxmikant Malharrao Subhedar, Advocate whom Vishwas B. Kher interviewed, was born in 1715 and died in 1802. Subhedar produced documentary evidence in support of his statement. If that be so, how could Sai Baba born around 1838 have been his disciple?

Swami Sai Sharan Anand has quoted Sai Baba as telling him that his guru was Roshan Sha Mia. Writes the Swami: "I marked that Baba was from time to time also using the word 'Roshan.' He used that word particularly when he told some parables. Then he used that word in the sense of 'light' meaning Knowledge as opposed to ignorance... Applying the same sense to Roshan in 'Roshan Shah' the name Roshan Shah would mean the Lord of Knowledge, the Universal Soul..."

"We do not however mean to suggest by the above interpretations that a person of the name Roshan Shah Mia did not exist... Accordingly, one should not be astonished if we say that Roshan Shah spoken of by Baba did exist in flesh and blood and Baba strenuously served him for over twelve years. It seems that Roshan Shah thereafter cast off his mortal coil and Baba buried him under or near the neem tree at present found in or near Navalkarwada...."

Then we have the testimony of Rao Bahadur H.V. Sathe who knew Baba. He has been quoted as saying: "Near Baba's favourite margosa tree there were the remnants of the old village wall. Baba told me: 'Pull down the wall and build.' Baba's suggestion was for building residential quarters there and for including the village wall in the construction. So I bought the land there and using the remants of the village wall built a *wada* enclosing or surrounding the margosa tree. Baba told me that the tomb, close to the tree over which now a part of the building has been erected... was that of his guru.* He gave me the guru's name. It ended with 'Shah' or 'Sa'. I have forgotten the rest of the name. It might be Venkusa.''

This information does not take us very far either. Venkusa might stand for Venkatesha or Venkateshwara or for Roshan Shah Mia. We are no closer to knowing who Baba's real guru was. Mr M.B. Rege, one time Judge of the Indore High Court has observed that "Sai Baba occasionally talked in mystic language and used parables freely—which, however, were construed in widely different ways by different listeners.''

Prof. G.G. Narke, professor of Geology at the Engineering College, Pune for many years has reported that he has heard Baba say: *"Maza guru brahman ahe"* (my guru is a brahmin). If that is so, how could anybody called Roshan Shah Mia—clearly a Muslim name—be his guru?

According to *Shri Sai-Sat-Charit* written by Govind Raghunath Dabholkar, Sai Baba is said to have stated: ''I stayed with my guru for twelve years. It is rare to find a person like my guru. He was a great *aulia* (spiritual master) and was the personification of love and kindness. How shall I describe his love? He was ever in the highest state of meditation (prayer) and was full of bliss. His was the serene wisdom free from things of desire. The school of instruction of my guru greatly attracted me. I lost my longing for home, the fetters of attachment were broken and I forgot everything including hunger and thirst. He became my all-in-all, home, father and mother. He expected nothing from me except unwavering faith and patience combined with courage. I was single-mindedly devoted to him. As a result he

---

* Arthur Osborne states in *The Incredible Sai Baba* that Sai Baba had indicated that the tomb under the margosa tree was that of his guru in a previous incarnation.

was highly pleased and ever protected me. Whether he was near or far, he looked after me as a tortoise looks after her young ones on the yonder bank by mere gaze and I never felt that I was separated from him. What I am is the result of my devotion and service to my guru. I did not have to look elsewhere for guidance."

This still does not explain who his guru was. But at least it has the ring of authenticity about it. Sai Baba spent approximately over twenty years or so of his early life in Marathwada before he came to Shirdi. Out of this time, he spent approximately half in the company of his guru and the other half in instructing a fakir in Aurangabad. And when he arrived in Shirdi he was a grown up man of about thirty, tempered in the discipline of *tapas* (austerity) and *sadhana* (practice).

The fact that Sai Baba's guru was a Sufi is not a matter of surprise; neither was it unusual for that period in Marathwada which was heavily under Muslim influence. There is a precedent of this kind in Marathwada. In the sixteenth century, Chand Bodhale, a sufi divine was the spiritual preceptor of Janardan Swami, who was in charge of the Daulatabad Fort. At the top of the fort one still sees the *samadhi* of Chand Bodhale. Janardan Swami (1504-1575 A.D.) was a great devotee of the deity Dattatreya and was the *sadguru* of Eknath (1533-1599) one of the foremost saints of Warkari sect in Maharashtra. Sai Baba who held Eknath in highest respect would say that excellent brahmins like Eknath were not to be found these days. Sai Baba also recommended Eknath's works such as *Eknathi Bhagwat* and *Bhavartha Ramayan* for regular reading to his devotees.

CHAPTER 2

MYSTICISM HAS NO GENEALOGY

If Sai Baba's guru was a *sufi*, what is sufism and what are its origins?

As in other religions, so in Islam there is a strong strain of ascetism and mysticism which is nothing more than the yearning of the human soul to have direct experience with the ultimate Reality.

Mysticism, it has been said, has no genealogy. The Prophet defined *ahsan* (the earliest term used for mystic experience in the Traditions of the Prophet) as follows: "You pray to God in a way that you have a feeling that you are looking at Him; if that be not possible, then you feel as if *He* is looking at you." No better explanation is possible.

Whether extraneous influences inspired the mystical movement in Islam or not—the beginnings of the movement can be traced back to the Koran itself—the fact remains that it had a profound impact on the religion itself. The two bedrocks on which the entire structure of mystic ideology in Islam rests are love of God and personal contact with Him.

There are two streaks in Sufism that immediately stand out. Asceticism and mysticism. One of the early scholar al-Hasan al-Basri has attributed to Jesus and David the austere practices that characterise Sufi ascetics, including the wearing of wool. Indeed, the very word *sufi* is undoubtedly derived from the Arabic word for wool and is believed to have been applied in the first place to a certain Abu Hashim, Uthman B. Sharik of Kufa who died about the year 776 AD. By the middle of the ninth century it had become the regular appellation of those who practised austerity. In the tenth century it had also acquired a theosophical connotation.

The sufi movement had begun in Basra and Kufa in what is now Iraq and spread to all parts of the Islamic world, notably to

Khorasan which, during the second half of the eighth century became an important focus of political and religious activity. It was in Khorasan, incidentally, that the plot was hatched which overthrew the Umayyads and established the Abbasid caliphate. To this remote province which had once been a flourishing centre of Buddhism, belonged the celebrated Ibrahim B. Adham, whose conversion to austerity became a favourite theme among later Sufis and has often been compared with the story of the Gautama Buddha. The question of whether Islam through sufism was ever influenced by Buddhism and thus indirectly by Hinduism has never been adequately probed, but merits study.

Sufism, like the Upanishads, calls for the giving up of desire as a means to attain God. This calls for the eradication of self-will. In some ways the Sufi conception of the passing away *(fana)* of Individual Self in Universal Being is almost Upanishadic. But *fana* is not the same as *Nirvana,* though both terms imply the passing away of individuality. *Fana* is accompanied by *baqa*— everlasting life in God. *Fana* involves the extinction of all passions and desires—the holding back of the senses as it were, advocated by the Upanishads. Indeed, Sufism has been described in such terms as: it is wholly self-discipline, it is to possess nothing and to be possessed by nothing, it is the control of the faculties and observation of the breaths. To attain *fana,* certain steps are prescribed, even as they are in the Raja Yoga. The first step is in moral transformation of the soul through the extinction of all passions and desires. The second step is a mental abstraction or passing away of the mind from all objects of perception, thoughts, actions and feelings through its concentration upon the thoughts of God (Here, the thought of God signifies contemplation of the divine attributes). The third step is the cessation of all conscious thought. The highest stage of *fana* is reached when even the consciousness of having attained *fana* disappears. This is what the Sufis call "the passing away of the passing away" *(fana-al-fana).* The Sufi mystic, like the Hindu in *samadhi,* is now rapt in contemplation of the divine essence. The final stage of *fana,* the complete passing away from self, forms the prelude to *baqa* which is continuance or 'abiding' in God. The Sufi who seeks the goal of union with Ultimate Reality *(fana'l-Haqq) calls himself a traveller (salik)* and advances by slow stages *(maqamat)* along a path *(tariqat)* to his final goal. The stages bear a resemblance to those prescribed in Raja Yoga.

There are seven stages to the ultimate goal: repentance, abstinence, renunciation, poverty, patience, trust in God and finally, satisfaction. These seven 'stages' constitute the ascetic and ethical discipline of the Sufi and must be carefully distinguished from the so-called 'states' *(abwal* plural of *bal)* which form a similar psychological chain. There are ten such 'states': meditation, nearness to God, love, fear, hope, longing, intimacy, tranquillity, contemplation and certainty.

The thinking of the Sufi is reflected in large measure in stories about Ibrahim B. Adham. A disciple once asked him for a definition of service. He replied: "The beginning of service is meditation and silence, save for the recollection *(dhikr)* of God." On another occasion, being informed that a certain man was studying grammar, he commented: "He is in greater need of studying silence." He is said to have prayed: "O God, Thou knowest that Paradise weighs not with me so much as the wing of a gnat. If Thou befriendest me by Thy recollection, and sustainest me with Thy love, and makest it easy for me to obey Thee, then give Thou Paradise to whomsoever Thou wilt."

In a letter to one of his fellow ascetics, he wrote:

"I charge thee to fear God, Who may not be disobeyed and in Whom alone is thy hope. Fear God, for he that fears God is great and mighty, his hunger is satisfied and his thirst is quenched and his mind is exalted above the world. His body is indeed seen to dwell among the peoples of this world, but his heart is face to face with the world to come...."

But asceticism for its own sake tended to become a rather joyless and negative attitude to the universe, even as the Buddha found out centuries before the Sufis conceived it. But when warmed by spiritual emotion it converted into an ardent fervour, rejoicing in hardship and delighting in ecstatic experience; subjected to the searching light of speculative reason, it was transformed into the hard discipline that was the necessary prelude to a proved theosophy, as A.J. Arberry noted in his excellent study of Sufism. The final development of Sufism took place at Baghdad which was to become the most important centre of Sufism as it had also come to be the focus of literature, theology, law and philosophy. The first Sufi author of the foremost rank whose preserved writings may truly be said to have formed to a large extent the pattern of all subsequent thought was al-Harith b. Asad al-Muhaasibi. He was born in Basra in 781 AD, but spent the greater part of his life in Baghdad. Contemporary with al-Muhaasibi was Dhu '1-Nun, the Egyptian born in 861 AD who uses the passionate language of the devoted lover as Raabi'a of Basra had done before him, and so fixed a tradition that was thereafter so prominent a characteristic of Sufi literature.

> I die, and yet not dies in me
> The ardour of my love for Thee,
> Nor hath Thy Love, my only goal,
> Assuaged the fever of my soul.
>
> To Thee alone my spirit cries;
> In Thee my whole ambition lies,
> And still Thy Wealth is far above
> The poverty of my small love.

This is the *bhakti* aspect of Sufism that so endeared itself to many in India who did not profess the Islamic faith. In a sense Sufism was the bridge between Islam and Hinduism wherever the two came in contact or conflict as in Marathwada and it was inevitable that often the line separating the Sufi *dervesh* and the Hindu *sanyasi* seemed thin indeed. For the Sufi, there is no fear of death because, like the Hindu mystic he does not see death as the end of man. As Reynold Nicholson put it, impersonal immortality of the human soul kindles in the Sufi an enthusiasm as deep and triumphant as that of the most ardent believer in a personal life beyond the grave. The great mystic Jalaluddin Rumi (1205-1273 AD), after describing the evolution of man in the material world and anticipating his growth further in the spiritual universe, utters a heartfelt prayer for self-annihilation in the ocean of the Godhead.

I died as mineral and became a plant,
I died as plant and rose to animal.
I died as animal and I was man.
Why should I fear? When was I less by dying?
Yet once more I shall die as man, to soar
With angels blest, but even from angelhood
I must pass on; all except God doth perish.
When I have sacrificed my angel soul,
I shall become what no mind e'er conceived.
Oh let me not exist! for Non-Existence
Proclaim in organ tones: "To Him we shall return."

Would it matter whether this state that is most desired by the Sufi is called *fana* or *nirvana* or *moksha*? Would it—or should it—come as a surprise that many people were often confused with Sai Baba, wondering what his origin—Hindu or Muslim—could be?

2

We will better understand and appreciate the nature of society in which Sai Baba was born and lived if we take a look at Medieval Deccan and what it was like in Marathwada at that time.

In 1296 AD, Allauddin Khilji raided the Yadava Kingdom of Devagiri and defeated the King, Ramadeva. Devagiri was annexed and became a part of the Khilji Dominion in 1313 AD. Between the years 1313 and 1347 Devagiri was ruled by the Khiljis and the Tughlaks. Tired of Muhammad bin Tughlak's erratic rule, his emirs rose against him, defeated the Imperial troops and succeeded in forcing their withdrawal from the Deccan. On August 3, 1347, Hasan ascended the throne at Daulatabad (former Devagiri) as Abdul-Muzaffar Allauddin Bahman Shah.

The period has been well described by Prof. H.K. Sherwani and Dr P.M. Joshi in their *History of Medieval Deccan (1295-1724)* Volume I. They state:

"The period between 1318 and 1347 (the establishment of the Bahmani Kingdom) was one of unrest and disturbances. It was during this period that the rigours of an alien rule were felt by the people and it was then that the poet-saint Namadeva said 'the earth was tyrannised by the Daityas' and the instances of idol-breaking and temple destruction mentioned by him and the Mahunabhavas are almost entirely restricted to this period. The close of the thirteenth and the beginning of the fourteenth century witnessed the influx of a large number of Muslim saints and holy men into the Deccan from Delhi. These were Sufi divines of different orders. Legend has it that in 1300, at the instance of Khwaja Nizamuddin Aulia of Delhi, a band of *seven hundred* Sufis left Delhi, came down south and established themselves at various centres in the Deccan. The leader of this band of missionaries was Mumtajabuddin Zarzari Zar Baksh who himself settled on the outskirts of Daulatabad at a village known as Khuldabad, where he died on 15 August 1309. He is said to have married a girl called Sonabai, the daughter of a petty local official of the Yadavas. On his death, his elder brother Burhanuddin Gharib Shah was directed by Nizam-buddin Aulia to wend his way to the Deccan. A wave of Sufi divines under Burhanuddin arrived in the Deccan in 1309 and spread all over the south. The mission of these Sufis was to spread and propagate Islam in Maharashtra and further south. Burhanuddin died at Daulatabad in 1338. By this time Muslim rule was firmly established in the Deccan. These missionaries acquired a following of non-Muslims, not all of whom were converted to Islam. Their work undoubtedly contributed toward stabilisation of Muslim rule in Maharashtra. Though, at first, conversion to Islam seems to have been voluntary, later on, as political power passed to Muslims, the conversion policy of missionaries and rulers perhaps assumed a comparatively aggressive form."

As Muslim divines settled down in the towns and villages of Deccan before the Khilji raid, they attracted many devotees. The *durgahs* of the Muslim saints who came into the Deccan in the 14th and 15th centuries also became holy places and acquired large followings. The most important and widely venerated Sufi saint of the Deccan was Syed Muhammad Gesu Daraz, whose mausoleum, a fine monument erected at Gulbarga by Ahmed Shah Wali, became a centre of pilgrimage for devotees spread far and wide.

The active presence of Sufis in the Deccan set two trends. One was ecumenic, in the sense that there was a strange commingling of Sufism and local beliefs. The other was the deep stirrings among Hindus for holding on to their faith in the context of an assault from a strange religion. That would explain the fact that most of the saints of Maharashtra come from Marathwada.

The saint of Gangapur, Narasimha Saraswati, a man of piety held in respect by all, who lived in those times appears to have been influenced by Sufism. As has been recorded in *The History of Medieval Deccan,* Narasimha Saraswati was an exponent of the Dattatreya School of Devotion, also known as the *Dattatreya sampradaya.* The deity Dattatreya is an ancient one, but Narasimha Saraswati revived its worship and founded a *sampradaya* to meet the demands of the times in which he lived—the second half of the fifteenth century. His main contribution to social and religious stream is that he bent this cult in such a manner as to be acceptable not only to various Hindu sects, but also to the Muslims many of whom, it may be remembered, were new converts. The deity became known to the Muslims as 'Shah Faqir' and gathered round it a number of followers. Dattatreya, so the legend goes, assumed the guise of a *malang* for these devotees. Also known as Shahdatta Allama Prabhu in various centres in the Deccan, the deity was an instrument in bringing about a synthesis of devotional thought among various communities of the people of the Deccan like the Lingayats (the Veerásaivas), the Muslims, the Anand Sampradaaya and the Giri-gosais. Shahgarh in Bir District as also Daulatabad became the main seats of Shah Faqir. Chand Bodhale, a Sufi divine who was the spiritual preceptor of Janardana Swami is supposed to have been the incarnation of Shahdatta Allama Prabhu. This title, incidentally, links up with the Lingayat concept of their deity Shah Allama Prabhu. The Lingayat sect was treated with consideration by Ahmed Shah Wali. The devotion of the followers of this sect to Ahmed Shah continues to this day and the 'Urs of the Wali' is celebrated with ceremonies at which the *jangam* or the Lingayat priest is one of the principal participants.

All this throws considerable light on Sai Baba's own universalism, if such as it can be called, because he lived in an atmosphere that was suffused with this universalism. We have the testimony of Ramachandra Chintaman Dhere who writes in his well-known work in Marathi entitled *Datta Sampradayacha Itihas:* "Dattatreya being the symbol of integration in Datta *sampradaya,* just as integration of Shaiva and Vaishnav tradition was effected in the said *sampradaya,* similarly an attempt at integration of Hindus and Muslims was also made. It is a matter of wonder that the beginning of this attempt is in the life history of Shri Narasimha Saraswati. Thereafter, in the background of Datta *Upasana,* integration of Hindus and Muslims was also attempted in the life time of Janardan Swami and Eknath. Chand Bodhale, the guru of Janardan Swami belonged to the Kadaria sub-sect and Shaikh Mohammad, a Muslim disciple of Chand Bodhale wrote a book in Marathi entitled *Yogasangrama,* expounding yoga and bhakti. Even though Janardan Swami was in the service of Muslims, his devotion to Dattatreya influenced the Muslim ruler and in his time the weekly holiday was observed on Thursday instead of on Friday. Janardan Swami constructed the samadhi of his guru on the Daulatabad Fort. In the following of Manek Prabhu of Humanabad (1817-1865), regarded as an incarnation of Dattatreya, there is a large proportion of Muslims. However, this attempt at integration, unfortunately, did not succeed. The following among Muslims which Datta *sampradaya* attracted was not because of the philosophy of Datta *sampradaya* but due to the aura of miracles and incredible supernatural powers surrounding the *siddhas* of Datta *sampradaya.* The Muslim following did not attempt to interact with their *guru-bandhus* (fellow disciples of a guru) of another faith at any other level except for their reverence for the *siddhas.* The life of Shri Narasimha Saraswati bears this out. As regards Manek Prabhu, it appears from his life story that he was sorely grieved and disappointed at this state of affairs. For the purpose of integration, some Muslim practices were incorporated in the Datta *sampradaya.* The importance given to music in *bhajans* (singing of devotional songs) was due to Sufi influence. The use of incense is also suggestive of the reproduction of atmosphere in Muslim religious shrines. While Dattatreya gave *darshan* in the form of *Malang* to Janardan Swami and Eknath he appeared to Narayan Maharaj Jalvankar disciple of Niranjan Raghunath, in the form of a fakir. That this Hindu divinity should find it necessary to assume the form of a Muslim reflects the intensity of Hindus for such integration".

Then we have to take the evidence of one Abdul, a devotee and servitor of Sai Baba who had the opportunity to watch Baba at close quarters because he lived with him for years. Born in 1869, three decades after Baba's own birth, Abdul was initially a servitor of Amiruddin fakir of Nanded. It is said that a mysterious event happened in 1889. Sai Baba appeared in a dream to Amiruddin, materialised two real mangoes in that dream and told Amiruddin to give them to Abdul and send him to Shirdi. Amiruddin did as he was told.

When Abdul came to Shirdi, Baba exclaimed: "My crow has come!" From the beginning Baba initiated Abdul in the task of service. It was Abdul's responsibility to keep lamps burning perpetually in five places in Shirdi including Lendi, Masjid and Chavadi. When Sai Baba went to Lendi, Abdul would keep two pots filled with water near his Master. Sitting opposite the *Nandadeep* at the Lendi, Sai Baba would make oblations of water in different directions. Sai Baba had charged Abdul with many other duties such as sweeping all the roads near the Masjid and Chavadi, washing Sai Baba's clothes at the stream near the northern boundary, fetching water etc. Abdul was also charged with cleaning the human refuse on the streets. No job was so menial that Abdul would not discharge it. For these services, Sai Baba undertook the responsibility for Abdul's spiritual progress. Abdul would read the Koran sitting by Baba's side. Some times Baba would open the Koran himself and ask Abdul to read from it or he would himself recite the *suras* from it. Sai Baba would also ask Abdul occasionally to remain awake the whole night and go on reading the Koran. Abdul would obey the instructions given to him by Baba right down to how many dishes he can have during his meals. Abdul's surrender to Baba was total.

Abdul dictated his thoughts to a primary school teacher who would take them down in Urdu. Abdul's unpublished works in Urdu clearly show beyond any shadow of doubt that Baba had a profound knowledge of Islamic religion and civilisation including Sufism, the Koran, *Sira* (the life of the Prophet), *sunna* (his code of conduct) *hadith* (the traditions), the *fakah* (dharmashastra), *shariat,* the *tarikat* etc, like any learned Muslim divine or Sufi shaikh. Baba was as comfortable in explaining Islamic works in all their significance as he was in explaining the Vedas, the Upanishads, the Gita and works of saints in *prakrit* (ancient dialects of North and Central India existing along with Sanskrit). Baba was familiar with the works of Sufi shaikhs of orders like Kadaria, Chistia, Suhrawardiya and Nakshbandi. In fact, Baba's range of knowledge was fantastic and incredible. In Abdul's manuscript there is one entry which says: "Friends, how is it possible to fathom the inner mind of Sai Baba if one cannot understand even the outward appearance (form) of Sai Baba? If it be said that he is a Muslim, his ears are pierced; if it be said that he is a Hindu, he dwells in a masjid, repeats the name of Allah Malik and distributes cooked meat as *prasad* (consecreated food). In his inner being, does he contemplate the Vedas, Puranas, the Gita or the Koran, Fakah? Only God knows. So Sai Baba's *leela* (sport) is wonderful. Amir, a Muslim devotee, wishes to sing the praises of Sai Baba, but does he have the capacity to do so? Sai Baba's *durbar* is that of a Kalandar (Muslim fakir). It is not a *math* of a Hindu saint. His slave Abdul regards him as his *Murshid* (guru)."

There must be some explanation for Baba's profound knowledge of both the holy texts of Hinduism and Islam. It is well to remember the times in which he lived. It is also said that he was illiterate. But if Abdul is to be believed, Baba could recite the *suras.* How come he could recite them if he had not learnt them by heart? Who taught him these things?

This leads one to the belief that he was indeed a disciple of a learned fakir for the best part of twelve years and learnt much from his master during that period, without the aid of books and through sheer memory. This, of course, is in India's ancient tradition of *smriti* and *shruti,* memory and recitation. Alternatively we must come to the conclusion that Baba knew everything and did not have to be taught. The first alternative seems more probable.

The point to it all is that he was immersed in the philosophy and tradition of both Hinduism and Islam and did not think either was alien to him. He respected each for its own sake and exhorted all by precept and example to be tolerant and charitable to others of another faith. When a Hindu who got converted to Islam came to his presence he is reported to have slapped him on his face and told him: "Aren't you ashamed to change your father?" One can be sure that if a Muslim convert to Hinduism had similarly appeared before him, he would have received much the same treatment and scolding.

3

Sai Baba is in the rich tradition of saints who are part of Maharashtra's history and culture. It seems also quite appropriate that Baba was born in Marathwada, which had seen Muslim rule over a long period of time.

Maharashtra together with Karnataka and Tilang-Andhra form the Deccan Plateau. These three states have a common calender known as Shalivahan Shaka and share a common cultural heritage. The dynasties of Shatavahanas, Rashtrakutas and Chalukyas held sway over Deccan during the first eleven to twelve centuries of the Christian era. Although the heroic struggles and beneficent measures of the rulers of these dynasties now lie buried in oblivion, we still have with us the noble monuments of Ellora and Ajanta and the temples of Badami, Aihole and Pattadakal and the stupas and sculptures of Nagarjunakonda and Amravati. The Deccan is where Indian temple architecture may be said to have been born.

The Maharashtra plateau was ruled since the latter half of the 12th century, from Devagiri, the modern Daulatabad, an ancient fortified capital. The city was built by Bhillana, the founder of the Yadava Dynasty. He died in 1191 AD and was succeeded by Jaipal who ruled till 1210 AD. He was followed by Singhana, a still more powerful monarch who fought the kings of Mathura and Kashi in the far north, conquered Malwa and extended his supremacy to the south as far as the Kaveri river on the banks of which he erected a triumphal column—all this quite an achievement for those times and place.

Toward the end of the thirteenth century there was a great flowering of talent in the Deccan. Sant Jnaneshwar wrote his imperishable commentary on the Gita known as the Jnaneshwari, the first literary work of major importance in Marathi, though some scholars insist in saying that they have detected Konkani words in Jnaneshwari. Obviously this was about the time that Marathi and Konkani went their different ways. Jnaneshwar certainly is considered the father of the Marathi language.

Then the Khiljis came upon the scene and the rule of Muslims began in right earnest. Between the years 1318 and 1347 Devagiri was ruled by the Khiljis and the Tughlaks, to be succeeded by other Muslim rulers.

The fourteenth century, however, saw the beginning of a new era in the history of the Deccan. For three hundred and odd years after 1318, till the rise of the Marathas under Shivaji, the whole of the Deccan, north of the Tungabhadra remained under the rule of Muslim Sultans.

Their administrative style did not vary a great deal. Murder was common and an accepted way to rise to power. Thus Muhammad Gawan, Vazir of the Bahmani Kingdom was murdered in 1481 following which there was a rapid decline in administration. The elements of disorder which had partly been removed by the powerful personality of that Minister made their appearance in forces more formidable than ever and hastened the process of disintegration.

Gradually the Bahmani Sultan was reduced to the level of a mere puppet. There followed finally the emergence of five states, collectively known as the Deccan Sultanate: the Bureed Shahi dynasty in Bidar, the Imad Shahi dynasty in Berar, the Nizam Shahi dynasty in Ahmednagar, the Adil Shahi dynasty in

Bijapur and the Qutub Shahi dynasty in Golconda.

It is interesting to note the origin of the word 'Bahmani'. According to the German historian Wilhelm von Pochhammer, the founder of the Muslim Deccan realm was a very singular personality. Born on Indian soil and therefore a native Muslim, he was brought up by a brahmin. Out of gratitude to the latter he changed his original name to Gangu (the name of his teacher) and named his family Bahmani (in pronunciation, the 'r' was left out!).

Von Pochhammer says that the first Bahmani ruler "symbolises the mixed type which came into existence through Hindus and Muslims living together." One gets an idea of the kind of 'synthesis' that went on in those times if one realises that the founders of the states of Berar and Ahmednagar came from old brahmin families who, for opportunistic reasons, had embraced Islam.

The Deccan Sultanates wanted to expand southward but they were held back by the Vijayanagar Empire which saw as its chief task the halting of the Muslim expansion. "We hear however," writes Pochhammer, "but little of serious attempts to convert people from Islam. What stood in the forefront was power politics." The growing might of the Hindu Empire was a threat to the existence of the Muslim states whose potential was inferior to that of the Hindus and was lessened further by being split up into different states. "At first," notes Pochhammer, "the plundering and carrying away of treasures played the main role, as the Bahmanis wanted money. The religious trimmings which manifested themselves in the shape of mass murder of the population soon wore off and disappeared altogether when all these states, for political reasons entered into an alliance with states belonging to the Hindu opposition."

Hindu-Muslim inter-face nevertheless existed at various times in a benevolent form. Thus while the Sultan of Bijapur, Yusuf Adil Shah was a 'pardesi' (foreign Muslim), he married a Maratha woman and administered his state in the spirit of the great Minister Muhammad Gawan, employed Hindus in state service and "can be regarded as one of the first Muslim rulers in the Deccan to carry into practice the principle of religious tolerance." But even then, the state religion was Islam in its Shia form which he had brought from Persia. One of his successors, Ibrahim Adil Shah (1534-1557 AD) went as far as to pay an official visit to his neighbour, the Emperor of Vijayanagar. This was the first example of a Muslim ruler treating a Hindu ruler as an equal.

Throughout the 14th and 15th centuries, Hindu-Muslim relations continued to have their ups and downs. If the period between 1318 and 1347 was one of unrest and disturbances under an alien rule—the saint Namadeva was moved to say that "the earth was tyrannised by Daityas"—there is at least one recorded instance of a Muslim governor ordering in 1326 A.D. the re-installation of a Shiva linga in the Madhukeshwara Temple at Kalyani and continuation of its worship.

Then there is the instance of Allauddin Ahmed II who "came very close to his Hindu subjects and was comforted in his last illness by the sage of Gangapur." *History of Mediaeval Deccan* notes that the *Gurucharitra* has eulogised the Sultan as one who was without caste, was a large-hearted ruler who showered generosity on his people without distinction of caste and creed. For all that, the Hindus were appalled at the slaughter of cows and the "occasional iconoclastic indulgences" of the alien rulers.

Students of history are familiar with the struggle between the Sultanates of Deccan and the Vijayanagar Empire, the ultimate clash between the two resulting in the Battle of Talikota and the destruction of Hampi, the capital city. Temples were vandalised, idols broken.

The Sutanates of Deccan were, in their turn, to pass into history with the coming of Mughal power from the north. By 1636 the Nizamshahi kingdom was wiped out. Bijapur kingdom ceased to be independent and became part of the Mughal empire in 1686. Golconda also suffered the same fate a year later in 1687.

During the regime of the Mughal Emperor Farrukh Sair, Niza-ul-Mulk Asif Jah was appointed as a permanent governor of Hyderabad in 1725 AD. In or about 1737, during the rule of

Mahammad Shah, Asif Jah seceded from the Mughal Empire and declared himself an independent king. Marathwada comprising the seven districts of Aurangabad, Jalna, Parbhani, Bhir, Nanded, Latur and Osmanabad and Berar consisting of the districts of Buldana, Akola, Amravati and Yavatmal became part of the Nizam's territory.

We get some idea of the Nizam and his territory from what Warren Hastings wrote in 1784. Of the Nizam he wrote: "His dominions are of small extent and scanty revenue; his military strength is represented to be most contemptible. Nor was he at any period of life distinguished for his personal courage or the spirit of enterprise. On the contrary, it seems to have been his constant and ruling maxim to foment the incentives of war among his neighbours, to profit by their weakness and embarrassments, but to avoid being a party himself in any of their contests and to submit even to humiliating sacrifices rather than subject himself to the chances of war."

Not only the first Nizam, but his successors as well, kept the Deccan political pot boiling until all of India came under the suzerainty of the British which was confirmed after the Sepoy Mutiny—also referred to as the First Battle of Independence—was put down. In 1857 Baba was all of nineteen years old.

4

Sai Baba was heir to the saintly tradition of Maharashtra that began with Jnaneshwar. The Maharashtra of Jnanadeva's time was a free Maharashtra, yet unmolested by Muslim invaders. The kings of Devagiri were still supreme. In Jnanadeva's own time the ruler at Devagiri was the Yadava king Ramadeva, a great patron of learning. Of this period R.D. Ranade has written: "On the whole, the Maharashtra preceding the days of Jnanadeva was a free, unmolested and prosperous Maharashtra, where no internecine strife reigned and where all was unity."

By the time Jnanadeva (Jnaneshwar) came on the scene (1275 AD) Maharashtra had seen the reign of Mukundaraja who was to make the first systematic attempt to make Vedantic principles available to the people in their own language, Marathi. His work *Paramamrita* discussed the nature of the physical body, the subtle body, the causal body and such other topics. Mukundaraja, however, was not just a philosopher but a saint as well. In the 9th chapter of his work he tells us in Yogic fashion the practical way to God attainment and in the 12th chapter he speaks of the great bliss that arises from spiritual experience.

Jnanadeva was born in 1275 AD. There is some controversy over the year of his birth. Some historians hold that he was born in 1271 AD. There is general agreement that he wrote his masterpiece Jnaneshwari in 1290 AD. If it is accepted that he was born in 1271, he would be 19 years old when he wrote his work whereas if we accept 1275 as the year of his birth, he would be just 15 years old when he wrote Jnaneshwari. Ranade has maintained that "it does not seem humanly possible that Jnanadeva could have written his great work when he was only fifteen." And he adds: "For a boy of nineteen years of age also to produce such an immortal work is a matter of no small difficulty. But if we were to choose between these two dates only, we had rather say that Jnanadeva was nineteen years old, than that he was only fifteen, at the time of the composition of the work." Jnanadeva whose elder brother and guru was Nivrittinatha (1273-1297 AD) was followed by Sopana (1277-1296 AD), Muktabai (1279-1297 AD), Namdeva (1270-1350 AD), Eknatha (1533-1599 AD) and Tukaram (1608-1650 AD). The last of the great Maharashtrian saints, however, until the arrival of Baba is Ramadas (1608-1681 AD).

But even before Jnanadeva was born two strong religious forces prevailed in the land: the first was the literature and influence of the Mahanubhavas and the other the great yogic tradition of the Nathas. Ranade has suggested that the Mahanubhavic contribution to religion was "of a peculiar kind" and that Jnanadeva "owed practically little to that tradition" having gone back to the original Upanishads, Gita and Bhagavata. There are conflicting views on the Mahanubhavas, some holding that they did not believe in the caste system, in the *Ashramas* or in slaughter of animals for *yajnas* and some holding exactly the opposite views. The Mahanubhavas believed in only one deity, Krishna, and not even in Vitthala of Pandharpur. Ranade, however, has said that "it cannot be gainsaid that the Mahanubhavas exercised a great deal of influence in their day and that Jnanadeva, so far from being a partisan or an opponent of them, took a more broad-minded and liberal view, going back to the fountain head of the Hindu religion."

The Nathic influence—of the yogic kind—was afloat in the country before the days of Jnanadeva. It is believed that Jnanadeva was greatly influenced by it and that it is reflected in his work. In any event it is certain that Nivrittinatha and Jnanadeva come from the same spiritual line of the great Gahininatha, as is more than once authenticated in the writings of both Nivritti and Jnanadeva themselves. Nivrittinatha was instructed by Gahininatha in spiritual knowledge, Gahininatha by Gorakhanatha and Gorakhanath by Matsyendranatha. However, there is no historical evidence to show when Matsyendranatha and Gorakhnatha actually lived.

Jnanadeva wrote four great works: the *Jnaneshwari* itself, the *Amritanubhava,* the *Abhangas* and the *Changadeva Pasashti.* Jnanadeva held his guru in the highest regard. As he put it: "Is it possible to add lustre to the sun? Is it possible to crown the *Kalpataru* with flowers? Is it possible to add a scent to camphor? How can the sandal wood tree be made more fragrant? How can one add a hue to a pearl? Or what is the propriety of giving a silver polish to gold? It is better that one should remain silent and silently bow to the feet of his master."

The *Jnaneshwari* is essentially an expositional work and follows the metaphysical line laid down in its prototype, the *Bhagavad Gita.* Just as the relation between Prakriti and Purusha forms one of the most important items of the metaphysics of the *Gita,* so is it one of the foundation stones of the metaphysics of the *Jnaneshwari.* Jnaneshwar takes up the problem of the *Kshara* (the mutable), the *Akshara* (the immutable) and the *Paramaatman* from the *Gita* itself. Jnaneshwar also teaches the doctrine of transmigration which is linked closely with the analysis of man's psychological qualities into the *sattvika,* the *Raajasa* and *Taamasa.* It is also Jnaneshwar's assertion that God cannot be known in His entirety. Again, as he puts it: "As a foetus in the mother's womb cannot know the age of its mother, as the sea animals cannot measure the greatness of the sea, as a fly cannot cross the heaven... similarly the sages and the gods and all the beings on the earth, being born of Me, cannot know Me."

For the sheer breadth of vision, its absolute metaphysic and exalted thought process, there is hardly any work in any language to exceed the *Jnaneshwari.* Jnaneshwar preaches the gospel of action. In a famous passage in the eighteenth chapter he says that people should participate in all actions that are necessary for them. As he put it: "Just as a traveller should never swerve from the path directed to him by the foregoing footprints, just as we should not leave the boat unless we have gone to the other bank of the river, just as we should not throw away a plantain tree before it has given us its plantains, just as we should not abandon a lamp before we have found out that which had been lost, similarly, until one becomes fixed in the knowledge of the Self, one should not grow indifferent to acts like sacrifice."

It is in *Amritanubhava,* though, that Jnanadeva expounds his philosophical teaching showing such a mastery and wealth of poetic imagery that Ranade has described it as "one of the greatest philosophical works in Marathi literature."

Jnanadeva had two brothers, Nivritti and Sopana and one sister, Muktabai. There are stories about how they were socially persecuted, and of the miracles that Jnanadeva performed. Jnanadeva took *samadhi* at a very young age; his brothers and sister too followed him not long after. Jnanadeva had his *samadhi* at Alandi. He was followed first by Sopana and then by Muktabai. The last to go was Nivrittinatha. Sopana's *samadhi* is at Sasawad, Muktabai's at Edalaabaad and Nivrittinatha's at Triambakeshwara.

Of the four children of the saint-householder Vitthalpant, Jnanadeva, of course, outshone his siblings. Muktabai is considered the greatest of the Indian mystical poetesses. Changadeva who comes at the end of the line, is a sublime illustration of the insufficiency of the life of mere Yogic power before a truly mystical attainment of God. Farquhar has rightly and most appropriately called Jnanadeva as the "Coryphaeus" of the whole *bhakti* movement of the Maratha country. Certainly, Jnanadeva's commentary on the Gita is regarded as the greatest of the commentaries that exist on that immortal poem.

A contemporary of Jnanadeva was Namadeva. Indeed Namadeva was to carry on the Vitthala *sampradaya* (tradition) long after Jnanadeva was no more. Namadeva was born at about the same time as Jnanadeva but he lived for more than half a century after him, during which time he became the pillar of the Vitthala *sampradaya* at Pandharpur. It was in his time that Pandharpur gained its great importance.

Not only were Jnanadeva and Namadeva contemporaries, they were brothers in a spiritual *sampradaya* and went together on a pilgrimage from Pandharpur. After Jnaneshwar's *samadhi* on October 8, 1296 Namadeva once again proceeded to the north to carry the message of *bhakti*. He stayed on in Punjab for twenty-one years and made many disciples of whom Vishnu-swami, Bahardas, Jallo, Laddha and Keso were the chief. In Ghuman in Gurudaspur district of Punjab, there is a *smarak-mandir* of Namadeva which is well-known as 'Gurudwara Baba Namadevaji' and a big fair is held there annually on the second day of the bright lunar phase in the month of *magha* (January-February). Namadeva composed many *padas* in Hindi, sixty-one of which have been included in *Guru Granthasaheb,* the holy book of the Sikhs. His influence on later saints in north India is evident from the references to him in the compositions of Ramanand, Kabir, Nanak, Rohidas and Peepa etc. Like Jnanadeva, Namadeva too wrote *abhangs* but the originals of those *abhangs* have not been preserved. Ranade has noted that an authentic collection of Namadeva's *abhangs* has yet to be made. It was during Namadeva's twenty-sixth year that Allauddin Khilji invaded the Deccan (1296 AD). That was to make a lasting impact on the minds of the Marathas.

In the beginning of his career, Namadeva, a tailor by caste, had led a lawless life, and once upon a time had killed eighty-four horsemen—no doubt a legend built to show his prowess. Namadeva was later to repent his evil deeds and become a devotee of God. He became one of the greatest of the early *Kirtana* performers. He developed the *sampradaya* of Pandhari as no other single saint ever did. All kinds of miracles have been attributed to Namadeva who saw God everywhere. While he was once eating a piece of bread, a dog appeared before him and ran away with the piece. Namadeva pursued it with a pot of ghee, praying that it should partake of that also. In the dog he had seen the presence of God.

What was Namadeva's philosophy? He supposed that the faculty of God realisation is a God-given gift. A cow gives birth to a calf in a forest; who sends the calf, asked Namadeva, to the udders of its mother? Who teaches the young one of a serpent the art of biting? Who teaches a *mogra* flower at the top of a creeper to be fragrant? Similarly, argued Namadeva, the faculty of realising God was native to man, and by that alone would one be able to realise God.

Namadeva wrote *abhangs*. In them he made his point about God realisation again and again. There was only one favour that we should ask of God, he said, and that was we should always think of Him, that we should always utter His name by our mouth, that we should always see Him with our eyes; that our hands should worship Him and our heads always placed at His feet.

Of the contemporary saints of Namadeva's time, Gora, the potter, takes first place. He was born in 1267 A.D., three years before Namadeva and about eight years before Jnanadeva. As he was the eldest of contemporary saints, he was called Uncle Gora. He was assigned the task of testing the spirituality of Namadeva by Jnanadeva and others. He was present at the Jnanadeva-Namadeva pilgrimage and was respected by all his contemporaries. The story goes that he was so filled with God-devotion that he once did not know that he had trampled his child. Gora often lost all sense of the body and felt as if he was possessed by a spirit.

Next in importance is Visoba Khechara, though Visoba was Namadeva's teacher. He was called Khechara in derision by Muktabai and Jnanadeva because of his lack of faith in bhakti marga initially. Legend has it that once when Namadeva went calling on him he found Visoba placing his foot on a *lingam*. Namadeva understandably strongly rebuked Visoba who is supposed to have told Namadeva to place his feet where there was no *lingam*. Behold! wherever Namadeva placed them, a *lingam* sprang up under them. Visoba had taught Namadeva a lesson that God dwelt everywhere. Indeed, Visoba was to berate Namadeva for boasting that he had seen God. That, he pointed out, was false knowledge. It was just not possible for anyone to meet God if he had not lost his ego. A man's bliss, said Visoba, was within himself. It did not lie in an external object. Discrimination (*viveka*) and dispassion (*vairagya*) were the ways open for the realisation of God.

Then there was Savata, the Gardener, who saw God everywhere in his garden. He wanted no attachment to his progeny. He was happy that he was born in a low caste as thereby he was saved from practising rituals. Addressing God he would say: "Placed as I am, I have neither ablutions to make, nor Sandhya to perform. Born in a low caste, I can only ask for Thy compassion."

Another contemporary was Narahari, the goldsmith. Narahari was a great devotee of Siva but under the influence of Jnanadeva he gradually came to welcome the Bhagavata line. Narahari was so convinced about the unreality of the world that he regarded it as merely a picture drawn upon the wall. As children built houses of stone and mud, only to destroy them, so did people engage themselves in worldly life only to take leave of it. Narahari spoke of the 'unstruck sound' that was for ever resounding in his heart, captivating him by it.

Three other contemporaries of Namadeva are worth mentioning in the litany of saints of that period: Chokha, the Untouchable, Janabai the maid and Sena the barber. Lastly there was Kanhopatra, the dancing girl.

Chokha was a resident of Mangalvedha, now a taluka in Sangli district. A great devotee of God in the form of Vitthala of Pandharpur, he could, however, only pray from outside the temple because he was an outcaste. When Chokha died—he was crushed under a wall that had collapsed—his bones were carried to Pandharpur and were placed in a samadhi before the front door of the temple.

Janabai was a maid servant of Namadeva as also his disciple who throughout her life served Namadeva as a menial in his house. But so great was her devotion to the Lord that to this day she is held in reverence.

There is a beautiful legend about Kanhopatra. She was beautiful beyond words and the king of Bedar wanted her. But she who found beauty only in her Vithoba refused to oblige the king. When the king sent for her she implored God to save her but when the king's men insisted on taking her away forcibly she decided to end her life. Her dead body was laid at the feet of the Lord and she was later buried to the south of the Vithoba temple. A strange tree sprung up on the place where she was buried. The tree remains and is worshipped by pilgrims.

Consider the saintly tradition of Maharashtra in which Sai Baba was born. We have a potter, a gardener, a goldsmith, an untouchable, a lowly maid, a barber and, miracle of miracles, the daughter of a dancing woman and herself a dancing woman. Not one from the upper castes. And they are all revered to this day.

We come, then to the fifteenth century and the time of Bhanudasa, (b. 1448 AD) a Deshastha Brahmin and probably a contemporary of the saint Damajipant. Bhanudasa's fame rests on one legend: that by the power of his prayers, he brought back the image of Vitthala from Hampi where the great Emperor of Vijayanagara, Krishnadevaraya, had taken it.

Bhanudasa was succeeded by Janardana Swami who was born in 1504 A.D. Janardana Swami who was in the service of Nizamshahi at Devagiri came to realise God through the grace of a guru Chand Bodhale. Janardana Swami died in 1575 A.D. at Dhaumya in Ahmednagar district on the border of Jamkhed and Shevgaon talukas where his *samadhi* can still be found to

54

this day and an annual festival is held there.

Eknath (b. 1533 A.D.) is the great grandson of Bhanudasa and lived to be 66 years old. A devotee of God from his very child-hood he was initiated by Janardana Swami. Eknath married a girl from Vaijapur called Girijabai, but his married life never came in the way of his devotion to God. It is true that he tells us in his *Chiranjivapada* that one should not sit among women, should not look at women or get shampooed by women, neither should one speak with women or permit women to share one's soli-tude, but he did not include his own wife in this category. Eknath's life was one of moderation. His daily spiritual routine was regularly and strictly practised. Eknath was a prolific writer and his literary work is voluminous. Ranade has described his commentary on the 11th chapter of the Bhagvata as his "most classical production."

Eknath held that the way of *bhakti* is easier than the path of knowledge, but it was sufficient by itself. As the sun requires no help to dispel darkness, so also *bhakti* (devotion) required no external help to destroy *avidya* (ignorance). Eknath held that intellectual knowledge is unnecessary for God realisation. Eknath illustrated this theory by the example of the milkmaids of Vraja. Those milkmaids were manifestly ignorant of any scriptural knowledge but by loving Him and even acting against the injunctions of the *shastras,* they realised their spiritual goal. Eknath also held that in matters worldly as well as spiritual, the help of the Guru was not only valuable, but indispensable. Eknath believed in meditation and insisted that even a single moment spent in meditating upon God could destroy tribulation, disease, obstacles, doubts, sins and egoism.

In a survey of the period of Eknath, Ranade says it is characterised by a "unique reconciliation of worldly and spiri-tual life, unattained either before or after." Janardana Swami was a fighter and a saint. Eknath was a householder and a saint. As Ranade has stated: "In this reconciliation of worldly and spiritual life, Eknath accomplished what had not been accomplished either by Jnanadeva or Namadeva before him or by Tukarama and Ramadasa after him. Jnanadeva and Rama-dasa had no wives and children and so we cannot say that they ever reconciled the worldly and spiritual life. Namadeva and Tukarama had wives and children, but, as in the case of Spinoza, God was to them a great lion's den to which all steps pointed but from which none returned. They were so absorbed in God that nothing else was of any value to them. Not so Eknath. He observed the Aristotleian mean in all things, was a man in whose life the principle of right judgment could be seen to have predominated at every moment. Eknath's life was unique and he derived this in no small measure from his teacher Janardana Swami himself.''

We now have to deal with two more Maharashtrian saints, Tukaram and Ramadasa. Tukarama was born in 1608 A.D. He passed away in 1650 at the age of 42. He had two wives: Rakhumabai and Jijaabai. His first wife died of starvation during a prolonged famine. A son named Santu also died about that time, Tukaram thereafter gave himself to spiritual readings. He was initiated by his guru Babaji in a dream. Tukaram experienced like other saints, the dark night of the soul till he attained God realisation. It was thereafter that he began to sing his *kirtanas*. He was hated by Rameshwarabhatta who, however, later became his disciple. Jijaabai was a Xantippe, often quarrelling with her saintly husband for not working for a livelihood and sustaining his family. But Tukaram suffered this in patience. It is said that Tukaram probably met both Sivaji Maharaj and Ramadasa at some point in his life. It is also said that it was Tukaram who told Shivaji to have spiritual instruction from Ramadasa. In due course Tukarama passed away and there is a story told that Tukarama ascended to heaven in a *vimana*. Ranade says that the story must have originated in the fact that there is no samadhi of Tukarama built anywhere, when there are *samadhis* of Eknath, Namadeva and Ramadasa.

Tukaram's *abhangs* are in a class by themselves. In them he poured out his heart in abundance. His humility became him. He wrote:

"Desire and anger have not yet lost their hold on my mind. They have taken a permanent lodgment in me..."

"I feel internally that I alone am a wise man. Save me or

otherwise I shall come to ruin." "Why hast thou brought me fame, O God? If a dead body be adorned with ornaments, of what use would it be to the body?"

"Why should'st thou have adorned my tongue with songs? For it takes me away from Thee." Tukaram is best understood through his *abhangs.* He was for ever in search of God. He found, however, that he would not be able to reach God merely by living in solitude. He very much needed the company of saints who would be able to give him the evangel of God. Tukaram would say that there was no townsman for him in this life. His city was planted in heaven. He often felt forlorn. He would say: "I so much pant after spiritual company. Wherever I look, in whatever direction I cast my eyes, I find empty space everywhere. Nobody tells the news of Thee."

On one occasion he said: "Give me the company of those who have an incessant love toward Thee, O God. Then I shall no longer tease Thee. I shall live near the feet of the saints and shall ask nothing of Thee. If Thou canst bestow upon me this boon, Thou will kill two birds with one stone. Neither Thou nor I shall be teased any longer. For this reason I am standing like a beggar at Thy door."

Over and over again he complained to God to accept him. He said: "When shall I be able to hear the words of the saints that Thou hast accepted me? Then alone shall my mind be at ease."

When none of these pleas helped Tukaram sought direct Grace from God. "Throw me not away. I am a dog at Thy door. I am sitting like a beggar before Thy house. Turn me not out of Thy mansion. Save me by Thy power, O God!"

Years after such pleadings, Tukaram was assured that they had been heeded. Tukaram, it is said, saw God's vision and bowed at His feet. Writes Tukaram: "I see God's face and the vision gives me infinite bliss. My mind is riveted on it and my hands cling to His feet. As I look at Him, my mental anguish vanishes. Bliss is now leading me to ever higher bliss!"

Tukaram had many mystic experiences. He could say with complete self-assurance: "God is pursuing me outright. I have fallen into the hands of God and He is using me as a menial without wages!"

To Tukaram finally came the mystic's highest experience, the indivisibility of man and God. As he put it: "I gave birth to myself and came out of my own womb. All my desires are at an end. When I became powerful beyond measure, I died at the very moment."

Again: "Deep has called unto deep, and all things have vanished into unity. The waves and the Ocean have become one. Nothing can come and nothing can now pass away. The Self is enveloping Himself all round. The time of the Great End has come and sunset and sunrise have ceased."

Increasingly, Tukaram saw unity all around. He wrote: "All men have now become God and merit and demerit have disappeared... My country is now the universe, I live in the whole world. There is nobody between Him and me. There is no chasm, my only resting place is the name of God. "

Tukaram notes that he saw his death with his own eyes. And he sang: "Incomparably glorious was the occasion. The whole universe was filled with joy. I became everything. Death and birth are no more. I am free from the littleness of 'me' and 'mine' "

The last of the Maharashtrian saints is Ramadasa. Ramadasa was born in 1608 A.D. When he was barely seven years old, his father Suryajipant passed away. At the age of twelve Ramadasa ran away from home. There are two stories connected with this incident. One is that he decided not to get married. The other is that his brother Gangadharpant refused to initiate him into the spiritual life because he was too young for that. In any event Ramadasa ran away from his home to find out God for himself. He is reported to have practised severe penance and religious austerities at Takali for a period of twelve years in the course of which he is supposed to have seen Sri Rama in a vision, who initiated him.

After finishing his religious austeries in 1632 A.D. Ramadasa devoted the next 12 years of his life travelling all over the country before settling down on the banks of the river Krishna.

It is believed possible that at one point in time he met Tukaram and Chhatrapati Shivaji. Shivaji was crowned king in 1674 A.D. after which, reports say, he visited Ramadasa at Sajjangad and lived there for some time. At Ramadasa's suggestion new images of Sri Rama, Lakshmana and Sita were ordered from Tanjore to be installed for worship in his shrine, at Sajjangad.

His most powerful disciple, of course, was Shivaji who wrote to him in 1678 A.D. thus: "Obeisance to my most high Teacher, the father of all, the abode of all bliss. Shivaji, who is merely as dust on his Master's feet, places his head on the feet of the Master and requests......" It is a long letter, placing before Ramadasa his problems, specially political.

Ramadasa's advice to Shivaji was "to adorn his body not by clothes and ornaments, but by shrewdness and wisdom." Ramadasa wrote to say that the Mohammedans were spreading oppression throughout India for a long time and that Shivaji should be on his guard. Ramadasa told Shivaji that when God once called a man His own, there was no knowing what he may do. His justice, his forethought, his ready wisdom and his knowledge of other peoples' hearts were all of them the gift of God. So was discrimination between matters which pertain to this world and those which pertain to the next.

"Historians differ as regards Ramadasa's influence on the political life of Shivaji," observes Prof. K.V. Gajendragadkar in Vol. II of *The Cultural Heritage of India*. "But the fact remains that the effect was mutual, and some of the later writings of Ramdas show a distinct dominance of political thought. This does not however mean that politics played an important part in his life and writings." Even saints are to a certain extent influenced by their physical and social environments. And as Ramadasa was born in a period of political upheaval, he could not but be somewhat affected by it. However, he regarded the realization of God as of primary and politics as only of secondary importance in life. He was a saint of practical temperament. As such he systematically organized his order and established his monasteries in Maharashtra to serve as centres of spiritual and practical activities.

Ramadasa wrote his famous *Dasabodha* in the Sake year 1581 (1659 AD). In it he noted what knowledge is *not*. Knowledge of sciences, even of the past and the future was not knowledge; it was certainly not wisdom. Real knowledge was self-knowledge, vision of the self by the self. Real knowledge was in knowing God, in cognizing His eternal form, in distinguishing the Real from the unreal. Where the phenomenal world hid itself, where the *"panchabhautika"* was at an end, there alone was knowledge. It went even beyond the Beyond and beyond the highest stage of speech. Ramadasa recommended meditation on the Name of God for remission of all sins. Self-knowledge was more powerful than all religious vows, than all religious charities, than all the different kinds of yogas, than various kinds of pilgrimage. There was indeed no limit to the merit of a man who had seen the Self. The true God was the pure Self who persists even when the body fell.

Ramadasa advised that one should search for the God that one cannot throw away. He decried blind faith which he termed ignorance. By ignorance, he said, we shall never be able to reach God.

Ramadasa asserted that God is the Inner Self and he dissuaded people from vainly following many gods. As he put it: "Images take us back to gods in the place of pilgrimage. The gods in the place of pilgrimage take us back to incarnations. The incarnations take us to the three deities Brahma, Vishnu and Mahesh—the Creator, the Preserver, and the Destroyer of the world. But the highest God is only He who presides over all these gods. He is the Inner Self. He is the real Doer, the Enjoyer... People miss this immanent God and follow vainly after other gods and then they come to grief because they are not able to find God in outer images."

Ramadasa held that Creation is unreality and that the only reality was God. He held too, that God was different from both body and soul. The body was made up of gross elements; the soul was of changeful qualities. The changeless Brahman was different from either. And he asserted that the Highest Principle must be reached in actual experience. God, he said can be realised even in this life. But for that, he added, an aspirant must have a *guru*. It was the *guru* who held the key to spiritual treasure.

5

To the list of saints of geographical Maharashtra we might add the saints of Karnataka whose influence was by no means meagre. Indeed we have to take the Deccan in its entirety because ideas don't take into account geographical boundaries. Like wind and water they move freely wherever there is a vaccum. We have, for example, the Dasas of the *Bhagavata sampradaya.* The Bhagavata *dharma* developed in the north and took deep roots in Bengal and Maharashtra. In the south, *dvaita* (daulistic) philosophy so enthusiastically taught by Madhvacharya, created a great awakening for God in the minds of his followers. The task of carrying Madhva's message to the general public, however, was undertaken by spirited missionaries, known as Dasas (servants). Their main mission was to take the greatness of the Lord to rich and poor alike in their own language, which was Kannada. The *Dasas*, writes Keshav M. Mutalik, in his monograph on Jagannath Dasa "did a yeoman's service in breaking the shackles of caste, creed and regionalism." They were socially oriented and dedicated themselves to the service of God and man.

The *Dasas* were instrumental in propagating the term *Dasa Koota*—the Fellowship of the Servants of God. They were different from *Vyasa Koota*—the Fellowship of scholars and pundits. There was no violent differences between the two in their training, approach and philosophy. Those who belonged to the Vyasa Koota laid stress on sanskrit learning and teaching. Those who belonged to the *Dasa Koota* took the message of Madhva to the people in their own mother tongue—Kannada.

There were three groups of *Dasas*. One group represented by Vijaya Dasa, Jagannatha Dasa and Venkatesh was mainly interested in Madhva philosophy and its preaching. The second group headed by Vyasaraya followed by Gopala Dasa and others created a literature meant for the brahmanical world in general. The third group consisted of Sripadaraya, Vadiraya, Purandara Dasa (and his sons) and Kanada Dasa who preached the ordinary code of morality for people of all castes and communities. All the Dasas however revered the name of Hari.

There are four distinct landmarks in the literature of the *Dasas,* based on the style and subject matter. The 13th century marked the origin of the Vaishnava Bhakti School or what is known as the Haridasa Koota. This literature was started under the guidance of Shri Naraharithirtha, the disciple of Shri Madhvacharya. This is considered the creative period.

Between the 15th and 16th centuries stalwarts like Sripadaraya, Vyasathirtha, Vijayendrathirtha and Purandaradasa helped in the growth and flowering of the Dasa literature. This is considered the 'classical' period. The 17th century brought to the limelight Shri Raghavendrathirtha and Shri Vedashathirtha. This period really stimulated the *Dasa Sahitya,* especially after the decline of the Vijayanagara Empire. Scholars consider the 18th and 19th centuries as the heyday of *Dasa Sahitya.* There were many great writers such as Vijayadasa, Gopaladasa, Jagannatha Dasa and Prasanna Venkatadasa. Their writings were polished and highly literary. This period in Dasa literature is considered the Didactic Period.

Mutalik classified the Dasa literature into seven major groups: (a) biographical (b) socio-religious (c) ethical and ritualistic (d) didactic and philosophical (e) meditative (f) narrative and eulogistic and (g) miscellaneous. The sources of the songs were the Vedas, the Upanishads, the Puranas as interpreted by Madhva and his followers. The *Dasas* sang in praise of Hari. Shri Hari is the supreme God who transcends all the trammels of *prakriti* and who lords over the entire universe of spirit and matter.

The post-Vyasaraya commentators of the *Bhagavata sampradaya* also propagated the *dvaita siddhanta* (philosophy of dualism). Their voice was heard both in Karnataka and Maharashtra. But the important thing is that the *Dasas,* through their music and song reformed a society that was then completely at sea. Vijayadasa especially came at a time when the spiritual thirst in man had reached the lowest level. To him and his disciple Gopaladasa the people of Deccan owe a great debt.

CHAPTER 3

THE UNKNOWN BEGINNING

It is futile to follow a controversy as to when exactly Sai Baba was born. While accuracy is to be applauded for historical reasons suffice it to say that Sai Baba was born towards the end of the third decade of the nineteenth century. By then the Maratha Power was clearly on the decline. By the end of the eighteenth century, as S.N. Quanungo has stated in *The History and Culture of the Indian People, Vol. 8,* "various forms of moral cankers were eating into the vitals of Maratha society—the popularity of erotic compositions of Anant Phandi and Ram Joshi, the wide-spread belief in witch craft, the great demand for the services of astrologers and marriage of infant girls." Quanungo noted that during this period "concrete instances are on record of excessive indulgences in sensual pleasures, drunkenness and frivolous enjoyments of the most degraded type on the part of top-ranking Maratha leaders like Peshwa Baji Rao II, Nana Phadnis, Daulat Rao Scindia and Yashwant-rao Holkar." The Marathas lacked the corporate spirit so essential for their national independence. To every one in that age his own fief (*watan*) was the only reality. The Maratha chiefs also failed to protect their subjects from excesses of their own armies which consisted of a motley crowd of Arabs, Sikhs, Rajputs, Rohillas, Abyssinians, Pathans and some Europeans besides Marathas. Peasants tended to turn toward anyone who could give them protection. The Maratha government was not influenced by the people and so the people, in turn, did not take any interest in its permanence. The cohesion of the Maratha people was not organic but artificial and accidental and therefore precarious. Nationalism of the 19th century was unknown to them.

Casteism also added to want of social cohesion. There was an infusion of racial and caste elements among the military leaders. Ramadasa's high ideal was lowered and the usual consequences followed. Thus, under the order of the Peshwas, the Paithan brahmins who refused to accept the verdict of the *sastras* were excommunicated. Nemesis was to overtake the destiny of the Maratha nation with the death of Ram Shastri in 1789, Hari Pant Phadke in 1794, Ahilyabai Holkar in 1795, Tukoji Holkar in 1797, Parashuram Bhau in 1799 and Nana Phadnis in 1800.

Importantly, the British had arrived on the scene.

During the four decades preceding the birth of Sai Baba one can say that chaos reigned supreme in India. Tipu Sultan in Mysore, the Nizam in Hyderabad, the Peshwas in Pune, the Maratha overlords and satraps in Indore, Baroda, Gwalior and elsewhere, the British on their way to conquest were fighting each other, the British alone having some clear concept of what they wanted.

War, despoliation by invading armies, absence of law and order and an abiding uncertainty characterised the decades. The Nizam, in whose territory Sai Baba was born, was weak and unable to hold his own against the wily and determined British who manipulated him to meet their needs and ends. As R.C. Majumdar has noted, "it was almost inevitable that the expansion of British dominions would leave behind a blazing trail of discontent and disaffection throughout India." That was not confined by any means to the ruling chiefs and royal families conquered by the British or annexed by them on other grounds. British rule was not favourably looked upon even by the people at large in any region where it was newly introduced, far less joyously welcomed, as many of the British writers and administrators would like us to believe. The arbitrary deposition of the ruler of Satara, the despotic coercion of the Scindia and similar other tyrannical acts generated a feeling of hostility and hatred against the British.

Indian industry was in ruins. Six years before Sai Baba was born, in 1832, one British historian, R.M. Martin was to observe thus: "By increase of export of cotton goods to India from Britain, many millions of Indo-British subjects have been totally ruined." When British goods flooded Indian markets and threatened wholesale destruction of Indian manufactures, the trading company which ruled India did not take any steps to prevent the catastrophe. From 1818 to 1836, the export of twist from Great Britain to India rose in the proportion of 1 to 5,200. In 1824, the export of British muslin to India hardly amounted to 6,000,000 yards while in 1837 it surpassed 64,000,000 yards. In 1834-35 the British Governor-General wrote: "The misery hardly finds a parallel in the history of commerce. The bones of the cotton-weavers are bleaching the plains of India." If this was the economic background to the birth of Sai Baba, what was the social background? The Charter Act of 1833 had compelled the East India Company to permit Christian missionaries to enter into their territory. This was to be the beginning of proselytising activities on the part of the missionaries. As Christopher Isherwood points out in *Ramakrishna:* "The British certainly had much to offer India that was valuable: medical science and engineering, the arts of the West, a clearly-defined legal code. Unfortunately, they brought with them also two creeds— scientific atheism and missionary evangelism—diametrically opposed to each other yet equally narrow and dogmatic.... The English missionaries attacked Hinduism as a polytheistic religion; a primitive tangle of cults and idolatry. In this they showed their utter ignorance of the Vedas, which state, again and again, that the substratum of all the many divine forms is Brahman, the one and indivisible.... The Catholics could not very well condemn the cult of holy images in theory, though they showed much zeal in destroying those which belonged to other creeds."

In schools run by Christian missions, the teaching of Christian doctrines was made compulsory in girls' schools. Hindus became the butt-end of vulgar jokes. One British journal was to write, referring to the names of girls such as Vishnupriya, Annapurna, Digambari etc: "What kind of conduct ought we to expect from these poor children, named by their parents after imaginary goddesses whose adultery, cruelty and gratification of their passions, as detailed by their own sacred writings, are so abominable?" Filthy abuses of Hindu gods and goddesses formed the main plank of the public preaching and propaganda of the Christian missionaries.

But there was another side to British rule—the abolition of *suttee* through legislation in 1829, the passing of the Widow Remarriage Act in 1856 and so on. For all that, the country was in a highly disturbed state. In December 1824 for instance, a brahmin, one Divakar Dikshit with a few associates, plundered Sindhi, about four miles to the east of Bijapur, and set up a regular government of his own. There were similar uprisings elsewhere. The cumulative discontent in many parts of India was ultimately to lead to the Sepoy Mutiny of 1857 which was cruelly put down. That year, Sai Baba was about 19 years old. He, surely, was aware of what was going on around him. It would be surprising if he weren't.

There is no reason to believe that the district in which Sai Baba was born was in any significant way different from districts elsewhere in regard to matters religious, political and social. Suttee, infanticide, child marriages, beliefs in superstition were a common factor. Poverty was endemic. Roads were in poor conditions and connected only the important towns; schools were few and far between. Education was for the privileged and even that could not have been of any meaningful value. Industry lay in ruins. Agriculture was by today's standards, primitive. Only the memory of past glory must have kept up the morale of the people.

His contemporaries were Bal Gangadhar Tilak who once called on Sai Baba in his later years and Mahadev Govind Ranade (b. 18 January 1842). Both were to rise to great heights. But Sai Baba was to become great in a different way.

Each of them went his own way. Sai Baba was born in what was then the Nizam's state. There is no record of his education, if he had any. In the village where he was born, there was no library and if there was a school, it has gone unrecorded. Books would not have been easily available and whatever Sai Baba learnt over the years must have been through lessons taught orally, by his gurus. Much of the information that we now have comes from devout sources like Swami Sai Sharan Anand, born as Vaman Prangovind Patel on 5 April 1889 in a well-to-do and educated brahmin family at Mota, a village in Bardoli taluka, famous for the peasant satyagraha of 1928.

A brief sketch of the life of this man may be relevant here.

Vaman's father Prangovind Lalbhai Patel was in the employ of the Excise Department (Salt Branch) of the Government of India. His mother Manigauri was the daughter of the well-known educationist Tuljaram Somnath. Vaman's grandfather had served as a *talati* in Navsari and was known as an honest, upright government servant who practised and enforced discipline. His grandmother Nandkuvar was a very religious lady as was his mother.

Vaman studied up to the sixth form in his village and for the VII Form he came to stay at Kheda with his uncle Ramgovind who was a head clerk in the Collector's office. From 1899 he commenced his secondary education at Ahmedabad where his father had been transferred. In 1903 his father was transferred again, this time to Bombay where Vaman joined the New High School (which was later to be re-named as Bharda New High School after a distinguished headmaster). Vaman passed his matriculation examination in 1905.

At that time there were three colleges in Bombay, Wilson, St Xavier's and Elphinstone. The fees charged by each were Rs 36, Rs 48 and Rs 64 per term respectively. As Vaman's father was a government servant he preferred to put his son in the government-run Elphinstone from which he graduated in Arts in 1909. Among his classmates and friends was Manu Subedar who was to become a member of the Central Legislative Assembly. Vaman passed his L.L.B. examination in 1911 and signed Articles with a solicitor's firm in Bombay known as Messrs Jehangir Gulabbhai & Billimoria.

According to the custom of that time, Vaman was married when he was barely 13 to a still younger Kalavati, the daughter of Ambaram Krishnashankar Shukla. From his childhood Vaman had a religious bent of mind which was nourished by the religious atmosphere in his household. In his childhood he learnt to recite *Ramraksha, Vishnu Sahasranaam* and *Aditya Hriday stotra.* When he was about five years old, his father was posted for some time at Dharasana Salt Depot where the family stayed in a tent. Sanitation was poor and Vaman came down with a bout of diarrhoea. He was hovering between life and death.

One evening as his mother sat outside the tent holding him in her lap, a fakir reportedly appeared in front of her as if from nowhere. Addressing the mother, the fakir said: "Your child is very fortunate." Replied the mother: "Fortunate? How fortunate? He has loose motions several times a day and we fear that he may not last even four more days." "Mother," replied the fakir, "say not that. The child is indeed fortunate. In his right armpit is a wart and a mole on his right side."

The mother had not noticed these marks before and when she examined the child, she found that the fakir indeed was right. If it amazed her, she did not show it; her anxiety was that for the life of her son. And she told the fakir so. "Fear not," said the fakir, "but take this *udi* and place it in the child's mouth. All will be well."

Swami Sai Sharan Anand records in his autobiography written in Gujarati entitled *Sainathne Sharane* and published posthumously in 1983 that thereafter his health improved rapidly and his parents were relieved. It is not recorded what happened to the fakir.

When Vaman was seven years old and was schooling at Kheda, he would visit early morning the temple of Somnath Mahadev with his mother and sisters where he often met a fakir who would playfully tease him. Vaman would often pass him on his way to school. In 1911, when Vaman first went to Shirdi he recognised at once that the fakir he knew at Kheda was none other than Sai Baba! Similarly, holding his palms apart Sai Baba once told Hari Sitaram Dikshit that he had known Vaman when he was that small—as small as a mouse. It was when Vaman recounted this to his mother that she told him about the fakir incident when he was a child.

When Vaman was in the Intermediate Arts class he lost interest in his daily religious rites such as *sandhya-puja* which he stopped performing, but he continued reciting *stotras* by force of habit after he had his morning bath. He would also read the Gita before retiring to bed and he found that these exercises gave him great strength. He was also convinced by studying *Neetishatak* and *Vairagyashatak* by Bhartruhari that the ideal of Aryavarta was the realization of God through renunciation. As he got first class marks in Logic in Inter Arts examination, Vaman chose Logic and Moral Philosophy as his subjects for study for B.A. R.S. Mars was then the professor of Logic and Moral Philosophy at the Elphinstone College. He was a great scholar of German and Greek and had read works of Kant in the original. As such he was very popular with students. The study of Kant's philosophy unsettled Vaman's mind and he wondered whether God really existed or was merely the creation of man's mind; whether the universe was sustained by a conscious creative power or was created accidentally. The more he thought the more he became eager and anxious to unravel the mystery of life and to see God face to face as Swami Vivekananda is reported to have done. It was when he was in this frame of mind that his father took him to Balakrishna Maharaj. Vaman told Balakrishna Maharaj that he would only accept him as his guru who would enable him to get direct perception of God. Now Vaman longed to meet a mahatma who would finally resolve his doubts.

His prayers were answered. His father who had just returned from a visit to Sai Baba told him that the latter was capable of meeting all his demands. So, on 11 December 1911, after he had given his second L.L.B. examination, Vaman left for Shirdi.

After his first meeting with Sai Baba, Vaman visited Shirdi frequently right up to 1918. However, his two visits in 1913 and 1916 were particularly significant and productive from a spiritual point of view.

Vaman went to Shirdi in May 1913 and Sai Baba detained him for nearly eleven months. Initially Sai Baba made him do *gayatri purascharan* to wipe off his past karma. He would also send him on his behalf to four or five houses seeking alms. He also put him through the necessary spiritual discipline, made him read *Jnaneshwari* and other spiritual works and gave him spiritual experiences. He treated him with affection and would call him by his pet name Babu. Then, one day, Sai Baba told him to go home. So Vaman returned to Bombay in March 1914 after eleven months.

Due to his long stay in Shirdi Vaman's period of articled clerkship was interrupted. On his return to Bombay he met Jehangir, the senior partner of the firm who told him that the period of 13 months earlier put in by him was wasted as his period of training had been interrupted. Jehangir said that Vaman would have to start all over again and put in two fresh years as an articled clerk.

About this time he received offers of employment—one as a police prosecutor and another as an assistant teacher in C.J.N.L. High School, Navsari. On the advice of Sai Baba he accepted the latter and served over a year in that post. At the time of the vacation that followed Vaman consulted Gulabbhai, another partner of the firm who advised him to apply to the Chief Justice of Bombay High Court for condonation of the break in his articles. On making the necessary application, an order was passed by the Chief Justice condoning the break and Vaman was thus permitted to serve for the remaining period of eleven months to complete his articled clerkship. This is said to be the only instance of its kind in the history of the Bombay High Court.

In October-November 1916, Vaman spent three weeks in Shirdi which were very important from his point of view for the valuable spiritual experiences he gained.

Between 1917 and 1935 the career of Vaman was full of vicissitudes. In 1923 he passed the Solicitor's examination and thereafter served in many capacities as solicitor, teacher and principal, very much part of the world and yet separate from it. Mentally he had given up his attachment to mundane matters. His wife passed away in 1951. A daughter died in 1978. Vaman turned his hand to literary activity in 1946 authoring religious books in Gujarati, chief of them being *Sai Leelakhyan* in 24 chapters and *Shri Sai Baba* containing 17 chapters.

Towards the end of 1953 he took *sanyas* at Dakor and came to be known as Swami Sai Sharan Anand. Thereafter he lived for 29 years an austere and virtuous life and attained nirvana at

Ahmedabad on 25 August 1982. It is said that Sai Sharan Anand had super-natural powers which he evidently used sparingly. His book *Sainathne Sharane* was published posthumously as were two other books *Brahma Parimal* (1986) and *Siddhamrit* (1987). Swami Sai Sharan Anand remains one of the best sources of information on Sai Baba. He wrote in Gujarati and his devotion to Sai Baba and his total faith in him comes through in every line he wrote. Some would consider him naive but nobody could ever call him insincere. He remains a true devotee, convinced that Sai Baba manifested himself by his self-existing power.

Let us think of some of the contemporaties of Sai Baba in order to better see him in the context of his times.

There is Afzal-ud-Daula, Nizam (1827-1869) who succeeded his father Nasir-ud-Daula, to the gaddi in May 1851. His Minister, Mir Turab Ali Khan, popularly known as Salar Jung, was a protege of the British. During the rebellion of 1857, the Nizam remained loyal to the John Company, although people were incited by 'rebel' sympathisers from time to time and several cases of insurrection were reported. These were ruthlessly put down.

During what were some of the most critical days for the Company, the Hyderabad contingent served with the British force in central India for thirteen months. The Nizam was persuaded by the Government of India to remove the Mughal Experor's name from his coinage, but an attempt to proclaim himself independent was viewed as a breach of friendship. After the suppression of the 1857 rebellion on behalf of the British sovereign, Viceroy Canning thanked the Nizam for his loyalty and bestowed many presents on him. By a treaty concluded in 1860 all territories assigned to the British, other than Berar, were restored to the Nizam.

Then there was the successor to Shah Alam II, Akbar Shah II who died in 1837. Syed Ameer Ali (1849-1928) claimed descent from the Prophet through the eighth Imam, Ali Raza. His forbears were prominent in the service of the Nawab of Oudh. Ameer Ali was educated at Hooghly College, Chinsura and later graduated in arts and law from Calcutta University. He is said to have been the first Muslim in India to take his M.A. degree. Ameer Ali was to go to England to be called to the Bar and in due course became a judge of the Calcutta High Court.

Surendranath Bannerjea (1848-1925) who rose to be a well known nationalist leader started as a member of the Indian Civil Service. Indomitable and undaunted, he was often referred to as 'Surrender not' Bannerjea. A political moderate, Bannerjea believed in the beneficence of British rule and advocated constitutional agitation as a means for achieving a representative form of government. Bannerjea held liberal social and religious views, advocated widow re-marriage and raising the age of marriage of girls. He has been described as a man whose most critical function was the transmission of ideas rather than creative thought.

Woomesh Chandra Bannerjee (1844-1906) was to become the first president of the Indian National Congress and the first Indian to contest an election to the British House of Commons. Twice he was offered a judgeship of the Calcutta High Court, but he refused the honour on "account of his poverty." His monthly income then was not less than Rs 20,000 whereas the salary of a judge was only Rs 4,000.

Himself a Hindu, he allowed his wife to embrace Christianity. A moderate in politics, Bannerjee placed great faith in the British sense of justice. Rich as he was, he is credited with financially supporting the Congress in its early days. It has been said that he "stood by the cradle of the Congress which he nurtured with parental solicitude and affection."

Annie Besant (1847-1933), a renowned theosophist, figures prominently in the history of the freedom movement in India and as the initiator of the Home Rule League. Of predominantly Irish lineage, Mrs Besant first came to india in 1893 where she lectured on Hindu religion and culture in several towns. Her slogan "England's difficulty is India's opportunity' became a catchphrase in the nationalist armoury. Her appeal was more to the English-educated middle classes. She gave the Congress its first flag which was green and red—a white portion with the spinning wheel was added later.

Syed Husain Bilgrami (1842-1926) was an eminent Muslim educationist and one of the first two Indians (the other being Sir K.S. Gupta) to be a member of the India Council of the Secretary of State in London. The programme for educational reform implemented in the erstwhile state of Hyderabad was largely structured by Bilgrami and almost all educational institutions in the state, barring perhaps Osmania University and New Girls' School, owe their origin to his efforts. Bilgrami exhorted his co-religionists to steer clear of the Congress and to concentrate on the educational progress of the community.

Romesh Chunder Dutt (1848-1909) belonged to a highly educated and cultured Bengali family. His father was one of the first Indians to become a deputy collector in Bengal. His two cousins, Aru and Toru Dutt became famous as accomplished scholars in French and English. A typical product of Macaulay's school of education, Dutt joined the Indian Civil Service and was later to write *History of Civilisation in Ancient India* as well as History of Bengali Literature. In 1899 Dutt presided over the fifteenth annual session of the Indian National Congress at Lucknow. A biographer has referred to Dutt's career as "an unanswerable demonstration" of the capacity of India to produce citizens of the highest calibre.

Incidentally, Thomas Babington Macaulay's famous Minute on Education which was to transform the Indian educational system for ever was written in 1835. A brilliantly argued essay for the retention of English education, Macaulay's Minute somewhat contemptuously discarded all 'oriental learning' as devoid of utility. When Sai Baba was born, probably nobody in Pathri ever had heard any sound in English! Sai Baba, let it be remembered, belonged to the pre-1857 generation. Gopal Krishna Gokhale was born in 1866 and Mahatma Gandhi in 1869. Only Bal Gangadhar Tilak was born in 1856.

Interestingly, one of the greatest names in Indian history, Rani Laxmi Bai of Jhansi was born in 1835, in the same decade as Sai Baba and one always wonders whether Sai Baba was aware of her great fight for independence. We have so little information on these matters, though, surely, Sai Baba could not have been unaware of what was going on in the political field.

Pherozeshah Mehta (1845-1915), a pioneering nationalist, one of the first Indians to secure higher western education was the first Parsi to acquire a Master's degree. Along with Badruddin Tyabji (1844-1906) and K.T. Telang, Mehta was to form the Bombay Presidency Association which, under his tutelage served as the organisational wing of the Indian National Congress.

It will be seen from this distinguished roster that it was not that education was unavailable to an Indian citizen either before or immediately after the rebellion of 1857. Not all of them mentioned came from rich families. Gokhale, indeed, came from a poor family. All of them did well. But there is no record that any of them were aware of the saint of Shirdi. Sai Baba lived in a different world.

It would seem that right from the beginning he was untouched by the events around him. There is almost a total lack of verifiable historical evidence about his early days. It is generally held that he left his home at the tender age of eight in the company of a Sufi fakir. The story has been recounted in an earlier chapter. It has been said that the fakir 'claimed' Sai Baba as his own, and that the parents of Sai Baba gave him away.

Answers to many pertinent questions about Sai Baba are found in the hallowed text of Shri Sai Satcharita composed by Govind Raghunath Dabholkar. It must not be forgotten, however that it is more in the nature of 'religious' text and the core of it is in essence a legend rather than historical truth for Sai Baba had become a legend in his own life time. For this reason, historical truth must be searched for elsewhere. This need has been largely met by books by two sanyasins, Swami Sai Sharan Anand and B.V. Narasimhaswami.

Says Shri Sai Satcharita: "Baba appeared first in Shirdi at the age of sixteen. He stayed at that time in Shirdi for three years. Then he vanished, only to surface in the Nizam's territory.

Thereafter he came with a marriage party to Shirdi and settled there permanently. He was then twenty years old. From that time onwards, he lived continuously for sixty years in Shirdi. This is known to all. In the year *shake* 1840, on the 10th of the bright lunar phase in *Ashwin* (October 15, 1918 A.D.), Baba breathed his last on the auspicious day of *Vijaya dashami.....*"

A detailed account of what Baba did in the three years of his first visit to Shirdi, how he disappeared and returned with Chandbhai Patil of Dhupkhed is given in Shri Sai Satcharit.

Baba who left his home in the company of a fakir arrived on the banks of the Godavari. One can only guess the route that the fakir took. There then were no highways, no railways, certainly no motor cars. A traveller would either have to take a bullock cart or walk the distance.

Those who are familiar with the terrain around Pathri will get some idea about how Baba travelled from an anecdote narrated by Baba himself:

"The path is from Pathri. From there Shailud (Sailu), Manoor (Manavat) and Jalnapur. I had been once (by that route). It took me eight days. By day I trod over the grass and slept at night in the grass. We walked step by step." Thus Baba reached Paithan-Aurangabad where he stayed for twelve years in a mosque and *guided* a fakir.

We do not know much about the first fakir who took Sai Baba along with him. Was he just a mendicant or a mendicant scholar? Where did the older man and his 'disciple' get their clothes? How did they live? Did they go begging from door to door? Did they have a roof over their heads while travelling? Sai Baba is reported to have slept in the grass. Of those years from the day Baba left home to the day he arrived in Shirdi, there is a painful blank.

Sai Baba's first arrival in Shirdi has been recounted in Shri Sai Satcharita. The story is as follows: There lived in a village called Dhoop, in Aurangabad district, a well-to-do Mohammadan gentleman by the name of Chand Patil. Once, while he was making a trip to Aurangabad, he lost his mare. He kept watch

76

for it for two long months, but there was no trace of his mare. Disappointed, he decided to return home. He had hardly walked some 5 miles, when he came upon an odd-looking man sitting at the foot of a mango tree. He had a cap on his head and he wore a *kafni* (long robe). Under his arm pit was a *satka* and he was preparing to smoke a *chilim* (clay pipe). Seeing Chand Patil passing by the man called out to him in a friendly sort of way and asked him to share his *chilim*. The man, who turned out to be a fakir asked Patil why he was carrying a saddle. Patil sadly said: "I have lost my mare." The Fakir replied: "But have you looked in the *nala* close by?" Intrigued, Patil went to the *nala* (a rude irregular stream or its dry bed) to find, to his utter surprise, that the mare was standing there—Patil returned to the place where the fakir was sitting, dragging the mare with him. "Have a smoke," said the fakir, quietly, getting the *chilim* ready. But two things were needed, fire to light the pipe and a little water to wet the *chhapi* (a piece of cloth through which the smoke is inhaled).

But even as Chand Patil watched, the fakir thrust his tongs into the earth and out came a burning ember as if by magic! Then the fakir hit the ground with his *satka* where-upon water began to ooze out. The *chilim* thereafter was lit and the *chhapi* wetted. Chand Patil looked on with fascination. A miracle had been nonchalantly performed right in front of his eyes and the fakir hardly seemed even aware of what he had done. Wonder-struck Patil requested the fakir to accompany him to his home and accept his hospitality. Patil was a village official and was a man of some importance. He told the fakir that his brother-in-law's son was to be married to a girl from Shirdi and would he care to accompany the marriage party? The fakir agreed. So off they went. The marriage ceremony went off without a hitch and Chand Patil and his party returned to Dhoop. But the fakir stayed on in Shirdi.

The fakir was Sai Baba.

Vishwas B. Kher who personally visited Dhupkhed, south-west of Aurangabad, in October 1982, wrote two articles in *Shri Sai Leela* of March and April 1985 under the title *The Miracle of The Mare* wherein he states that the aforesaid account in

Shri Sai Satcharita seems to be based on hearsay. He records that "there is only one Muslim family in the whole village and it comprises the descendants of Chand Patil. Chand Patil had no issue. Chandbhai's cottage is in ruins and is not habited. In the cottage nearby lives Gulabkhan the son of Chand Patil's brother Ansarkhan. He is about eighty years old. His wife Umarbi is also alive. Gulabkhan's son Lalkhan, is about fifty. We learnt from him that Chand Patil died about forty five years ago and within five years thereof Ansarkhan at the age of one hundred and four, breathed his last." The actual encounter between Sai Baba and Chand Patil took place according to Gulabkhan near the twin villages Sindhon Bindhon, 24 kms South of Aurangabad. "Chand Patil then returned to Dhupkhed along with Sai Baba. Sai Baba camped in the maidan by the bank of Yelganga river on the outskirts of Dhupkhed and spent his time under the trees or wandering around in the forest. It is not possible to say definitely how long Sai Baba was in Dhupkhed. According to Lalkhan he passed some years in Dhupkhed and then accompanied the marriage party of Chand Patil to Shirdi where the sister of Chand Patil got married to Aminbhai's son Hamid." This version agrees broadly with what is stated by Ramgir Bua (called as Bapugir by Sai Baba) in his statement dated 1st December, 1936 to B.V. Narasimhaswami. Ramgir Bua was then seventy-six years old. Ramgir Bua says that he was a boy of about 8 or 10 studying in the village school when Sai Baba first arrived in Shirdi. Sai Baba then appeared to be about 25 to 30 years of age. Ramgir Bua had heard the wonderful tale of the Miracle of the Mare from Chand Patil's lips.

The marriage party had alighted in Shirdi at the foot of a banyan tree—not an uncommon occurance those days when housing was difficult if not unheard of. The tree was in a field close to Khandoba's Temple. The carts were unharnessed in the open coutyard of Khandoba's Temple and the members of the marriage party descended one by one. The fakir, too, got down. Bhagat Mhalsapati who owned the temple saw the fakir and said to him: 'Ya Sai!' (Welcome, Sai!) The name Sai stuck. Nobody, neither Chand Patil nor Bhagat Mhalsapati had obviously bothered to ask the fakir his name. He was addressed as Sai. And Sai he became. At least that is one theory. Some hold that it is implausible. According to Narasimhaswami when Sai Baba arrived in Shirdi, he found Khandoba's Temple which belonged to Bhagat Mhalsapati, a man of orthodox views. Mhalsapati took Sai Baba as a muslim and would not, therefore let him enter the temple. So Sai Baba had to camp in the courtyard of one Aminbhai, a short distance from the temple. Narasimhaswami believes that it is inconceivable that Mhalsapati would have addressed a simple fakir as Sai, which means, Lord, Master, God or fakir. The other theory is that people addressed him as Sai because they mistook him for a fakir.

Indeed even in the matter of what Sai wore when he first arrived in Shirdi there are differences of opinion. Mhalsapati has been quoted as saying that when he first saw Sai Baba, his kafni was of ochre colour as was his cap and *dhoti*. One Kashiram, a tailor, is subsequently reported to have stitched a green kafni and cap for Baba. Are these made-up stories? Ochre is the colour of the Hindu sanyasi. Green is the colour favoured by Muslims. Another report has it that later on Baba took to wearing white *kafnis* and a piece of white cloth round his head. That would be a neutral colour. However, it is claimed that at the time of Baba's nirvana, a green cap was found in a bundle of clothes that Baba often used as a pillow. That bundle is now in the possession of the *sansthan*.

It is quite possible that because he was refused admission to the temple, Baba found it convenient to stay in Shirdi's *masjid*. But even here, accounts vary. One account has Baba quarrelling with the son-in-law of Mohiddin and in consequence removing himself to a nearby forest of babul trees, on the outskirts of Shirdi. There is no confirmation available, either, of Baba's dancing with *ghungarus* tied round his ankles. It is claimed that Baba had a good knowledge of music and he was often heard to sing bhajans in his melodious voice. One M.B. Rege, a former Judge of the Indore State High Court had the rare fortune of listening to Baba sing. According to Rege, Baba not only could sing well, but could correct anyone who got their *ragas* wrong.

At the time that Baba was staying in the *masjid* there lived a saint in Shirdi named Devidas. Baba apparently liked his company. Later they were joined by another saintly man called Jankidas. It is also said that a *Vaishnav* householder saint from Puntambe by name Gangagir was a frequent visitor to Shirdi. When Gangagir watched Baba for the first time, he is reported to have said: "Blessed is Shirdi that it has this precious jewel. This is no ordinary person. Lucky and meritorious Shirdi is indeed to have him!" Baba, then, was still in his teens. But to many he struck as someone extraordinary.

There are many stories about Baba's early days in Shirdi. One concerns a wrestling bout that Baba had with one Mohiuddin Tamboli. Baba lost and reportedly look to wearing a *kafni* as a result. Ramgir Bua emphatically states that Sai Baba did not wrestle but had a quarrel with Mohiuddin's son-in-law, a *mantrika,* as a result of which Sai Baba resorted to the jungle about a mile or two away from Shirdi.

Another story says that at Shirdi, Baba came into contact with a *mahatma* and, looking upon him as his *guru,* served him for twelve years with his heart and soul. Baba has been quoted as saying: "My *guru* would sit at one place. He would never leave his seat and would even perform all his bodily functions right at the same spot. Feeding him and cleaning up the place were my responsibilities. Whatever you see in me is the result of that service."

As his *guru's* time for taking samadhi approached, it is said that Baba constructed an edifice under the neem tree to the left of the *guru padukasthan* and spent many years in the underground cell *(hypogeum)* opposite, in loving memory of his guru. This *samadhi* was first noticed when Rao Bahadur Sathe, the owner of the place, who was all ready to erect a staircase to the verandah of the upper storey of the edifice. When asked what should be done about it, Sai Baba's reply was: "Do not disturb it. It is the samadhi of my ancestors. Make a bay-window and construct the staircase over it. God will bless those who burn live incense before it on Thursdays and Fridays." The underground cell when first noticed extended from Sathewada to the Masjid and the *chavadi.* There was a small door behind the *chavadi* for exit. In those early days, Sai Baba once said, he grew matted hair which was so long that it touched the ground. Pointing to the column near the *dhuni* in the masjid, Sai Baba is also reported to have said: "There was an underground cell where I would spend the day. Though people would move about near by, I would not come out. Only when a virtuous man came, would I emerge and hold discourse with him."

Many have asked the question: who was Baba's guru? As in the matter of Baba himself, there is no reliable information about him. In Chapter 26 of *Bhakti Saramrit* (originally written in Marathi), Das Ganu has inferred that the name of Baba's guru may have been Venkusa. Based on this information, Narasimhaswami imagines from the obscure and uncertain replies which Baba gave to a first class magistrate in a theft case that he had stated the name of his guru as Venkusa. But there seems to be no correct information on this score.

But there can be no two questions but that Baba had a guru and that they were fond of each other. Sai Baba would often say: "For a human being, the guru's place is preeminent. By keeping utmost faith in him alone, everything is obtained. A devotee's entire strength is due to his guru. Devotion to the guru is superior to devotion to gods or goddesses. The guru is the supreme being." And he would praise and commend devotion to guru.

Does that meet the question though? Writing in Shri Sai Leela (April 1976) Vishwas B. Kher, who has done much research on the matter, has come to the conclusion that Das Ganu's inference that Shri Gopalrao Keshavrao Deshmukh (1715-1802) could possibly have been Baba's guru is absolutely wrong as Gopalrao was born much before Baba's time. Kher also avers that it is doubtful whether such a person as Roshan Sha Mia ever existed to be Baba's guru. Then could it be that Baba really had no guru? Kher answers this as follows: "Just as Tukaram had a glimpse of his guru Babaji in his dream or as Ramdas had revelation of Shri Rama, similarly Sai Baba may have had, for all we know, direct perception of the Divine, Venkatesh, Roshan or by whatever name you call it." According to Bahinabai, saint-poetess and disciple of Tukaram, the *guruparampara* (regular succession of gurus) of her Master is,

Jnaneshwar - Satchidanand - Vishwambhar - Raghavachaitanya - Keshavchaitanya - Babaji - Tukaram. Incidentally, Satchidananda was a scribe of Jnaneshwar for his famous composition Jnaneshwari.

However, when queried further about his conclusion, Kher told this writer: "I have been pondering for a long time over the problem of the guru of Sai Baba. I have revised my earlier opinion and finally come to the conclusin that a sufi divine was the guru of Sai Baba. The name of the Sufi divine is not known.

Sai Baba had left his home for good at the age of eight in the company of a fakir as revealed by him to Swami Sai Sharan Anand and Mhalsapati. Sai Baba had also told Swami Sai Sai Sharan Anand that he had lived with his guru for twelve years. Further that his guru was a mahatma who had taken him in hand and moulded him. This finds confirmation in the account given in *Shri Sai Satcharit*."

According to *Shri Sai Satcharit,* Baba is supposed to have said: "I stayed with my guru for twelve years. It is rare to find a person like my guru. He was a great *aulia* (spiritual master) and was the personification of love and kindness. How shall I describe his love? He was ever in the highest state of meditation and was full of bliss. His was the serene wisdom, free from things of desire. The school of instruction of my guru greatly attracted me. I lost my longing for home, the fetters of attachment were broken and I forgot everything including hunger and thirst. He became my all-in-all—home, father and mother. He expected nothing from me except unwavering faith and patience combined with courage. I was single-mindedly devoted to him. As a result he was highly pleased and ever protected me. Whether he was near or far, he looked after me as a tortoise looks after her young ones on the yonder bank by mere gaze and never felt that I was separated from him. What I am is the result of my devotion and service to my guru. He satisfied all my highest urges and I did not have to look elsewhere for guidance."

That is a remarkable statement and cannot possibly be more explicit.

Sai Baba spent approximately over twenty years or so of his early life in Marathwada before he came to Shirdi. Out of this period he spent approximately half the time in the company of his guru and the other half in instructing a fakir in Aurangabad. And when he arrived in Shirdi, he was a grown up man of about thirty, no doubt tempered in the discipline of *tapas, sadhana* and austerity.

It will be seen from this that the evidence even of Baba's arrival at a certain age is conflicting. Did he come when he was just sixteen or when he was about thirty and above? What exactly did he learn from his guru? The Gita? The Koran? How to become a *siddha*? In Shri Sai Satcharit, at the time of his arrival in Shirdi, he is described as a "fair and handsome lad." A lad of thirty? Consider the evidence of the aged mother of Nana Chopdar, a resident of Shirdi: She is quoted as saying: "Initially, this fair and handsome lad was seen sitting under the neem tree. People were astonished at the sight of this beautiful youth. He practised severe austerities. Cold or heat did not affect him. When first sighted he was a knower of *Brahman*. Even in his dreams he was desireless. His renunciation was firm as if he had abandoned *maya* (illusion) completely. People from far and near came for his *darshan*. By day he kept no company; he was not afraid of darkness. Where could this youth have come from was the thought that filled the minds of all. His form was so comely that it would be a case of love at first sight for anyone. He did not visit any household. He was mostly seen sitting under the neem tree. Everyone would wonder on seeing this personification of renunciation."

A story is also told about the underground cell, and is attributed to Nana Chopdar's mother.

"An astonishing thing happened one day. It was the day of Khandoba's Fair. Two to four persons began to shiver, heave and chatter as if possessed by the spirit. People started asking them questions (as was customary). They wanted to know who Baba's parents were and whence he came from. The spirit replied: "Get a hoe, dig at the place I point out and you will know." One man brought a hoe and began to dig at the spot opposite the neem tree as pointed out. After digging for some time at the place, a layer of bricks was noticed. Below the layer of bricks was found one of the pair of discs of a quern. On removing the stone disc, an underground cell was seen which was plastered with lime and in its four corners were four lighted *samais* (upright lamps usually made of brass or silver). A *paat* (a low wooden stool), a *gomukhi* (a glove shaped like the mouth of a cow used for covering the hand while telling the beads) and a rosary were also found there. The spirit said: "This boy practised penance here for 12 years." Then people plied Baba with questions and Baba answered: "This is the shrine of my guru. Take care of it."

Over and over again, one comes across the question: how did Sai Baba become what he became? One can establish the fact that he had a guru—whoever he be. One can establish the further fact that there was a great deal of rapport between guru and *shishya* (disciple). But beyond that we come to a wall. What did the guru teach his disciple? Was there a regular 'academic' session between the two? Did the guru teach Baba by rote the entire *Koran* and the *Gita*? Was there any discussion between the two? Was there ever any disagreement between the teacher and the taught? How did Baba attain *siddhi* powers? A facile answer to such questions would be that the guru was merely symbolic, that Baba did not really need a guru as he was *swayam-siddha,* self-realised and that the matter of his having a *fakir* as a guru is just an example of *maya*—illusion. The *fakir* may have been a guru, but Baba did not really need him, except to fulfil a phase of one's life where having a guru is important. There have been references in many biographies of Baba that he practised 'austerities' and 'penance'. What did these austerities consist of? Doing without food and clothing? Living in the open? Sitting in a trance as if in deep meditation? Gautama, the Buddha, we know, sat under a *bodhi* tree and practised penance until one day, the truth dawned on him. In Baba's case we have the bodhi tree substituted by a neem tree. It couldn't have been leafy enough to provide Baba some shade. We know that Baba often confined himself to an underground cell. But what exactly is the nature of his *tapas*? At what stage in his life did he find his truth? Information on all such questions is at best sketchy or derivative, based on chance remarks that Baba made into which much has been read by devoted followers. We draw a blank when it comes to knowing at what stage Baba realised that he could work miracles. Was it at the instant of his guru's passing away? We know the time when Sri Ramakrishna Paramahansa (1836-1886) literally initiated Swami Vivekananda, then still Narendra Dutta (1863-1902), into knowledge of God. Sri Ramakrishna was an early and Vivekananda a later contemporary of Baba who outlived both. But while there is so much available about Sri Ramakrishna, thanks, mainly to a disciple and about Vivekananda, even of his *parivrajaka* times, much of what we know about Baba has to be judged by the test of reason.

At the time that Baba went to Shirdi, it was an insignificant village, in Kopergaon taluka of Ahmednagar district of the composite Bombay Province upto 1960. In the Bombay Gazetteer (Vol XVII) of Ahmednagar district published in 1884, it is mentioned in a chart of 'Kopergaon villages, 1883 and is grouped under 'Taraf Korhale thirty villages' where it is spelt as Shirdhi. Speaking of the one and only road in Kopergaon taluka to Malegaon, the Gazetteer says: "This road (from Ahmednagar) enters the Kopergaon sub-division in the 45th mile from Ahmednagar near the village of Ashtagaon and passing through the villages of Rahata 49 miles, Shirdi 52½ miles, Nighoj-Nimgaon 54 miles, Kopergaon 60½ miles and Yesgaon 65 miles, enters the Yeola sub-division of Nasik in the sixty seventh mile. The Godavari river at Kopargaon is crossed by a wire-rope ferry."

Sai Baba attained *Nirvana* in 1918 and Shirdi thereafter generally faded out of public memory until the sixties and seventies of the twentieth century when it suddenly shot into prominence and Sai Baba's shrine began attracting large crowds so that in the Gazetteer of India of Maharashtra State, Ahmednagar district, published in 1976 it was considered sufficiently important for seven and a quarter pages to be devoted to it.

Our only source of information of what Shirdi was like in

Sai Baba's own time (1868-1918) is an article contributed by Balkrishna Vishwanath Dev, *Mamledar* which was published in *Shri Sai Leela* in 1932. Dev first went to Shirdi in 1910 for Sai Baba's *darshan.* Later he recorded his impressions. He noted that the name 'Shirdi' is actually a corrupt form of 'Shiladhi' or 'Shailadhi' and that at that time the village had about 400 houses big and small, two wells, a Marathi school upto the seventh standard as well as a Marathi Mission School, two *panmalas,* two orchards, one flower garden, nine temples, two masjids, one dharamshala, one sugar mill, one flour mill, one water mill and that the total population was 2,568, the Hindus being divided into the following castes: Brahmins, Marwadis, Marathas, Dhangars (shepherds), Malis (growers of fruits and vegetables), Sonars (goldsmiths), Sutars (carpenters), Lohars (blacksmiths), Kumbhars (potters), Parits (washermen), Mahars, Mangs, Chamars (leather workers and tanners), Kolis, Bhils (scheduled tribes), Guravs and Vadars. They constitute quite a miscellany. Shirdi may have been insignificant, but it seems to have been prosperous. The presence of potters, blacksmiths, carpenters and other craftsmen indicates that Shirdi was eminently self-sufficient in the Gandhian sense of the term. There is no reference to any bookshop. Presumably there wasn't any in the village. We have no idea of the percentage of literacy or of the circulation of any newspaper or whether anyone in the village ever read anything.

Mrs. Tarabai Sadashiv Tarkhad, wife of Sadashiv Tarkhad, Manager, Raja Bahadur Cotton Textile Spinning and Weaving Mills, Pune in a statement made in 1936 has said: "In those days Shirdi was a neglected hamlet without any lighting, sweeping or other conveniences of civilisation. It has had some improvements since. But when I was there, the streets and passages were all dark and unlit at night. On the outskirts of the villages there was a thick growth of prickly Babul trees."

If that was so in the second decade of the 20th century, one can well imagine conditions in Shirdi when Baba first went there to settle down. They must have been horrendous! Sai Baba arrived in Shirdi around 1868. The political configuration of India had changed. Peace had been established in the country.

Land settlement was to follow. The rebellion of 1857 was a distant memory.

Sai Baba, of course, had nothing to do with politics. There is no indication ever of his having discussed the nature of the rulers, their benevolence or otherwise. His concerns were with matters of the spirit. He had a set routine. Every morning he would go out for alms and stand in front of the houses of Bayajabai Kote Patil, Patlibua Gondkar, Nandram Savairam (obviously a marwadi), Appaji Kote and Narayan Teli (oil presser) who would dutifully give him his day's needs. It is clear that he had won their hearts and their respect. In those early years he was yet to gather a band of devotees. The alms-gathering of the day over, Baba would be back in his masjid, bothering none, and none evidently bothering him. A mad fakir he was considered to be, but even mad fakirs had their uses. In a village that did not boast of having even an ayurvedic doctor—allopathic medicine, of course, was still to come to India in its present shape—a fakir sufficed, since he was believed to have magic powers. In any event what was a fakir for, if not to help those around him? So many villagers would go to Baba with their trifling health problems like fever or a stomach ache believing that he could cure them. We learn that at first Baba would administer to them some indigenous remedies. How come he was aware of them? Where did he learn about their curative properties? Or was this knowledge part of the education imparted to Baba by his guru? Or, again, was Baba administering those simple remedies from hearsay? At what point in time did he shift from prescribing herbal and other remedies to giving his patients *udi* from his *dhuni*?

In later years he was to freely distribute the *udi* (ashes of the sacred fire that perpetually burnt before him) and many have testified that partaking of the *udi* had miraculous results. We will discuss the miracles later. The point is that the ashes by themselves could not have had any medicinal properties. How could the same ashes cure a variety of ailments? Was it a matter of faith-healing? Baba was not one to play on the credulity of the simple villagers who had put faith in him. Then was it a part of what Baba's devotees call his 'leela', a word that is somewhat hard to define but suggests divine action that is beyond man's comprehension?

Throughout all those sixty years he lived in Shirdi, the man never changed. Age took its toll all right. The hair greyed, where once he lived practically alone, hundreds now came to see him and got his blessings. If once he had to ask for alms, in his later years food came to him unasked and unsought. Yet until two days or so before his end he followed the fakir's routine. Often he would mumble to himself and many believed that may be he was a little touched in the head. He assumed no spiritual airs, nor was it necessary. He had come to be addressed as Sai Baba. The dictionary meaning of 'Sai' or 'Sain' is: Lord, God, Husband (Beloved), Fakir. Kabir, the weaver saint, has frequently used the word 'Sain' in his *sakhis* and *dohas,* in the sense of 'Lord' or 'God'. Sri Ramakrishna is quoted as saying that the Perfect Man among the *Shaktas* is called Kaula, among the Vedantins as Paramahansa and among the Vaishnavas of Baul sect, *Sain.* Incidentally, the literal meaning of the word 'Baul' is 'God-intoxicated devotee' and a Baul is a minstrel or mendicant of one of the Vaishnava sects in Bengal. Among the Kartabhaja Sect are four classes: the Auls, Bauls, Derveshes and Sains. The highest attainers among them were the Sains. Or, should we say, Sais? Our Baba certainly was a Sai and deserved the appellation, though, as we have seen earlier, it is given spontaneously, as in a form of greeting.

Baba never left Shirdi, except for a brief period; he never went round expounding a philosophy or preaching to the people. Of course he addressed people who came to see him. But Shirdi was his entire world. His needs were few. Till the day of his attainment of *nirvana* he retained his simple, sparse, habits. Even though it became unnecessary for him to seek alms, he would accept whatever was offered to him by his devotees who kept increasing in number as the months and years rolled by. But this he did as a concession to the feelings of the men and women who thronged round him. He never changed his mode of dress. The *kafni* was all he wore. He did not have a wardrobe. It would have looked ridiculous if he had one. It was useless to provide him with a new set of clothes since he would give it away as soon as he received it. The *kafni* stayed on his body until it was torn and tattered. Such pictures of him as are available show his *kafni* torn in the sleeve.

But the crowds of devotees was a matter of the future. In the early seventies Baba was still very much alone though he enjoyed visits from virtuous men. He had ceased to administer simple medicines and thereafter the villagers kept away from him. There was a period in Baba's life when he was 'god-intoxicated'. He would sleep at night on a narrow wooden plank about 10 inches broad suspended from the rafter of the roof and secured by rags. At the head and foot of the plank, *pantis* (earthen saucerlike receptacles filled with oil and a cotton wick to serve as lamps) would be lighted. No one ever saw Baba either getting on or off the plank, but he would be noticed lying on that ramshackle 'bed'. It became the talk of Shirdi until Baba, in disgust, got rid of it. Many years thereafter Baba told the story of his penance to Kakasaheb Dikshit who was moved to say: "If you are so fond of sleeping on the plank, I will get one suspended for you rightaway so you could use it tonight!" Baba replied: "Never mind, how would it do for me to sleep up while Mhalsapati by my side lies on the ground?" Whereupon Dikshit promised that he would get a plank up for Mhalsapati also. To which Baba replied: "Kaka, it is not for any ordinary man to sleep on a suspended plank. He wouldn't be able to get any sleep. And who can do without sleep?"

And then Baba added: "I tell Mhalsapati to keep his hand on my heart and watch the continuous *nama smaran* which goes on there. I tell him to wake me up the moment it stops. But you know, Mhalsapati falls asleep while doing this. His hand becomes heavy as a stone. How then can he sleep on a plank? He alone who is ever watchful and awake and absorbed in devotion can sleep as I do on a suspended plank."

Baba would also hint at the sounding of the drum of the beginningless eternity within the soul, which is referred to by *yogis* as *anaahat* and by Sufis as *saut-e-sarmadi,* in order to draw attention to the fact that the loving devotee is ever watchful and every single breath of his is accompanied by *nama-smaran* (remembrance of the name of the Lord).

Swami Sai Sharan Anand has written: "It is not only in his heart but from every limb, every bone and every pore of his body did this *anaahat* sound emerge. In an ordinary individual his limbs and bones are in a state of torpor. But in Sai Baba's body these were not only active but permeated with the divine essence and so he claimed that though, one day, he may not be any more in flesh and blood "my bones will assure you from the grave, my tomb will communicate with you and will sway with him who surrenders to the spirit (in it)." Baba also said: "Do not ever think I will be lost to you. Remember me with intense devotion and you will be blessed."

In addition to sleeping on a suspended plank that was too narrow for comfort, Sai Baba apparently observed other *hatha yoga* practices. It is said, for instance, that he would go to the stream north of the masjid in privacy, take out his intestines, clean them and hang them up for drying—totally unbelievable but the legend has persisted. Similarly it has also been said that he would practise the more difficult act of *khand yoga* (severance of various limbs of the body) at night in the masjid. Were anyone to visit Baba at the masjid at certain hours of the night, there would be no Baba in the vicinity, but only several limbs in different places! If his head were at one place, his hands would be at another and his trunk at yet another and so on. In the morning Baba was whole and back again as if nothing had happened at night.

It is not clear why he should be indulging in such yogic practices and to what purpose. What was he trying to prove? How often did he indulge in this *khand yoga*? Did he have to practise it? It is clear that he was not trying to convince anybody about his *siddhi* powers. In any event he was having a steadily increasing band of devotees and Baba neither needed nor wanted nor sought popularity for its own sake. What, then, can be the explanation for such practices? The orthodox explanation, still unconvincing except to those who want to be convinced is that this was "a play of Sai Baba's yogic powers."

The question can be asked: If he was so powerful, why did he give up the practice of administering ayurvedic medicines? One report has it that he stopped giving these medicines after one of his patients died and the explanation given is that the man had not followed the prescribed regimen. It is said that after this particular incident Baba stopped prescribing medicine but instead took to giving *udi* to those who came to him.

It is said that after he ceased to prescribe medicines his life style changed drastically. Now he began to wear tattered garments and begged for alms as many times and as often as he liked. He would carry a *dhoti* on his shoulder and gathering one end of it, he would convert it into a *zoli* (bag) and put dry *bhiksha* (offerings) like rice, *bhakri* (unleavened millet bread) in it. In another hand he would carry a tumbler in which he would accept all liquid or semi-liquid substances like *amti,* cooked vegetables, chatni, milk, curd etc. He would then keep all that he had received on his rounds in a *kundi* (open-mouthed jar). Crows, dogs and cats would take away morsels of food from the *kundi,* since it was never closed, and neither Baba nor anyone would shoo them away. The person sweeping the masjid would also take away ten or twelve *bhakris* without anyone questioning him. If any poor, hungry or unexpected visitor arrived, he or she would be fed from the same *kundi.* To keep visitors away, Baba sometimes would feign anger. So the villagers called him a mad fakir and did not go his way or trouble him. But there was one pious Maratha lady who knew his worth. Bayajabai. She somehow seemed to have understood the worth of Baba and his spiritual eminence. She vowed never to take any meal unless Baba was first fed. By day Baba would be either near his *guru-samadhi* or in the fields or in the jungle near by or in Nimgaon. No matter where he was at any given time, Bayajabai would religiously carry Baba's meal in a wicker basket held over her head, seek him out and feed him. Years later Baba was to favour her son Tatya Ganpat Kote and help him out of his difficulties, raise him in the eyes of society and ultimately, it is claimed even lay down his life in exchange for Tatya's. Mhalsapati who first addressed Baba as Sai and took him to his village introduced to him his two friends Kashiram Shimpi and Appa Jagale. This trio received all sadhus, *gosains, bairagis* (renunciates), fakirs and such other holy men who would visit Shirdi and served them. The three became·Baba's devotees who gave them their all. It is they who arranged for his stay in the masjid.

In those early days Sai Baba did not accept *dakshina* (cash offerings) from anyone. He wouldn't even accept it from Kashiram which would drive the faithful devotee to tears. To Kashiram, he was the donor and Baba the recipient. Baba knew this too well. So Baba went on a new tack. Repeatedly he would ask Kashiram for *dakshina*. At first he would be happy to receive only a pice (1/ 64 part of a rupee) but slowly he started raising his demand. The time soon came when Kashiram could not give any more. In a larger sense his financial position deteriorated and no one would lend him money. His plight was miserable. It was then that Kashiram realised that both the donor and recipient were fractions of his radiance and that Baba must have reduced him to penury in order to get the message across to him. It is said that the day Kashiram realised this, his financial affairs started to show marked improvement. Thereafter, whether Baba asked him for *dakshina* or not, he never lost his equanimity.

Kashiram was a vendor of clothes and on bazaar days he would set up his shop in nearby villages. Once while he was returning from Naur Bazaar he had an encounter with an armed party of Bhil free-booters. Kashiram gave away all that he had except a small bundle with which he would not part. The plunderers thought that the bundle contained the most valuable things and hence to be prised out of him. Actually the bundle contained only powdered sugar which Kashiram always carried with him to feed ants. So when the Bhils tried to snatch it away from him, he resisted them stoutly. He picked up a sword of one of the looters that had been thrown to the ground and put two robbers to death. But a third robber hit him on his head with an axe. Kashiram lost consciousness and fell to the ground. Believing him to be dead the rest of the robbers fled. Kashiram, however, was not dead. He regained his consciousness after some time. Such was his faith in Sai Baba that instead of trying to find a doctor he reported himself to Baba who treated him. Within a few days, Kashiram was restored to normalcy. For his bravery, Kashiram received a sword as an award from the Government of Bombay.

What Kashiram did not know, but came to know later was that even as he was fighting the robbers, back in Shirdi, Baba was uttering cries of distress and hitting himself on his mouth like a man possessed. Those who watched him could not understand what the matter was but believed that he was reacting to something far away. Which he was, indeed. The coincidence was eerie. Baba was going to the rescue of his devotee as only he could. No man could have survived single-handedly the onslaught of a gang of armed robbers. But Kashinath did. It was taken as a sign of *guru-kripa*—the infinite mercy of the guru.

Many years after this incident, Kashiram passed away on *Ekadashi* Day, considered auspicious by Hindus. Appa Jagale similarly died after serving Baba for many years. Only Mhalsapati survived right up to the *samadhi* of Baba.

The masjid was where Baba would sleep every alternate day. On such day Mhalsapati would give Baba company. He would go to the masjid around 9 p.m. and sit the whole night through, conversing with Baba, while reclining against a pillar. If Mhalsapati dozed off, Baba would wake him up. This went on for fourteen years. Tatya Patil was yet another who joined the duo. They would be conversing the night through. Their discussions have gone unrecorded.

On the full-moon day in the month of *Margashirsha* (November-December) in the Sake year 1807 (1885 A.D.) Baba had a severe bout of asthma. He summoned Mhalsapati and told him: "I am entrusting my body to your custody. I am going into *samadhi*. Please take care of the body for three days".

Saying that, Baba went into *nirvikalpa* samadhi. As instructed, Mhalsapati stood guard by the body which was motionless. For all one knew he was dead. At least that was what the villagers thought and were it not for the vigilant Mhalsapati, they would have taken the body for ceremonial burial. Actually some people were heard muttering about making the necessary funeral arrangements. But Mhalsapati would not hear of such things. He sat there by Baba's body. On the third day Baba returned to normal consciousness and everyone was happy. Mhalsapati practically became Baba's *alter ego.* There was one other person close to Baba and that was Abdul. Born in 1869 Abdul was a servitor of Amiruddin fakir of Nanded. A mysterious event took place in 1889. Sai Baba appeared in a dream to Amiruddin, materialised two real mangoes and told him to give those mangoes to Abdul and send him to Shirdi. On his arrival in Shirdi, Baba exclaimed: "Well, my crow has come!"

From Abdul's unpublished works in Urdu, it is clear that Baba had a profound knowledge of Islam, *Sira.* (the life of the Prophet Mohammad), *sunna* (his code of conduct), *hadith* (traditions), the *fakah, shariat* and the *tarikat.* Just as Sai Baba could explain, elaborate and comment with deep insight into the meaning of the Vedas, the Upanishads, the Gita and the works of saints in *prakrit,* similarly, he was equally at ease with all the Muslim religious works and traditions, including the writings of Sufi shaikhs or orders like Kadaria, Chistia, Suhrawardiya and Nakshabandhi. In fact his range of knowledge was fantastic and incredible, passing all comprehension.

Baba was a unique blend of all faiths and observed no barrier of religion, sect, race, sex, caste, creed, language or nation. He confirmed each devotee who came to him in his own faith and spiritual practices suited to his level of individual development. The story has been recounted—this has been referred to before—of how he slapped in the face a Hindu convert to Islam saying: "Aren't you ashamed to change your father?" Muslim fundamentalists disliked him and yet stayed to honour him for his spiritual eminence as an *Aulia* of the highest order. Today his shrine is a place of pilgrimage for lakhs of devotees of diverse faiths. That is the measure of Baba.

He is everyman's Baba, a friend to his devotees who come flocking to Shirdi.

★★★

CHAPTER 4

THE MERCY OF THE TRUE GURU

He (the true guru) removes the veil from the eyes, and gives
the true Vision of Brahma:
He reveals the worlds in Him, and makes me hear the unstruck Music.

—One Hundred Poems of Kabir
translated by Rabindranath Tagore No. XXII

It is the mercy of my true Guru that has made me know the
Unknown;
Kabir says: The guru is great beyond words and great is the
good fortune of the disciple.

—One Hundred Poems of Kabir
translated by Rabindranath Tagore No. XXVII

Inasmuch as Baba was totally devoted to his guru in thought,
word and deed, he expected the same devotion from his disciples. He would often tell Nanasaheb Chandorkar that these
days there were too many gurus around. But a guru's responsibilities were onerous. Until the disciple attained salvation,
the guru had to follow him from birth to death, ultimately to set
him free. By merely giving advice one did not become a guru.
There were many erudite scholars who could give plenty of
learned discourses but that did not make them *adhyatmic*
(spiritual) gurus. As observed wisely by Mouni Sadhu,
Sadgurus or 'the Masters' as they are called, 'come on this
earth very rarely and there are many false ones posing as
genuine. They are easily recognizable for every man possessed of common sense and discriminative experience. An irre-
proachable and saintly life is the best proof of Mastership.' Only
he was a guru who did not rest merely by reading lessons to his
disciple but watched over him carefully to see how faithfully the
imparted lessons were being followed. The guru also had the
responsibility of encouraging his disciple in spiritual exercises

and correcting him wherever it was found necessary and to set him on the virtuous path and monitor his progress from birth to birth until the latter was liberated. The claim has been made that for that reason Sai Baba attracted, by visible and invisible means, all those persons who were bound to him by ties of past births *(rinanubandha)*. This could be a matter of opinion but there is no doubt that as far as Baba himself was concerned he maintained a hawk's eye on all his disciples, pulling them up sharply if he found them straying from the straight and narrow path of righteousness. He once told Nanasaheb Chandorkar: "If any one calls on you for help in a public cause, do whatever you can. If you are not in a position to help, or do not wish to help, decline courteously but never make fun of him who comes seeking your help, neither be cross with him. Will you remember this?"

Nanasaheb said he would. But he was soon to be tested.

Whenever Nanasaheb went to Shirdi from Kopargaon on his way he would visit Dattatreya Mandir for the Lord's *darshan* and spend some time there. He would also have a word with the Mandir's caretaker.

Once, being pressed hard by the caretaker, Nanasaheb agreed to make a payment of three hundred rupees to the former towards the cost of constructing a *ghat* (landing platform with steps). The caretaker was very pleased.

A few days later Nanasaheb planned to visit Shirdi again, but found that he could not raise the sum of money he had promised to the Mandir's caretaker. To avoid the embarrassment of reneging on his promise, Nanasaheb took a circuitous route to go to Shirdi. The by-road was in a bad condition, there were thorns and brambles along the way and Nanasaheb's foot bled. He managed to reach Shirdi but in considerable distress.

The welcome he expected from Baba, however, did not materialise. Instead, Baba was in a foul mood, and was silent. Had he offended Baba, Nanasaheb asked. "Yes, you have," thundered Baba, "you feared that the caretaker would ask you for the promised monetary help and in consequence you missed the *darshan* of Dattatreya. You also took recourse to a by-road instead of coming by the regular one. Is this how you follow my lesson? If you did not have the three hundred rupees on you or you could not arrange for the money in time, what harm was there in telling the truth to the caretaker? Where was the point in taking a circuitous road, only to get hurt by thorns and brambles? Why should I talk to you?"

It was one of the few occasions when Nanasaheb was to become aware of Baba's omniscience. He had to abjectedly, apologise for his fall from grace and promise never to repeat that behaviour again.

But Baba astonished Nanasaheb by testing him once again. He had cautioned Nanasaheb that always he should give according to his capacity. "If the recipient is not satisfied, decline politely to give him anything more. But never lose your temper neither exercise your power nor show off your wealth!"

As in the past, Nanasaheb had agreed to follow these instructions. But once again he was to stumble.

It so happened that one day a beggar woman came to Nanasaheb's residence in Kalyan, seeking alms. The household never turned away a beggar and on this occasion, too, this beggar was offered the customary alms.

"But I want bhaajani," demanded the woman. Bhaajani is flour made of four or five kinds of grain that Nanasaheb's wife herself used to grind.

Nanasaheb's wife should have been alerted by this demand but perhaps it did not occur to her that this beggar woman was someone extraordinary. In the circumstances she handed out a small amount of bhaajani to the beggar.

"I want more," said the beggar woman.

Rather peeved, but still being the good housewife, the lady of the house poured out another couple of handfuls into the beggar's bowl.

"I want still more!" now demanded the beggar.

At this Nanasaheb's wife lost her temper. She said: "You take what you are given and clear out!''

The beggar woman refused to budge. She would get what she asked for or she would not leave.

At this the lady of the house called her husband for help.

Nanasaheb felt outraged that a mere beggar woman should have the insolence to demand more when his wife had been charitable enough to make a reasonable offering. He called his *chaprasi* and ordered him to drive the beggar woman away. The woman shot back a reply that was to haunt Nanasaheb. ''If you don't want to give me what I asked for, don't! But do you have to get the *chaprasi* to throw me out? Why, I'll leave on my own!'' Saying which, she left.

The incident was forgotten.

A few months later Nanasaheb went to Shirdi for Baba's *darshan.* As on an earlier occasion, he received the cold treatment. Baba was cross and would not speak to Nanasaheb. ''What have I done to merit your anger?'' Nanasaheb asked disconsolately. ''What have you done, you ask?'' Baba said angrily, ''why should I talk to someone who keeps breaking his word? Did you have to order a *chaprasi* to throw out a poor beggar woman merely because she asked for sufficient *bhaajani?* At worst she would have sat in front of your doorstep before leaving of her own accord. Couldn't you have talked sweetly to her yourself? Where was the need to threaten a woman with force?''

For a moment Nanasaheb had no idea what Baba was talking about. Then he remembered the incident of the beggar woman and her insistent demand for more *bhaajani* than what was offered to her. And he felt full of remorse. Faithful as he was to Baba, he now realised that one never could tell when one would be tested—and how.

It was a lesson he was to forget never again.

Baba often said: ''For a human being, guru's place is pre-eminent. By keeping utmost faith in him, by being devoted to him alone, everything is obtained. A devotee's whole strength is what the guru gives him. Nothing more, nothing less. Devotion to the guru is superior even to devotion to gods and goddesses. Indeed, consider your guru as the Supreme Being!"

And he would praise and commend devotion to guru.

From among those who came for his *darshan* he would gladly tell the ones whom he considered as seekers, about his own guru's powers, kindness, single-minded contemplation or unexcelled changeless state of meditation and his own singular service to his peerless guru. Similarly, he would clearly explain the two great precepts of *bhakti yoga* pointed out by his guru and would commend to the seekers to faithfully adhere to them.

As he put it, food, pleasure and merriment, happiness and sorrow in life were dependent on one's *prarabdha* (karma, constituting the occasion of the present birth). When Nanasaheb established that he was a true seeker of spiritual emancipation and not mere worldly pleasures, Baba spoke to him of these two precepts or steps. It is said that it was through Nanasaheb that many devotees came to know of them and that was how knowledge of the same was communicated to Annasaheb Dabholkar, author of *Shri Sai Satcharita*. We will trace that incident and Baba's easy and superb way of imparting instruction.

Once Dabholkar was sitting by Baba's side. In his presence Baba told one Sathe who had finished one *parayana* (reading) of *Gurucharitra* that he should complete one more *parayana* thereof so that God would favour him and liberate him.

Dabholkar was peeved. There he was, a man who had been reading the Gurucharita for some forty years and never had Baba promised him liberation from the endless cycle of births. And here was this Sathe who was being promised liberation almost overnight as it were!

Poor Dabholkar. He reckoned without Baba's powers to know what was going on in his mind.

Unexpectedly, Baba told Dabholkar: "You go now to Madhavrao Deshpande and get fifteen rupees." Dabholkar did as he was told. He went to Deshpande and gave him the message. But Deshpande replied: "How can a poor man like me have money to give to Sai Baba? Moreover, how am I qualified to instruct a person like you?"

To soften his inability to pay the fifteen rupees sought from him, Deshpande related to Dabholkar some of his personal experiences as also the experiences of some others like Radhabai with Sai Baba. Once Khashaba Deshmukh's mother Radhabai had come to Shirdi along with some others to get Baba's darshan. For her it was devotion at first sight. She felt instinctively that if only Baba would become her guru, she could advance spiritually. But she was rather scared to put the issue directly to Baba. She decided that if she could not get a 'mantra' from the lips of the Master, she would at least fast. So she did—for three days running. In the process she became weak. One devotee felt concerned for her condition and went and informed Baba that if the old woman was not pacified, she may die.

So Baba called her, and bade her sit next to him and said: "Mother, I will tell you the truth. My guru was a great Master full of kindness. I served him with all my being, but he would not favour me with a mantra. I had an intense urge to receive a mantra from him and felt that I must never leave him. He had accepted me as a disciple from the staft. He had taken two pice from me. My desireless guru never wanted material wealth. But he demanded two things: shraddha or nishta (faith, trust) and saburi (courage combined with patient waiting). I gave these two pice to him at once. It is rare to find a guru like mine. I would look at the living embodiment of devotion and love ever lost in meditation, with admiration, day and night. In the process I lost all sense of hunger and thirst. He became the centre of my observation, attention and meditation. If he were out of my sight, I would be restless. My guru had no other expectation from me except shraddha and saburi. I had already committed them to him. So he never neglected me and ever protected me from danger. Sometimes I would stay in his company and at other times away from him. Yet he looked after me with a kind eye just as a tortoise nourishes her young one by her mere sight. I speak the truth. My guru never initiated me with a *mantra.* So how will I initiate you or give you a *mantra*? But follow this fundamental precept of singular trust and courage and do not torture yourself by fasting.''

Radhabai got the point. She gave up her fast and took the normal life of devotion and faith.

When Deshpande finished the narration, Dabholkar realised that Radhabai's story, too, had a lesson for him. If Radhabai was denied a *mantra* why should he get a promise of salvation from Baba? It became clear to him that Baba had sent him to Deshpande just to get an indirect lesson on what to expect and what not to, from Baba. He was wise enough to imbibe the lesson meekly.

Baba would often say, *"Mi kan funkanara guru nave. Mi kanala dasanara guru nave. Amche gharane nirale ahe."* (I am not a guru who babbles through the ear. Our traditions are different). What did he intend to convey thereby? The explanation of this statement can be obtained from one of the *dohas* of Kabir where in he states that the real guru is he who teaches the way to the Unlimited. The said doha is as under:

Kanfunka guru hadd ka, behad ka guru aur;
Behad ka guru jab mile, lahai thikana thaur.

(The guru who babbles through the ear teaches the limited. The guru who teaches the way to the Unlimited (Supreme Being) is very different. When you meet the guru who knows the Supreme, you are able to realize the Self).

Baba had special ties with Nanasaheb Chandorkar. When Nanasaheb was the Collector's Personal Assistant in 1887, the *Kulkarni* of Shirdi had often to go to the Collector's office in Ahmedanagar in connection with work pertaining to land revenue. On such occasions Baba would send word through the Kulkarni to Nanasaheb, inviting the latter to come to Shirdi. Baba was often heard to say: "I will willy nilly drag any one who is my man here, even if he is hiding in the seventh nether world."

Baba felt towards Nanasaheb as he would towards a devotee. At first Nanasaheb spurned the invitation. What did he have to do with a fakir? But when pressed to come for the third time, Nanasaheb obliged.

He had his doubts about Baba. What sort of a man was he? Was he a fakir or a sadhu? But once having agreed to visit Baba, Nanasaheb set aside all his thoughts. He put on his alpaca jacket and set out to Shirdi. On the way he remembered that one should not go empty handed while calling on a saint or a house of God. He had not taken anything with him in a fit of absent-mindedness and the thought that he will be seeing Baba empty-handed bothered him. He knew that Shirdi was too small a village to buy even a bunch of bananas. But when he put his hand in his pocket he realised that he had with him a small packet containing almonds and sugar—something that he always carried with him. At least, he thought, he could place this packet, howsoever insignificant, before the feet of Baba. The thought consoled him.

On reaching Shirdi with his companions, Nanasaheb bowed low before Baba and placed before him his small offering. He could not help feeling embarrassed, though. He especially noticed about twenty five devotees seated around Baba and it seemed ridiculous that all he could give to Baba were a few almonds and a few sugar crystals! But a miracle had taken place. There seemed enough in the small packet for all the assembled men to receive their quota as *prasad*!

For all that, Nanasaheb was curious to know why Baba had summoned him so insistently. Baba came straight to the point. "Nana," he said, "there is a special relationship between us that goes back to four births. You are not aware of it, but I am. That is why I called you! You are my responsibility!"

And then Baba added: "Come again to me—but at your convenience."

To Nanasaheb it seemed an odd invitation. But he bore it in mind.

Not long after the incident, an epidemic of plague broke out at Ahmednagar. The Collector wanted Nanasaheb to get inoculated against plague so that he would by that act set an example to the people who were suspicious of inoculation. Inoculation had just come to India and many were hostile to the idea of having some foreign liquid injected into their body.

It was then that Nanasaheb decided that he would go to Shirdi and ask for Baba's advice. Baba's counsel was to the point. "Do as the Collector tells you," He said, "and get inoculated. There is nothing to fear!"

So back to Ahmednagar Nanasaheb went, this time to get inoculated against plague. His example proved contagious and everyone in the Collector's office followed suit. Their lives were saved.

Nanasaheb thereafter was to call on Baba almost every fortnight whenever he was in the vicinity of Shirdi. The two would spend a whole night talking about the Gita or spiritual matters.

It is claimed on behalf of Sai Baba—and he himself made it clear in so many words—that he manifested himself for the sake of advancing on the righteous path, those who were connected in their past lives with him. There were many whom he contacted on his own and influenced their lives by his company, love and words of advice. There was the time he won over by his love, a learned fakir of Ahmednagar named Javar Ali and then humbled his pride of being a *murshid.* This fakir had settled down in Rahata, five kilometers from Shirdi. He was well-versed in the Koran. He began constructing an *idgah* (place of worship) in Rahata but, in the process, attracted the charge of having 'polluted' the temple of Veerabhadra. So he came to stay in Shirdi with Sai Baba.

Javar Ali was a sweet talker and soon impressed the villagers of Shirdi with his learning. It appeared as if Baba's friendship with him had increased. When Javar Ali shifted his residence to Rahata again, Sai Baba accompanied him. He served Javar Ali in every way, even going to the length of carrying water for him. Baba would thereafter visit Shirdi occasionally and that made his many devotees apprehensive about Baba leaving Shirdi for ever. So they went on a deputation to Rahata. When they reached Rahata, Javar Ali was out and Baba was alone. He told the deputationists: "It is good that the fakir is not here.

He is a hot-tempered man and if he knows that you have come here to take me back, he will curse you.''

But even while they were conversing, Javar Ali arrived and good-naturedly asked the Shirdi villagers: "What, have you come to take this lad away? If you wish to do that, take me also with him!" He said that because he had come to depend on Baba for the personal services rendered by him. The villagers consented and so both Baba and Javar Ali returned to Shirdi.

Then an unfortunate event took place. Javar Ali and the sadhu Devidas engaged in a debate in which the former was defeated. Crest-fallen Javar Ali slipped away to Vaijapur. He was to return to Shirdi only many years after, deeply chastened and filled with repentance for having considered himself a *murshid* and Baba only his *chela*. Humbly, he saluted Baba.

As Baba was wont to say, it is comparatively easy to put away the pride of wealth, but it is harder to give up the pride of learning, wisdom and righteousness. Javar Ali considered himself to be quite a learned man and he prided himself on the fact. Baba took his time to bring him to his senses, not directly, not aggressively, but through another agency and in the fulness of love.

And that was how he also treated Upasani Baba who was hoping to gain liberation through mortification of the flesh. Baba had his own gentle way to dissuade Upasani Baba and to bring him to Shirdi and to show him the path to salvation.

Baba would often test the depth and sincerity of his devotees in unforeseeable ways. One of his devotees, Hari Sitaram alias Kakasaheb Dikshit had turned his back on a flourishing legal practice and a promising political career to serve Baba with body, mind and wealth (*tan-man-dhan*). Once Baba was to test his faith in a strange way. He found a goat, practically on its last legs, tied to a post near the masjid. A fakir was at that time visiting Baba, by name Bade Baba. "Bade Baba," said Sai Baba addressing his visitor, "would you like to kill that goat with one stroke?" Bade Baba demurred. So Baba asked Madhavrao Deshpande to get a knife and finish the job. Deshpande went looking for a knife and found one with Radhakrishna Aii who, however, refused to part with it when she learnt the use it was going to be put to. She was a religious lady who wanted no goat's blood on her hands!

In the meantime, Dikshit happened to come on the scene so Baba shifted his attention to poor Dikshit and said he should despatch the goat. Dikshit's faith in Baba was total and he was not going to be the one who would refuse any of Baba's requests. He could never imagine that Baba would ever ask him to do something wrong or sinful. So promptly he went to Sathe Wada, obtained a knife and returned and was about to wield it when Baba stopped him. "Let it be, Kaka," he told Dikshit, "don't kill the poor animal!" And he teased him, saying: "some brahmin *you* are, wishing to kill a goat! Don't you have any compunction?"

Dikshit threw away the knife and looking at Baba, said: "Baba, you should know me by now! Your word is my *dharma*! I know of no other religion. What you say is law for me!" Whereupon Baba said: "Very well, then. Let me do the killing myself. Take this jug of water!" Baba said he would resort to the *halal* way of killing an animal.

But he did not. He waited, while Dikshit and the others watched, wondering what Baba was up to.

After a time, Baba said: "It is better you take this goat to the fakir's *takia*." There in due course, the goat died a natural death. But Baba had used it to test his devotees' faith. Out of them, Dikshit alone was not found wanting. Dikshit regarded the actions of his Master, who dwelt in the perpetual state of spiritual consciousness beyond mind and feelings, that is, beyond the illusion of the world and separate being, as infallible. This knowledge explains the absolute confidence and obedience to Sai Baba offered by a true and intelligent devotee like Dikshit.

He was often cryptic in his utterances as many noted. Once, a devotee, Deo, Mamlatdar of Dahanu came to Shirdi. Such were his official duties that he seldom found time to read religious books. Often he would start with Jnaneshwari but there would be interruptions, much to his annoyance. Then it occurred to him that he would do this reading only at the bidding of Baba, so that no obstacles would come his way. In that frame of mind, he came to Shirdi.

One of the first to greet him was Balakram Mankar. Mankar had fully dedicated himself to Baba's service and he had made Shirdi his home. Baba had even permitted him to dress as he dressed: in a *kafni* and a scarf round his head. Baba had extended this privilege only to three devotees, one of whom was Mankar. Naturally word had gone round that these three were the favoured of Baba.

Innocently, Deo asked Mankar: "Tell me, how did you earn the grace of Sai Baba?" "I will let you know tomorrow," said Mankar and proved true to his words. Then Deo again asked him: "How did Sai Baba inspire you to do *upasana*? (objective meditation). Please tell me about it!"

But before Mankar could utter a word there came a message from Sai Baba that he wanted to see Deo immediately. So Deo went to the masjid. It was as if Baba was waiting for him near the compound wall. On seeing Deo, Baba asked: "With whom and about what were you conversing?" Deo answered the question truthfully enough.

"Give me twenty five rupees as *dakshina*!" Baba demanded abruptly.
Deo gave the amount readily.
"Let's go inside the masjid," said Baba.
Together they went in.
Deo was wondering what was going on when Baba suddenly turned round angrily and said: "That strip of cloth in which I tie *dakshina* is stolen!"
"What strip of cloth?" Deo asked innocently.
"Look for it! It must be somewhere!" Baba ordered.
Deo dutifully looked for that bit of cloth in every corner of the masjid, but it wasn't to be found anywhere. He told Baba so.

"You haven't found it, you say? Then you yourself must have stolen it! Did you have to come to Shirdi to steal?" Baba thundered.

Deo did not know what to say. Far from stealing the cloth, he had not even seen it. Besides, why would he want to steal money with which he had voluntarily parted? Baba seemed to be in a wild temper.

"Go back to the Wada whence you came! I don't want to see you!" Baba told the bewildered man. There was nothing else for Deo to do except to obey. Crestfallen, he left the masjid premises.

A couple of hours later Baba called some of his devotees around and said to them in a gentle voice: "Poor Deo. I must have hurt his feelings. But I could not help getting angry because a theft had indeed been committed!"

Then he summoned Deo again and told him: "Now give me more *dakshina*!"
Meekly Deo obeyed.
Then Baba turned to him and looking him in the face, said: "What were you doing in the Wada?"
"Nothing," said Deo, meekly.
Baba said: "In that case, make a habit of sitting regularly in the Wada for reading *pothi*."

Then he softly added: "When I am waiting here to give you a whole *jari shela* (a lengthy piece of shawl woven with gold linings to be draped loosely over the shoulders) what is this bad habit of stealing a shred of clothing?"

For a while Deo blinked but suddenly a smile came over his face. It had dawned on him that what Sai Baba was referring to was his brief conversation with Mankar about meditation on *Brahman*. Did Deo have to get his knowledge second hand from Mankar when Baba himself was waiting to enlighten him to the fullest? The brief conversation was likened to theft while Baba was willing to give an entire shawl in the form of direct enlightenment. What Baba had wished to emphasize in his strange behaviour was that when the ground was ready for sowing, the guru on his own would lead the devotee to higher levels. It was not necessary for the devotee to seek wisdom second hand, thereby achieving nothing. It merely inhibited progress.

Thereafter Deo had free access to Baba. Day after day he would read Jnaneshwari and provide his own exposition of that great work. Before the completion of one year, on Thursday, 2 April 1914, Deo had a pleasant experience. He dreamt of Sai Baba. He saw Baba sitting on the upper storey of his home. Asked Baba: "Do you understand the *pothi*?"

"No," replied Deo.
"When will you understand?" Baba asked again.
Overcome by emotion, Deo replied: "It is no use reading the *pothi*, Baba, unless your grace descends on me."
Came Baba's reply: "Then sit by me and read it in my presence."
"What shall I read?"
Baba said: *"Adhyatma."*
Then Deo commenced reading the *pothi*, still in his dream.

Soon thereafter, the dream ended and Deo woke up. He had felt the grace of Baba on him. He was mightily pleased.

2

Incidentally, *Upasana* is of two types: *Ahamgraha upasana and pratika upasana. Ahamgraha upasana* or meditation may be on *Saguna Brahma* (Brahma in form) or *Nirguna Brahma* (form-less Brahma). In both cases, Brahma is regarded as not different or separate from Self, i.e. as its own Self. But when the presence of deity is invoked by religious rites in an object without soul, meditation on such an object is called *Pratika upasana*. It is claimed that by *ahamgraha upasana*, Brahma loka can be attained, but it cannot be attained by *pratika upasana*.

Upasanas enumerated in the Upanishads such as Shandilya vidya, Bhooma vidya, Sat vidya, Dahar vidya, Upakoshal vidya, Anandamaya vidya, Akshar vidya are all forms of Ahamgraha Vidya. The object of all these *vidyas* or *upasanas* is realisation of Self or Brahman. A seeker may select any of these *vidyas* or *upasanas* of his choice and then should stick to it until the Self is realized. This is the rule of *Ahamgraha Upasana*.

If a seeker goes after many *vidyas,* his attention will be divided and thereby his spiritual progress will be retarded or interrupted. Once the object of *upasana* is realised, study of other *upasanas* will become unnecessary and redundant.

Pratika Upasana is meant for the fulfilment of worldly desires. Hence the above rule of *Ahamgraha Upasana* is not applicable, to it. And for the satisfaction of various desires, *upasana* of more than one object or gods is permissible.

Single-minded devotion of a *sadguru* is meant for self-realisation. Worldly desire can be fulfilled by devotion to *sadguru,* gods or goddesses.

[3]

It is said that even a material object which comes into contact with an individual whose heart beats continuously day and night in tune with Logos, bursts into speech. Many are the means open to a *sadguru* who is omnipresent (literally, envelops the atom, dust, individual and universe) and protects his devotees by manifesting in gross, subtle, large or atomic form.

In order to lose consciousness of the body, to experience that the self is not the body, but separate from it, yogis resort to many practices, like enduring the heat of the sun or fire, sleeping on a bed of nails, living only on air without intake of food, remaining naked, consuming five kinds of fire etc. But Baba's means to experience this truth were unique. He believed that his body was that of a single-minded devotee or servant of God. So, should he find a devotee suffering from an ailment, Baba would take the *karma* of the devotee upon himself and thus remove the devotee's ailment. Thereby even if the *bhakta* had to go necessarily through his *prarabdha karma,* the intensity of it would be considerably reduced to make it bearable.

What is considered impossible by science is possible for a yogi and the effect of such power has been experienced by Sai Baba's many devotees' wives even! At the time of their delivery, Baba would say that he experienced the pain himself.

And by the time he told of his pains and moaned and groaned in the masjid, the delivery pains of the women would begin to subside and they would give normal birth to a child.

In 1911, when a plague epidemic broke out even in Shirdi, seven or eight buboes were noticed on Baba's body and he began to get fever. Noticing this, the devotees were concerned and asked him what was the remedy for its cure. Baba would then suggest that burnt cotton wool should be dipped in ghee and applied to the buboes. He followed this remedy himself and assured his devotees that he was safe and he would live and that, nobody in Shirdi would come to grief either. He had taken upon himself the calamity that had affected Shirdi. As it turned out no one died of plague in Shirdi. More remarkable was the fact that inspite of so many buboes on his body there was no change in his daily routine—his morning and evening rounds, his visits to Lendi, the begging of alms and sitting in meditation in the masjid.

At that time, Sai Baba's devotee, Dadasaheb Khaparde had suspended his legal practice and was staying in Shirdi. As long as Baba would not permit him to leave, he was determined to camp there. One day Khaparde's young son got high fever and was in great pain. The boy's mother was frightened as there was an epidemic of plague around. One day when Baba was on his evening round, Mrs. Khaparde asked Baba to bless her son. Baba said: "Mother, do not fear. The sky is overcast with clouds and it will soon rain and the sky will be clear." So saying, he raised his *kafni* to show four egg-sized buboes on his legs and added: "Look, I have taken the ailment of your son upon me. You have nothing to fear. I am suffering all this for your son and he will be all right soon." Mrs. Khaparde was relieved and the boy was cured as assured.

On Dhana trayodashi Day the same year, Baba was sitting in the masjid opposite the *dhuni* stoking the fire. Suddenly Baba put his hand in the fire and sat quietly. When the devotees in the *sabhamandap* outside saw what was happening, one of them rushed in and clasping Baba round the waist, pulled him back. Seeing the burns sustained by the whole hand, the devotee asked him in great distress: "What have you done?" Hearing this, Baba suddenly came to his normal consciousness and said: "What shall I tell you? A child sitting on its mother's lap fell into the fire. I pulled her out. While doing so my hand was burnt. Let it be. But the life of the girl was saved."

Later it was learnt that at that time, the wife of a blacksmith while blowing the bellows of the fire-place, accidentally lost control of her child whom she was holding with one hand, causing the child to fall into the fire cauldron. It was Baba who pulled it out before the child got burnt. In the process it was Baba who sustained burns.

As soon as Nanasaheb Chandorkar heard of the incident, he rushed to Shirdi along with Dr. Paramanand of Bombay. Sai Baba however told him that God was his physician and he did not want the services of any doctor. He preferred to have his burns dressed up by a devotee suffering from black leprosy who gently covered the burns with ghee and had them bandaged with a leaf. The healing took place in good time.

It had become second nature with Sai Baba to take up the karmic suffering of his devotees and thus lighten their burden. This service of devotees he would regard as service to God; he considered himself fortunate on that account. That was evident in one of his dialogues with his devotees, one of whom told him: "We are blessed by your darshan." But Baba told the assembly: "Brothers, I deem myself fortunate that I came to know you, and I am grateful to God for it."

There was something of Christ in Baba who would not, probably, have liked the comparison, not because it did not match but because of his inherent humility.

Baba did not say: "In as much as you do it to one of the least of these, you do it also to me," but his work illustrated it. A lady once asked him to come and take food with her and he consented. As may be imagined, she prepared special dishes with great care and devotion and with all the culinary skills she possessed. But even before she could serve Baba she found to her horror that a stray dog was making away with the dishes. Angrily she drove away the animal. When she went to invite Baba, however, he said he had changed his mind. "You drove me away when I wanted it," he said enigmatically to the shocked woman, "and now I don't want it."

Very often he would speak symbolically and it needed some one who knew his ways to interpret his language.

A lady described her first visit to him, when she was about eighteen. A devotee's spectacles had fallen off when he was bowing down to Baba and another devotee who watched it offered the suggestion that since the spectacles had fallen at Baba's feet, they should be presented to him. "No," said Baba, "I don't need spectacles. I've got a pair. They cost forty rupees."

Every one knew that he did not possess spectacles. The lady who told the story was puzzled until her father explained to her that by spectacles he meant sight or self-realization and by forty rupees Baba meant the forty years he had been working at gaining self-realization.

Even when performing cures he would say something that would leave his devotees puzzled. Once Deshpande was bitten by a snake. All that he could do was to rush to see Baba. But even as he was rushing up the masjid's steps he heard Baba shout: "Don't come up, brahmin! Go back, get down!" Even at that instant when fear gripped him, Deshpande did not dare disobey Baba. So he stood there in instant freeze, waiting for Baba to give his next order. A moment later Baba spoke again, this time in a gentle, kindly voice. "Come up, now. The fakir is gracious to you. You will recover!"

The 'Fakir' was Baba's way of referring to God. Deshpande then learnt that in the command not to come up, Baba had been addressing not him, but the poison that was entering the bloodstream!

During the Christmas of 1909, a Medical Practitioner went to Shirdi with a friend who was a *tehsildar*. The doctor was an orthodox brahmin and was strict in his religious rites like bath, performance of *sandhya* etc. Besides, he was a great devotee of Sri Rama. The doctor besides felt it unbecoming of him as a brahmin to prostrate before a Muslim fakir for he thought Baba was a fakir. The *tehsildar* however assured the doctor that he would not be asked by anyone in Shirdi to prostrate before Sai Baba and that Baba himself expected nothing of the kind. So the doctor very reluctantly accompanied his *tehsildar* friend to the masjid.

When they reached the entrance to the masjid, however, it appeared to the doctor that Shri Ramachandra himself was sitting before him whereupon he prostrated before the divine presence that was none other than Baba himself! On coming out of the masjid, the doctor narrated his experience to the *tehsildar* and then and there resolved that unless Baba blessed him (with spiritual experience) he would neither touch any food nor go to the masjid.

On the fourth day of his fasting, the doctor met a friend of his from Khandesh unexpectedly and forgetting his resolve went along with the latter to the masjid. When the doctor prostrated before Sai Baba, the latter asked him, "Well, doctor, why have you come? Who called you?" The doctor's embarrassment can well be imagined. But he had his reward. That same night in his slumber the doctor experienced an indescribable bliss, a state of mind that lasted for a fortnight, even after his return home. Thus he had been recipient of Baba's grace.

Like this staunch devotee of Sri Ramachandra there was another, a man called Mule Shastri, who was attached to his guru. He had once been to Shirdi to see Gopalrao Buti, a rich *Malgujar* of Nagpur who was devoted to Sai Baba.

Mule Shastri had not intended to halt at Shirdi for long and was planning to return to Nasik after seeing Buti. That he did and then, on the spur of the moment, he went along with some others to visit Sai Baba. It happened that at that time Baba was distributing bananas as *prasad* to those assembled in the masjid.

Mule Shastri had studied the six *darshanas* (philosophies) and was proficient in astrology and palmistry. He extended his hand to take up Sai Baba's palm but Baba paid no attention to this move but, instead, placed four bananas in Mule Shastri's hands. Mule Shastri accepted the *prasad* and made no mention of his wish to read Baba's palm. He returned to the Wada where he was staying, had his ritual bath and wearing a silken dhoti he sat down for the *agnihotra* ritual.

In the meantime, Sai Baba started for the *lendi* and remarked: "Take *geru* with you. I have to don the ochre-coloured robe today." No one round him understood the significance of this remark. By the time Sai Baba returned it was time for the noon *arati*. Bapusaheb Jog who conducted the *arati* asked Mule Shastri whether he would accompany him to the masjid to witness the *arati*. Mule Shastri had strong scruples about pollution by touch and he was reluctant to leave his *agnihotra* to go to the masjid.

At that time Sai Baba was seated in the *masjid and arati* was about to commence when he said: "Go to the brahmin who has newly arrived and get *dakshina* from him." So Buti approached Mule Shastri for *dakshina*. The latter was busy with his *agnihotra* and had his mind on it but out of deference to Buti, he accompanied the latter to the masjid with his *dakshina*,, but lest the masjid should pollute him, he remained at a distance in the *sabhamandap*, saluted Sai Baba and showered flowers on him. Then a strange thing happened. While everyone saw Sai Baba in his seat, Mule Shastri saw his guru Gholap in ochre-coloured robe instead. He was, to say the least, perplexed and astonished. Gholapguruji had expired several years earlier. Mule Shastri did not know whether he could trust his eyes. Was he really seeing his guru Gholap, or was he in a dream. He pinched himself to see whether he was awake or asleep. So overcome was he with emotion that he ran up the steps of the masjid and embraced the feet of his guru and stood up with his hands folded. Others began reciting the *arati* while Mule Shastri, his eyes half-closed also sang, but this was *arati* to his own guru.

By and by the *arati* was over; the singing stopped. Mule Shastri stopped singing. What he now saw before him was Sai Baba, sitting in his usual place and gently asking for *dakshina*!

It was a revelation to Mule Shastri; thanks to Sai Baba, he had the *darshan* of his own guru, Gholap. Overjoyed and with tears streaming down his cheeks, Mule Shastri prostrated himself before Sai Baba. He was to tell this story again and again to whoever was interested.

Sai Baba would wear a kafni made of coarse *manjarpat,* tie a piece of cloth round his head and grow a beard. While people addressed him as Sai Baba, Hindus who visited Shirdi weren't always sure how to treat him. Was it right and proper to accept him as a spiritual guide or guru? Those who accepted him became his permanent devotees. Among them was one Megha, a brahmin from Marwar who was domiciled in Gujarat. Megha came into contact with another devotee of Sai Baba, Rao Bahadur Hari Vinayak Sathe, when the latter was a Deputy Collector of Kheda District. Megha was a brahmin only in name. He knew next to nothing about *gayatri* and much less about *sandhya puja, brahma puja* etc. Sathe took him in his employ and entrusted him with the daily puja of Shiva. Sathe made him aware of his ignorance, explained to him the duties of a brahmin and taught him *gayatri mantra*. The mutual affection between them increased and Megha accepted Sathe as his guide.

Time passed. One day Sathe described to Megha the greatness of his sadguru Sai Baba and said with a good deal of feeling: "I desire that my guru who is Shiva personified should be bathed with Ganga water and worshipped with due religious rites. I am much pleased with your progress and feel that if you were fortunate enough to come in contact with my guru you will be blessed."

Megha in his ignorance asked: "To what caste does your guru belong?" Sathe replied: "I do not know his caste. Both Hindus and Muslims claim him as their own. His permanent abode is in a masjid, a *dhuni* is perpetually lighted before him and to that fire he offers the oblation of the alms he receives."

Megha was aghast. He mumbled, "As he resides in a masjid and Muslims consider him as their own, he must be a Muslim. How can a *yavana* ever be a guru?"

Sathe did not know what to say. But he advised Megha at least to go to Shirdi to see Sai Baba for himself. Shortly afterwards, Megha undertook the journey. He was to receive a surprise.

As he was about to step into the masjid he heard a roar from Sai Baba who assumed a ferocious look, picked up a stone and shouted: "How dare you step in? I am the lowest of *yavana* and you are a high class brahmin! Go away, go away before you get polluted by my touch!"

Megha was stunned. Ahmednagar was far away from Kheda and yet Sai Baba had come to know what he said in his private conversation with Raosaheb Sathe! But there was no time to think. Sai Baba had chased him out of the masjid. Megha ran out. But what he did not realise was that Sai Baba's anger was feigned. All that he wanted to convey to Megha was that he was aware of what the latter was thinking about. Shortly thereafter Sai Baba appeared to be pacified and Megha was allowed to come to the masjid freely. Megha stayed in Shirdi for many days and served Sai Baba. He observed Baba's powers, his way of life from close quarters but yet could not put his firm faith in him. He returned to Kheda but fell ill and was confined to bed. One day he went for Shiva's darshan but instead of the *pindi* he only saw Sai Baba. Now he longed to return to Shirdi. So soon after he recovered he proceeded to Shirdi. When he called on Sai Baba, the latter got him to do *gayatri purascharan*. This time Megha not only relished his life in Shirdi but came fully to believe in Sai Baba and became his staunch devotee. Indeed, he began worshipping Baba in the belief that Baba was Shiva incarnate. Day and night Megha would do *japa* of Shankar. He did not mix with others. He was straight-forward and simple. He always wore a joyous expression on his face. In Shirdi there was no tree to provide him with *bela patra (Aegle marmelos* or *Crataeva religiosa)* which is sacred to Shiva. So Megha would walk some 1½ miles every day to fetch the bela leaves, worship all the village gods and then return to the masjid to worship Sai Baba.

Initially, Baba never allowed anyone to worship him. Whenever anyone approached him with plans to worship him, Baba would get angry. But when he saw the pure devotion of people like Mhalsapati he relented. Mhalsapati was to be followed by other devotees like Nanasaheb Chandorkar's son.

Megha did his puja in style. The routine never varied. A mile and a half of walk to get the bela leaves, worship of the village gods and then on to the masjid. On one occasion, Megha could not worship at the shrine of Khandoba since the doors to the temple were closed. So Megha came straight to the masjid but before he could commence the worship of Sai Baba, the latter stopped him saying: "Stop. There has been a breach in your daily practice. Go, complete the puja of *all* the village gods and only then return!" Megha, taken somewhat by surprise, said that he could not complete his day's routine because Khandoba Mandir was closed. "Never mind," replied Sai Baba, "go again. The doors of Khandoba are now open. Finish your puja there. The *arati* here can wait!" And that is exactly what happened!

Experiences such as this merely strengthened Megha's faith in Sai Baba. Once, on a *makara sankranti* day (the passage of the sun from Sagittarius to Capricorn) Megha felt the desire to bathe Baba with the waters of the Godavari river (eight miles away from Shirdi) for which he obtained Baba's permission after much persuasion. On the appointed day Megha got up earlier than usual and made his way to the banks of the Godavari and filling the copper vessel with the river water returned to Shirdi.

Sai Baba, however, did not seem anxious for the bath. He did not stir from his seat. The noon *arati* over, all the devotees returned to their homes. Now Megha addressed himself to Baba.

"Baba," he said, "it is afternoon now, please do get ready for your bath."

Sai Baba replied: "What has a fakir like me got to do with Ganga jal?" (Baba always referred to the Godavari water as Ganga).

Megha refused to budge. He had not trudged sixteen miles to be so rebuffed. So he said: "I know one thing. Shankar (Shiva) is propitiated by a bath with Ganga water. Today is *Sankrant*. So I must bathe my Shankar with Gangajal, shouldn't I?" Giving in to importuning, Sai Baba said: "Very well. As you please. I will remove my head cover. Pour just a little water over my head; that would be as good as bathing the whole body.''

Megha's enthusiasm knew no bounds. Permission received, he joyously shouted 'Har Ganga, Har Ganga!' and emptied the entire copper vessel on Sai Baba's head. He thought he had achieved his purpose of bathing all of Baba's body, head downwards. But he reckoned without Baba. For what he saw was something entirely different. Only Baba's head was wet and the rest of the body was bone dry. There was not a drop of water on Baba's *kafni*.

The sight brought Megha to his senses. He had disobeyed Baba in emptying an entire pot of water on him. But Baba had saved him from the blame of violating a guru's orders. He felt relieved.

Sai Baba later was to give Megha yet another incomparable experience which was to win him over completely.

A year had passed since Megha had begun to serve Sai Baba. One day, in the early predawn hours when Megha was fast asleep, Megha saw in his dream the figure of Sai Baba who threw consecrated rice on his bed, saying: 'Megha, trace the *trishul*' and then vanished. Megha woke up and found consecrated rice all over his bed. Where could it have come from? The door to his room was bolted from the inside, but Baba had obviously got in.

Unable to get an explanation to this phenomenon, Megha went to the masjid and narrated his experience to Baba. ''What should I do now? Shall I trace the *trishul* (trident) according to the vision I had, where your picture is hung up?'' Megha asked.

''What vision? Did you not recognise my voice?'' queried Baba. ''I did,'' replied Megha, ''but I thought it couldn't be you, as my room was bolted from inside.''
''Bolted from within?'' Baba countered. ''Do I need open doors to get into rooms? I have neither shape nor size. I am omnipresent.''

The same day, in accordance with Baba's instructions, Megha drew with red lead, a *trishul* to the right of Sai Baba's picture. Next day a Ramadasi from Pune arrived in Shirdi and presented a *Shiva linga* to Baba. Megha happened to be present at the occasion. So Sai Baba said to him: "Look, Lord Shiva has come. Take care of him!" Megha was overwhelmed on receiving the *Shiva linga*. Now he had no doubt whatsoever that Sai Baba was a *sadguru,* Lord Shankar himself and considered himself blessed indeed that he got an opportunity to serve Him.

For a long time he resided in Shirdi and served Baba faithfully. When he died Baba said: "He was my true devotee" and arranged for his funeral obsequies, including, as was customary, the feeding of brahmins.

Hearing reports that Sai Baba distributed a lot of money among the poor, a party of four Ramadasis (consisting of the husband, wife, daughter and wife's sister) on their way to Banaras broke their journey at Shirdi. They first had Baba's *darshan* and during their two days' stay found to their joy that Sai Baba daily distributed amounts ranging from fifty to a hundred rupees. The family—with the exception of the wife—became greedy and thought that perhaps if they extended their stay in Shirdi and ingratiated themselves to Sai Baba, they would be well off. With that in mind they would sing *bhajans* every day in Baba's presence. Only the wife was selfless. Once, after the noon *arati* Sai Baba gave the wife darshana in the form of Sri Rama wielding the bow. To the devout woman this was a moment of great joy and tears flowed freely from her eyes.

When the family returned to their little habitation, the wife was asked what made her cry. Her explanation only brought ridicule from the husband. But that very night, the husband dreamt that he had surrendered himself to Sai Baba and admitted to him that he had considered Baba to be a Muslim who was attempting to convert Hindus to Islam.

Baba reminded the husband that he worshipped the *panja* (the iron hand of Mohammadans representing the five Holy Personages) at home and on the occasion of marriage worshipped Kadbibi—a Muslim divinity. The husband repented and begged of Sai Baba to give him *darshan* of Ramdas Swami. That request was granted—still in the dream. When the husband woke up, he realised the divinity of Baba who transcended all differences such as caste and religion.

The family stayed on for a while in Shirdi, now freed of greed. The four members continued to sing *bhajans* but now it was out of pure devotion. Not long after they were on their way to their original destination—Banaras.

Then there was the foreign-educated medical officer who similarly believed that Sai Baba was really a Muslim. This doctor was similarly to have *darshan* of a mixed Hindu-Muslim divinity in his dream that was to remove all his doubts. The divinity was clothed in white and a piece of white cloth was tied round its head. And the doctor heard the divinity say: "Sainath Maharaj and Dattatreya are both one. Do not be guided or deceived by external appearance or dress. Identify the inner reality and perceive it."

The doctor's faith was strengthened by this event which occurred in his dream. It is said that an ailment from which he was suffering for some six months also subsided following his taking of the *prasad* he received from Sai Baba. Thereafter, the doctor accepted Dattatreya as his *ishtadaivat* (chosen deity, personal god).

One out of two visitors from Goa who came for Sai Baba's darshan also had a similar experience. This individual had vowed to offer his first month's salary to Shri Dattatreya if he secured a job. Then he secured employment on a monthly salary of Rs 15. With years of service his pay, too, had increased and at the time of his visit to Sai Baba it was Rs. 700 per month. A princely sum in those days and the man had nothing to complain about; but there was one lacuna: he had forgotten to keep his vow and was not released from his debt to Dattatreya.

Like everyone else, this man also went for Sai Baba's darshan and prostrated himself before him.
Sai Baba, sternly: "Give me my fifteen rupees!" The man paid the amount. Seeing this his companion prostrated before Sai Baba and offered thirty five rupees to Baba. But Sai Baba would have none of it.

Madhavrao Deshpande who was watching this now asked, "Baba, why this discrimination? You asked for fifteen rupees in the first case and this man is offering you thirty-five rupees voluntarily. Why are you refusing the amount?"

"You do not understand," Baba replied. "I take nothing from anybody. This masjid, Dwarkamai, only asks for nothing more than what is due, and only to the extent of the debt. Nothing more, nothing less. What do I need money for? I have neither a household nor samsar. I am totally detached." The man had forgotten his vow to pay his first month's salary to Sri Dattatreya—a vow he had not kept. The amount was a bare fifteen rupees. And that was all that Sai Baba had asked for. Not thirty five, not seven hundred. Just the amount the man had said he would pay, but hadn't. And it was all that Sai Baba had asked for—what was due to Dattatreya.

Chastened, but very happy and relieved, the man had paid the fifteen rupees and felt that he had discharged an overdue debt. Kakaji Vaidya had an experience of the oneness of Sai Baba with Saptashringi Devi of Vani in Nasik District. He was the priest of Saptashringi Devi and regarded her as his Chosen Deity A calamity had befallen him and he had become restless. So he entered the Devi's Temple and prayed to Her intensely. The Devi was pleased and appeared to him in his dream and told him that he would get his peace of mind if he approached Sai Baba. Kakaji had no idea who Baba was and was somewhat befuddled. Perhaps, he thought, Lord Tryambakeshwar was what Saptashringi Devi was referring to and so he went to Trimbak for the Lord's *darshan*. Every day, on waking up, he would first have *darshan* of Tryambakeshwar and after a bath perform *rudrabhishek*. He did this for ten days but there was no change in his condition and his mental anguish remained unabated. So he returned to Vani and again taking the Devi's *darshan* complained piteously: "Why did you send me to Trimbak? I am as unhappy as ever. I appeal to you to help me!"

That night Kakaji had another dream. The Devi appeared to him again and said: "The Baba I referred to is Sai Baba of Shirdi, Go to him!"

Kakaji woke up wondering where Shirdi was and how to get there. In the meantime it so happened that an astrologer visiting Shirdi had told Madhavrao Deshpande's younger brother Bapaji that because his elder brother Madhavrao had not fulfilled the vows of his mother, he had incurred the displeasure of Saptashringi Devi. When Bapaji reported this to Madhavrao the latter remembered that in his childhood he was once seriously ill and his mother had vowed to take him to get darshan of Saptashringi Devi. On another occasion when his mother had developed tumours on her nipples she had vowed to present two silver nipples to the Devi if she was cured. Madhavrao had promised his mother on her death-bed that he would fulfil her vows but his *ishtadaivat* (personal deity) was sadguru Sai Baba and he told Baba: "You are our Saptashringi Devi. Please accept these silver nipples in fulfilment of my mother's vows."

But Sai Baba would not have them. The vow was to make the presents to Saptashringi Devi and he felt he could not substitute for her. He advised Madhavrao that he should personally go to Saptashringi Devi Temple and place the offerings at her feet. Accordingly, Madhavrao proceeded to Vani and in his search for the priest, arrived at Kakaji's house. It was as if all this had been pre-arranged. There was Kakaji looking for Sai Baba and here was Madhavrao who had come straight from Shirdi. Kakaji was overjoyed. After Madhavrao had fulfilled both the vows of his mother, he and Kakaji started for Shirdi. As soon as Kakaji arrived in Shirdi he went for Sai Baba's *darshan.* He neither asked for anything nor did he wish to converse with Baba, nor did Baba bless him. For Kakaji, Baba's *darshan* sufficed by itself and he was finally at peace with himself. But the incident also showed the essential unity of Baba with Saptashringi Devi.

Similarly Sai Baba showed his identity with Akkalkot Swami, the famous saint whom many considered as an incarnation of Datatreya. Once Harishchandra Pitale, a resident of Bombay went to Shirdi with his wife and son to get Sai Baba's *darshan.* The son was epileptic and medical treatment had been of no help at all. Pitale thought that the only "remedy" was the *darshan* of a holy man.

About this time Das Ganu was popularising the name of Sai Baba through his *kirtanas.* That made Pitale all the more anxious to visit Shirdi which he did along with his wife and son.

Pitale had hoped to put his son at the feet of Sai Baba but the son fell at the feet of Sai Baba all on his own. But even as he did so the poor lad collapsed foaming profusely at his mouth. Pitale was very upset while there were tears in his wife's eyes. It was as if they had insulted Sai Baba. But Baba was re-assurance itself. "Take him back to your place," he told the parents in a re-assuring tone, "he will revive after half an hour. Do not worry."

The boy revived and the parents went back to Sai Baba for his *darshan.* They decided to stay in Shirdi for a few days. On their day of departure they went to Sai Baba, prostrated themselves before him and sought his permission to leave. Baba wished them well, gave them *udi* and then, taking out three rupees from his pocket told them: "I had given you two rupees before. Now keep these three rupees along with them for *puja* and you will be blessed!"

That had been Pitale's first visit to Shirdi and he had no recollection of being given two rupees earlier but he said nothing and returned home eager to find out what the reference to the two rupees meant. He narrated his experience to his aged mother and wondered whether she could enlighten him.

Pitale's mother thought for a while and said: "What Sai Baba told you is true. Even as you took your son to Shirdi for Sai Baba's *darshan,* your father had taken you to Akkalkot for the *darshan* of the Akkalkot Swami. The Swami was so pleased with your father's devotion that he gave him two rupees suggesting that he keep them for daily worship. As long as your father was alive the two rupee coins were in the shrine and your father would worship them with faith. But after his passing away the articles used in *puja* became the play things of children who had no faith in God and who were ashamed to do *puja.* In the years that have elapsed the two rupees were lost. Never mind.

But now know that in the guise of Sai Baba you have met Akkalkot Swami. Give up your doubts, remember the devotion of your father and now that you have three rupees given to you by a holy person worship them with devotion." To his credit, Pitale followed his mother's advice with devotion.

At the time of *nirvana* of Akkalkot Swami, Keshav Naik had asked him: "Maharaj, to whom should I and my son Rama-chandra look for guidance after you have gone?" The Swami hurled his leather *padukas* at him and said: "Worship these and go to Shirdi in the district of Ahmednagar where there is my incarnation. Give him your love in the same way as you have given me and you will not be in want of anything." After Akkalkot Swami took *samadhi* (1878) Keshav Naik with his son Ramachandra went to Shirdi. There both of them had Sai Baba's *darshan*. At Baba's behest Ramachandra plucked some leaves of the Neem tree which Baba asked the Naiks to eat. To their surprise the bitter leaves tasted utterly sweet! They remembered that at Akkalkot, the Swami had rendered part of the Neem tree in his *mutt* sweet. Here at Shirdi, Sai Baba had demonstrated his oneness with Akkalkot Swami in a novel way!

It was Sai Baba's practice to convince every visitor, whatever his chosen deity, that he was fully identified with Him or Her. A Parsi contractor of Nanded in the state of Hyderabad called Seth Ratanji Shapurji Wadia had an experience of this in an incomparable way.

Wadia was rich but he had twelve daughters—and no son. He was pining for a male successor. He had great faith in Das Ganu who asked him to travel to Shirdi for Sai Baba's bless-ings. Wadia came to Shirdi and went directly to the masjid with baskets of fruits and flowers as offerings, had Sai Baba's *darshan* and then addressing him said: "I have heard of your fame. I have come to take refuge in you for I know you help those in distress."

Baba told him: "Well, you have come at last. Give me whatever *dakshina* you wish to give in addition to Rs. 3 / 14 / 0 (three rupees fourteen annas) that you have already given me and your desire will be fulfilled."

Wadia gave a substantial sum as *dakshina,* received Baba's blessings and returned to Nanded. He called on Das Ganu and narrated his experience in Shirdi but added that he did not quite understand the reference to Rs. 3 / 14 / 0.

It was then that Das Ganu reminded him that after the latter had decided to pay a visit to Shirdi, a saintly person, Maulisaheb had come to the Wadia household where he was presented with garlands, fruits and served a light repast and the expense on that account may be worked out. When they totalled the amount spent on Maulisaheb, it was found that it came exactly to Rs 3 / 14 / 0. As to so many others in different situations, this came to Wadia as a revelation and a surprise and the conviction grew on him that there was some power that watched on every act of an individual and registered it. But what to Wadia was most satisfying was that his next child turned out to be a male.

People of all faiths called on Sai Baba and that included Christians as well. All were agreed that Sai Baba had divine powers that they could not explain. Chakra Narayan was a Christian. In 1918, he was Police Fauzdar at Kopargaon. In a statement that was recorded he wrote: "I was not a believer in Baba. We were watching Baba through our men. Even though I watched him sceptically, I ended up having a high regard for him. First and foremost was the fact that he was not moved by women or wealth. Many women would come to him and place their heads on his feet and sit before him. But he remained unmoved. There was no question of his casting a lustful glance at them. He was clearly and unmistakeably unattached. About money and financial dealings also, we watched him. People gave him money voluntarily. He never showed any signs of displeasure or anger at people who did not give him anything. The same held good about his begging for alms. He did not care for what he received. Whatever he got he gave away liberally. When he died, we took possession of whatever cash he had. It amounted to only sixteen rupees! Yet every day he was giving away hundreds of rupees. Often we noticed that he gave away more than he received. Wherefrom came the excess funds? We had no means of knowing or finding out. I have concluded that he has divine powers beyond my ken."

A Christian nurse working in Thakar Hospital in Girgaum, Bombay had an experience of the unity of Sai Baba with the Holy Ghost even after he had passed away. Her boss rejected her application for leave to go to Shirdi. Instead of grumbling, the nurse merely took to the chanting of Sai Baba's name in the privacy of her home. By and by she noticed a change in the boss's attitude towards her until finally, of his own accord, he let her go. Similar stories have been recounted which Swami Sai Sharan Anand has recorded in his book *Shri Sai Baba*.

Muslims visiting Sai Baba regarded him as a *Pir Avaliya* of a high order and respected him accordingly. There is an ancient belief among Muslims that an *avaliya* never dies. Such an experience was given by Sai Baba thirteen years after he laid down his body to Rajabally Mohammad, a Khoja contractor. Rajabally's she-buffalo became ill and inspite of the treatment of a veterinary surgeon, showed no improvement in its condition. Rajabally remembered Sai Baba and administered Sai Baba's *udi* to the buffalo as a result of which the ailing she-buffalo recovered fully.

There are many other stories on the same lines.
There is the story of Abdulla Jan, a Pathan from Tarabel in Hajra district of North West Frontier Province who had an educative experience. After Sai Baba was no more, Abdulla, who had accepted Sai Baba as his *murshid*, felt frustrated and dejected of heart and he left for his home. On his way in Swat Valley he came across the tomb of Syed Akunbaba, a descendant of the Prophet. While lying down near the tomb Abdulla prayed to Akunbaba to take him under his protection. That very night he had a dream in which he saw Sai Baba seated in a chair near his head. Sai Baba did not say anything. But Abdulla realized that though Sai Baba was no more physically, he continued to take care of his devotee.

Similarly, a broker called Amir Shakkar had an experience which convinced him that Sai Baba was an *avaliya* of a high order. When Gopalrao Gund and Damuanna Kasar decided to hold in consultation with prominent men in Shirdi an annual fair and asked Sai Baba when it should be held, the latter suggested the day of Rama Navami. So every year on Rama Navami Day, a procession is taken upto the masjid and flags are put up. Muslim devotees, too, according to their custom take a *sandal* procession through the village upto the masjid. Sandal means levigated and powdered sandalwood. This is placed in a metal vessel of a certain form and size and incense is burnt before it and *agarbatti* lighted and it is taken in procession upto a holy place and then palm impressions of levigated sandalwood are put at that place.

Amir Shakkar would organise with pomp a *sandal* procession every year. After him his widow had continued the practice. The flag procession of Hindus and *sandal* procession of Muslims are organised on the same day and followers of both faith participate in each other's procession.

Equal regard and respect for religions was a precept of Baba's life.

But there were dissidents and those who questioned Sai Baba's way of life. Thus, in 1894, some intolerant Muslims in Shirdi summoned the Kazi of Sangamner and positioned themselves near the masjid armed with lathis for obstructing the devotees going in for worshipping Sai Baba. In the meantime Mhalsapati who worshipped Sai Baba daily, came with his articles of *puja*, but noticing the well-armed crowd that stood menacingly in front of the masjid decided to worship Sai Baba mentally and from afar when Baba himself called him in to proceed with the rituals. The armed crowd stood transfixed and could not prevail against Baba and never again did they indulge in such fundamentalist behaviour.

Twenty years after this incident, a fundamentalist Pathan who also did not like what he considered were Hindu practices complained to Baba and asked his permission to massacre all Hindus sleeping in the chavdi. Baba told him no one was to blame and if he wanted to kill, he might begin by slitting Baba's throat first.

While this temporarily put off the Pathan, he continued to bear a grudge against Baba. So, one day, taking an opportunity when nobody was around, the Pathan swung at Sai Baba with his hefty stick. Baba merely glanced at him and caught him by his wrist. The Pathan felt powerless and collapsed to the ground. He could not even get up without the help of two persons. Crestfallen and ashamed he had to concede Baba's supernatural powers. He also realized that it was not for him to judge Baba according to his own concepts of what was right or wrong.

CHAPTER 5

AND THE FIRE DIED DOWN

What is a miracle?

The dictionary defines a "miracle" as "an effect in the physical world which surpasses all known human or natural powers and is therefore ascribed to supernatural agency." It is said that for those who believe in miracles, no explanation is necessary. And for those who do not believe in them, no explanation is possible.

There is the story of the sceptic who would not believe in any explanation. "Suppose," he was told by his friend, "that I jump from the tenth floor of my building, land on the ground, casually stand up, dust my trousers and walk away, would you believe that to be a miracle?"

"No," said the sceptic, "I would think it is just one of those things."

"Well, suppose," said his friend, "I climb a little higher, say to the fifteenth floor and jump down and, as in the previous instance, get up and walk away as if the fall was of no import, would you concede that as a miracle?"

"Not at all," countered the sceptic, "I should call it a coincidence."

"Well suppose," said his exasperated friend, "I go still high and jump out of the twenty fourth floor and as in the previous two incidents, walk away unharmed, would you' at least then concede *that* as a miracle?"

"Miracle?" said the sceptic, tossing his head contemptuously, "not at all. I should call it a bloody habit!"

No. The sceptic will never believe in miracles. But there have been reports down the ages of persons who had supernatural powers and who exercised these powers. Jesus Christ performed miracles. He walked on water. With a few loaves and fishes he fed the multitudes. He raised the dead. They called him the Son of Man. He described himself as the son of God whom he called Father in Heaven. He certainly had supernatural powers. It might be asked, as the thief who had been crucified along with him did ask, why, if he was the son of God, he could not escape the Cross. Why was he accepting suffering when he had relieved so many of it?

In India we are aware of *siddhas* who wielded supernatural powers; but in their time they, too, had to die. Of what use, then, were such supernatural powers, if one could not save oneself from death?

Is spiritual bliss or attainment in conflict with supernatural powers? Indeed, are supernatural powers obstacles to the attainment of spiritual bliss? One answer is that when a seeker strives diligently for the realization of God he gets supernatural powers which try their utmost to entangle him in the web of temptation. But if the seeker remained steady in intense meditation of God he was rewarded with the state of godhood. Once he attained that state, no *karma* would then stain him. But were a seeker to use the supernatural powers that he has won prior to his attaining godhood, for mundane purposes, he would be the loser. Godhood would ever elude him. Sai Baba always used to be in a state of *sahaj samadhi,* ever in tune with the Divine. If he performed miracles, it would have been, as it was said of Sant Tukaram, "for the welfare of the world" but never for self aggrandizement.

Long before Sai Baba's fame spread, he was fond of burning lights in his masjid and other mandirs. But for the oil needed in those little earthenware lights that he lit, he depended on the generosity of the grocers of Shirdi. He had made it a rule to light *pantis* (earthenware lights) in the masjid every morning and he would call on the grocers for small donations. But there came a time when the grocers tired of giving oil free to Sai Baba and one day they bluntly refused to oblige him, saying they had no fresh stocks. Without a word of protest Sai Baba returned to the masjid. Into those earthenware lamps he poured watur and lighted the wicks. The lamps continued to burn deep into the midnight. The matter came to the notice of the grocers who now came to Sai Baba with profuse apologies. And won't Sai Baba kindly pardon them?

Sai Baba pardoned them, but he warned them never to lie again. "You could have refused to give me the oil, but did you have to say you didn't have fresh stocks?" he admonished them. But he had made his point.

Once, harvesting in Shirdi had been completed and the food-grains of the entire village had been stored in a yard. The summer was on. The heat was intense as only those know who have lived in Shirdi. One afternoon Sai Baba summoned Kondaji Sutar and said to him: "Go, your field is on fire!"

Frightened, Kondaji ran to his field and frantically looked around for any sign of fire. There wasn't any. He returned to the masjid and informed Sai Baba that he had looked everywhere but had found no trace of fire and why did Baba have to frighten him?

Unfazed, Baba said: "You better turn back and look again."

Baba was found right after all. Kondaji noticed that a sheaf of corn was indeed on fire and smoke was billowing from it. A strong wind was fanning the fire and word had gone round to the villagers who now came running to the scene.

"Sai Baba," the people shouted, "help us, help us put the fire out!"

Thereupon, Sai Baba walked casually towards the yard, sprinkled some water on a stack of sheaves and said: "There now! The fire will die down!"
And so it happened.
Was it a miracle?

There was that other occasion when many thought that the masjid which housed Sai Baba itself was due to be consumed by fire from flames which leapt up from the *dhuni*. All that Baba did was to take some swipes at a wooden pillar in front of him. With every blow the flames subsided and the fire died down.

"Mirac ious," said his devotees. Often they would notice him stirring some hot concoction over the kitchen fire not with a ladle but with his bare hands. There never was a time when his hand was scalded. What supernatura! powers did he have?

On yet another occasion, Sai Baba was partaking of food with three of his devotees in the masjid when, without any cause for provocation, he exclaimed: "Stop!" Then, as if nothing had happened, the four continued with their meal. Lunch over and the dishes cleared, they stepped out of the masjid when large chunks of the ceiling fell on the very spot where they had been seated only a few minutes earlier. Did Sai Baba's powers extend even to inanimate matter, the devotees wondered.

Instances have been quoted by his devotees of how Sai Baba commanded the rains to stop and the winds to cease. There is the story of one Rao Bahadur Moreshwar Pradhan who had come to Shirdi to take Sai Baba's darshan along with his wife. As the couple were about to leave, it began to rain heavily. Thunder and lightning rent the air. As the Pradhan couple looked round in dismay, Sai Baba prayed. "Oh Allah!" he intoned, "let the rains cease. My children are going home. Let them go peacefully!" The storm thereupon ceased, the downpour became but a slight drizzle and the Pradhans were able to reach their destination safely.

When Sai Baba first came to Shirdi it boasted of no basic facilities. There was a well but only in name. It had no natural spring water and if ever there had been one, it must long ago have dried up. Water had to be fetched from a distance. When, therefore, Sai Baba gave his permission to the villagers to celebrate Ram Navami Fair the big problem facing the organizers was one of water supply. So what should they do but go to Sai Baba with their problem?

"Oh yes," said Sai Baba, "so you want plenty of water, do you? Here, take this and drop it in the well and wait and see."

"This," turned up to be a platter of leaves on which some prasad had been placed along with the remnants of alms Baba had received earlier in the day.

132

The villagers had no qualms about doing as they were bid. Their faith in Sai Baba was total. No sooner had that platter of leaves been dropped in the well, it is said, water rose from the bottom as if by divine command and completely filled it. And great was the rejoicing of the people.

One report has it that word spread that the 3-year old daughter of a poor man called Babu Kirwandikar had fallen into the well and had been drowned. When the villagers rushed to the well they saw the child suspended in mid-air as if some invisible hand was holding it up! She was quickly pulled out. Sai Baba was fond of that child who was often heard to say: "I am Baba's sister!" After this incident, the villagers took her at her word. "It is all Baba's *leela*" the people would say philosophically. They could offer no other explanation. These were instances of things they had seen with their own eyes. It was not second-hand information they had gathered. Sai Baba was to them as real as their homes and their fields and their cattle and the distant hills.

Das Ganu once had an unforgettable experience. On a festive occasion, he sought Baba's permission to go to a place called Singba on the banks of the Godavari to have a bath in the holy waters.

"No," Baba replied resolutely, "where is the need to go all the way when the Godavari is here right at my feet?"

Das Ganu was vexed. He was willing to concede that Ganga (and Baba frequently referred to Godavari as Ganga) rose from the feet of Sri Narayana himself, but his faith was not deep enough to believe that the waters of the Godavari could spring from the feet of his master.

Baba who was reading Das Ganu's mind decided that this was the time to strengthen Das Ganu's faith. He told his devotee: "Come closer to me and hold the hollow of your palms at my feet!"

As soon as he did so water flowed freely out of the toes of the master's feet and filled the hollow of Das Ganu's palms in no time. His joy knew no limits. He sprinkled the water on his head and his body and distributed some more among assembled devotees as *tirtha*. He was so overcome that he was inspired then and there to write a *pada* (a poetic composition) in Marathi addressing Sai Baba:

The Song of Das Ganu

Oh Supreme sadguru, boundless is your power
and marvellous your deeds!
You are the ship transporting the ignorant
across the Ocean of Life. (*refrain*).

You became Veni Madhav Himself and
made your feet Prayag.
And manifested the Ganga and the Yamuna
from your two toes.

You are Brahma, Vishnu and Shiva, the
quintessence of the three Gunas
And on this earth, you manifest as Sai,
the powerful.

In the early morning you become Brahma, and
spiritual knowledge flows from you.
And sometimes resorting to the quality of *tamas*
you assume the terrible form of Shiva.

Sometimes like Shri Krishna, you indulge in
child-like pranks;
And, at times, you become the fabled swan in
the lake of your devotees' minds.

Considering your fondness for *gandha,* how
can you be called a Muslim?
And yet, if you are a Hindu, how do you dwell
happily in a mosque?

If rich, why should you go asking for alms?
And yet, how can you be called a fakir
when you put Kuber to shame with your generosity?

If your house be a mosque, why does it
have the sacred fire of the Hindus

Burning continuously in the *dhuni* which
produces the *udi*?

From morning devotees in their simplicity
worship you.
At noon when the sun is overhead, your
arati is performed.

Devotees stand all around you like
attendants of Gods;
And holding *chowrie* and *chaamar* wave them over you.

Trumpets, *dhols, pipani, shahanai*
and bells resound.
And *chopdars* wearing belts proclaim
your glory at the gates.

And at *arati* time on your divine seat
You look like Lord Vishnu
And at dusk as you sit before the *dhuni*
you appear as Shankara.

Such *leelas* of the Trinity
manifest in you
Are experienced by us daily
O Baba Sai!

Even so my mind
wanders idly!
O steady it
I implore you!

Vilest of the vile, and a great sinner I
take refuge at your feet!
O Supreme guru, ward off the three-fold
afflictions of your devotee, Das Ganu!

Sai Baba had the power to appear in dreams of his devotees
and actually give them material things which the devotees
found in their bed on waking up. To a childless woman, Sai
Baba gave in her dream a coconut with his blessings and said
to her: "Partake of this coconut and you will get a son!" This
incident was narrated by the woman herself when she had

come to Shirdi to attend the Ram Navami Fair with her new-born son for Baba's darshan.

Another experience of this kind was given to Fakir Amiruddin, former *murshid of* Abdul, Sai Baba's personal attendant. Sai Baba appeared in Amiruddin's dream and said: "Take these two mangoes, hand them over to Abdul and instruct him to come to Shirdi." On waking up Amruddin found the two mangoes in his bed!

Sai Baba possessed the *annapurna siddhi*. He could infinitely multiply the amount of food available to feed the multitudes. Purandare once went on a Good Friday to Shirdi when Sai Baba said to him: "I will come to your place for a meal."

"I am blessed," said Purandare, "but what shall I prepare for the meal?"

"Some rice," replied Baba, "a little *kichri, shira,* and one or two vegetables, all for two or three fakirs, you and I."

Accordingly Purandare made purchases in the bazaar and asked his wife to prepare the dishes. After the noon *arati* was over, Purandare returned to his home. Shortly afterwards five fakirs came along and told Purandare that more were to follow. Determined not to let anyone go unfed, Purandare told his wife to cook some more. When the first five fakirs left after thoroughly enjoying themselves Purandare found twenty fakirs at his door asking to be fed. Purandare turned to his wife. His wife went back to the kitchen but to her infinite surprise she found that the vessels were still full! Cheerfully she fed the twenty, but when they left there were ten more fakirs waiting their turn at the door. But the Purandares had no difficulty feeding them either. The vessels never seemed empty!

By now Purandare realised that Sai Baba had not come, so he went to the mosque to invite him. But Sai Baba said: "You want me to eat more? I have already had my fill!" and turning to some devotees he said jokingly: "But I frightened this gentleman!" Purandare thereupon gave Baba a *vida* (a betel leaf rolled with some areca and lime) and *dakshina* and the latter said: "Go now and have your meal with Bala Shimpi with whom

136

you are staying."

The family now had its meal but there was still so much food left that Purandare took the rest back to Bombay to distribute as *prasad* to other devotees.

There is yet another story on similar lines told about Sai Baba's *siddhi* powers. Balaji Nevaskar as well as members of his family were all devotees of Sai Baba. Once there was a *shraaddha* ceremony at Nevaskar's and three times the number of expected guests turned up for meals. Nevaskar's wife was unnerved. She spoke about her anxiety to Nevaskar's mother. The lady was not fazed. She prayed to Sai Baba, put some of *udi* she had kept with her in the cooked food and covered it with a piece of cloth. Sai Baba did not fail his devotee. Everything went off well without any hitch. There was plenty of food for all the guests and there was enough left-overs for the entire family to eat.

Such incidents are indeed miraculous and remind one of Christ's miracles of the loaves and fishes. But there are other incidents that are best described as the result of faith. There is the story of the eldest son of Raghunathrao Tendulkar, his wife Savitribai and their son Babu, residents of Bandra, a suburb of Bombay. An astrolger who had read Babu's horoscope had made the prediction that Babu's stars were so bad that very likely he would not succeed in his final year medical examination. Babu who heard this felt disappointed and was slack in his studies. Savitribai understandably was upset. On a visit to Shirdi she confided her predicament to Sai Baba and sought his guidance. Baba was very forthcoming. "Tell Babu," he advised Savitribai, "to keep aside his horoscope and have faith in me. Ask him to study as usual, appear for his examination with a calm mind and surely he will succeed."

Babu did as he was bid and appeared for his examination. But nevertheless he felt that he had not done well. Disappointed, he stayed away from orals. The first day passed off uneventfully. On the second day as Babu was having his lunch, a friend dropped by and told him that his absence had been noticed by the Oral Examiner who wanted to know what the matter was. When the Oral Examiner was apprised of Babu's fears he in turn sent word to the boy that he had indeed passed his written tests and that he should not absent himself from Orals. Delighted, Babu presented himself for Orals, did well and was declared to have passed his examination. Miracle? Hardly. But faith, no doubt, had played its part in Babu's success. Devotees have also testified to the calamities that befell them when they disregarded Baba's advice. One, Aurangabadkar who was preparing to leave Shirdi was told by Baba: "What work is so important that you have to go? You will break your bones!" But the skies were clear and there was no sign of storm. So Aurangabadkar decided to leave. He had not proceeded very far when heavy rains prevented him from going further.

Then there is the story of the *Keertankar* who, disobeying Baba left for the station when he had been specifically told: "There is plenty of time for the train to arrive; have your meal and then go!"

Baba had correctly visualised that the train would be late. And the *Keertankar* had to stay hungry for the rest of the day!

Abdul Rahim Shamsuddin similarly would not listen to Baba. On his way, one of the *tonga* wheels broke and he had to wait in the night for two hours before succour came. And the succour came from Baba himself who thoughtfully sent another tonga lest Abdul Rahim and his wife spend an entire night shivering in the darkness and prey to any lurking dacoits.

"Be content with half a loaf of bread that you get here, do not go away out of greed for more," was the advice Baba gave to Tukaram Barku who left Shirdi and went to Karaji, 20 miles away for work on the road. There Barku developed fever, had to give up his job and return to Shirdi to be lovingly taken care of by Baba.

Kaavaji Patil of Andheri desired to construct a temple in memory of his father. He sought Baba's permission to build a temple to Vanidevi at a certain place. Baba said "No." When Kaavaji asked him again, Baba said "No" for the second time. When Kaavaji kept pestering him, Baba replied: "In spite of my saying 'no' to you repeatedly, you keep asking me the same question. If you want to build the temple, go ahead and face the consequences.''

Kaavaji went ahead on the advice of some quack and Baba said nothing more. But even as work on the construction of the temple began plague broke out in the vicinity. Kaavaji gave up the idea of installing an idol of Vanidevi and looked for another goddess to be installed in the temple. But then he fell sick and· was confined to bed for two years. Finally he came back to Baba.

Baba told him: "Stick to your family deity and don't look for other goddesses. Worship the god that your ancestors have worshipped.'' Kaavaji now took Baba's advice. And all went well.

Then the story is told about a Sai devotee who went on a pilgrimage to Rameshwar, with his wife and sister-in-law. Their first halt was at Madras in a Gujarati *dharmashala*. The sister-in-law was particular about observing pollution taboos and began to grumble about the situation in the *dharmashala*. So her sister told her: "The arrangements here are good enough but you keep grumbling. What would you do at Shirdi? There even orthodox persons particular about pollution taboos also place their heads on Baba's feet without any reservation.''

The sister-in-law who was no devotee of Baba said sarcastically: "If that is so, I prostrate before Sai Baba right here!''

That seemingly had its repercussions. Shortly thereafter the sister-in-law developed shooting pains in her limbs; neither massage, nor fomentation helped. She could not even get up from her bed. The family was due to leave Madras the next morning, for train reservations had already been made. But there was no way the sister-in-law could accompany her sister and brother-in-law. The two ladies were deeply worried and all night they discussed how the calamity could have befallen on one of them. The married sister joked about it. "Only this morning you said that you could prostrate before Sai Baba right in Madras without having to go to Shirdi! May be Shri Rameshwar wants you to prostrate before him also from Madras!''

The words hit their target.

Very contrite by then, the sister-in-law said that if the shooting pain in her legs went away and she can complete her pilgrimage to Rameshwar, she would thereafter go to Shirdi for darshan of Sai Baba. It was sincerely meant.

By early morning, the pain was gone. The sister-in-law felt immensely relieved. She kept her tryst with Rameshwar and later she kept her vow to go to Shirdi. No more would she slight Baba.

The newly-married wife of Aba Samant invited the wrath of fire by her insult of Sai Baba. One day Samant bought a sari and gave it to his wife, saying: "This sari has been given to you by Sai Baba." Samant's wife had no faith in Sai Baba. She said: "What has Sai Baba got to do with this sari? You worked hard and earned money and out of your earnings bought this sari. Where does Sai Baba come in the picture?" Somewhat cross she kept the sari on a box and went ahead with preparations for the evening's dinner. Dinner over she said to her husband: "Anyway, let me see what the sari looks like," and she went to pick it up. She was to get the surprise of her life. For, while the outer packing was intact, inside all that the poor girl was to find were charred pieces of cloth!

Full of anguish for her lack of faith in Sai Baba and her arrogance, the wife did not know what to do. She still had her doubts but the charred pieces of cloth were not to be ignored. She prayed. "Baba," she said, "if I get a new sari tomorrow, I will know that it was wrong of me to say the things I said earlier! Forgive me!"

She must have been forgiven. Unexpectedly the next morning, some one who owed Samant ten rupees came to return the debt and out of that, Samant bought his wife a new sari. At that instant Baba had a new devotee.

But easily the most outstanding miracle that Baba performed was to revive the dead. The daughter of the maternal aunt of Vasudeo Sitaram Ratanjankar who had come to Shirdi had this experience. The girl was having high fever and the doctors said that she had developed tuberculosis. Medical help was of no avail and all hopes had been practically given up. She was given *udi* but she wanted Baba's darshan and so, despite her precarious health she was brought to Shirdi.

But Baba was furious that the girl should have been put to so much inconvenience and let off a volley of abuse. "Place her on a *kambal* (coarse blanket) and give her only water," he ordered. His orders were obeyed. The girl survived for seven days on a water diet. On the eighth day she breathed her last, early in the morning.

She died just about the time that Baba was to get up. He had been sleeping at the *chavadi* but that day he did not get up at his regular time. No one tried to wake him up. Nevertheless funeral arrangements had to be made. The family was distraught and the womenfolk began weeping aloud.

Suddenly they noticed that the girl given up as dead was stirring. In another few seconds people around her observed her yawning and looking bewildered. When the initial shock was over, they heard her tell her tale. She said she was being forcibly led by a dark man when she called for Sai Baba in her distress. She saw Baba come with his staff and belabour the dark man who let go of her. Baba thereafter led her to a *chavadi*. She had never been to the *chavadi* where Baba habitually slept, but she described it in vivid and accurate terms.

While this conversation was going on in Dikshitwada where the Ratanjankars were staying, others at the *chavadi* were wondering why Baba was still asleep, which was very, very unusual of him. That had never before happened. Baba was always up early and his oversleeping was unheard of.

Then they were to witness yet another incident. Without warning, Baba woke up suddenly, shouting loudly and hitting the ground with his staff. Then just as suddenly he ran in the direction of Dikshitwada. By now everyone around had come to know what had happened.

Often Baba would grant his devotees their prayers for a son. It was one thing that some of his devotees most ardently prayed for. Several cases of childless couples begetting sons have been recorded. There was Babasaheb Dengle of Nimgaor whose brother had no sons. Believing that his first wife could bear him no children, he had married again but that didn't help either. On Babasaheb's advice he went to Shirdi and received Baba's blessings.

There is the instance of Gopal Gund who had married thrice but had children by none of his three wives. He sought Baba's blessings and was amply rewarded. He got a son. To express his gratitude, Gund offered to have the masjid where Baba was staying, repaired. Baba would not give his permission. But he suggested that the Hanuman Temple, adjacent to the masjid which was in a bad state be repaired instead. Gund readily agreed to do so. It is said that it was at Gund's suggestion that an annual fair was first held on Ram Navami Day in Shirdi in 1896-97.

Damodar Savalaram Rasane, a bangle merchant of Ahmed-nagar had no sons even though he had two wives. He was a Sai Baba devotee for many years. Then an interesting thing happened. In 1900 a devotee sent Baba a parcel of quality mangoes from Goa. Sai Baba picked out eight mangoes from the lot and distributed the remaining among children. Noticing that eight mangoes had been set aside the children wanted to have them as well. But Baba told them: "I have to give them to Damya."

"Why Damya? He is not here, is he?" the children queried.

"But he is on his way!" replied Baba.

Actually Rasane was on his way, but the children managed to steal four of the eight mangoes and got away with them. Not long afterwards Rasane arrived in Shirdi and went for Baba's darshan. Baba said to him: "Here, take these mangoes which I have kept for you and die!"

As Rasane did not understand the meaning of Sai Baba's words he was frightened. So Baba said: "Do not eat the mangoes yourself but give them to your second wife. Thereby you will have sons. Name the first one Daulatshah and the second one Thanashah." Rasane took the mangoes reverentially and gave them to his second wife to eat. After a year she gave birth to a son. A year and a half later, she gave birth to another son. In all she gave birth to eight sons, of whom only four survived!

Rasane performed the thread ceremony of Daulatshah at Shirdi. In later years Daulatshah had many offers from rich merchants for marrying their daughters. But Baba had advised Rasane that he must choose a girl from a poor family. Daulatshah had one son from her but the child died after an epileptic fit. Daulatshah became very dejected. He went to Shirdi and after taking darshan of Baba's samadhi—for by then Baba had passed away—he prayed for just one son who will live long than for many who would die soon.

It has been recorded that Daulatshah saw Baba in his dream and Baba said: "I took away your son because he was born in *mool nakshatra* (one of the 27 asterisms in the moon's path). I will give you a good son. Do not worry."

Daulatshah returned from Shirdi and called for his dead son's horoscope that he had really not cared to see before. He found that Baba was indeed right. The boy had been born in *mool nakshatra.* But then Daulatshah had another son who lived long.

Rao Bahadur Hari Vinayak Sathe became a widower in 1900. At that time he was 45 years old. He had two daughters. His relatives pressed him to remarry but he would excuse himself saying that he would remarry only if a holy person assured him that he would beget a son by his second marriage.

In 1904 Sathe was transferred to Ahmednagar district and he took the opportunity to visit Shirdi to get Baba's darshan. Having taken darshan, Sathe stood mutely before Baba. The *mamlatdar* who had accompanied Sathe assured him. Sathe took Baba at his word and remarried. The first two children he had by his second marriage were daughters. But the third child turned out to be a son. And great was his happiness.

Shantaram Balwant Nachane went for Baba's darshan in 1915 along with his wife. All the children that were born to the couple had died young. As *dakshina* Nachane's wife offered Baba a coconut which he promptly placed in her *oti.* Even as he did tears were welling out of Baba's eyes, inexplicably. The couple left. In 1919 a son was born to Nachane's wife under *moola nakshatra,* not an auspicious sign. As the child was born after Baba's *nirvana,* he was named Kaluram. When the child was barely two years old, the mother passed away.

Kaluram was about five years old when he was noticed to do spiritual exercises as if he was continuing an interrupted life in a previous birth. He would often go into *samadhi*. He had written the mantra *Rama Hare Rama* more than a hundred thousand times. Standing before Sai Baba's picture he would perform *arati*, listen to the reading of religious works like *Hari Vijaya* and say: "Krishna comes to play with me!" Gadge Baba had come to visit him in 1924. Once the boy faulted his father for not meditating on Sai Baba and pointing to the picture of a dog on a gramophone record of His Master's Voice suggested that his father listen to Sai Baba's voice with the same intense concentration as the dog itself.

Kaluram died at the tender age of eight of abdominal dropsy. When his end approached Kaluram called his father to his bedside, asked for a copy of *Jnaneshwari* and opening it at Canto 13 asked the elder to read it. When his father started crying, Kaluram cheered him and said: "What is there to cry about? Read the 13th Canto aloud for me. I am going today."

It was only after Kaluram died that Nachane began to understand the tears of Baba as he dropped the coconut in his wife's *oti*. It was obvious that Baba had foreseen the events of the wife's death and the end of the child yet to be born. Nachane subsequently remarried and had three sons who survived. The girl he married had been approved of by Baba in a dream that Nachane's mother had.

Govind Narayan Shinde of Harda had seven daughters and no son. On the suggestion of a friend he had vowed before the *padukas* of Gangapur that if he got a son through the grace of Dattatreya he would take the child for *darshan* of Dattatreya at Gangapur. He got a son within a year but he failed to fulfil his vow. Seven years thus elapsed. Shinde, along with the friend at whose suggestion he had taken the vow had an occasion to go to Shirdi. He quickly got his come-uppance from Baba.

Looking at him in his face Baba said: "How come you have become so arrogant? Don't you know that you were not

144

destined to get a son? Out of my own body have I given you one!" So saying he looked at Shinde's friend and asked: "Isn't that true?" Shinde apologised to Sai Baba and was quick thereafter to fulfil his vow. It was a way of showing on Baba's part of his oneness with all deities.

Chhotubai, wife of Rao Bahadur Moreshwar Pradhan had once been to Shirdi along with her husband's sister. Looking at Chhotubai Sai Baba said in the presence of all: "She is going to be the mother of my Babu!" Had he mistaken Chhotubai for her sister? Those present sought a clarification. Still pointing to Chhotubai, Baba said: "She is the one who will be my Babu's mother." At that time Chhotobai was not pregnant but within a year she gave birth to a son who was named Babu. At the age of four Babu had a serious illness. A Telangi brahmin named Madhav Bhatt was then staying with the Pradhans. He used to do *pooja* and *japa* for the welfare of the Pradhan family. He was deeply concerned with Babu's sickness and thought that Pradhan had invited this calamity upon himself by serving a Muslim fakir (Sai Baba). But Bhatt had no courage to give expression to his private views. One night Madhav Bhatt had a dream in which he saw Sai Baba sitting on the stairs with a staff in his hand. He said to Bhatt: "What do you think? *I* am the owner of this house!" Bhatt did not reveal this dream to anyone. As it turned out, Babu's illness became more acute. Bhatt got frightened and going up to Sai Baba's picture hanging on the wall said loudly for all to hear: "If by 4 p.m. Babu's condition improves sufficiently to take him down to the ground floor, I will admit that you are indeed Dattatreya!"

Within minutes Babu's fever began to come down and at 4 p.m. Babu himself asked to be taken down to the ground floor for playing. Bhatt now was convinced that Sai Baba was none other than Dattatreya. He offered Rs 120 to Sai Baba as *dakshina*. Being childless he also vowed to give Sai Baba Rs 108 if he begot a son. When a son was born to him, he kept his word.

Sapatnekar, a *vakil* (pleader) of Akkalkot had a similar experience. When he was reading law, he first heard of

Sai Baba from a fellow-student, Shevade. Shevade and he were exchanging notes after giving an examination when Sapatnekar found that his friend's answers were all wrong. "How will you ever become an L.L.B.?" Sapatnekar asked Shevade. The latter replied: "My Sai Baba has told me that I will fail this time but will pass on the second attempt. I have full confidence in him."

"Who is this Sai Baba? Where does he live?" Sapatnekar asked in idle curiosity. Shevade supplied the information. And he reiterated his faith in Baba. Sapatnekar could hardly suppress a smile at what he thought was blind faith.

But then on his second attempt Shevade did pass!

For ten years Sapatnekar and Shevade had no contacts with each other. In the meantime Sapatnekar got married and started his legal practice. His wife bore him a son who, however, died at an early age, leaving the father desolate. At that point in time he remembered his brief conversation with Shevade and decided he would go to Shirdi.

So one day, accompanied by his wife and a brother, Sapatnekar went to Shirdi and went for Baba's darshan. Each took a coconut as an offering to Baba.

But Baba had no time for them. *"Chal hat"* (go away!) was his only response. Every time Sapatnekar saluted him, the response was still the same. Disheartened, he asked an old devotee of Sai Baba, Bala Shimpi to accompany him. But still Baba seemed as angry as ever. This time he said: "Go away immediately!"

Sapatnekar thereupon, left. His mind was in turmoil. At the end of a year he decided to go on a pilgrimage to Gangapur and then to Varanasi. But then it happened!

Two days before the day of departure Sapatnekar's wife had a dream in which she saw a fakir, a piece of cloth tied round his head, sitting under a neem tree. She herself was going to fetch water but she heard the fakir tell her: "My dear girl, why do you labour in vain? I will get your *ghaagar* (brass or copper vessel) filled with clean water." She had never been addressed like that before, so Sapatnekar's wife moved away from the fakir as fast as she could, but the fakir now followed her. At that point she awoke. Believing that the fakir could not be anyone else than Sai Baba the Sapatnekar couple decided to go to Shirdi instead of Varanasi. When they reached the masjid, they learnt that Baba had gone to the nearby stream. So the couple waited for him to return. Not long afterwards Baba returned and took his usual seat in the masjid whereupon Sapatnekar's wife went towards him and bowed low. Baba seemed pleased. He told a woman devotee sitting by him: "My hands and feet, stomach and waist have been aching a great deal these last few days. I tried several remedies but to no avail. Now my pain has suddenly vanished!"

Sapatnekar's wife was astonished when she heard this. For Baba was describing her own ailment!

She had now become a Baba devotee but Sapatnekar had his doubts. Yet, like a man torn by the tragedy of his son's death, he wanted peace at the feet of Baba but the latter still would not have him. "Chal hat!" was his only response. In desperation Sapatnekar went to Baba when he was alone and clutched his feet in despair. Baba now relented and blessed him.

Even as Sapatnekar was doing *charan seva* (pressing of feet) to Baba, a shepherd woman came to see him. To her Baba recounted Sapatnekar's problems starting with the death of the latter's son. "He accuses me of having killed his son," Baba told the Shepherdess, "but why does he come here and bewail that I strike down others' children? Let it go. I will see to it that he gets another son!"

Then Baba addressed himself to Sapatnekar. "These feet of mine" he told Sapatnekar, "are very ancient. Have complete trust in me. Do not worry. Your wish will be fulfilled." Sapatnekar was overjoyed and stayed on in Shirdi for many days. When the time came for him to leave Sai Baba asked him for *dakshina* of two rupees which Sapatnekar had already decided in his mind to offer. Then Sai Baba placed a coconut in the *oti* of Sapatnekar's wife. In a year's time she bore her husband a son. Husband, wife and son called on Baba to express their gratitude.

Instances have been recorded of childless couples or couples desiring a son having their desires fulfilled. Though Baba himself is no more largesse continues to come its way to his devotees who have faith in Baba. Baba himself has once said: "After I pass away, my *samadhi* will protect my devotees".

2

In his best-selling book *Meditation* Mouni Sadhu has recounted a statement made to him by Ramana Maharshi on the nature of miracles. The fulcrum of all miracles, Ramana Maharshi is quoted as saying, is "the dynamic power of consciousness". The basis of all supernatural phenomenon was the active consciousness. Spirit ruled matter. The Maharshi told Mouni Sadhu: "Jesus, the man, was utterly unconscious of being a separate finite personality when He worked His miracles and spoke His wonderful words. It was White Light, the Life, which is the Cause and Effect, acting in perfect concert. My father and I are one!"

The state which allows the incredible miracles to be performed is the *Sahaja Nirvikalpa Samadhi* the perennial or eternal state of spiritual Superconsciousness or Hyperconsciousness accessible only to those who have finished their earthly evolution and learned all its lessons and hence have nothing more to know. Referring to the unlimited spiritual powers associated with the *Sahaja* state, judging by Ramana Maharshi's own, Mouni Sadhu says: "Although he did not like to show them in any way, these manifested themselves as knowing all the three sub-divisions of time; being able to read the innermost depths of human consciousness; being visible in different places at once; assisting decisively in the spiritual advancement and enlightenment of those who truly turned to him, as to their Master and guide; promoting the hidden

148

faculties in his devotees, and leading them to *Samadhi* in an unobtrusive and sure way; purifying their minds and turning them towards spirituality, instead of the illusions of the visible earthly existence, and supervising their spiritual growth even after leaving his physical body, according to his own promise 'not to abandon us' after death. Involuntarily the great words of Christ come to mind: 'I will not leave you orphans, I will come to you.'"

Of the state lower than *Sahaja,* the *Kevala Nirvikalpa Samadhi,* which can be of long or short duration, after which a man inevitably returns to his normal awareness of the physical world, Mouni Sadhu says: "*Kevala Nirvikalpa Samadhi* may well be accompanied by certain psychic powers called *Siddhis* by Hindu occultists, such as clairvoyance, clairaudience, magnetic forces which can be used for the cure of certain diseases, and so on."

"In *Samadhi* there is no such thing as 'time', that is, the sequence of events. There all is *One,* at the same moment, if we can say so. No past, no future, only the glorious eternal *Present* extending into infinity."

Everything is possible for him who has Faith.

Mouni Sadhu's theory is that where there are powers acting beyond the limitations of the physical laws, there must be an advanced consciousness acting behind them. He has two explanations for miracles:

1. They are the result of the application of some Laws of a superior kind *unknown* to us in our limited world.

2. They may be the results of a direct act of the Creative Consciousness which imposed those Laws, but which is above all of its creation and Laws. The manifested creation is subject to the law of cause and effect. But the Spirit is far above and beyond any laws, those which we know as well as those about which we have not the slightest premonition. To us what lies beyond our limited knowledge is like a miracle.

The range of miracles depended solely upon the range of consciousness operating behind them.

With regard to the first explanation, Mouni Sadhu has a further explanation. As he puts it, "All that we are performing in our three-dimensional world would be an unbroken chain of miracles to, say, a being limited to only two dimensions." The world superior to the lower realms (planes), namely, mental, astral and physical ones, is beyond our time (three mortal sub-divisions—past, present and future) and space. As the drama of the manifested universe operates, apart from the planes conceivable for us and also beyond them, it cannot be translated into words. In the higher (transcendental) state of consciousness, this problem is solved individually, but cannot be communicated by words and thoughts. "The Primary Will" can neither be explained nor conceived in the limited terms of the thinking brain. Can we think of a "superior dimension" which could explain miracles? To anyone living in that "superior dimension" adds Mouni Sadhu, "our most advanced techniques, such as space travel and atomic energy would appear like clumsy inventions and conditions of life of stone-age men." P. D. Ouspensky, a thinker of considerable depth, tried to reconcile occult phenomena with science and proposed to explain the 'miracles' as actions deriving from superior dimensions." In Physics, time viewed as lengthlike quantity is considered as the fourth dimension. However, referring to this concept, Mouni Sadhu cautions in his book *Samadhi* that "the reader must not follow the theories of some thinker-mathematicians of the beginning of this century, who supposed that the fourth co-ordinate (added to the three coordinates officially used in trignometry) is *just that of time!* It is not so, because although time still exists in the higher planes, in them it has quite a different meaning, and cannot be fully compared with *earthly time.*" Ouspensky believed that there could be five or six dimensions of which we are not aware of but which could explain a miracle in simple terms.

But the key to miracles, one believes, still remains Faith.
Sri Ramakrishna explained it this way. Speaking to one of his disciples, the Paramahansa said:

"You must have heard of the power of Faith; Ramachandra was God Incarnate. You know how he had to build a bridge across the sea. But Hanuman, the great lover of the Lord, had infinite faith in the power of His Name. He repeated it and behold, he found himself at once on the other side! Here you see the power of faith; the Lord himself had to build a bridge while the devotee who had faith in His Name needed no bridge to carry him across."

But to sustain miracles, faith too had to be sustained. Sri Ramakrishna Paramahansa recited another story to prove that point. He said:

"Another devotee wrote the name of Rama on a leaf and handed it to a man who wanted to cross the sea, saying: 'Fear not, my friend, have faith and walk across the deep. But mind you, do not show any want of faith; for then you will be drowned.' The man tied the leaf within the folds of his cloth. He went his way, walking on the sea. As he went, he was seized with a desire to look at the writing. He brought out the leaf and read the name of Rama (God) written large upon it. At this he thought to himself: 'Only the name of Rama? Is that all?' And at that instant when he lost his faith, down he went into the water!"

In his book *Living With the Himalayan Masters,* Swami Rama has many stories to tell about the power of faith. One of them is about how his Master, a *siddha* saved a drowning man. This is how Swami Rama tells the story:

A learned man from Rajasthan once came to my ashram at Uttarkashi. He was a well-known pandit. He was on a pilgrimage to Gangotri in the Himalayas. He was then about seventy years of age. One day he wanted to take a dip in the holy river Ganges but did not know how to swim. The river was just a short distance from my ashram. He saw that monkeys on the other side were jumping into the water, diving and coming up. So he thought: "If monkeys can dive in and swim, why can't I, an educated man, do it?" Thereupon he jumped into the water and started drowning. One of my companions saw him drowning and began shouting. I rushed out and asked: "What happened?"

He replied: "That man is drowning."

I rushed to the river. I was worried. I thought: "Is somebody

going to be killed in front of my ashram?" When I got there, the old man was sitting on the bank gasping for air. After he caught his breath, I asked him what happened.
He said: "I was taken by the currents."
"Then how did you get out?" I asked.
He said: "A Swami pulled me out."
I asked him who it was and he gave an exact description of my master. I had only one picture of my master and had never showed it to anyone. But in this case I wanted to verify whether it was indeed my master who had pulled him out, so I showed that picture to him.

He said: "Yes, that's the man. After I had gone under three times, I went down to the bottom and started inhaling water. I thought: 'If this is a holy place, somebody will help me' and then suddenly somebody pulled me out of the water and *he* is the very one."
I told him: "You were hallucinating."
He said: "No! I have so much faith now that I must find this man and stay with him. I shall never go back home."
I asked: "What will your family say?"
He said: "My children are grown up. I'm going to the Himalayas." And he left.
My gurudeva sent word to him on the way not to come until he was better prepared. Now he lives some twelve miles away from our monastery where he spends his time in meditation...

Many of the stories recounted by Swami Rama have a parallel in reports of the miracles wrought by Sai Baba. Obviously, Swami Rama's *gurudev* had powers to work miracles. He recounts this story of how he and his gurudev once found themselves in Etah, in north India. They stopped at Etah railway station and the gurudev went to the station master and said: "My child is with me and he is hungry. Please give us some food." The Station Master went to his home but his wife cried: "You know that our only son is suffering from small pox and all that you can think of is giving food to these wandering sadhus! My son is dying! Go away!"
The wife told her husband that if the sadhu was a real one, he surely could cure the child!

The Station Master came back with a long face and told the guru what happened. The guru decided that he would visit the Station Master's home and see the child.

The child had abscesses all over his body and even on his face and puss was issuing from them. The guru told the parents: "Don't worry, in two minutes your son will be completely well."

He took a glass of water, and walked round the cot on which the boy was lying. He did this three times and then drank the water. Then he looked at the Station Master's wife and said: "He's getting well, don't you see?"

To everyone's amazement, the abscesses began to disappear from the body, but to the absolute horror of Swami Rama who was then all of twelve years old, the abscesses began to appear on his guru's face! Swami Rama was terrified and started to cry. But his master said: "Don't worry, nothing will happen to me!"

Within two minutes the child's face and skin became perfectly clear and Swami Rama and his guru left the house until they came to a banyan tree. There they sat and soon the abscesses on the guru's face disappeared, even as they began to appear on the trunk of the tree. But even the tree abscesses disappeared after ten minutes.

Comments Swami Rama, echoing Mouni Sadhu's words:
"When individual consciousness expands itself to cosmic consciousness, it becomes easy to feel delight in suffering for the sake of others. For him it is not suffering though the ordinary people think that he is suffering. When one's consciousness remains limited to the individual boundaries only, then the individual suffers. Pain and pleasure are a pair of opposites experienced when the senses contact objects of the world. Those whose consciousness has expanded beyond the sensory level get freedom from this pair of opposites. There are techniques for voluntarily withdrawing the mind from the senses and focusing inwards to reveal the centre of consciousness. In such a state of mind, one is not affected by sensory pleasure or pain. Such a one-pointed mind also creates a dynamic will which can be used for healing others. All such healing powers flow through the human being from the one source of consciousness. The moment the healer becomes conscious of his

individuality that spontaneous flow of healing power stops. Healing is a natural power in man. The healing of others is possible through that will power which is not interrupted by the lower mind.''

3

Sai Baba, as we have seen, had the power to heal. And he frequently took on the illnesses of others on himself out of his infinite love and compassion for his devotees. No two saints are alike, except, perhaps, in their capacity to give. Each has his distinct characteristic.

Once, all of Shirdi was affected by an epidemic of cholera and fears were entertained that many may die. But they reckoned without Sai Baba.

He had his own way of meeting the situation. And this is exactly what happened. In the masjid there always was a sack of wheat, a scuttle-basket and a quern. This was put to use.

Baba woke up one morning, finished his morning ablutions and took out from the wheat sack several measures of the grain. He then spread an empty sack on the ground, put the quern on it and hammered its peg firmly into position. He then rolled up his sleeves and squatting on the ground began grinding the wheat.

Devotees watched him in silence. They had not seen him at this job, but they dared not question why he was now at it. News, as it frequently happens in a village, spread and men and women came rushing to the masjid to see what was happening. It did not seem right to some of the older women that Baba should be grinding wheat when they were around. So they gently edged Baba away, snatched the quern-peg from Baba's hands and went ahead with the grinding. Baba was visibly angry and as usual let go a few words. The village folk were quite accustomed to that, too, and did not mind. Baba's anger subsided—if indeed he was angry, since often he would feign anger. About eight pounds of wheat were thereafter ground. But what was the purpose of making flour if Baba was not going to use it? So the women decided that they would carry home the flour. Till then Baba had contented himself merely with watching the scene but as the women began to pack the flour to take it home he burst into another bout of angry words. Speaking in the local lingo he said: "Are you all mad? Where are you taking the flour to? Does it belong to your father? Go take your share of the flour to the village boundary and cast it on the bank of the brook!" For a while the women fretted, but Baba's orders were not lightly to be cast aside. So they did as they were told: they went to the village boundary and cast the freshly ground flour on the bank of the stream flowing at the edge. The miracle happened. Not a single person died of cholera thereafter.

Then there is the story of Gopalrao alias Bapusaheb Buti, a devout devotee of Sai Baba. He had made Shirdi his residence to be close to Baba. Once he came down with a severe bout of diarrhoea and vomiting. Medical treatment was of no help and Buti was frightened. Baba heard of this and sent for Buti who came to the masjid with great difficulty and sat down. Sai Baba merely raised his finger and said: "Mind you, from now onwards you will not go for evacuation of bowels and vomits."

Buti did not know what to say. On the one side was his physical helplessness; on the other were Baba's orders which he dare not disobey. But such was Baba's power that both motions and vomits stopped instantly. On another occasion, Buti was asked to take *kheer* made of walnuts, almonds and pistachio as a cure for cholera. But it worked. Buti, incidentally, was a disciple of the well-known saint of Berar, Gajanan Maharaj. He was a barrister and his work took him to many centres. On the direction of Sai Baba he had constructed a *wada* of black stone and the oblong space forming the central portion of the *wada* was left open. Buti wanted to build a temple in that space but not long after, Sai Baba passed away. According to his wish his body was interred in the middle of the oval over which a samadhi has been built.

Bhimaji Patil of Narayangaon in Junnar taluka, Pune district, suffered from tuberculosis and the disease was in an advanced stage. Bhimaji would vomit blood every now and then. He gave up all hope of living. In a letter to Nanasaheb Chandorkar, he gave an account of his condition and said that his one last desire was to see Nanasaheb.

Nanasaheb was touched by Bhimaji's letter. They were friends. The best way of helping his friend thought Nanasaheb, was to invite him to Shirdi and ask him to take refuge in Sai Baba. When Bhimaji came to Shirdi, he was in no condition to walk. He had to be lifted and brought to Baba's presence in the masjid. Nanasaheb Chandorkar and Madhavrao Deshpande were both present on the occasion. Seeing Bhimaji, Baba told Madhavrao; "Oh Shama, how many thieves will you bring and set upon me? Is this proper?"

But Bhimaji placed his head on Baba's feet and prayed: "Take care of this helpless man!" Baba was filled with compassion and told Bhimaji: "Give up your worries. As soon as you put your feet in Shirdi, your misery has ended. The fakir here is very kind. He is the protector of all. Now go and retire to the house of Bhimabai and stay there. Within a day or two you will experience remission of your sickness."

By then Bhimaji was already feeling energetic. He went to Bhimabai's house where the floor, just got ready, was still wet but he did not want to disobey Baba's instructions and spreading his bedding fell asleep.

He dreamt heavily. In one dream he was caned on the back by the teacher of his childhood. In another dream he felt a stranger sitting on his chest and levigating it with a stone. At the end of the dreams he slept peacefully. But when he awoke, he noticed to his surprise complete well-being. He was a new man in good health. Happy beyond words he went to the masjid to prostrate himself before Baba to express his gratitude.

Sometimes Baba would astound even his most devoted disciples by the kind of far-off remedies he would suggest. Once when Bala Ganpat Shimpi came down with malaria he went to Baba and said to him: "What sin have I committed that I should suffer thus? Have mercy on me!" Baba had a great sense of humour and he would often joke with Shimpi who was his personal tailor and would stitch his kafnis. This time he said "Tell you what. If you feed cooked rice and curds to a black dog near the Laxmidevi Temple, you will be cured of your malarial fever and shivering."

Shimpi wondered for a moment whether Baba was pulling a fast one on him. But such was his faith that he went home and found some cooked rice and obtained some curds to go with it. But what was the guarantee that he would find a *black* dog near the Laxmidevi Temple? He had never seen one there.

But he took the rice and curds to the Temple and there he found a black dog wagging its tail as if expecting him to come! He fed the dog and at that instant his fever left him! Baba's ways were, to say the least, very odd and one never could foretell what he would do. Lakshmanrao alias Kaka Mahajani came down with *cholera morbus* accompanied by severe diarrhoea. His visits to the masjid became occasions of distress. One day Baba suddenly turned fiercely angry, something that often terrified his devotees who would run away. This time Baba caught hold of Mahajani and said: "Why are you running away? Stay here!" Some one had left a bag of peanuts behind and now Baba took out a few peanuts and fed them to Mahajani. He also ate a few himself. When they had exhausted the stock Baba told Mahajani: "I am thirsty, get me some water!" He drank some and also made Mahajani do so. Then he told him: "You may now go. You are cured. But get back those people who ran away. It is time for *arati!*"

Sometimes Baba would cure a patient just by blessing him. On other occasions he would suggest wholesome remedies. For spasmodic griping, for instance, he prescribed eating a piece of *barfi* with ghee.

But those who mistook Baba's "remedies" as infallible would come to grief. Obviously it was not what Baba prescribed but the secret power behind that prescription that effected the cure. Madhavrao Deshpande who was administered a concoction successfully to cure his piles repeated that dose on his own without reference to Baba who had originally prescribed it to him, when he had a repeat attack of piles. But this time it did not work. Only, his condition became serious. Dejected he went to Baba who must have known what Madhavrao had done to cure himself. So he teasingly addressed him as Vaidyaraj and asked him how he was feeling. Madhavrao had to confess to what he had done. This time Baba administered something else and Madhavrao was cured.

On yet another occasion, Madhavrao was bitten by a poisonous snake on his little finger which turned black while his entire body turned a dull red. His uncle Nimonkar suggested that Madhavrao be taken to Baba immediately. But when the two went to the masjid, they were greeted with abuse. "Do not come up *Bhaturdya* (a contemptuous term for a brahmin)," Baba thundered. "Away with you!"
Shocked at this treatment, Madhavrao sat down mutely. When Baba calmed down, he rose and approached Baba who said: "Don't lose heart. The merciful Lord will protect you. Go and sit quietly at home. Have faith in me and do not fear."

When Madhavrao left, Baba summoned Tatya Kote and asked him to take a message to Madhavrao. "Tell him," he said, "*not* to sleep. Ask him to move about the house. Ensure this much."

Then turning to Dikshit, Baba said: "See that Madhavrao does not sleep!"
Madhavrao had to go sleepless that night. But his suffering ended. It was then that Madhavrao realised that Baba's orders originally to him not to "come up" was directed not at him but at the poison in the little finger.

Sometimes Baba could be quite abrupt. Bapusaheb Jog had been bitten by a scorpion and the pain was intense. Jog went to Baba. Baba asked: "Bapusaheb, what is it?"
"A scorpion has bitten me," replied Bapusaheb.
"Oh that," said Baba, "go home, it will be all right."
Bapusaheb did as he was told. But even as he was leaving the masjid, the pain had ceased. Sometimes Sai Baba would caution a devotee about a forthcoming danger and would also save him from it. Balasaheb Mirikar, Mamlatdar of Kopergaon and son of the Sardar while on tour of Chithali decided he would visit Shirdi for Baba's darshan. When he went to the masjid Sai Baba enquired about his well-being. Then he told Mirikar: "Do you know our Dwarkamai?" When Mirikar failed to

understand what Baba was alluding to, the latter said: "Oh! Dwarkamai is this very masjid. She makes him who ascends her steps fearless. This masjidmai is very kind. He who comes here reaches his goal!"

When Mirikar was about to leave, Baba asked him: "Do you know the long baawa?"
Then holding his right elbow by the palm of his left hand, he turned his fist and remarked: "He is so fierce. But how can he hurt the children of Dwarkamai? What can he do with the Protector?"
Then addressing Madhavrao who was sitting there, Baba said: "Shama, please accompany Mirikar to Chithali."

Mirikar protested saying that Madhavrao should not be asked to take all that trouble and requested Madhavrao to return. When Baba heard of this, he merely said: "What do we lose? Whatever is destined has to happen."
But Mirikar had second thoughts and he requested Madhavrao to accompany him which the latter did. When they reached Chithali, Mirikar learnt that two of his superior officers who were also to arrive had not come. So he and Madhavrao retired to the Maruti Temple where a peon spread a bedding for them.

It was there, while Mirikar was busy reading a paper that a snake slid up to him without his being aware of it and coiled itself round his waist. It was only when the peon noticed it and raised a hue and cry that the snake unwound itself and dropped to the ground where it was killed. Mirlikar only then remembered the sign made by Baba and the assurance given by Baba that "the children of Dwarkamai" would be protected. There are other stories involving snakes—apparently there were plenty of them around Shirdi—and Baba's protective net he threw to save his devotees from them It was just that Baba could foresee the future and when he saw danger to his devotees he would warn them in time.

Shantaram Balwant Nachane, first clerk to the Shirastedar of Kurla was a devotee of Sai Baba. In 1913 when he was at Shirdi, Baba said to him: "Beware of a mad man." Nachane did not understand what Baba meant by that, but he remembered the warning. In 1914 when Nachane was engaged in performing his daily puja at home, an insane person was standing at some distance from him. Though deranged, the man was considered to be harmless so no one took much notice of him. But that day he suddenly entered the room where Nachane was doing his puja, grasped him by the neck and began to shout: "I will drink your blood!"

Nachane thereupon quickly hit the mad man in his mouth with one of his puja implements and while the two were struggling, other members of the household rushed in and separated the two, but not before Nachane fell down unconscious. It was a matter of touch and go.

Nachane kept the information to himself but when he was next in Shirdi, Sai Baba said to Anna Chinchnikar who was sitting by him: "See, Anna, Nachane has come. He almost got strangled by a mad man. I had to save him. If I do not save my own children, who else will?"

Once it happened that while Nanasaheb Chandorkar was riding in a tonga in Poona, the horses turned wild, stood on their hind legs and overturned the carriage. Nana, however, escaped without a scratch. At that very instant in Shirdi, Sai Baba was heard to say apropos of nothing: "Nana was involved in an accident and could have been killed. But how can I permit him to die?"

On another occasion, Hari Sitaram alias Kakasaheb Dikshit was taking Sai Baba's darshan when Baba said to him in his quiet way: "Kaka, don't worry. I will bear all your burden!"
Dikshit had not come to Baba with any personal problem and he was rather intrigued by Baba's remarks. But it was only when he returned home some days later that he learnt that his seven-year old daughter was playing with her toys when she happened to overturn the cupboard containing them and barely escaped with her life. The wooden cupboard was heavy and could have crushed the child. She escaped with some minor bruises.

A woman devotee from Bombay and her son had come to Shirdi and were taking Baba's darshan when Baba told the boy to sit on a *chatai* and ordered him not to move without his permission.

Exactly at 3 pm a huge, ugly and hideous woman jumped over the fence and entered the masjid shouting: "I want to take away this boy!" Sai Baba ordered her out but she tried to snatch the boy whereupon Sai Baba administered her such a hard kick that she ran out screaming, and vanished out of sight. Baba later explained that the woman was the goddess of cholera and he was expecting a visit from her. Hence his admonition to the boy not to stir from the place.

There is a story told about how, as late as 1951, with Baba gone 32 years, he was still aiding those who had faith in him. In this case it was a case of a woman who was possessed by an evil spirit. The woman was Sushilabai, wife of Babasaheb Sakharam Sule who would often swoon as if she had epileptic fits and would be unconscious for hours together. She was finally taken to Baba's *samadhi* where she was given *tirtha* and administered *udi*. On her own she later circumambulated the *samadhi* but not before informing those who had led her to it that the spirit of a Bhil woman had taken possession of her. The *tirtha* and *udi* cured her for ever.

Then there was the occasion when Sai Baba came to the rescue of Raoji Balakrishna Upasani's son who was so ill that doctors had given up all hope for his survival. That night Upasani was fast asleep when he had a dream. In the dream he saw Sai Baba applying *udi* to his son. Addressing Upasani himself, Baba said: "Now don't worry. Your son will perspire in a couple of hours and his condition will improve. When he has completely recovered, bring him to Shirdi."

Upasani woke up and saw that it was 2 pm. He kept watch over his son and everything transpired as Baba had said, to the surprise of the doctors.

A couple of days later, Upasani received a letter from Madhavrao Deshpande in Shirdi. Deshpande said Baba had told him that he had been to Dhulia to see his friend. "Which friend?" Madhavrao had asked and Baba was to reply: "Upasani." And Madhavrao wrote: "Baba has now asked me to write to you asking you to come to Shirdi and bring your son along.''

There was no way of informing Baba when Upasani would arrive in Shirdi, but as soon as the son was completely recovered, Upasani started on his journey to Shirdi with his wife and son. On the way, however, there was delay caused by a tongawallah who came late. At Shirdi, the afternoon *arati* was due to start, but Baba asked everyone to wait for a while. He told Madhavrao: "Wait, your relation from Dhulia is due to arrive!''

Upasani came late but the *arati* was held up as Baba wanted Upasani to be present. As soon as Upasani arrived with his wife and son, Baba hugged the young boy and said: "Do you know when you were very sick, I had visited you in your home?''

Instances have been recorded of people suffering from all sorts of ailments being cured by the mere darshan of Sai Baba. Was it a matter of faith cure? The cures were often effected in strange ways. A six-year old child suffering from chronic asthama was asked to take a puff at Baba's *chillim*. The child was cured then and there. Epileptics were cured by the mere sight of Sai Baba. Sakharam Krishna Pangarkar, who was suffering from acute liver complaint and could hardly eat, found his health restored after hardly a week's stay in Shirdi during which he had Baba's darshan regularly. Baburao Ingle who had wet eczma on his face was cured after he had gone round Baba's samadhi 108 times.

The story is told of Vithalrao Yeshwantrao Deshpande who was blind. He was a devotee of Sai Baba. Accompanied by his grandson he went to Shirdi and appeared before Baba for his darshan. And he said: "Sai Baba, I have come for your darshan, but I cannot see!'' Baba replied: "Who said you cannot? Of course you will be able to see!'' and at that instant Vithalrao's sight was restored! It was plainly a miracle.

Another blind man was found standing in the *sabha mandap* and singing bhajans. This between 1912 and 1915 was his regular practice. Gradually, it is said, his eyesight was restored. When it was completely restored, the man put his

162

eyesight to good use. He completely memorised the *Gita* and Jnaneshwar's *Anubhavamrit* and he would sit in the same *sabha mandap* and recite these holy books until 1952.

A dumb girl got back her power of speech. She was injured in a car accident and was hospitalised. Though her wounds healed she lost her speech. In spite of nine long months of treatment there was no improvement. She was administered *udi* personally handled by Baba and she immediately recovered her voice and speech. Rajalakshmi, daughter of one T.R.S. Mani of Kumbhakonam, was born dumb and until she was nine years old there was no change in her condition. Her father then began praying to Sai Baba and he was ordered to go to Shirdi with his daughter. The family had darshan of Baba's *samadhi* on 28 March 1942. No sooner had the daughter come close to the *samadhi* than she was heard to say: "Sai Baba, Sai Baba!" She had received the gift of speech.

Baba received strange requests from his devotees. A Muslim devotee of Baba came to Shirdi and asked that the sentence of death pronounced against a brahmin friend should be set aside. Baba blessed him and asked him to stay in Shirdi for a few days. During the fag end of the stay the Muslim received news that his friend had been acquitted in appeal and the death sentence had been automatically set aside! Baba, as we have noted earlier, had the gift to look into the future which is illustrated by the following story. One Chandrabai R. Borkar was living with her husband in a small town called Asavali near Nasik. Asavali was on the railway line and the couple could often hear the sound of trains passing by.

One day Mr Borkar came down with high fever after returning from his office. There was no one in the house except the couple and no medicine was immediately available at that time of the evening. Around 2 a.m. as Mr Borkar dozed off, Chandrabai also went off to sleep after keeping vigil by her husband. In her sleep she dreamt of a fakir who came up to her and told her: "Bai, do not be frightened Your husband will perspire shortly. Apply the *udi* you have in your home to him. But don't allow your husband to leave the house before 11 a.m."

Chandrabai woke up to find that her husband was indeed perspiring. She wiped his perspiration and narrated her dream to him.

Mr Borkar, however, had no faith in such stories and next day early in the morning he went to Asavali station. Just at that time the Mail from Manmad and the Passenger from Bombay were moving in opposite directions. Mr Borkar who was standing by the side of one track had not noticed the Mail steaming in and was knocked off his feet by the Mail and fell on the third track. Chandrabai had accompanied her husband to the station and when she saw what happened she loudly uttered Baba's name before herself falling down unconscious.

By then railway porters rushed to her and revived her. She was informed that her husband had not been killed but had, however, sustained severe injuries in his leg. Mr Borkar was taken to his home where Chandrabai applied *udi* to the injured leg and bandaged it. When he became conscious, Mr Borkar asked: "Where am I? Our house is pervaded by a fakir." Chandrabai said to him: "Don't be afraid. He is our Sai Baba. He had instructed you through me not to venture out but you wouldn't listen. Even then he saved you. Take courage. Baba will make you well."

Mr Borkar's faith in *udi* was limited and so the next day the railway doctor was summoned and he did what he thought was needed to be done. A fresh bandage was applied to Mr Borkar's leg but it did not help. The pain increased. The leg had been fractured. Mrs Borkar stayed by her husband's bedside as long as she could and finally went to bed. Once again she had a dream. Again the same fakir appeared in it. This time the fakir said: "What you want the leg to be damaged permanently? Apply a mixture of coconut, dough and *udi* over the leg and bandage it. Then foment it with a mixture of leaves (of a certain medicinal plant), salt and turmeric and jowar."

Disregarding the railway doctor's instructions, Chandrabai followed the instructions she had received in her dream. To Mr Borkar's surprise, the bones healed and he regained use of his injured leg. He became thereafter a firm believer in Baba.

4

You and I, Arjuna,
Have lived many lives.
I remember them all:
You do not remember.

—Bhagavad Gita IV, 5 (Translated by
Swami Prabhavananda and Christopher Isherwood).

Even as Krishna remembered his past lives, so did Baba. There is the instance of Babu, a young devotee dear to Sai Baba. Sai Baba loved him deeply. Babu was the nephew of Ganesh D. Kelkar, father-in-law of Rao Bahadur H.V. Sathe. He was employed as a clerk at Kopargaon and Yewale, under Mr Limaye, an assistant to Rao Bahadur Sathe. Following a dream Babu left home and came on foot to Shirdi for Sai Baba's darshan. He would serve Baba in many ways and was thus dear to Baba. Babu paid more attention to the service of Sai Baba than to his clerical duties, a sore point with his employer.

Whenever Mr Kelkar would complain to Baba about Babu's laxness, Baba would soothingly say: "Let it be, let it be; let him continue to serve me."

Then one day Babu came down with high fever and his end was near, but all that Sai Baba would do was to ask Mr Kelkar: "Is he still alive?" as if he did not expect him to be. Babu died at Shirdi at the age of 22, leaving behind a childless widow.

Not long afterwards, as predicted by Baba, Chhotubai, wife of Pradhan, gave birth to a son who was named Babu. That child was brought to the presence of Sai Baba when it was four months old. Sai Baba fondled it and said: "Babu, where had you been? Were you tired of me?"

Ganpatrao Narke was a professor in Poona Engineering College. During 1913-1914 he stayed at Shirdi for some length of time. Once in his dream Narke had Baba's darshan and saw a person looking like a labourer standing close to him. Pointing to the labourer Narke heard Baba say: "See this friend of your last birth? One's condition changes according to one's karma!"

A few days after his dream Narke was sitting beside Sai Baba in the morning when a labourer carrying a load of firewood on his head came to the masjid. Looking at him Narke felt he resembled the labourer he had seen in his dream and wondered whether he indeed was the friend of his last birth! Immediately Sai Baba said to him: "Go and give your friend two rupees for the load of firewood." That was a lot of money in those days and Narke was a little hesitant. But Sai Baba told him: "This is the one known to us in our preceding birth, is he not?" Narke's doubts were immediately dispelled. Swami Sai Saran Anand himself has recounted a similar instance that was personally known to him.

On one occasion Sai Baba expressed his knowledge of the preceding birth of two she goats. One morning as he was returning from *lendi* he brought two she goats paying sixteen rupees for each. Tatya Kote and Madhavrao Deshpande did not approve of the high price which they considered was far in excess of market rates, which were hardly two rupees a goat. Sai Baba listened to his devotees but without arguing with them merely said: "Buy two seers of pulse from the grocer, feed one seer to each of the two goats and return them to the shepherd." Accordingly, the goats were fed and duly returned to the shepherd.

This strange behaviour perplexed Tatya Kote and Madhavrao Deshpande, but Sai Baba told them: "In their last birth they were human beings. They were two brothers with whom I was well acquainted. Initially they were affectionate toward each other. They lived and worked together. Then, by a quirk of destiny they fell out. The elder brother was lazy while the younger one was hard working. The younger brother, in the circumstances, acquired considerable wealth. The elder brother became envious of his sibling and plotted to do away with him. When the plot came to light there was fight between the two. Each hit the other and as a result of the wounds each sustained, they both died within a few days. Now they are born as goats. I recognised them and felt pity towards them and wanted to give them shelter. That is why I fed them at my own expense. However, at your suggestion, I let them go so that the effect of *karma* can work out without my interference."

On another occasion, Sai Baba recognised in a giant serpent about to swallow a frog, two people he knew in a previous birth. He went towards the serpent and said in a loud voice: "Oh Veerbhadrappa, this enemy of yours Chanbasappa has become a frog and in order to pay off old scores you have become·a serpent. But won't you forget past enmity even now? Aren't you ashamed? Give up your hostility and be quiet!"

This happened on the banks of the river and in the presence of a passer by. When Sai Baba finished speaking, the snake dropped the frog from its jaws and quietly slid into the waters and vanished from sight. The frog, too, hopped into a near by thicket and disappeared.

The passer-by was tremendously impressed and wanted to hear from Sai Baba the story of Veerbhadrappa and Chanbasappa. And this is what Sai Baba told him:

"Five to six miles from my place was a holy shrine of Mahadev which was in a state of disrepair. With the intention of renovating the temple, all the devotees collected a large sum of money. A sowcar of that town was requested to look after the renovation and the money collected was handed over to him. The sowcar was honest and he kept the collection in a separate account. But being a born miser he would not put in any of his own money for the renovation. The work of repair started and some progress was made but there was a shortage of resources. Then the devotees said to the sowcar: 'What is the use of your moneylending if you do not help out the renovation work when it is needed? We will coax the people to contribute once again but please see that the work is completed.'

"Again the collection box went round but this time the sowcar was slow in getting on with the renovation work. Some days later the sowcar's wife had a dream in which she was directed to arise and complete the dome of the temple and was assured that Shiva would give her hundred times the amount of expenditure incurred.

"Next morning she recalled her dream to her husband but he belittled her and paid no attention whatsoever. However, he resumed the repair work until there was nothing left in the till.

Still, he himself would not part with his own money. Some days later his wife had yet another dream in which she heard a voice say: 'Out of your *streedhan* donate whatever you wish to. As you have faith, a piece given by you willingly is worth a lakh.'

"The wife thereupon decided that it is now her job to help the completion of the temple renovation and decided to sell the ornaments given to her by her father. This upset the *sowcar* and he thought of a way out. A helpless woman had mortgaged her land with the *sowcar* for a loan of Rs 200. It was a piece of uncultivated waste land. So, valuing the ornaments of his wife at Rs 1,000 he purchased the ornaments himself and instead of giving her cash, decided to transfer the land in his wife's name. He said to her: 'Take this land worth Rs 1,000. Donate it to Shankar, so that he may be pleased with you.'

"The *sowcar's* wife agreed and donated that land to the Shiva Temple. After some years, during the constellation *kruttika* (third of the lunar asterism) it rained heavily. There was a storm and the *sowcar's* wife was struck by lightning. The whole structure sank and the *sowcar*, his wife and the woman who had originally mortgaged the land died after a few years.

"The *sowcar's* wife was born as the daughter of the *pujari* at Shankar's Temple and was named Gauri. The woman who had mortagaged the land was begotten as a son by the *Gurav* of Shankar's Temple and was named Chanbasappa. The *sowcar* was born in a brahmin household in Mathura and was named Veerbhadrappa. I had great affection for Gauri's father, the priest at Shankar's Temple. He would always visit me and we would talk of many things far into the night. He would also bring Gauri with him and she was devoted to me. When Gauri reached marriageable age her father made all efforts to find a husband but something or other came in the way. So her father was worried. I would assure him that a spouse would come to her door on his own.

"Now let us turn to Veerbhadrappa. As Veerbhadrappa was born in a poor family, he decided to leave his home to seek his fortune. He wandered and supported himself by asking for alms or by doing physical labour. In the course of his wandering he arrived at the household of the *pujari* of the Shankar Temple. He was liked by all and with my consent the *pujari* gave his daughter in marriage to Veerbhadrappa.

"Veerbhadrappa stayed in his father-in-law's house and improved in his health after his marriage. When the *pujari* passed away, he bequeathed the land to his dear daughter Gauri. By God's grace the land appreciated in value. A purchaser agreed to pay a lakh of rupees for the land of which he paid half on the spot and the balance was to be paid in annual instalments of Rs 2,000 plus interest over 25 years. The deal was approved by all except Chanbasappa. He said that as *Gurav* he had the first claim over the money received by Shankar and as such he should receive half the annual interest. Veerbhadrappa flatly declined to entertain Chanbasappa's demand. The two had a heated argument and the dispute came to me for arbitration. I told them both that the real owner of the land was Shiva-Shankar. The land ought not to be utilised for any other purpose. It was therefore right that neither of them should covet the land. It was for Gauri to decide. If they acted according to her wishes, they would be happy. Veerbhadrappa had also no authority to act independently.

"Hearing this Veerbhadrappa called me names and alleged that by declaring Gauri as the owner I wished to establish my hold over the land. I was stunned at this accusation. The same night Gauri had a dream in which Shankar appeared and instructed her: 'All this money is yours. Don't give anything to any one. As regards the permanent arrangements, do as I tell you. For the temple expenditure Chanbasappa's wishes may be respected as I have full trust in him in this regard. For other things do nothing without consulting the Baba in the masjid.'

"Gauri apprised me of her dream and sought my counsel. So I said to her: 'Keep your capital to yourself. Give half the annual interest to Chanbasappa according to divine guidance.'"

While we were thus conversing, Veerbhadrappa and Chanbasappa came there quarrelling. In spite of being told about Gauri's dream it had no effect on Veerbhadrappa. He abused the opposite party to his heart's content. Then he had spasms and in supervening delirium he would gabble and rave and say to Chanbasappa: 'When I get you alone I will make mince meat of you.' In fright Chanbasappa would clasp my feet and I would assure him. Later Veerbhadrappa died and due to enmity in his previous birth he was born as a serpent. Chanbasappa was my devotee but he shrank in terror and died of shock. So he was born as a frog. In the form of a serpent Veerbhadrappa chased Chanbasappa in the form of a frog and it was when I heard the frog's piteous call that I came to save him. The principle of *karma* is relentless in its operation."

Sai Baba once told Nanasaheb Chandorkar that their relations went back to four births. On another occasion he identified Shri Sai Sharan Anand and Balakram Mankar as having in a previous birth resided opposite each other in caves doing penance. Of Shri Sai Sharan Anand himself Sai Baba said in open durbar that he had known him "from very early times." About Mrs Chandrabai Borkar who practised the vow of *Kokilavrata* he had said: "Wherever I go she comes in search of me. She is a sister of mine in seven births." It was the *siddhi* in Sai Baba which recognised past births.

CHAPTER 6

'MOTHER' BABA'S CONCERN

Devotees of Sai Baba are agreed that the protection he provided to them and continues to do to this day is total and encompasses everything from spiritual enrichment to the more mundane warding off of their financial difficulties.

Rao Bahadur S.S. Dhumal, B.A., L.L.B. a Nasik Pleader was a staunch devotee of Sai Baba who did not take any important step without consulting the latter. He states: "I was holding the office of Revenue Member of the Dewas State from 1 September 1930 to 9 April 1932 and I was the *karbhari* of the Surgana State from the end of 1932 to August 1933. Every time I returned to Nasik, I would resume my legal practice and got on as well as I did before, without having to idle even for a day. Baba's kind help on the financial side was manifested in a peculiar incident while I was in Surgana.

"I was seated one day to have my meal when the Chief of that State walked into my room. I apologised for my inability to leave the seat to accord him a proper reception or even to offer him a fitting chair seat. But he did not seem to mind. He quickly walked into the next room, gazed a while at the portrait of Sai Baba that was hanging on the wall and returned to my dining room and quietly announced that as of then I was being awarded an increase of fifty rupees in my salary. I had never asked for the increase. This grant of an increase in my salary within a fortnight of my appointment and without any request from me can only be explained by his having been with Baba in my *pooja* room. Evidently, 'the child's welfare was the concern of mother Baba'.

Now, every advocate worth his salt works hard at his profession and Dhumal was no exception to this. But there was this difference: in Dhumal's case his trust in Baba was complete and he subjected his ego to Baba. This was fully rewarded even in instances where eminent lawyers would not dare to appear.

In 1911-12 there was a criminal case from Shirdi. Raghu, a servitor of Sai Baba and five others were arraigned on a charge of outraging the modesty of a Marwadi lady. There always were party and factional feelings in Shirdi as in most villages. In this case, Raghu and his friends were convicted on the direct evidence of a "number of eye-witnesses" and sentenced to 6 months in jail.

Tatya Kote's sympathies were on the side of the accused. He took a copy of the judgement and the case papers to eminent lawyers like the Hon. G.S. Khaparde, H.S. Dikshit and retired Magistrate Rao Bahadur H.V. Sathe. All found the judgement strong and discouraged going in appeal. Tatya Kote went to Sai Baba who simply told him to go to Dhumal. So to Dhumal he went. Dhumal however suggested that it would be advisable to engage counsel from either Bombay or a prominent lawyer from Ahmednagar where the appeal had to be filed. Tatya Kote, however told Dhumal that it was Baba's wish that he take up the case. Dhumal now could hardly say no. So he wrote out an appeal memo after going through the papers carefully and took it to the District Magistrate at his residence. The Magistrate went through the appeal, studied the papers and pointed out that the judgement was strong. Undeterred, Dhumal replied that that could well be but in this instance note had to be taken of village factions.

Said the Magistrate: "Do you think so?"
To which Dhumal immediately replied: "Think? I am more than sure of it!"

The Magistrate was no stranger to the working of village factions and was worldly-wise. He gave the matter a little thought and then accepted Dhumal's appeal memo and wrote out his judgement acquitting all the appellants. Then he said, apropos of nothing: "How is your Sai Baba of Shirdi? Is he a Moslem or a Hindu? What does he teach you?" Dhumal replied that Sai Baba was neither a Moslem nor a Hindu but was above both and that he could not state what his teachings were, to know which, he must go in person to Shirdi.

Dhumal then started on his way to Shirdi. About that time Sai

Baba remarked to his devotees sitting near him: "I will show you some *chamatkar* (miracle)." The devotees however had something else on their minds. H.S. Dikshit's daughter had died that very day and they hastened to her funeral.

When they returned, there was Dhumal telling one and all that Raghu and his friends had been acquitted on appeal. It was then that it dawned on the devotees what the *chamatkar* was that Baba was referring to earlier in the day.

There was another criminal appeal which Dhumal won but again which he attributed to Sai Baba's grace.

A charge had been levied against three brothers of causing grievous bodily hurt to a man. The injured party had been treated by a quack who was neither a qualified nor certified doctor, in his private nursing home, for over three weeks. Dhumal who was engaged for the accused-appellants filed an appeal memo and a bail application. The Sessions Judge who was a senior British officer remarked on hearing Dhumal that the case against the appellants was strong and he was not going to allow bail. Dhumal's thoughts turned to Sai Baba and turning to the Judge Dhumal said that the evidence for a bone being broken was that of a quack and that the prosecution evidence was interested and unreliable. The three appellants were agriculturists and if they were to remain in jail their work would suffer in their absence. On the other hand, Dhumal argued, if their sentence was indeed confirmed they surely would be sent to jail anyway. Why not, then, at least give the appellants bail?

This was thereupon granted. When the case came up for argument Dhunal argued for a reversal but then wound up with a prayer for a reduction of the sentence. Somewhat riled the Judge remarked that if Dhumal were merely asking for the court's mercy, he need not have taken so much time to contest the conviction. But inscrutable are Sai Baba's ways—Dhumal won!

When the Public Prosecutor was arguing the Judge wanted to know how he made out a case of grievous hurt as the opinion of an unqualified man, a quack was inadmissible as to the breakage of a bone. The Public Prosecutor retorted that the injured man had been in a Nursing Home for twenty days. The Judge's reaction was quick and sharp. "Do you realise that you are arguing before a Sessions Judge and not a Third Class Magistrate?

The Public Prosecutor fell silent. The appellants were acquitted much to Dhumal's delight.

Similar have been the experiences of two Advocates, Chinubhai Vadilal Shah of Ahmedabad and Harshadbhai P. Mehta of Baroda.

Then we have the experiences of Sadashivrao Tarkhad and Sadashivrao Dikshit. In 1915 Sadashivrao Tarkhad lost his job and remained unemployed as managerial positions were not easily to be had. It was then that he came to Shirdi and stayed there. When the time came for him to take leave of Sai Baba, the latter said to him: "Go to Bombay via Poona." As the railway fare to Bombay via Poona was more than for the direct Manmad-Bombay route, Mrs Tarkhad was a bit hesitant to take the advice. But Sai Baba's order was clear. Also, their faith in Sai Baba was total. So they proceeded to Poona and halted for a night at a friend's place. There they learnt that a millowner was looking for a manager who had experience in handling labour. Tarkhad called on the millowner and he was offered the job as Manager of Raja Bahadur Mills.

Hari Sitaram alias Kakasaheb Dikshit's younger brother Sadashiv, a lawyer by profession, began his practice in Nagpur but with disheartening results. Sai Baba suggested that Sadashiv go to Bombay. That did not seem to work and Sai Baba was again consulted. It was decided that Sadashiv should join Kakasaheb's own firm of Solicitors. That did not help matters either. Could Sai Baba have been wrong? That worried Kakasaheb, but he advised his brother to have patience until Diwali.

Then matters took a strange turn. A friend of Kakasaheb came to him and said that Cutch State required a highly reliable officer for their bank with a knowledge of Gujarati. Can he suggest his brother's name? asked Kakasaheb. The suggestion was welcomed and as a result Sadashiv was appointed on the princely salary of Rs 1,000 a month and he served his office till his retirement.

Another person who had faith in Sai Baba, obeyed his orders and obtained a good job was Prof. Narke who was the son-in-law of Gopalrao Buti, Malgujar of Nagpur. Narke was a scholar from C.P. & Berar having passed his M.A. in 1905. Between 1907 and 1909 he was at Calcutta to receive training in geological survey. He was sent out in 1909 by the Government of India to Manchester University where he got his M.Sc. in Geology and Mining and returned in August 1912.

Trained as he was in natural sciences, Narke believed in knowledge based on verification. He had carried Jnaneshwari with him during his studies abroad which he read assiduously. His faith in Sai Baba grew gradually by his own experience and he would abide by his advice whether in temporal or spiritual matters.

As a geologist and mining engineer Narke would get prospecting jobs intermittently. There were times when he would get several offers simultaneously when he would approach Sai Baba for guidance. Sai Baba would always say: "Go to such and such a place and Poona" stressing Poona every time.

In 1916 Narke had to choose between an offer from Banaras of a professorship and a prospecting job in Burma. Sai Baba told him to go to Burma—and Poona; Narke would laugh within himself when Baba would mention Poona, considering that Poona could never have a job for a mining engineer.

Then it happened. In 1917 came an announcement that the College of Engineering in Poona wanted a Professor of Geology. Sai Baba advised Narke to apply for the post. Of applicants there were many and some of them had the backing of influential personages. But it was Narke who got the job. The appointment came through in 1918 and in a year's time came the confirmation as well. Baba had been vindicated.

The worldly cares and ambitions whether of the higher or lower income groups are similar. Cholkar, belonging to a lower middle class family could secure no permanent appointment without passing a departmental examination. He vowed to go to Shirdi for Sai Baba's darshan if he were successful. And he worked hard. He passed his examination and secured the job. His salary, however, was low and he could not save enough to make his pilgrimage to Shirdi. So he decided to abjure sugar from his diet until his vow was fulfilled.

A few months passed. Cholkar saved enough to make the journey and he was beside himself with joy that he could make it at last. He had Baba's darshan and was invited to sit close to him. At this point Baba summoned Bapusaheb Jog who was around and told him: "Take Cholkar home and serve him many cups of highly-sugared tea!" Bapusaheb wondered at this strange order and it was only when Cholkar told him of the vow that he had taken that he could appreciate it.

Govind Dhondo Pansare of Sholapur who had vowed to go to see Sai Baba if he passed the Vernacular Final Examination, the prescribed qualification for appointment as a primary teacher, had a similar experience. He passed the examination and got the job. And naturally he went to Shirdi. Baba's first question to him was: "And what do you do?"

"The job of a teacher which you gave me!" replied Pansare respectfully.

In 1913 the new Head Master of the Primary School at Shirdi, Daji Vaman Chitambar was concerned about the low standard and general attitude of the pupils and complained to Kakasaheb Dikshit that whatever reputation he had gained as a teacher would now be lost in Shirdi thanks to his lazy students. The students, however, had their answer pat. They would fall back on Baba's *udi* to help them in the examinations! In time the examinations began and the Deputy Inspector was present on the occasion. That day all the students went to Sai Baba and received his *udi*. When the examination results were announced not a single pupil had failed! Never in all his career had Chitambar seen cent per cent results. He could not believe his eyes. But he started believing in Sai Baba.

176

Dr Tendulkar's father Raghunathrao and mother Savitribai were both devotees of Sai Baba who had published a book of songs in Marathi titled *Raghunath-Savitri Bhajan Maala*. Raghunathrao was getting on in years and his eyesight was getting weaker by the day. Worse, he would often have epileptic fits. So he applied for long leave preparatory to retirement from Graham Trading Co. which he had served for many years. The last salary he had drawn was Rs 150 a month. Raghunath Rao was worried about the future. Even were he to get a pension it was unlikely to exceed Rs 75 a month which was hardly enough to meet his monthly expenses.

Fifteen days before Raghunathrao was to retire, Sai Baba appeared in a dream to Savitribai and told her: "I intend giving Raghunathrao a pension of Rs 100. Would that be all right?" Replied Savitribai: "What is this you ask us? You are our sole refuge. You will do what is proper!"

On the day Raghunathrao was to retire, his boss, a kind-hearted man told him: "Raghunathrao, we have decided you should get a pension of Rs 110 p.m." And that was that. Though Sai Baba either out of humility or out of a clearly perceived policy ascribed all beneficent things done for his visitors and devotees to God, he sometimes would disclose his own authorship in words. An example of this is the case of Daji Hari Lele, District Inspector of Land Records at Nasik who was proceeding to Shirdi to see Sai Baba. On his way he dropped by at the Library in Kopergaon and saw the Gazette. Therein he discovered that he had received a raise of Rs 25 in his salary. In time he reached Shirdi and bowed to Baba who told him: "It is only yesterday that I gave you twenty five rupees. Go, bring me my *dakshina*." Lele then went to Sathe, told him his story and borrowed the money to pay Baba.

Another instance of this kind was that of Somnath Shankar Deshpande, son of Nanasaheb Nimonkar, a great devotee of Sai Baba. Somnath was a Police sub-Inspector at Kopargaon and Shirdi was within his jurisdiction. As soon as he got his monthly pay packet he would send two rupees by Money Order to Sai Baba. That was his father's order and possibly his own vow. When Somnath once went to Shirdi in the company of his father, Sai Baba asked him for a *dakshina* of ten rupees which he promptly paid. It did not seem to have any significance at that time. But about six months later, he received information that his pay had been increased by ten rupees from the day that Sai Baba had asked for Dakshina for that same amount.

It is not that Sai Baba advised every one to take up employment. Naranlal Motiram Jani, an employee of Sai devotee Ramachandra Vaman Modak, along with his mother had come for Baba's darshan a few days before the latter's *mahasamadhi*. Baba casually told Jani's mother: "We do not have to serve any more. We have to do independent business." Thereafter Jani left his job in Nasik and opened a Boarding and Lodging House and called it Anandashram which flourished by Baba's grace.

Ramachandra Sitaram alias Balabhau Deo, an assistant teacher in a local board school also did the work of a stamp vendor, which interfered with his teaching. Knowing Deo's bright future Sai Baba would detain him in Shirdi beyond vacation periods. So Deo had to give up his teaching post. Thereby he was able to stay in Shirdi as long as he liked and only attempted to do stamp-vending whereby he could earn as much as twenty to twenty five rupees a day. When he became old he got his license of stamp-vending transferred in the name of his son and thus his son's well-being, too, was ensured by Baba's grace. Janardan Moreshwar alias Haribhan Phanse of Dahanu had an amusing and pleasant experience of how Baba looks after the maintenance and protection of one who takes refuge in him and puts all his burden on him. Haribhau was tired of carrying the burden of his family and with his mother's consent he went on a pilgrimage to Rameshwar. But on his way he felt the need to pay his respects to a holy person. Shirdi was on obvious place to visit and so Phanse made a detour, met Baba, bowed to him and decided to stay at Shirdi for a few days. A week passed on, Phanse was still at Shirdi. At that point Baba called him and said: "Go, go home for Rameshwar is starving these last seven days. If you don't go, you will intend doing one thing and something else will happen." Phanse thereupon decided to return home to find that his mother was starving. He decided to cancel his visit to Rameshwar and stayed back.

He had brought back some *udi* from Shirdi which he now used to great effect. One of the patients he cured by giving him *udi* was suffering from cholera. The man was cured. Phanse's fame as a *vaid* spread quickly.

Once he had to go to a Marwari in a neighbouring village called Bhopali. The marwadi's brother was very sick. Medicine prescribed by the local government medical doctor had no effect. Seeing a devotee of Sai Baba visiting him, the Marwari told Phanse: 'I understand you do Baba's *bhajan*. Well, if my brother is cured at your hands, I will believe that Baba is powerful. Not otherwise."

Phanse examined the patient whose condition was none too good. He did not relish the idea of staying at the Marwadi's residence but as it was getting dark by then, he had no choice.

He had his dinner in the house while preparations for a *bhajan* session were being quietly made. The patient himself sat quietly gazing at a picture of Baba. It was announced by the family that the patient would be administered medicine only by Phanse who panicked. He knew that he was no real *vaid.* What should he do in the circumstances? He decided that he would think it over and went to sleep. At night Phanse had a dream in which Baba told him what the patient was suffering from and what the remedy was.

Still Phanse hoped that he would not have to be found out as a charlatan and demanded Rs. 200 as fees hoping that the Marwadi would show him the door. Instead, the Marwadi agreed to pay the sum. Phanse now had no choice but to prescribe the remedy that Baba had suggested to him in his dream. The medicine worked!

True to his word the Marwadi brought him the agreed-upon sum but Phanse would not accept it, saying: "I did nothing, my guru did everything." Thereafter he returned home. The Marwadi felt bad that he was not able to pay what was due from him. So he went to Phanse's home and finding that he was not in, left his costly *jari* turban behind. When Phanse found that out his first thought was to send an equivalent amount of money to Baba. In the meantime, Baba passed away.

This was still on his mind when he finished his usual *bhajan* the following Thursday. That night, in his sleep Baba appeared to him and said: "There is a famine going. Sell that jari turban and from the money realised from the sale buy rice and get into trading. You will find it profitable."

Phanse did as he was told and not long after he was having a turnover of between Rs 50 to Rs 60 thousand and making a good profit which Phanse ascribed to Baba's grace.

V.C. Chitnis had also benefitted by having darshan of Baba's *samadhi.* His services had been terminated and he was in distress. S.B. Nachane suggested that he go to Shirdi and have the darshan of Baba's *samadhi.* Believing that he had nothing to lose, he took Nachane's advice and learnt, to his great delight a few days later, that he had been re-instated in his job.

Fauzdar Joseph of 45, Turner Road, Bandra had a very difficult criminal case to detect. He prayed for help. Sai Baba came to him in a dream and gave him explicit directions on how to proceed. Acting on those directions Joseph was successful in detecting the criminal.

Baburao Boravke of Saswad near Poona also had a very pleasant experience. His parents died when he was but a child. Taking advantage of his position, his uncle and other relations misappropriated his father's property and Boravke had to give up schooling to take up employment. One of his maternal uncles who lived in Shirdi cultivated sugar cane in his farms and made jaggery out of it. He had become a devotee of Sai Baba. Boravke heard the fame of Sai Baba from his maternal uncle and became eager to see him. He managed to get a ticket upto Kopargaon and decided en route at Ahmednagar station not to take food until he had Baba's darshan. Alighting at Kopargaon station he travelled three miles by tonga upto the banks of the Godavari and had by then only three annas (12 paise) left in his pocket. Shirdi was still eight miles further up and he realised that he did not have sufficient fare for the tonga ride. So he decided to foot the distance.

His maternal uncle's farm was on the way. He stopped by it and his uncle's wife asked him to have his meal before going for Baba's darshan, but Boravke told her that he would eat on his return from Shirdi.

At the Lendi near Shirdi he met his maternal uncle who also pressed him to have his meal before going for the darshan, but to all such pleadings Boravke had the same reply. So the maternal uncle gave him a rupee and with this Boravke proceeded to the masjid. After the darshan, Sai Baba enquired after Boravke and asked him for the *dakshina*. When Boravke expressed his helplessness, Sai Baba asked him to look into his pocket. The one rupee Boravke had he now gave to Baba. But he was so taken in with Baba that he decided to stay on in Shirdi and work on his uncle's farm. His daily routine now was, farm work and regular Baba's darshan.

Days passed. One day a friend of the uncle from Kopargaon called at the farm and noting the improvements on the farm asked who was responsible for transforming its face. The maternal uncle promptly replied: "My nephew." Impressed by what Boravke had done, the uncle's friend offered to take Boravke as a partner to which the uncle gave his consent.

From that time Boravke began attending to the farms of both his maternal uncle and his partner. The production of jaggery increased considerably and fetched good prices and hence good profits. Boravke who had come to Shirdi with three annas in his pocket for Baba's darshan now had a lakh of rupees as his share when accounts were written at the end of two years. Convinced that all this was possible only as a result of Baba's grace, Boravke decided to stay not far away from Shirdi and built a bungalow on a plot of land he purchased close by.

Vithoba Mhadba Fand through his faith in Sai Baba, even after the latter's *mahasamadhi,* was able to get a job. Fand had some formal education. He applied for a job to the Railway Engineer but it was of no avail. His maternal uncle, Kashinath Dube, who was a devotee of Sai Baba asked him to worship

Baba's picture. A sceptic, Fand agreed to do so on condition that he should get an experience of Baba's prowess within two months.

A month after he commenced his puja, a vacancy arose in the Railways Engineer's office. Fand applied again. In the meantime a new officer had been put in charge of the office. Fand was recommended by a devotee who knew the new officer well. In all there were three applicants including Fand. One applicant was an ex-exmployee with ten years' experience and the second was the son of the *avval karkoon* (the seniormost clerk). The ex-employee's application for reappointment was rejected. The other two applicants were asked to appear for an examination. Fand was apprehensive as his educational qualification was rather low. But his maternal uncle suggested that Fand apply some *udi* to himself before appearing for the examination. It turned out that the other candidate did poorly whereas Fand came out with flying colours. He got the job. He attributed his success to Baba. Nagesh Atmaram Savant learnt of Sai Baba in December 1923 by reading Sai Leela magazine. Baba's *leelas* intrigued him. Two years later he went to Nasik for training at the Police School but his studies did not attract him. His mind was set on Baba and he would often pray to Baba for guidance. He even managed to get a picture of Baba to worship him. He failed in his departmental examination.

Now those who fail are not given a chance of becoming a Sub-Inspector and Nagesh continued to serve as *acting* sub-inspector for about five years. He was unwilling to go back to Nasik again as it would have been financially ruinous. Such was his faith that he took it for granted that Baba would somehow give him a permanent posting even without having to pass an examination.

He would go to Shirdi every year without fail during Baba's *punya-tithi* which fell on Dussera Day. In July 1929, as a special case, he was exempted from appearing for his examination and given a permanent posting as Sub-Inspector.

Devotees narrate many instances of how, by acting on Baba's advice, many of them earned money or were saved from incurring losses and how, by disregarding his advice they also suffered losses.

Damuanna Kasar of Ahmednagar was one of the two persons who hoisted a flag on Dwarkamai on Ram Navami Day. One of his friends wrote to him inviting him to join in forward trading in cotton. Damuanna wrote to Baba seeking his advice. Baba's advice was to the point. "Sheth Damuanna is unhinged. He should be satisfied with what he is getting. Ask him not to run after a lakh of rupees."

The advice was conveyed to Damuanna who was disappointed on reading it. Cotton prices were shooting up day by day. Therefore Damuanna personally visited Shirdi, bowed to Baba, sat down to perform *charan-seva* (pressing of legs) and in his mind wondered whether if he were to offer a percentage of his profits to Baba he could get Baba's consent for going into business.

But Baba had read his mind. He merely said: "Bapu, I am not in any of your transactions." Damuanna felt like a boy caught in the act of stealing and was ashamed. He gave up the idea of trading in cotton while his friend berated him for taking a fakir's advice and missing a golden opportunity to make a million. But all of a sudden the market crashed and Damuanna's friend suffered a great loss. It was a lesson that Damuanna was not to forget in a hurry.

Bayaji Appaji Patil of Shirdi was a devotee who used to get during the last fourteen years of his life four rupees every day from Sai Baba. From his savings he purchased 84 acres of land. Once he disregarded Baba's advice and came to grief. Sai Baba had advised him not to plant sugarcane in his land as others had done. However, yielding to temptation he planted sugarcane and suffered a loss of over Rs 300.

Mangesh Shivaji Satam, resident of Bagtala in Deogad taluka of Ratnagiri district heard of Sai Baba's reputation after the latter's *mahasamadhi*. He bought a photo of Baba and started worshipping it. Whenever he had to make an important transaction in business he would seek Baba's direction by casting lots before him. In 1921 he thus sought direction on the question whether he should trade with the same party with whom he had dealings for many years. Baba's answer was 'No.' Satam was unhappy with it. He disregarded Baba's advice and soon enough got into trouble. Finally he craved Baba's pardon and as a token of his submission resolved to send five rupees to Shirdi. Thereafter matters improved for him.

A theft in the house of Vaman Chintaman Mule's house in Pimpalgaon was satisfactorily solved and all stolen property recovered when Mule, fast asleep, was woken up from his dream by Sai Baba in time to shout for help. In 1924 a devotee by the name of Ganpat Dhond Kadam was protected by Baba from robbers. Kadam was travelling by train with his family from Nasik to Manmad. At Nasik a number of Bhils got into his compartment and sat by him. Kadam then was engrossed in reading *Bhaktimarg Pradeep* by Lakshman Ramachandra Pangarkar. Noticing the people around him he thought may be they would like to hear him sing bhajans. So he began singing. Hardly five minutes passed when Kadam noticed that the Bhils were jumping out of the moving train one by one. Puzzled Kadam went to the door to see what was happening and saw to his surprise that the Bhils were running helter skelter as if some one was chasing them! Not realising what it was all about he returned to his seat when he noticed an old fakir sitting opposite him. "Very strange," Kadam told himself, "there was no one sitting opposite me a moment before but now here is an old fakir materialising as if from nowhere!"

The thought had hardly entered his mind when the fakir vanished from sight! Was it an illusion? A miracle? Kadam was still brooding over it when he arrived in Shirdi and called on Baba for a darshan. The first thing that Baba asked him was: "Well, did you travel safely?" It was then that it dawned on Kadam that Baba had saved him from a gang of robbers.

Sai Baba had similarly protected the Telegraph Master of Veena Railway Station in Kapadvanj taluka of Nadiad district, one Ratanlal Ganpatlal Dave from thieves. Dave had been transferred from Veena to Nadiad and the day before his departure he was feted by his friends. The Dave couple retired to bed late at night and soon was fast asleep. It was then that a thief entered his house sure that a box of jewels would have been around packed and ready to be transported to Nadiad. Unluckily for the thief Mrs Dave woke up but she was too frightened to see the thief. Then her child woke up and started to howl which startled the thief who tried to run away but stumbled against a bucket and woke up Dave in the bargain. The thief, however, made good his escape. But nothing had been touched. Dave had been woken up in time.

There is the story of a man who had money stolen from him by brahmin employee of 35 years' service. All his savings had been stolen and he was broken-hearted. One day as he was sitting on the verandah of his home in a dejected manner he saw a fakir passing by to whom he told his sad story. "Why don't you visit Shirdi?" the fakir told him. The fakir also advised him to give up an item of food and to go to Shirdi when the stolen money was recovered. As it happened, the man who had stolen the money felt remorse and came back to his employer and not only begged for forgiveness but returned the money as well. The man thereupon visited Shirdi to obtain Baba's darshan.

Dr Madhav Ramachandra Tagare of Dashrathwadi had a strange experience on 14 May 1952. His war bonds worth Rs 2,500 had matured and money was due to him from the Post Office. He placed the War Bond certificates along with other papers in his bag and set out for Kopargaon by a bullock cart. While he was engaged in conversation with another person in the cart, he did not notice the bag which fell out of the cart. When they were crossing Naradi River he found that his bag was missing. There was only one thing to do: get down from the cart and walk backwards for about two miles in search of the bag. He did not find it; he did, however, notice a man driving a kerosene cart picking up something from the road, but it did not occur to him that it could be his bag. He returned home, in great distress and prayed to Sai Baba. In his troubled state of mind, however, he heard some one gently say: "Don't worry."

Next morning he was to visit a friend who was ill. Dr Tagare examined his patient, prescribed him some medicine and by way of small talk he told him about his missing bag. He did not notice a girl standing not far away who apparently heard the conversation. The girl turned out to be the daughter of the kerosene cartman who had chanced to pick up the bag the previous day. Now the girl brought the bag and laid it at Dr Tagare' feet. It had been tampered with but when Dr Tagare opened it, he found all his papers intact. Apparently the cartman had prised it open to see what the contents were and had come to the conclusion that some papers were not worth stealing. Dr Tagare was naturally overjoyed and attributed this to Baba's grace.

Similar experiences have been related by Mrs Kamalabai Pednekar, a nurse and one Kanoba Hari who had gone to Shirdi to test whether Baba was truly a saint who could work miracles. He arrived in Shirdi wearing a new pair of sandals and a *jari* turban on his head. Before he entered the masjid, he put away his pair of new sandals at an inconspicuous place, lest they be stolen. But when he returned to the corner after having Baba's darshan, he found his sandals missing. He was too embarrassed to ask those around whether they had seen his sandals. He sat down for his afternoon meal, but could not enjoy it. As he was washing his hands he noticed a boy with a pair of sandals held at one end of a stick going round crying: "Hari ka beta, jari ka pheta." Kanoba called him and said that the sandals belonged to him. But the boy said: "Sai Baba's orders, sir. These sandals are to be given only to him who is the son of Hari and wears a turban of jari. Satisfy me about these two conditions and the sandals are yours!" Kanoba who had taken off his turban when he was having his meal now took it out and showed it to the boy and said that his father's name was indeed Hari. Satisfied, the boy handed him his sandals. How Sai Baba could have known that Kanoba's father was named Hari puzzled Kanoba but then quickly came to the conclusion that Baba was giving him an object lesson in his own way.

A clerk in a well-known firm in Bombay embezzled funds of the employer and disappeared. In his peregrination the culprit

186

arrived in Shirdi. A devotee of Sai Baba was the manager of the firm. The owner had obtained a warrant of arrest issued to be served on the clerk. A search was conducted at many places but it had not revealed the whereabouts of the embezzler. So the Manager-devotee thought of consulting Sai Baba in the matter. When the Manager arrived in Shirdi he found, to his astonishment, the culprit sitting by the side of Baba! The Manager was worried. Should he have the culprit arrested in Sai Baba's presence or should he allow him to escape which latter course would be tantamount to disloyalty to his employer. However he was relieved when the embezzler himself admitted to his guilt and sought Baba's blessings. On Sai Baba's advice, the culprit accompanied the Manager and admitted to his guilt before his employer. Thus the matter was satisfactorily resolved through Baba's grace.

The financial position of Hari Sitaram alias Kakasaheb Dikshit, Solicitor, deteriorated during the latter half of his life and he was indebted to the extent of Rs 30,000. The creditor was pressing hard and the period of repayment of loan was due to expire in four days. Yet Dikshit had no way of making the full repayment. That night Dikshit dreamed that the creditor demanded immediate repayment and he assured the creditor, saying: "Do not fear that your loan will not be repaid. I have my resources. I know Sir Chimanlal Setalwad, Sir X and Sir Y. So you have no reason to fear."

Shortly thereafter he woke up and remembered the dream. He was aghast at his stupidity in relying on poor human support even of distinguished men and failing to recognize that his only sheet anchor was Sai Baba. Filled with remorse he entreated Sai Baba with tear-filled eyes to forgive him for his lack of faith. Thereafter he felt assured that Baba alone would help him.

And how could Baba fail a devotee in the hour of his need? Yet, as the day for repayment neared Dikshit saw no signs of money forthcoming. With just one day more to go, the son of a deceased intimate friend called on him and wanted advice on how a sum of Rs 30,000 he had, should be invested. On learning Dikshit's financial difficulty the young man pressed upon Dikshit to accept the deposit and said that he would not be true to his father if he failed to help him with an accommodation at the time of dire need. Help had come to Dikshit in the most unexpected way!

A Muslim farmer was worried about paying off a loan of Rs 500 which he had taken for the improvement of his farm. While digging, he came across a rock, for blowing up which he applied twice to the Collector for a permit to buy explosives. Both his applications were rejected. Disheartened the farmer approached Sai Baba. Baba merly told him: "Let Nanasaheb (Chandorkar) come and I will tell him."

During Nana's visit to Shirdi, the farmer reminded Baba of his promise. So Baba told Nana: "Give this man's application to the Collector with your recommendation so that his work will be done." Nana was aware of Baba's powers but he felt that the farmer's application would still not be entertained. However, Nanasaheb took the farmer to the Collector, placed the former's application before him and told him that two earlier applications had been rejected. Whereupon the Collector asked the farmer why he was so insistent on using explosives. The farmer said: "Saheb, I have taken a loan of Rs 500 from the government. I wish to improve my farm and pay off the loan. Without a well I cannot improve the farm and without explosives the well cannot be dug. If you do not grant the permit, how can the well be dug and without a well how can I pay off the loan?"

The Collector saw the point and granted permission for the farmer to buy his explosives.

There are still other instances of devotees receiving help in unexpected ways. Dattoba Tulsiram Chavan, the grandson of Bhausaheb Shirsathe had given a loan on interest to a person. Chavan, was planning to visit Shirdi but some financial diffi-culties came in his way and he almost gave up his travel plans. But then the man who had borrowed money from him came personally to return it and Chavan felt as if Baba wanted to see him. He made his trip to Shirdi with pleasure and anticipation.

We have the experience of Bapusaheb Jog who, while in service, had advanced a loan of Rs 1,400 to a relation of his wife. The amount remained unpaid for over a dozen years despite regular reminders. Jog's earnings were about Rs 200 a month but when he retired on pension he felt the need for the cash he had long ago parted with. Jog had settled down in Shirdi and one day sought Baba's advice on whether he should personally call on his debtor to recover the money. "But where is the need?" asked Sai Baba, "The money will come to your doorstep. Why are you in such a hurry?"

Nothing happened, though. Jog kept pestering Baba but would always get the same reply. One day, in despair, Jog told Baba: "It is over twelve years now since the man took the money and not a pie has been returned. Why should he come now to my doorstep, as you say, to bring me the money?"

Baba merely repeated what he had said on previous occasions. Jog gave up thinking that he was doing nobody any favour by grumbling. Some days later, to his utter surprise, the debtor came to Shirdi with a couple of his friends and put up at Jog's residence. Jog understandably was stunned and recollected Baba's words. To his surprise he learnt that the debtor had only brought Rs 1,400 with him but not the interest on it as expected. He demanded the interest. The debtor did not have it with him. The man pleaded with Jog's wife to intercede on his behalf. It did not help. Finally they agreed to take the matter to Sai Baba who ruled that Jog should forego the interest but accept Rs 1,400. Jog accepted the verdict. At least, he felt, he had got back the principal, without having to take recourse to legal proceedings. Jog offered the entire amount to Baba who only accepted a token sum and returned the rest to his devotee.

2

Hari,
Thou didst remove the afflictions of Thy devotees.
Thou didst spare the shame of Draupadi
By continually lengthening her dress.
Thou didst assume the form of a Man-Lion
To save thy devotee Prahlad.
Thou didst save the elephant from drowning.

Mira is the servant of Lal Giridhara:
He has removed all my afflictions.
—Mirabai (The Devotional Poems translated by A.J. Alston)

As in other instances, Sai Baba often went to the rescue of his devotees when they badly needed his help.

The wife of Hari Vinayak Sathe was placed in a awkward situation when her husband and father gave her conflicting directions. Were she to obey her father, she would invite her husband's wrath. And vice versa. Sai Baba saved her from her dilemma. On Sathe's instructions his father-in-law had bought land comprising some 20 acres for a sum of Rs 1,200 for Sathe. Once when Sathe was in Shirdi he felt a pressing desire to visit his land but his father-in-law did not approve of the idea as he was afraid that if the widow of his nephew came to know of it she would demand a share in the land. So he declined to accompany Sathe.

Sathe had called for the bullock cart of Tatya Kote Patil and asked his wife to accompany him. She had earlier agreed to do so but on her father's entreaties, she changed her mind. Sathe was furious and taking the whip out of the cartman's hand was about to whip her when Megha was seen running towards him. Baba, said Megha, wanted to see Sathe immediately. When Sathe stood before him, Baba said: "What is it? What has happened?"

Sathe realised that Baba had noticed how he was about to whip his wife, through his inner eye, and felt ashamed. Baba told him, "Your land is where it is. Where is the need to visit it?" Sathe calmed down and prostrated before Baba and sought his forgiveness.

Baba came to the rescue of the wife of Nanasaheb Nimonkar in her predicament. Nimonkar's son at Belapur was ill. So Nimonkar asked his wife to go to Belapur and check on her son but told her not to linger on but return the very next day. The next day was *amaavasya* and she knew that she would not be allowed to travel that day. Yet she did not want to stay on in Belapur against her husband's wishes. When the time came for her to leave she went to the masjid accompanied by her husband and bowed to Baba. Baba told her: "Go, go soon and return in four days' time after spending them happily with your son." Nimonkar who was standing close by got the message. He dared not countermand Baba.

Govind Damodar Pant of Palaspe Panvel in Kolaba (now renamed Raigad) district had a problem getting his daughter married. He met many eligible young men but none came up to his expectations. On the suggestion of a Baba-devotee Pant took a vow that if his daughter got married in fifteen days he would visit Shirdi. It turned out that the son of one Hardikar from south Hyderabad on his own came to Palaspe in search of a suitable bride, decided Pant's daughter was just the girl for him and the marriage took place not long after. To Pant's credit he kept his vow.

Govind Narayan alias Baba Samant tried hard to fix up the marriage of his elder daughter but without any success. In such an anxious state of mind he woke up one night, lighted a lamp before Baba's photograph and prayed to him fervently. Next day Samant got word about an eligible young man, the son of the late Bhaurao Dabholkar and not long afterwards an alliance was agreed upon much to Samant's happiness and relief.

Sai Baba had also helped the tehsildar of Sunel in Holkar State, one Keshav Rege Amin. His financial condition was not much to speak of but he desired that his daughter should be placed in a well-to-do family. He tried hard in Indore, Ujjain, Bombay, Thane and other places but failed in his expectations. Then he went to Baroda and with a relation of his he went to the homes of two prospective bridegrooms. At one of these places deceit was sought to be practised on him by substituting for the prospective weak bridegroom a handsome healthy young man for the purpose of fixing up the marriage. This deceit was discovered in good time and the girl was saved from future disaster. Then Sai Baba appeared in Amin's dream and asked him to proceed to Jirapur. At first Amin was baffled but in a few days' time he found himself transferred to Jirapur. Not long after he settled down he learnt that the son of Nabars of Soyat, some ten to twelve miles away from Jirapur was eligible. Amin went with his daughter to Soyat and the groom liked the girl, as did his parents. Marriage was fixed and Amin was relieved of his anxiety.

The experience of Gopal Ganesh Shriyan was that Sai Baba continues to take care of his devotees even after his *maha-samadhi.* There was an understanding since seven to eight years between Shriyan and the father of a prospective bride-groom that the son would marry Shriyan's elder daughter. Relations between the two families were cordial. The boy had passed his matriculation examination and was studying in college. The boy's father became greedy and asked for a large sum of money as dowry and since Shriyan was unable to raise it, relations between the families stopped and the engagement was broken off. Shriyan prayed to Sai Baba who assured him that all would be well and his daughter would be surely married to the same boy!

Then it came to Shriyan's ears that another party was prepared to offer a huge dowry to the boy's father. Shriyan was worried but Baba again appeared to him in his dream and assured him that his daughter would be married to the same boy in two years' time.

And so, miraculously, it happened. The father of the boy himself came to Shriyan with the marriage proposal before the end of two years and the marriage took place without any hitch. Shriyan did not ask for an explanation. He believed in Baba's grace.

It would seem that it did not matter whether the person seeking help was a true devotee or someone in plain distress asking for Baba's help. An instance is cited of a young man who was vacillating to marry a girl who had been recommended to him. He could not make up his mind. The girl's mother was espe-cially upset, that her daughter's marriage was held up because a man could not say either yes or no. She prayed before a picture of Baba, but it was more a challenge and a reproach to Baba than a prayer. "They tell me you help them through your mysterious powers. Why then don't you help me? My daughter continues to remain unmarried and I am worried. If you really are all that powerful, show me by way of a letter from that man giving his consent to marry my child."

She couldn't believe her own eyes when next day the postman delivered a letter from the fellow agreeing to the marriage. It was solemnized within a few days.

Abdul of Nanded had left his home and served Baba in Shirdi for 45 years. He passed away in Shirdi on 2nd April 1954. Abdul's mother was very eager to get her grandson married. Elders of one household conveyed in clear terms that they did not wish to give away their daughter in marriage to the son of a fakir. When Abdul's mother approached Sai Baba with a complaint he assured her: "Do not be worried. The boy will get a good bride and everything will fall in its place in good time." And so it happened. Grandmother and grandson had been visiting some friends where they met a person who showed keenness in giving his daughter in marriage to the boy. The man was specifically told that the boy's father was a fakir. "That is of no moment," said the man and gave his second daughter away in marriage even when his eldest daughter was still to be married.

Adam Dalal of Naopada, Bandra, was anxious to arrange for his son's marriage. He would talk to Sai Baba about it from time to time. Baba would put off the discussion on the topic every time. Some three years later Baba suddenly gave his permission but Adam did not have the money but just ten days prior to the date fixed for the marriage he not only got a job but some advance payment as well. Adam was a happy man.

Similar experiences have been related by devotees and they all add up to the same thing: Baba's timely help when everything seemed to crumble around one. Laxman Govind Munge of Main Road, Nasik, received the help he needed when no one, not even his closest relatives were willing to extend assistance to him. Often people in distress would challenge Baba in their distress, half disbelieving that he would ever come to their help. But he did. A father who had been separated from his son for many years met him—call it by chance or attribute it to Baba's grace—on a railway platform at Thane almost by accident only to fall into each other's arms. The son of a Parsi merchant was missing and the father spent over four thousand rupees to trace him but failed. Finally he took refuge in Sai Baba and enquired through a letter when the missing boy would be found. He received a reply from Shirdi saying that according to Baba the boy had gone south, was happy and would return on his own. The boy did, after a few days. He had been to Madras.

Capt. Dr. Hate of Gwalior was a staunch devotee of Sai Baba. One evening a person came to him and said that both he and his wife were distressed because their son had left his home and was not traceable. Dr. Hate told the man to go to Shirdi for Baba's darshan. The man vowed that if his son was found he would certainly pay a visit to Shirdi. After some time he received a letter from his son in Mesopotamia that he had joined the Army without informing anyone and was now returning home. When the news was conveyed to Dr. Hate he told the man: "First go to Shirdi." But the man spurned the advice and went, instead, to Bombay to receive his son. It turned out, however, that the son was ill and needed treatment and so he was brought to Dr. Hate. The latter castigated the man for not going to Shirdi first and relenting, gave the man a rupee which he said shoud be offered to Baba as *dakshina.* Dr. Hate, however, hoped that the coin would come back to him blessed by Baba, but he did not mention that to the man.

Not long afterwards the man went to Shirdi along with his wife and son, had Baba's darshan and presented Baba with the rupee. Baba took it in his hand, looked at it for a moment and then quietly returned it saying that it should be given to its owner! When Dr. Hate received it his joy was great. He received Baba's *prasad.*

A Parsi gentleman had a son who was insane. The son's condition was so pitiable that the father could not bear to see it and hence got him admitted in to an asylum. Hearing of Baba's fame, the gentleman went to Shirdi for Baba's darshan. Baba blessed him and said: "Go, your son will get well. Take him home."

The gentleman was taken aback. He was not sure whether the Asylum authorities would release his son but when he returned home he found a letter from the very authorities which said that the young man was losing weight and that it would be advisable to get him admitted elsewhere. The gentleman was happy to bring his son back as Baba had instructed. As it turned out on his return home the young man's condition improved rapidly and after some days he recovered completely and joined his father in his business.

Sakharam Hari alias Bapusaheb Jog who would attend to *arati* of Sai Baba asked permission of Sai Baba to go to Nasik for performing the obsequies after his mother's death. Baba postponed giving permission. When Jog felt that the matter could not be delayed any longer he said to Baba: "I must go to Nasik this afternoon," to which Baba replied: "We will see in the afternoon." Jog was anxious because there was no brahmin belonging to his branch of Vedas in Shirdi. However, in the afternoon, a learned brahmin belonging exactly to Jog's branch of Veda arrived unexpectedly in Shirdi. It was then that Jog realised why Baba had delayed giving permission. The obsequies were performed in Shirdi itself at the hands of the learned brahmin.

When Neelkanth Ramachandra Sahasrabuddhe first went to Shirdi Sai Baba asked him for a dakshina of Rs. 12 and annas eight. Later as Sahasrabuddhe offered to Baba five rupees received by Tatyasaheb Nulkar by Money Order from Ramachandra Vaman Modak, Baba told him "Keep the money with you. You will require it for your expense." So he kept the money with himself. He was required to go to Jalgaon from Shirdi on his way back home and he was falling short exactly by five rupees for the rail fare—the amount he had been asked to hold on to!

A pensioner teacher, a devotee of Sai Baba, living at Chandoli in Ambegaon taluka of Pune district used to grow potatoes and sell the crop to government. In 1945 the potato crop was infested and no one was willing to offer him more than Rs. 200 for his crop. He had incurred expenses amounting to Rs 400 and was in distress. He never failed to pray to Sai Baba thrice a day and vowed to go to Shirdi every Thursday. One day a government officer came to inspect his crop, adjudged it good and offered to purchase the lot for Rs. 600. Where once he feared a loss of Rs. 200 he now made a neat profit of Rs. 200.

Bhikaji Mahadeo Bidwe, a peon of Shri Sai Baba Samsthan of Shirdi received by way of salary Rs. 36 per month. His sister Chabutai was sick for about three months. Her condition took a serious turn on 5 December 1951. Bhikaji wanted her to be examined by a good doctor. But how could he call a doctor for domiciliary visit on his meagre salary? So, putting his burden on Sai Baba and ever remembering him, he was doing his duty in the office when an old devotee, a doctor, came in to make an equiry. Bhikaji did not recognise him but, stangely enough, the doctor recognised Bhikaji whereupon Bhikaji asked the doctor whether he would examine his sister which the doctor gladly agreed to do after which he prescribed the necessary medicines.

Once Nanasaheb Chandorkar was restless as a seeming conflict between devotion to his father and devotion to his guru was raging in his mind which resolved itself peacefully for which, in his heart, he thanked Sai Baba.

Like Nanasaheb, his father Govindrao, too, had once been a deputy Collector. He owned a house in Kalyan and enjoyed a high standing in the town. Govindrao developed hostility towards some Muslims over some matter as a result of which he gave instructions to members of his household not to have any truck with Muslims. At that time Nanasaheb was out of station on duty. On his return he came to know about his father's instructions. Nanasaheb was now in a fix. For while he was ready to sever relations with all other Muslims, as far as Sai Baba was concerned, though he was regarded by many ignorant people as a Muslim, Nanasaheb was not willing to sever his connections with him. At the same time he did not wish to offend his father. Caught in this dilemma, he considered talking over the matter with his father but by then omniscient as Sai Baba was, the latter had prepared the ground for conciliation. So, when Nanasaheb raised the matter of his special relation with Sai Baba, the old man said: "Just as Sakharam Maharaj is my guru, so is Sai Baba your guru. So even assuming that he is really a Musalman, you should continue to visit him without any reservation." So pleased was Nanasaheb on hearing this that he burst into tears.

Sai Baba was pledged to satisfying the desires of his devotees for the darshan of saints and God. Nanasaheb Chandorkar was convinced of this as a result of a unique experience. Nanasaheb was then the Mamledar of a taluka near Pachora in East Khandesh. There is a shrine called Padmalaya about ten to twelve miles from Pachora. A realised soul named Govindbua stayed in the jungle at a distance of about a mile and a half from the shrine. Govindbua would go into the temple early morning and after attending to the worship of Gajanan look after the visitors to the shrine and retire to his monastery at 10 pm. His intake of food consisted of some 18 tolas of tea a day. Nanasaheb felt a strong urge to have darshan of Govindbua and told his friends about it. The day for a visit to the shrine was fixed up. As his party missed the train by which they planned to travel, they reached Pachora late in the evening. The road to Padmalaya passed through a forest. So, taking a guide, they started on foot for Padmalaya. It was a dark night and the road was uphill and down dale. Since the meal they had in the morning, none had eaten anything and they had brought no snacks with them. After covering about six miles Nanasaheb was very tired. He had no energy to go further and the party stopped for rest. What was to be done? Pachora by this time was well behind and it would be well past 10 pm. by the time they reached Padmalaya. Moreover no one lived in Padmalaya. Govindbua would have retired to his monastery in which case who would be there to provide food and shelter? Finally Nanasaheb got up and remembering Sai Baba, he prayed fervently to him. So alternately praying and walking and resting, the party reached Padmalaya after 10 pm. But even as they arrived, Govindbua came out of the shrine with a goblet of steaming tea—just what Nanasaheb had prayed for!— and asked: "Has Nana come?" Nanasaheb and others greeted Govindbua respectfully and wondered how come he had stayed back at the shrine though it was well past 10 pm. Govindbua artlessly replied: "I received a message just a while ago from Sai Baba that Nana will be arriving here on foot from a long distance and in a tired condition, that he would be very hungry and that a goblet of tea should be kept waiting for him. So I had brought this tea for you!'' The entire party was served tea but no matter how much they drank, there still was some tea left! Baba had taken care of them.

During the 1909 Christmas vacation R.B. Modak thought of going to Khandesh via Shirdi. So he purchased railway tickets from Poona to Dhond and Dhond to Manmad. Then taking baskets of fruits and flowers with him, he and his wife and children arrived at the station fifteen minutes before the train's departure well ahead of time. Modak had the luggage weighed and then putting his wife and children in the women's compartment was looking for a place for himself and the luggage when the guard sounded the whistle and waved the green flag. Modak was in a panic. He requested the guard to charge him the difference between the second and third class fares and permit him to sit in a second class compartment. But the guard paid no attention and the train began to move. Modak was dejected and remembered Sai Baba. Suddenly the Station Master appeared on the scene and asked Modak what he wanted. When Modak explained his difficulty, the Station Master raised both his hands as a signal for the train to stop and made arrangements for Modak to board the train and even got a porter to load Modak's luggage into the compartment.

Vasudev Narayan Desai had a similar experience after the *mahasamadhi* of Sai Baba. Desai had decided at short notice to take a party of about fifty persons to Navsari for his daughter's marriage. A compartment could not be therefore reserved in advance. The Ticket Collector told Desai before the train started that an entire compartment could not be provided for the party. So Desai found himself in a fix. He prayed to Sai Baba fervently when the Head Ticket Collector arrived on the scene to whom Desai explained his predicament. "I'll help you," said the Head Ticket Collector and got a compartment reserved from Baroda, opened, which was to have gone empty. The entire party was thus providentially taken care of.

At Gholvad station a fakir entered the compartment and with one leg placed across the other very much as Baba himself would, asked: "Well, you are all accommodated, aren't you?" Desai said they were. "Such is Allahmia's doing," saying which the fakir alighted from the compartment and vanished!

A clerk serving in the Port Trust was required to find several bills earlier returned by the Customs Office as they were called for again by Customs. Failure to produce the said bills would have resulted either in incurring the displeasure of his superior or even in losing his job. The clerk began praying to Sai Baba.

The clerk had been told to submit the bills but despite his desperate search he could not find them. On the day he was expected to submit the bills he went to his office much ahead of time to pursue the search when, to his surprise, he found the bills, all neatly tied up in a bundle, right on his table! The bundle was not there when he left office the previous evening and that morning he was the first to reach his office. No human agency could have placed that bundle on his table. It was then that the clerk realised that Baba had answered his prayers.

The biggest calamity for a middle class householder is to be charged with a criminal offence and only a person who has undergone the bitter experience of a false criminal charge knows the agony of anxiety, mental torture and financial loss which he has to suffer. Many devotees of Sai Baba have been saved by him from such a calamity. Thus, a police officer was charged with the offence of extortion of money. He took refuge in Sai Baba and vowed to go to Shirdi for Baba's darshan if he were acquitted. He was. And he kept his vow.

Once a Muslim doctor had come to Shirdi to stay for a few days. During that period somebody instituted a criminal case against him and he was served with summons. On the day previous to the hearing of the case, the doctor asked Baba's permission to leave so as to attend to the summons. Baba, however, suggested that he only leave the next day. The doctor, in the circumstances could not be present in court on the day he should have been there but he learnt subsequently that the judge had examined the plaintiff and the witnesses first, found that there was no *prima facie* case against the doctor and dismissed the case.

Once, when a party in Shirdi village, hostile to Appa Kulkarni, filed a complaint against him of misappropriation of funds, the Deputy Collector called him over for an explanation. Appa was frightened and approached Sai Baba. Baba told him: "The Deputy Collector is at Nevase. First go to the temple of Mohiniraj at Nevase, bow to the Lord and give your explanation to Him and then go the Deputy Collector's office to answer his query." Appa did as he was told. The official heard him out and decided that he was innocent and discharged him. Appa returned to Shirdi brimming with happiness and told Baba what happened and praised him. "Praise me?" asked Baba, "what did I do? It is Narayana who gets things done. He makes impossible things possible for a devotee." It was alleged against Adam Dalal of Bandra that in a mortgage transaction, his bond in favour of mortgagor was fabricated. Adam was alarmed and went for Baba's darshan. Baba assured him and said: "All will be well." And so it happened. The mortgagor was committed to sessions in which Adam became a witness for the prosecution and was freed from anxiety.

Once, before jesting and joking took an ugly turn, Sai Baba by a remark of his applied the healing touch which ended a controversy. Two devotees were engaged in serving Sai Baba when their faces almost came into contact with each other. One of them, an old lady known as Mavshibai told the other, also an older man: "What, you want to kiss me? Old man, have you no sense of shame?" Hearing this Anna Chinchanikar was visibly agitated. But Sai Baba intervened and addressing Anna he said: "Why are you so highly agitated? What is wrong in kissing the mother?" There was laughter on all sides with the two serving devotees joining happily in it.

Domestic events, one would call them and such they were. Baba, in a sense was the paterfamilias, the *karta,* the elder in the house who often gave orders and got things done. It was all the same, whether they were young or old, men or women. Baba would intervene in their quarrels or rebuke them when they lost their temper or pacify them when the situation called for it.

His help was sought in all kinds of situations. One man came to him saying that he was the victim of witchcraft, Baba blessed him and thereafter witchcraft ceased to have any effect on him. A father brought his son to get Baba's darshan. The son had appeared for the Vernacular Final examination and inquired of Baba whether he would pass. "You will pass with 114th rank," Baba replied off-hand. And so it turned out! He appeared in a dream to a railway servant who was planning to visit Shirdi and told him not to come. The man had definitely decided to make the trip but called it off. It was just as well for just then workmen were thinking of going on strike and had he gone out of station he would have been suspected of colluding with the strikers. Baba's advice to him to stay put was timely.

On one occasion Sai Baba told Raghuvir Bhaskar Purandare to build a house. Purandare did not have the wherewithal to do so, but what was considered impossible somehow came to pass and when the bungalow was finally built, Purandare also got a good tenant.

Small or minor examples of assistance, perhaps, but he seemed to be with his devotees and at their beck and call. Sadashiv Dhundiraj Nayak wanted to attend a marriage of a friend's son but was reluctant to go as his mother was seriously ill. Baba sent word to him indirectly that he could conveniently attend the marriage as his mother was due to pass away much later. She died as Baba had predicted, on an *Ekadashi* day.

There is the story of Uddhavaeshabua alias Shyamdas of Dahanu who had taken a party on a pilgrimage to Dwarka and on the way lost the tickets. Stranded, he prayed to Baba who appeared in a dream to Uddhaveshabua's son Gopal Giridhar and told him to send his father money immediately as it was needed. The fakir in the dream was so vivid that Giridhar even woke up and went looking for the fakir. At first Giridhar took no action, but when the fakir appeared to him in his dream a second time he sent a money order to his father who was agreeably surprised to get it. It was Baba in action again.

Indeed, when Uddhaveshbua was back in Shirdi, Baba remarked: "I arranged to send you money, didn't I?"

CHAPTER 7

IN THE TRUE SAINT'S DURBAR

The highest relationship is one of love:
The plain simple fare of Vidura He preferred
   to the delicacies of Duryodhana.

He relished the berries tasted by Shabari
   and established bonds of love.
Out of love Hari served the King and
   even became a barber.

In Rajasuya sacrifice of Yūdhishtir
He cleared the left-overs,
And out of love, forgetting His divinity
   drove the chariot of Arjuna.

The bonds of love grew in Vrindavan
   where He danced with Gopis.
Surdas is not worthy of His grace
Why should he be vain?

Wealth is respected in the world but in the *durbar* of the true saint, who is Lord personified, it is loving devotion which is honoured. And so it has been with Baba. It was the day of Ramanavami Fair in 1913-14. There was a terrific rush in Shirdi for Sai Baba's darshan. The Mamledar, Police Inspector and other officials were present to maintain *bandobast*. Sai Baba sat in his usual place in the masjid while the crowd outside was milling around waiting for an opportunity to get Baba's darshan. Among the crowd was an old woman who kept saying: ''Please have pity on this poor old woman, O Sai Baba, and give me your darshan.'' But there was no way she could see Baba for a long time. Luckily for her, Ramachandra Atmaram Tarkhad who chanced to pass by saw her, heard her plea and out of respect for her age arranged to give her priority over the rest.

The moment she saw Baba she called out to him and embraced him warmly. Tears rolled down her eyes and for some time she was choked with emotion. Placing his hand on her head Baba made minute enquiries about her household and told her: "Mother, I have been waiting since long for you. What have you brought for me?"

The old woman replied: "Baba, I had brought one *bhakri* and two onions with me. After I had walked and walked, I got tired and sitting by the stream in the morning, I ate half the *bhakri* and one onion. Now I have only half the *bhakri* and one onion left which please accept!"

So saying she untied the bundle in her sari and gave the remnants of her meal to Baba who ate them with great relish, saying: "Mother, the *bhakri* has never tasted better!" Tears welled in the old woman's eyes and Tarkhad could scarcely contain his. Once R. B. Purandare started for Shirdi with his wife. Giving her two brinjals, Mrs. R. A. Tarkhad requested her to make a dish of *bharit* and another dish of *kaacharya* and offer them to Baba. On reaching Shirdi, Purandare's wife did as she was told. First she made the *bharit* and offered it to Baba but then Baba said: "When we get *kaacharya* we shall have our meal." Brinjals at that time of the year were a rarity and Baba was all the more insistent on tasting what had been prepared for him by the love and care of his devotees.

Sai Baba also showed recognition of Mrs. Tarkhad's love for him in December 1915. Balakram Mankar, a devotee of Sai Baba passed away in Shirdi. Mankar's son called on R. A. Tarkhad before proceeding to Shirdi to perform the obsequies of his father. Mrs. Tarkhad thought of sending something with Mankar's son as an offering to Sai Baba. Nothing else was available in the house except one *pedha*. She sent that *pedha* with Mankar's son. On reaching Shirdi he went for Baba's darshan but forgot to carry Mrs. Tarkhad's *pedha* with him.

"Have you brought anything with you for me?" Baba asked.
"Nothing," replied the young man.
After a smile, Baba again asked: "Is anything given for me?"
"No," replied the young man.

For the third time Baba asked: "Did the mother not give you something for me before you started on your journey?"

The young man suddenly realised that he had indeed been given *pedha*—just one—but still something given with love and he apologised to Baba and rushed back to his lodgings and brought the *pedha*. Baba ate it with relish.

In 1915 when Shantaram Balwant Nachane Dahanukar was leaving for Shirdi, V. S. Samant gave him a coconut, a little packet of sugar and two annas (8 paise) as offering to Baba. Nachane offered the coconut to Baba, but forgot to give him the two annas. When after taking Baba's darshan, Nachane asked permission to leave for Bombay, the latter said: "Go from Chithali but why have you retained two annas that you should have given to this poor brahmin?" (meaning himself!)

Nachane realised that he had not given that small *dakshina* that Samant had asked him to give Baba on his behalf. He now gave it. Baba teased him, "Never accept any responsibility. But if you have, discharge it to the fullest!" Nachane got the point all right! On 13 September, 1918, Annasaheb Dabholkar, the author of *Shri Sai Satcharit* had a dream. Accordingly he sent with a devotee going to Shirdi, 100 leaves of piper-betel, some areca nuts and eight annas (half a rupee). As the devotee was late by two days in starting for Shirdi the piper-betel leaves dried up. Nevertheless, the devotee offered them to Baba with due explanation. As Baba rose from his sent his attendant wondered what was to be done with the dried leaves. Should they be given away? Should they be kept aside? "Keep them aside," Baba advised. He was not going to throw away something that a devotee had brought with love.

Sai Baba once appeared in the dream of the wife of a postal official at Burhanpur who had never before visited Shirdi. In the dream Baba was standing at her doorstep asking for a meal of *khichri*. The woman woke up and looked around, wondering whether there was some one at the door—the dream was so vivid. Later in the morning she told her family about her dream.

A few weeks later her husband was transferred to Akola. While in Akola the couple visited Shirdi and served Baba for a full fortnight. One day, while preparing *khichri* for *naivedya* (consecrated food) she went to the masjid. At that time the curtain had been drawn as Baba was having his meal and his privacy was always respected. Love, however, knows no fear or bounds and pulling the curtain aside the lady entered with the *thali* of *naivedya*. As soon as Sai Baba saw her, he said: "Come, come! Bring me the *khichri!* I have been waiting for it!" and taking the *thali* from the lady's hands, he ate mouthfuls of the *khichri*.

This was something unusual. Baba seldom partook of *naivedya*. How come, then, that he was not only breaking his own rule but really enjoying himself? Some one asked the lady's husband who then narrated the story of his wife's dream. It was as if Baba had waited just for the *khichri* prepared by the lady.

Dr Keshav M. Gavankar has stated that in 1912 when he was seven years old, he was very sick. Medical treatment as well as tantric practices were of no avail. For two months he had lain semi-conscious in bed and doctors gave it as their opinion that he would have to be operated. His parents were against an operation as they were afraid that he may die. At this time Y.J. Galwankar, Annasaheb Dabholkar's son-in-law had just returned from Shirdi. Galwankar was a close friend of Gavankar's uncle. He advised application of *udi* and worship of Sai Baba and a vow to be taken that if Gavankar got well, he would pay a visit to Shirdi. The instructions were followed to the full and Gavankar got well, but it took five years for the vow to be fulfilled. When Gavankar went to Shirdi and *naivedya* of *pedhas* was offered on his behalf to Baba, the latter returned five *pedhas* and ate the rest. "Why have you declined the five *pedhas*?" a devotee asked him. "That is one *pedha* for each of the year that Gavankar kept me hungry!" Baba replied. Baba, clearly, had known of the vow.

Once Sai Baba appeared in the dream of Capt Dr Hate of Gwalior and asked him: "Have you forgotten me?" Prostrating before Baba, Hate went into his garden, gathered fresh *walpapadi* (a sort of beans), prepared a soup of *walpapadi* with undressed rice and went to offer it to Baba when he awoke. Hate had an intense urge to offer *naivedya* with *walpapadi* to Sai Baba but could not make the journey to Shirdi leaving aside his work. So he wrote to a friend in Bombay requesting him personally to go to Shirdi and offer *naivedya* with a *walpapadi* dish and said he was remitting money by money order. The friend thereupon went to Shirdi where a vegetable vendor brought the out-of-season *walpapadi* much to his surprise, prepared the dish as instructed and offered it to Baba. There were other dishes besides that were being served to him, but Baba would have none of them. The only dish he accepted that day was the one with *walpapadi*. It was as if he wanted to show his appreciation of a devotee's resolution.

Sai Baba's flow of love continued uninterruptedly even after he took his *mahasamadhi*. Sagun Meru Naik had an experience of this in 1922-23. He had a dream in which he saw that the *naivedya* of butter-sugar which used to be offered to Baba in earlier times at the morning *arati* had been stopped. So he enquired of the Samsthan and it was confirmed that the practice had been discontinued. Sagun knew that Baba liked butter a great deal. So, at his own expense, he began offering *naivedya* of butter-sugar at the morning *arati,* a practice that since then has been followed.

When Das Ganu, along with his party (which possibly included Pundalikrao) returned from Jagannath Puri, he happened to meet Vásudevanand Saraswati, *alias* Tembe Maharaj. He told Tembe Maharaj that he would be going to Nanded via Shirdi, whereupon Tembe Maharaj gave him a coconut to be handed over to Baba with his *pranaams.*

When Das Ganu's party reached Shirdi, Baba remarked to Madhavrao Deshpande: "This Das Ganu is a big thief! He ate the sweetmeat which my brother had sent to me!"

Das Ganu did not understand what Baba meant and asked: "What sweetmeat?"

"A thief and contumacious at that!" retorted Sai Baba and added: "Didn't you consume the coconut meant for me?"

At that point Das Ganu recollected that Vasudevanand had indeed given him a coconut to be delivered to Baba and he had forgotten to hand it over.

Das Ganu felt properly ashamed and prostrated before Baba, admitted to his guilt and promised to bring another coconut to replace the one he had consumed on the way. Baba told him: "My brother, considering you trustworthy gave you that thing. Now see what you have done!" And then he went on: "You appear to hold yourself guilty because your ego considers yourself as the doer. Actually, I felt like meeting all of you and the coconut offering was only an excuse! What's wrong if you consumed that coconut? You are all my children! So when you ate what was meant for me, you, in fact, offered it to me! Understand that I have received it! What has happened is all according to my wish. Offer me both merit earned and sin committed so that you will be liberated."

Sai Baba would see through his inner vision the *sattvic* desire of a devotee and would satisfy it. Thereby the true of love of a devotee could get nurtured by watering it with faith. Once Hari Sitaram alias Kakasaheb Dikshit came to Shirdi at the commencement of *navaratri* all the way from Nagpur and stayed on till dusserah. He had no fruit with him for the worship of Sai Baba and so he was somewhat downcast. Some time later Sai Baba distributed grapes brought by a devotee. Dikshit gave some grapes from his share back to Baba which the latter ate. Dikshit's troubled mind thus was set at peace. In 1918 on the day of *Gurupoornima* no *tambool* or *vida* could be found for Baba's *puja*. In the afternoon Baba called Dikshit and asked him to get three or four *vidas*. When Dikshit brought them, Baba ate one of them as if to say that the deficiency at the time of the *puja* has been set right.

Surveyor Govindrao Oak of Andheri and Krishnaji alias Annasaheb Agashe went to Shirdi to get Baba's darshan, and stayed there for three days. Before departing both of them purchased a photograph each of Baba for themselves which were kept in a bundle. On the way home Govindrao felt that it would have been better if he had purchased one more photograph for his brother. When the bundle was opened at home, to everyone's surprise, they found three photographs instead of the two they had purchased! They ascribed it, naturally, to Baba's *leela*.

Chhotubai, wife of Rao Bahadur Moreswhwar Pradhan had time and again experienced Sai Baba's response to her loving devotion and the protection he gave her. Once all her children in her household got measles. The youngest of them was very weak. His condition became serious and he developed high fever. Doctors gave up all hope for his life. Chhotubai sat by her child, day and night, praying to Sai Baba, repeating his name over and over again. Tired, she dozed off. She dreamt. In her dream Baba appeared and told her: "What are you doing? Your child is well. Have no fear. Early in the morning around 6 a.m. he will ask for food. Give it to him."

She woke up, looked around her, but there was no Sai Baba around. Her child was fast asleep. His temperature steadily was coming down. At the break of dawn he woke up and asked for food as Baba had said he would. Within a few days he had completely recovered. On another occasion, Chhotubai received advance intimation from Sai Baba, again in a dream that another child of hers might soon be down with a bout of epilepsy. At the time she had the dream, her child was perfectly fit but the dream came true. Only, she was prepared to face it, as was her family. The child suffered for four days but then, after that he never had any recurrence of epilepsy.

Once Pradhan's elder son had typhoid. The elder sister of Chhotubai, vowed to take Chhotubai's son to Shirdi if he got well. The fever took its course and subsided after a fortnight. A few days later the boy was permitted to sit up in bed. Against medical advice the elder sister now started for Shirdi with Chhotubai and her son. On their way the boy again fell ill and understandably Chhotubai was frightened. Should anything happen to the boy, she would not only be blamed but would be the laughing stock of her neighbourhood. Her elder sister was no less peturbed. Had they made a mistake in taking the boy to Shirdi just to keep a vow, when, in fact, he should have been convalescing? When they alighted at Kopargaon station a man came to them and asked: "Shall I get you a tonga?" The boy heard this and asked: "Have we already reached Sai Baba's home? Then help me to sit up!"

Chhotubai felt his arm; the temperature had gone and all seemed well. The boy wanted to sit but Chhotubai took him in her lap. On reaching Shirdi he was taken to the masjid. Sai Baba held him up with both his hands and made him stand. Chhotubai was afraid that after being in bed for a long time, the boy may now collapse. But he didn't. Instead, he stood firmly and ate a banana and a mango given to him by Baba. Then, as if to remind Chhotubai of her fears, Baba said: "Well, will the world laugh at you for having taken the risk of bringing the boy here?"

Once Baba stopped Chhotubai while she was engaged in worshipping him and told her: "Stop. Go home, your *puja* is there!" Accustomed to obey, Chhotubai stopped midway during her *puja* and went home to find her son bawling and refusing to quieten down. Baba had sensed the child's unease and had sent Chhotubai to soothe him. It was only after she had succeeded in doing so did she return to the masjid to resume worship. On another occasion Chhotubai saw Baba in her dream. Baba said to her: "Look, I have come here for your sake. Now offer *haldi-kumkum* at my feet!"

Nanasaheb Chandorkar interpreted the dream as meaning that Chhotubai must get silver *padukas* made and have them stepped on by Baba with both his feet so they were consecrated. He advised her that the *padukas* could then be installed in her puja-shrine. Chhotubai followed Chandorkar's advice, had silver *padukas* made and took them to Shirdi. When she went to the masjid she found that Baba would place only one foot on the ground at a time. How could she tell him to put both feet down to oblige her? But she did not have to tell him. When Baba saw her, he immediately placed his other foot on the ground, directed her on which *paduka* should be placed where and let her worship him. As Chhotubai bent down to pick up the *padukas,* Baba took both of them in his own hands and offered them to her, remarking to Chandorkar: "Nana, look, she is cutting both my feet and taking them away!"

Pandurang Bendre desired that he should have Sai Baba's *padukas* for his daily *puja.* So he had silver *padukas* made and took them to Shirdi. When he approached Sai Baba, Kaka-saheb Dikshit was sitting by him. Bendre handed over the *padukas* to Dikshit. When the latter was about to give them to Sai Baba, the latter said: "Give him the *padukas*!" That made Bendre very unhappy. He returned with the *padukas* in the afternoon and gave them to Madhavrao Deshpande to be handed over to Sai Baba. This time Sai Baba not only received them but personally handed them over to Bendre along with a coconut. No man could then have been happier.

In 1913 when Atmaram Haribhau Chaubal went to Shirdi for Sai Baba's darshan, he took with him silver *padukas* which he had specially got made to order. When he showed them to Baba, the latter took them in his hands and remarked: "How beautiful!" Then he inserted his two great toes in the *padukas* and added: "How nice they look! Take and keep them in your puja-shrine and worship them." And so he did.

In 1930 on the thirteenth day of the waning moon in Ashwin (October-November), Chaubal woke up early in the morning and wanted to have the *darshan* of the *padukas* but found that one of the *padukas* was missing. The *padukas* had been installed on a low wooden stool. The missing *paduka* was not found either under the stool or anywhere near by. It deeply disturbed Chaubal.

Nevertheless he continued to worship the remaining *paduka* but a couple of months later he found that the other *paduka* was missing as well. Nowhere could it be traced. This was very distressing. Chaubal and his family wondered whether they had incurred the displeasure of Baba and that thought was even more distressing to them. Chaubal, however, decided that he would go to Bombay and order for a new pair of *padukas* but they were not readily available. Disappointed Chaubal returned home and contented himself with worshipping a picture of Baba.

Then it happened. Chaubal worried himself every day about the *padukas* and Baba must have realised that Chaubal's devotion was unflagging. One fine morning, when Chaubal entered the puja room as usual he found to his tremendous surprise the missing *padukas* neatly placed under the wooden stool as if they always belonged there! Great was the sense of relief and joy in the Chaubal household.

Sai Baba would accept things sent to him with love and guide his devotees. The wife of Vinayak Shankar Giridhar had an experience of this kind. When Giridhar went with his friend to Shirdi, she sent with him a garland of roses strung together by her. When Giridhar garlanded him, Baba said: "This is a garland of love." As was his wont, he hardly wore the garland for more than a couple of seconds. But it was evident that he was quite pleased. That same night he appeared in a dream to Giridhar's wife and told her: "The garland which you sent me is one of love. Continue to garland me often." Those whom Baba wanted to see, he saw to it that they came to him from no matter where. Lakhmichand of Delhi was first employed at the Churchgate office of the then B.B. & C.I. Railway and later with Ralli Bros. In 1910 he saw in his dream a bearded sadhu surrounded by his devotees. He bowed to him respectfully. Later Lakhmichand went to the house of Dattatreya Manjunath Bijur for kirtan by Das Ganu. According to his usual practice, Das Ganu had kept a photograph of Sai Baba before him while performing *kirtan*. As soon as Lakhmichand saw the photograph he identified it as that of the sadhu whom he had seen in his dream! He sought more information about Baba. But he was a stranger to Shirdi and did not know whom to go with to have Baba's darshan.

But one day, around 8 p.m. Lakhmichand's friend Shankarrao came to his home and said: "Would you like to come with me to Shirdi? I was planning to go to Kedgaon, but now I have changed my mind. I would like to go to Shirdi."

It was as if his prayer had been heard. Lakhmichand borrowed fifteen rupees from his paternal cousin and started for Shirdi. On the way Shankarrao performed *bhajan*. They met a couple of Muslims with whom Lakhmichand made enquiries about Baba. Their replies goaded Lakhmichand yet more to see Baba. He wanted to buy some guavas at Kopargaon but in his excitement he forgot to do so. It was after they crossed the Godavari that he was reminded of his wish. But just then he saw an old woman with a basket on her head. He learnt that she was carrying guavas—just what he wanted. He picked the best of the lot and paid for them but when the old woman learnt that they were meant for Baba she cheerfully suggested that Lakhmichand take the remaining ones too and give them to Baba on her behalf.

When Lakhmichand arrived in Shirdi he went straight for Baba's darshan. Looking at Lakhmichand Baba said: "They perform *bhajan* on the way and then ask others about me! Why should they do that? They should see everything with their own eyes! That will show them whether their dream is true or false. Also, what was the necessity of coming to Shirdi on borrowed money? Is your desire satisfied now?"

Lakhmichand suddenly realised that Baba was speaking about him and his friend and about how he happened to come to Shirdi and what happened on the way.

When Lakhmichand visited Shirdi a second time, a thought crossed his mind that Nanasaheb Chandorkar and Kakasaheb Dikshit were old devotees and big wigs. If a garland were to be offered to Sai Baba through them, surely Baba would accept it. So, instead of personally seeking to garland Baba, Lakhmichand asked Chandorkar to do it for him. But Baba interrupted him and told Lakhmichand: "So *you* are not a big wig? Of course you are. Now come forward and garland me yourself and offer me *naivedya* etc." Poor Lakhmichand. How would he have known that Baba could read his mind?

Ramlal lived in Bombay. Sai Baba gave him darshan in his dream and asked him to come to Shirdi. Ramlal had never seen or heard of Baba before and wondered why he should be summoned to meet a fakir. The next day as Ramlal was walking along the road he saw a picture of a man resembling the person he had seen in his dream in a shop. Ramlal went in to inquire from the shopkeeper who the man was. The dream had been so vivid that Ramlal felt impelled to go to Shirdi on the strength of what the shopkeeper had told him about Sai Baba. He not only went to Shirdi but he stayed there till Baba's *nirvana* in 1918.

Sai Baba helped in ingenious ways those who wished to have his darshan. One such instance is that of Ganesh Gopal Mahajani of Samantwadi, Thane, who was keeping indifferent health and was debilitated. His pious mother desired that her son should have the darshan of a Mahatma like Sai Baba and Mahajani agreed with her. He had heard of Baba's fame. But he was a poor man, working as a clerk in Makanji Khatau Mills on a salary of Rs 15 a month which was about equal to what he would have to pay for going to Shirdi and returning. The spirit was willing, but the cost was prohibitive.

It turned out that a water pump in Shirdi went out of order and R.A. Tarkhad, the Manager of the Mills decided to send his engineer to Shirdi to have the pump repaired. Mrs Tarkhad also decided to go to Shirdi with the engineer. Mahajani came to know of it and he went to Dadar station to see off the engineer and Mrs Tarkhad and taking along with him a garland and some fruits to be presented to Baba.

Mr Tarkhad, too, had come to the station to see his wife off. When he saw Mahajani with a garland in his hands meant for Sai Baba, Mr Tarkhad told him: "Would you also like to go to Shirdi? I have an extra ticket here with me that was meant for a member of my family who can't make it. You are welcome to it!" Mahajani gladly accepted the kind offer and sent word to his mother that her cherished wish was about to be fulfilled thanks to the charity of his Manager. Mahajani was never to forget his visit to Shirdi and his *darshan* of Baba.

Even after Baba's *mahasamadhi* devotees often found that obstacles in their wish to visit Shirdi would mysteriously disappear. Anandrao Dolas of Kandivli had an experience of this kind, on 10 March 1952. He desired to be present for the Ramnavami Festival at Shirdi. So he asked for his head clerk's permission and applied for a month's leave in advance. As it turned out Anandrao's own assistant fell ill and his application for leave was turned down. But Anandrao was a determined man. He prayed to Baba to get his leave sanctioned and made it clear that he would rather resign than not be present at the Ramnavami festival at Shirdi. The resolve made, he went to his office the next day and asked the head clerk whether he would change his mind. "You can have your leave but make it short—just a fortnight!" was the answer. For Anandrao that was enough. His prayer had been answered.

Ramachandra Vithoba was a student devotee whose one desire was to go to Shirdi. He saw his friend Dattu, son of Bapusaheb Shirsathe preparing to go to Shirdi and felt sorry that he could not go himself because he did not have the money. His mother lived in Talegaon and there was no one around who could pay for his travel expenses. But a couple of days before Dattu was to leave, Ramachandra's mother unexpectedly came to town and realising that he wanted so desperately to get Baba's darshan agreed to give him the necessary money. It only strengthened Ramachandra's faith in Baba.

Bapusaheb Shirsathe, a devotee of Sai Baba desired that his whole family should go to Shirdi for Sai Baba's *samadhi darshan.* One of his sons who was a government official agreed to accompany him. However, the other son was a non-believer and flatly refused to accompany his parents. His father was pained but felt that Sai Baba would bring him round. The wife of the non-believer son was with her parents at Ahmednagar at that time. As the non-believer son was travelling to Ahmednagar he got down at the earlier station and was strolling on the platform when he saw, to his surprise that his wife was there! She had decided to go to Shirdi to be with her parents-in-law! So, willy-nilly he also went with her to Shirdi. The atmosphere there was to change him.

The nephew of Dr D.M. Mulky, a medical practitioner was being treated for osteomyelitis by the best surgeons of Bombay but without any effect. The boy's wound in the bone however was fully healed by the *udi* and—it is claimed—by the loving and merciful *drishti* (glance) of Sai Baba. Dr Mulky had himself vowed twice earlier when he was cured of two ailments but he had not kept them. Once he even went as far as Manmad to keep his vow but was dissuaded by an anti-Baba tirade from a booking clerk. He therefore decided to spend his remaining leave in Alibag. For three consecutive nights he heard in his dream the words: "Do you still have no faith in me?" That induced him to go over to Shirdi but he did not feel it right to leave a case of typhoid behind. Finally he said to himself that if the temperature of his patient came down that very day, he would start for Shirdi the next day. To his surprise the patient's fever came down the same afternoon and he left for Shirdi. He stayed in Shirdi for four days. On the last day he made his *pranaams* to Baba who gave him the information that when he reached home he would find on his table an order saying that he has been "transferred to Bijapur on promotion." And so it happened. That was to make Dr Mulky a confirmed believer in Baba. The story of how Sai Baba's great devotee Hari Sitaram Dikshit alias Kakasaheb Dikshit was inspired to go to Shirdi and how Baba facilitated his visit is both amusing and delightful. When Dikshit was in London, he tripped and impaired his foot while getting into a train. In 1909 Dikshit spent a few days in his bungalow at Lonavla when he chanced to meet a co-alumni Nanasaheb Chandorkar, at Elphinstone College, Bombay, after many years. They exchanged notes about the events in their lives during the intervening years. Then Nanasaheb asked Dikshit: "Do you really desire that you should be cured of your limp? If you do, come with me for my guru's darshan. He can not only take care of any physical ailment but can show you the true path to God."

Dikshit took Nanasaheb at his word. He obtained all the necessary information about Shirdi and when he visited Ahmednagar during his election campaign, he decided to go to Shirdi after the campaigning was over. He was staying with his friend

Sirdar Mirikar and wondered whether he or some one else could accompany him to Shirdi.

Meanwile, in Shirdi itself, Madhavrao Deshpande received a telegram saying that his mother-in-law was very ill in Ahmednagar. Madhavrao rushed to see the lady but to his immense relief found, on arrival, that she was greatly improving. But news of his coming to Ahmednagar reached Mirikar who felt that Madhavrao was the right man to take Dikshit to Shirdi. He got in touch with Madhavrao who readily agreed to be Dikshit's escort. The two left for Shirdi the same night by train. Madhavrao regaled Dikshit with tales of Baba's doings. The two hardly had a wink of sleep. Dikshit was quite thrilled and wanted to know more about Baba. Early in the morning they reached Kopergaon and who should they see there but Nanasaheb Chandorkar! Unknown to Dikshit, Chandorkar had also planned to come to Shirdi and this was a happy re-union!

Later, when Dikshit met Sai Baba, the latter said: "I sent Madhavrao to Ahmednagar knowing that you wanted to come!" You could have knocked down Dikshit then with a feather! He was to become a staunch devotee of Baba, built a *wada* in Shirdi and came in close contact with his guru. Eight years after the *nirvana* of Baba, Dikshit suddenly passed away while travelling in a Bombay suburban train singing the praises of Baba.

Joshi of Thane who could not go with his friends and family to Shirdi, vowed that unless he had Baba's *darshan* at home, he would not accept him. Joshi was to experience that, too! It happened thus: a Konkani gentleman went to have Baba's darshan. As he was taking leave, Baba told him: "Would you do something for me?" "Of course, I would!" the gentleman replied. Whereupon Baba gave him a packet of *udi* and told him: "Go by the Mail. And whoever asks you for an inch of space on the seat, give him this packet!" The gentleman thought this was a strange request.

He told Baba: "Your wish shall be fulfilled. But if I don't meet any such person on the train, I will let you know by post!"

The gentleman then left. He travelled by the Mail from Koper-gaon and till he arrived at Kalyan no passenger ever asked him to move a bit. He did not know then that the Mail would halt at Thane. Under the impression that nobody from there to Bombay would be getting in, let alone ask for an "inch of space" the gentleman was about to write a post-card to Baba when the train came to a halt at Thane. The compartment was now getting full. Just as the train was about to move, a man came panting in and noticing that the gentleman's child was sleeping next to him pleaded in an earnest voice: "Can you give me an inch of space to sit, please? I am feeling giddy!"

The Konkani gentleman picked up his child, held it in his lap and told the man: "Do please sit down!" He then handed over the packet of *udi* to the man and recounted Baba's instructions to him. He was overwhelmed. He accepted the *udi* with reverence as if Baba was giving him *darshan* in absentia.

In 1921 Raosaheb Y.J. Galwankar started with his family on a pilgrimage to Kashi and Prayag. After visiting many a holy shrine and bathing in holy *kunds* and rivers, he arrived at Prayag where he was taken to all the holy spots. At Bharadwaj Ashram, he was filled with a desire to have *darshan* of a holy person and silently prayed to Baba for it. He had told his guide that besides seeing holy spots, he was anxious to see holy persons as well. They had hardly left Bharadwaj Ashram when the guide stopped the *tonga* and pointing to a venerable man with a long beard, said: "This *mahatma* visits Prayag but rarely, may be once in many years. He is known widely for his saintli-ness. He does not allow people to approach him and does not accept money." Considering that he had only a few minutes ago prayed to Baba to give him a chance to meet a holy person, Galwankar thought meeting this holy man was a heaven-sent opportunity and the guide's protests notwithstand-ing he alighed from the *tonga* and approached the *mahatma*. But far from showing any annoyance the saintly figure wel-comed Galwankar with raised arm by way of blessings and said: "Come, child." Galwankar's mother, wife and other ladies in the party also approached the *mahatma* despite the guide's protest and were also blessed. Galwankar had barely three annas (18 paise) in his pocket which he now took out and offered to the saint. Much to the surprise of the guide, the *mahatma* accepted the coins with evident pleasure. Little did the guide know that Galwankar was a staunch devotee of Sai Baba, that Baba was in touch with saints everywhere through his astral body and fulfilled the good desires of his devotees.

In 1928 Justice M.B. Rege of the Indore High Court went to Dakshineshwar to see places and things of interest. He hired the services of a man to act as his cicerone. The cicerone showed him the idol of Kali that Shri Ramakrishna Parama-hansa worshipped. Rege took a long look at the idol but was also anxious to have a look at the tiny image of Ramlal that sported with the Paramahansa as a living boy and asked the guide to show it to him. The guide took him to one of the temples and pointing to a huge image, said: "This is Ramlal." Rege replied that it could not be but the guide said he should know: he was the local man and knew better than Rege who was a stranger to the town. Rege fell silent. Just at that juncture, a *pujari* happened to pass by and noticing Rege solicitously asked him whether he could be from the Deccan. Rege replied that he was. At that the *pujari* offered to show him round and provide him with all the necessary information in detail. Rege was reluctant to accept the *pujari's* services. But the latter insisted, saying that he was not expecting any monetary offering. He explained his persistence saying that he had been instructed in a dream the previous night that a devotee from Deccan would be coming the following day and he was to take him round all the temples and help him in worshipping the various gods. Assured, Rege accepted the *pujari's* help. The latter even permitted Rege to enter the *sanctum sanctora* in many temples and offer worship. At one point Rege said he had asked his previous guide to show him the image of Ramlal and he had been deceived. "I will show you the right one," replied the *pujari* and not only showed Rege the tiny idol but let him even handle it. Rege's wildest expec-tations had thus been fulfilled. Rege attributed it to the grace of

Sai Baba. Madhavrao Deshpande had an expectation of the fulfillment of his *sattvic* desire. Once Baba simultaneously received pressing invitations to the thread ceremony of Kakasaheb Dikshit's son and the marriage of the older son of Nanasaheb Chandorkar. Instead of attending the ceremonies personally Baba deputed Madhavrao Deshpande to attend the thread ceremony at Nagpur and the marriage at Gwalior. As Banaras was not far from Gwalior, Madhavrao planned on a pilgrimage to both Banaras and nearby Gaya. When he mentioned this to Baba, the latter said: "By all means go. I will make the pilgrimage to these places too but return ahead of you."

Madhavrao borrowed a hundred rupees and was on his way. On the road he met Appa Kote. On learning that Madhavrao was going to Banaras he immediately joined him though he had no money on him.

But matters were smoothed out. As presents Dikshit gave Madhavrao two hundred rupees and Chandorkar another hundred rupees. The father of Chandorkar's daughter-in-law also gave a present of yet another hundred rupees. Mr Jatar, the father-in-law also made arrangements for Madhavrao's stay in Banaras and in Ayodhya. Madhavrao spent two months and twenty one days in these two places and after visiting Prayag, proceeded to Gaya. In the train he heard there was an outbreak of plague in Gaya. The train reached Gaya at midnight. Madhavrao and Kote spent the night in a *dharamshala*. The following morning a *panda* who met them told them to hurry up as all the other pilgrims were on their way. Madhavrao asked him guardedly whether there was an epidemic of plague in his locality. The *panda* assured him that there was no plague whatsoever as they could see for themselves. The *panda* took Madhavrao and Kote to his spacious house and allotted them a room. They were pleased with this hospitality but what pleased them even more was the picture of Sai Baba on the wall. At the sight of that picture Madhavrao was so overcome that tears began to flow from his eyes. The *panda* thought that he was crying because of his fears of the plague and suggested that if

Madhavrao did not trust him, he could check with anyone else. "But please don't cry!" the *panda* said.

Madhavrao had to explain why he was in tears. It was seeing the picture of Sai Baba so unexpectedly he said that made him cry. But how come, he asked the *panda* that he had put Baba's picture on the wall?

"Oh," said the *panda,* "that is easily explained. You know, some twelve years ago, I had a paid contingent of a couple of hundred pilgrims from Manmad and Puntambe. From them I heard about Sai Baba and decided to go to Shirdi. I had Baba's *darshan.* It occurred to me that I should have a picture of Baba. I was inquiring about where to find one when I saw the kind of picture I wanted in someone's house. I asked whether I could have it and it was presented to me."

It was at this point that it suddenly struck Madhavrao that that "someone" was himself and that it was he who had presented the picture to the *panda.* Twelve years had passed and he had forgotten all about the incident!

When he revealed his identity to the *panda* it was now the latter's turn to be pleasantly shocked. Both were overjoyed and recounted the event. The *panda* remembered how hospitable Madhavrao had been and said he would like to repay it in some small measure. The *panda* was personally wealthy and maintained a stable of elephants. Now he summoned one and offered it to Madhavrao while he himself rode in a palanquin. The *panda* showed him around, led him to Vishnupad where he arranged for *puja* and *abhishek* to the deity and *pindadaan* (offering of rice balls to the manes of ancestors). None could have been happier that day than Madhavrao who attributed all the help he received to Sai Baba's *leela.*

The story of Shri Sai Vishwa Mandir in Tarkas Bhuvan on Relief Road in Kalupur area of Ahmedabad has similar overtones. Ramshankar Tripathi apprised his close friend Linubhai Sayyad of his personal experiences following a visit to Shirdi. Linubhai had similar experiences and the two of them felt that they should share their experiences with others. So in August 1948 they decided to form a Mandal. Initially the two would meet at a place and sing *bhajans*. About that time they heard of Sheth Ratilal Chimanlal Shah and his devotion to Baba. They called on him and told him about their hopes of setting up a Mandal. Sheth Ratilal suggested that they could use the third floor of his house for the purpose. And thus was the Sai Mandir in Tarkas Bhuvan formed where every Thursday there is a programme of *stavan* (songs in praise), *bhajan* and *swadhyaya* followed by *arati*. Since 1948 there has been a marked increase in the number of devotees so that the hall is kept open the whole day long. Now there are plans to shift the Mandal to a bigger building.

Vasantrao Vishnushastri Panashikar was an orthodox brahmin who did not believe in the omnipotence and oneness of Sai Baba with *Brahman*. He was opposed to the keeping of a photograph of Baba in the Vitthal Mandir at 129 Fanaswadi, Kalbadevi, Bombay, but that opposition was soon to melt away after he felt the power of Baba personally. That led him not only to establish Shri Sai Seva Sangh in Bombay but to donate *padukas* to those devotees wishing to worship them. One pair was ceremoniously taken to Ahmedabad from Bombay by train and at every station en route devotees came to honour them with *bhajans, puja* and *arati*.

Many devotees have had their wish-fulfilment, thanks to Baba's grace, even when they were physically separated from him and only he could know of their innermost thoughts. When Smt Krishnabai Prabhakar first came for Baba's *darshan,* he gave her a four-anna coin as a present. Krishnabai kept it in a casket and would worship it. One day Krishnabai gave away the coin inadvertently in order to purchase a coconut from a woman vendor. When she realised what had happened she became most unhappy and began to pray to Baba. In the evening what did she find but the woman vendor at the door saying: "Bai, you gave me a coin from your *puja*. I don't want to keep it.". Krishnabai was overjoyed and took back the coin but gave another one to the vendor instead.

Whenever anyone visited Shirdi it was Baba who decided when they should leave. Always he took their interests into consideration. When Wagle, a government servant went to Shirdi for Baba's *darshan,* he felt like extending his stay but was in two minds as his leave was due to expire. Baba realised it and told Wagle: "Why are you afraid? Have no anxiety. There is no need to worry."

On the fourth day Baba summoned Wagle and told him: "You can leave today."

Wagle returned to Bombay worried that his superiors may question him for extending his leave without permission. But nothing of that sort happened. It was as if nobody really cared.

The case of Kaka Mahajani was quite the opposite. He went to Shirdi with the clear desire of staying for a week and participating in the Gokulashtami festival. But the day he arrived in Shirdi and went for Baba's *darshan,* the latter asked: "When are you going back?"

Mahajani did not know what to say! But he managed to reply: "Whenever you ask me to." Baba said: "Leave tomorrow."

Mahajani left for Bombay the next day. When he reported for work he was told that the Managing Clerk had suddenly fallen ill and the senior partner of the firm had mailed a letter to him the previous day asking him to return from Shirdi immediately!

Baba's love was not limited to human beings but also extended to the animal world as well. A bull in Shirdi was dedicated to Lord Shiva and was allowed to roam about freely and graze on any land. It turned out to be a nuisance, entering fields and gardens and causing damage. The villagers therefore decided to have it sent to a *pinjrapole* at Yeola. The bull was entrusted to Bhiku Marwari along with the money and he took it away for being placed in a *pinjrapole.* Not long afterwards he returned and reported to the villagers that he had discharged the task assigned to him.

That very night Sai Baba appeared in a dream to Bayaji Appaji Patil and said: "Why are you sleeping? I have been tied at the door of a butcher." Bayaji woke up. The dream was so vivid that he decided to consult others in the village. They concluded that the bull could not possibly have been taken to the *pinjra-pole* but must have been taken over to a butcher. So Bayaji was asked to check on the whereabout of the bull. He went to Yeola and inquired of the two *pinjrapoles* there whether they had admitted a bull. The answer was No. Then Bayaji went round and looked for the bull at the butchers' quarters. He saw it and quickly recognized it. Inquiries revealed that Bhiku Marwari had sold the bull to a butcher for Rs. 14 and it was due to be butchered that very day. Bayaji got it released, and returned home. Bhiku Marwari was charged with cheating, was duly convicted—the evidence against him was overwhelming—and sentenced to two months' imprisonment. And rightly did he deserve it. But what comes through in this incident is Sai Baba's concern even for a bull.

Baba's concern for his devotees extended even to minor matters. Once Shankarrao Gavankar and Lala Lakhmichand of Bombay went to Shirdi for Baba's darshan. They were ascending the steps of the masjid only to find Baba in a terrible temper. Notwithstanding Baba's mood Shankarrao went up only to be ordered out. Feeling deeply hurt, Shankarrao and Lakhmichand left the masjid fully resolved not to return unless specifically called for by Baba. They had hardly gone two minutes when a message came to them that they were wanted by Baba.

The boss of Kaka Mahajani, Shri Dharamsey Thakkar went to Shirdi to pay his respects to Baba. Baba gave Thakkar a bunch of grapes which contained the usual seeds. Thakkar had a positive dislike for such grapes but out of respect for Sai Baba he quietly ate them, spitting out the seeds into his palm without Baba's knowledge. Baba, however, knew of it through his inner eye and he offered Thakkar another bunch of grapes from the same lot which turned out to be seedless. Baba had thus given to Thakkar an experience of his power and inner knowledge.

A tailor in Shirdi named Martand was very sick. There was no one at his home to take care of him. He suffered quietly with no help from anyone. One day he was seen lying on the roadside as Sai Baba was passing by. Noticing him Baba told Martand who was quite conscious that he should go to Nanasaheb Dengle of Nimgaon where he would be taken care of. So Martand managed to go to Nimgaon to see Dengle who turned out to be very considerate. He told Martand: "Consider this as your own house and stay here. Yesterday night Sai Baba appeared to me in a dream and asked me to take care of you. Don't worry." Martand was deeply touched by this spontaneous burst of hospitality and stayed on in Dengle's house until he got well. He received all the necessary nursing during his long illness.

Baba barely left the limits of Shirdi. If at all he did so it was to go to Nimgaon and Rahata. Khushalchand Seth of Rahata was a devotee of his. Once Sai Baba felt like meeting Khushalchand Seth whom he had not seen for some time and said to Kakasaheb Dikshit: "Take a tonga to Rahata and tell Khushalchand Seth that it is many days since he met me and ask him to call on me." Dikshit went by a tonga to Rahata and met Khushalchand even as he was getting up from his after-noon nap. Kushalchand said: "Just before you came he gave me *darshan* in my dream and also the message which you have brought from him. I wish very much to come to Shirdi but my son has gone out with the cart."

Dikshit told him that Baba was aware of that and that's why he had sent a tonga to fetch Khushalchand. Not at all surprised, Khushalchand readily accompanied Dikshit to Shirdi and had a happy chat with Baba.

Sai Baba made no distinction between one devotee and another and should one think that he was being looked after less favourably Baba would endeavour to set right the balance. Baba would always say that in his durbar there was no differen-tiation between one devotee and another. R.V. Modak and Prof. G.G. Naike had an experience of this. Seeing Sai Baba smoke a chillum given him by Narke, Modak felt that he should receive a chillum of Sai Baba's at his own hands so that he could keep it in his daily *puja.* The following day when Modak went to the masjid for *darshan,* Sai Baba asked Madhavrao to give two chillums to Modak. Similarly, once when Prof. Narke was in Shirdi, he saw another devotee being entrusted by Sai Baba with the task of collecting noon *bhiksha.* Narke felt that he was not as advanced as the other devotee and possibly that could be the reason why he was not entrusted with that honour. One can well imagine his surprise, then, when the following day the task of collecting the noon *bhiksha* was allotted to him by Baba. Baba had read his mind. More, Baba was telling him that he was not loved any the less.

Every devotee felt that he was dearest to Sai Baba. Once, Mr M.B. Rege, Judge of the Indore High Court decided to visit Shirdi during the time of Ramnavami and to present Baba with a costly gift. He purchased for Rs 85 a fine lace-embroidered muslin of Dacca type, produced at Chander which could be neatly folded into a 6" × 6" × 1" packet and made up his mind that if Sai Baba indeed cared for his love, he should not return the same to him but should retain and wear it.

Normally, each devotee went and presented his cloth openly to Sai Baba which was placed on him and then attendants would take it off and return the same to the person who made the gift. When Rege bowed to Sai Baba, he shoved the tiny packet under Baba's mattress. None noticed what was beneath the mattress (*gadi*). When Baba got up he said: "Clear off all that lies on the *gadi* and dust it". When, however, the *gadi* was removed, attendants found that there was a small packet underneath. Baba picked it up and said: "I am not going to return this. It is mine!" He then wrapped the embroidered muslin round his shoulders and pointedly remarked to Rege: "Don't I look nice in this?" Rege considered himself blessed.

That was not the first occasion Baba had shown his affection for Rege. Three years earlier, Rege had come to Shirdi for *guru purnima day.* On his way at Manmad he saw local devotees each having a basket of flower garlands. He was pained at the thought that he had never thought of also getting garlands for his guru. When they reached Shirdi all the devotees except Rege garlanded Baba who admitted sadly that he had no garland to offer, whereupon Baba lifted all the garlands round his neck and offered them to Rege saying: "All these are yours."

The Honorary Magistrate of Harda in Madhya Pradesh, Krishnarao Narayan Paralkar would feed every year a hundred brahmins in remembrance of Lord Dattatreya. If, for any reason, he could not feed a hundred brahmins in any one year he would feed two hundred the next year. In accordance with this practice he decided, in 1925 to feed two hundred brahmins. The decision was taken on a Monday and the actual feeding was to take place on a Saturday. On Tuesday, around 5 a.m. while he was performing *bhajan*, Paralkar heard an inner voice that said: "If you feel that I should participate in the meal on Saturday, invite Kakasaheb Dikshit."

Paralkar was in two minds. He knew that the voice belonged to Sai Baba. But Dikshit was living in Bombay. Would it be proper for him to summon Dikshit all the way from Bombay just to have a meal? While he was thus hesitating came the clear answer at *puja* time: "Why are you confused? Write a letter to Kakasaheb Dikshit and feed him along with the brahmins and thus know that you have fed me!"

Unquestioningly, Paralkar wrote a letter to Dikshit. Dawned the Saturday but there was neither any letter from Dikshit nor had he arrived. So Paralkar with tears in his eyes approached Sai Baba's photograph and prayed to him; having done that he had a bath and sat down for his *sandhya*. Just then a telegram was received from Dikshit saying that he was arriving with Madhavrao Deshpande. Paralkar was overjoyed. He went along with his friends to the station to receive the honoured guests. Dinner that evening, served to two hundred brahmins and two associates was something to be savoured. Everyone knew that Baba was present among them.

CHAPTER 8

NANA IS IN TROUBLE

By doing *keertan* with loving devotion, the devotee experiences that the Lord manifests Himself.

— *Naradasutra*

Our religious scriptures tell us how the Lord came to the rescue of his devotees in their time of distress. He honoured the *hundi* of Narsi Mehta, to Eknath He came in the form of a servitor, for the sake of Damaji, he became Vithu Mahar. He helped Janabai in grinding, pounding and other jobs. He rescued Draupadi from dishonour as Dushyasana tried to disrobe her. Many are such stories, to prove that the Lord is the devotee of His devotee.

And so it has been with Sai Baba. For the sake of Nanasaheb Chandorkar Sai Baba once assumed the form of a wood-gatherer, another time that of a *mahar* and yet another time that of an office peon.

During the first incident Nanasaheb Chandorkar who was in Ahmednagar district in the summer season had started for the fair held on Mount Harishchandra along with his office crowd. By the time he had climbed half the 'distance it was noon. Nanasaheb's throat was parched; the afternoon sun was harsh and Nanasaheb found himself panting. His companions looked for water near about but none was to be had. Nanasaheb was therefore advised to climb slowly with frequent pauses for rest in order not to fatigue himself. Nanasaheb, however, felt very weak and in no condition to do any further climbing. He wished that Sai Baba was there.

Somewhat annoyed, his companions said: "Nana, Sai Baba is not here, so get on steadily with patience and grit." Nanasaheb, however, gave no heed to them and would not budge an inch.

Meanwhile, back in Shirdi Sai Baba remarked to Madhavrao

Deshpande who was sitting next to him: "Nana is in trouble."
At the same time Nanasaheb noticed a bhil carrying a load of
wood on his head and asked him where he could get some
water to drink. The bhil casually replied: "Just below the rock
you are now sitting on. There's the water!" When the rock was
lifted, clear water sprouted. Nanasaheb had his fill and slaked
his thirst and went ahead, considerably refreshed, as if nothing
happened. After some days when Nanasaheb went to Shirdi,
Madhavrao asked him: "Were you in some trouble on such and
such a date?"

"Why?" Nanasaheb asked.

Madhavrao then narrated what Sai Baba had told him that day
at Shirdi. It was then that Nanasaheb realised that the bhil
whom he met was surely Baba.

The second incident took place when Nanasaheb went from
Shirdi to Kopergaon during an eclipse to have a dip in the
Godavari. As soon as the eclipse commenced a mahar came
shouting: *"de daan sute grahan"* (give in charity and the
eclipse will pass off). Nanasaheb gave him four annas. At that
very moment showing a four anna coin to a devotee sitting by
him in Shirdi, Sai Baba said: "See, I have brought these four
annas from Nana!" After Nanasaheb returned to Shirdi when
asked how much he had given in charity for the eclipse, he said
that he had given four annas to a mahar! When Baba's
comment that day to a devotee was relayed to him, he knew it
was Baba who had come in the guise of a mahar.

The third incident occurred when Nanasaheb was a Mamlatdar
at Jamner. His daughter Minatai had severe labour pains as the
time of delivery was drawing near. So Chandorkar family
prayed to Sai Baba for smooth and safe delivery. No one in
Shirdi knew anything about this except Sai Baba who through
his inner vision was aware of Minatai's pain. The passionate
cry for help from a devotee reached the Lord without delay.

While all this was happening, in Jamner, Ramgirbua in Shirdi
felt an intense desire to visit his place in Khandesh. So he
approached Sai Baba for permission to go. Sai Baba addressing him by his pet name, said: "Bapurgir, do you wish to go?

Do go, but rest for a while and then proceed. First go to Jamner. Halt at Nana's place, meet him and then go further."

To Madhavrao Deshpande, Baba said: "Copy out the *arati* of Adkar for Nana." Then, handing over a packet of *udi* to Ramgirbua he said: "Give this packet and the text of the *arati* to Nana."

Ramgirbua said to him: "I have only two rupees with me. How can I go to Jamner with just this amount?"

Sai Baba replied: "Go with your mind at ease. Everything will be provided."

With faith in Sai Baba's words Ramgirbua left. In those days there was no railway connection right up to Jamner. Alighting at Jalgaon the journey onwards had to be made by other transport. Ramgirbua purchased a ticket up to Jalgaon. The fare was Rs. 1-14-0. He reached Jalgaon by 2-45 am. He had now only two annas in his pocket. So with an anxious mind he walked out of the station when he saw at a distance a robust man with a beard and whiskers and dressed in breeches and a buttoned-up tunic. He wore a turban and had boots on. The man approached Ramgirbua and asked: "Who is Bapugir of Shirdi?" Ramgirbua advanced and said: "Why, I am Bapugir of Shirdi. What do you want from me at this hour of the night?"

Replied the be-turbanned man: "Chandorkar saheb has sent me with a tonga. Please get into it and let us go!"

Ramgirbua felt tremendously relieved. The tonga sped along merrily. At the break of dawn the tonga stopped at Baghoor, near a stream. Unyoking the horse, the driver took the horse to the water. Then he brought water for both himself and Ramgirbua to drink and spreading out a repast of mangoes, *gulpapadi* (a variety of cake made with *gur*) and *pedhas* before Ramgirbua, invited the latter to have his breakfast. Ramgirbua was suspicious about the driver's caste. Sensing his distrust the driver told him: "Sir, I am not a Muslim. I am a garhwali Rajput. There can be no objection to sharing food with me. Moreover, these refreshments are sent by Nanasaheb for you."

Relieved, Ramgirbua shared his morning meal with the driver

and soon after they were once again on the road to Jamner. When they reached Jamner, and within sight of Nanasaheb's kacheri (office) Ramgirbua alighted to relieve himself. When he returned and looked around for the tonga—he found that the tonga, the horse and the driver had all disappeared in thin air. It was unbelievable.

Quite surprised, Ramgirbua walked up to the kacheri and learning that Nanasaheb was at home, went to his residence and sat on the verandah. When the news of his unexpected arrival reached Nanasaheb he hurriedly came out to welcome his guest. Ramgirbua handed over to Nanasaheb the text of the arati and the packet of udi given by Baba. At that moment Nanasaheb's daughter was in insufferable pains and navachandihavan was being performed and Saptashati was being recited. Nanasaheb called his wife and gave her the udi to be immediately given to Minatai and meanwhile Nanasaheb himself started reciting the arati sent by Sai Baba. At that moment came a message from the delivery room that as soon as the udi was given Minatai had safely delivered a child. Nanasaheb felt a great sense of relief and turned to Ramgirbua who said: "Just to satisfy my curiosity, where is the tonga driver? And where is the tonga?"

Nanasaheb did not understand what Ramgirbua was talking about. Tonga driver? Tonga? What was he talking about? Said Nanasaheb, "Which tonga? How was I to know that you were coming, for me to send a tonga to fetch you? I did not send any tonga for you!" Listening to this, Ramgirbua was astonished and narrated to Nanasaheb the full story of his travel right from the start. Nanasaheb too was agape with wonder and realised that it was all the work of the Master.

For the wife of Ramachandra Atmaram Tarkhad Sai Baba assumed the forms of a hungry dog and pig. Eating the food offered by Mrs. Tarkhad, he expressed satisfaction and stressed the duty of a devotee to offer food to a guest, whether it be a human being or any creature, animal or bird, present.

It so happened once at Shirdi that it was mealtime and food was being served in thalis. A dog was hovering around and

Mrs. R. A. Tarkhad gave it a *bhakri* to eat. Just then a hungry pig came grunting and Mrs. Tarkhad served a *bhakri* to that beast too. She fed the animals without having any second thoughts. The act came to her naturally. In the afternoon when she went for Sai Baba's *darshan* he said to her: "Mother, you fed me today and I was filled. I was hungry and you satisfied my hunger. Always act thus. This is the way to practice kindness. Give food to the hungry and all will be well. Rembember this to your very end."

Mrs. Tarkhad did not quite understand what Baba was talking about. He had not come to her home and she had certainly not fed him. So she said: "How could I have given you any food? I am a dependant woman in Shirdi and eat whatever I get on payment of money!"

Baba replied: "You served me *bhakri* with love. When you sat down for your meal, a dog suddenly appeared before you and you fed it. Then came a dirty pig all covered with mud. You fed it, too. I am one with both of them. In as much as you fed them, you fed me!" This very truth Sai Baba taught Lakshmibai Shinde, in his inimitable way. After his evening prayer Sai Baba was once standing facing south, in the direction of the Marwadi's house and shop. There were several other devotees with him. In the meantime, Lakshmibai Shinde came and bowed to Baba. Baba said to her: "I am hungry." Lakshmibai replied: "In that case I will make a *bhakri* for you and bring it. I shall be back soon."

She returned home, quickly made the *bhakris* and returned to the masjid along with a side dish. She served the simple fare on a leaf-plate and placed it before Baba. Baba quickly took the plate and placed it before a dog hovering in the background. Lakshmibai was naturally upset. "Baba," she said, "what is this you have done? I went post-haste to make *bhakris* for you to eat but now you have given them to a dog! I thought you said *you* were hungry! What kind of hunger is this? You did not taste even a bit of what I brought you! I fretted for nothing!"

Baba looked at her and said: "Why grieve for nothing? Know that when you feed a hungry dog, you feed me. All living

232

creatures are alike in hunger. Therefore those who feed the hungry, whether man or beast, in fact feed me!"

Sai Baba looked not only after the material well-being of a devotee but also his spiritual welfare. One morning Sai Baba told Mrs. Jog: "Tai, a she-buffalo will come to your backdoor in the afternoon. Feed her well with *puranpolis* with ghee applied to them."

Mrs. Jog faithfully prepared *puranpolis*, offered *naivedya* to Sai Baba and in the afternoon noticed a she-buffalo standing at her backdoor as predicted by Sai Baba. Mrs. Jog was at first happy that the animal consumed *puranpolis* to her heart's content but was upset when in a short time the buffalo sat down, was indisposed and died on the spot! Frightened, she examined all the vessels used for cooking, including the one in which *puran* was cooked to see whether any extraneous material had fallen into them. She noticed nothing of the kind. She was thoroughly fazed. If the buffalo had died as a result of being overfed, the sin of its death would be on her head. From a strictly mundane point of view, if the owner of the buffalo came to know that it had died after being fed on *puranpolis,* he could hold Mrs. Jog responsible for the death of the animal. The protector of devotees is ultimately the Lord. So she took refuge in Sai Baba and apprising him of the facts admitted that she was disconcerted. Baba assured her that there was no reason to worry. He said: "The owner cannot harass you. Spiritually you have committed no wrong. There was only one desire left in the buffalo; to eat *puranpolis.* I satisfied its desire, working through you. The she-baffalo will now be released from its *yoni* (class or nature) and will be born again and merit a good birth. There is no need for any anxiety on your part."

It was a revelation to Mrs. Jog and an insight into Baba's way of functioning. Sai Baba once assumed the form of a black dog for Bala Shimpi as well as Mhalsapati, ate rice at their hands and cured them of chronic fever. There is the case of Hansraj who suffered from asthma. In order to prevent him from eating curds, Baba took the form of a cat and lapped up the curds in the kitchen. Hansraj, noticing the cat lapping a whole bowlful of curds gave it a couple of resounding blows. Baba was to show the marks on his body to his devotees.

While Upasanibua was staying in the Khandoba Temple, for accepting the *naivedya* Sai Baba assumed the form of a dog but Upasani shooed him away Sai Baba later brought this incident to the notice of Upasani.

The son of Ramchandra Atmaram Tarkhad was a sincere devotee of Sai Baba. Once his mother wished to go to Shirdi and the son wanted to accompany her. There was, however, an impediment in his way. He worshipped and offered *naivedya* to a photograph of Baba regularly. Who would do the *puja* and offer *naivedya* in his absence? The father undertook the responsibility. Relieved, the son went with his mother to Shirdi and stayed there for some days. One day, when mother and son went for Baba's *darshan,* he said to them: "I had been to Bandra today as I do every day, but I got nothing to eat or drink and had to return hungry. The door was closed, yet I entered freely. Who was to stop me? The owner was not at home. I had to suffer the pangs of hunger as I was not fed. I had to turn back in the heat of the sun."

The son at once realised that his father must have forgotten to offer *naivedya* to Baba's photograph. He immediately wrote to his father and learnt that on the day Baba said he had been to Bandra, the father had indeed forgotten to offer worship and *naivedya.* to Baba's photograph. What Baba had done was to gently remind the family that it should not be remiss in remembering him for whatever reason.

Sai Baba also assumed form not only to counsel his devotees but also to gladden their hearts. In 1918 Gulveshastri went to Shirdi for Sai Baba's *darshan*. He brought *Gangajal* and performed *abhishek* to Sai Baba with it. Then he asked Baba's permission to leave for Sajjangad to attend to Ramnavami celebrations. Baba told him: "But I am there as well as here!" Gulveshastri proceeded to Sajjangad but to his surprise he found Baba was there too! Promptly, Gulveshastri performed *charan-seva* whereupon Baba vanished!

Similarly, when Damodar Ghanashyam Babre, alias Anna Chinchnikar had come to stay in Shirdi and his wife was alone at her home she had cause to be alarmed and frightened because of the outbreak of plague. Baba appeared to her several times to assure her that all would be well.

Once, when R. B. Purandare's wife was unwell, Sai Baba appeared before her, gave her *darshan,* applied *udi* to her forehead and saved her. On the day of *Vastu Shanti* (house-warming) when Purandare started home with Baba's photograph, it was as if Baba himself was accompanying him, such was the exhilarating feeling he gave to Purandare. Again—and no matter how impossible all this may seem—when Purandare's mother and wife felt an intense desire to go to Pandharpur for the *darshan* of Vithoba-Rakhumai, Baba made that *darshan* possible in Shirdi itself. A case of hallucination? Hardly.

The mother of Shankarrao, a friend of Shantaram Balwant Nachane was a devotee of Vithoba of Pandharpur. She went to Shirdi and for some reason found that she could not proceed to Pandharpur. But the *udi* given to her at Shirdi turned into *abir* (fragrant powder composed of sandal, zedoary, cyperus, rotundus etc) and she felt that Shirdi was Pandharpur, no less.

Police sub-inspector Somnath Shankar Deshpande, son of Nanasaheb Nimonkar, once stayed in Shirdi in the absence of his father to serve Baba. It is said that while Madhavrao Deshpande was sitting on a step of the masjid and Sai Baba was seated in his usual place, Sai Baba suddenly appeared to Somnath in the form of Maruti! On another occasion Baba appeared before Adam Dalili of Bandra as a brahmin and asked for a favour. Dalili gave the brahmin two annas and sent him away. On another occasion still, unbeknownest to Dalili, Baba came as a Marwadi, claiming he was hungry. This time Dalili gave him four annas and suggested he go to a hotel and buy himself a lunch. Next time Dalili went to Shirdi, Baba pointed him out to his disciples and said: "When I went to see this man, he sent me to the Marwadi hotel to eat!" Dalili might well be forgiven if he felt thoroughly flabbergasted!

A devotee, one Haribhau Keshav Karnik while travelling from Shirdi to Pandharpur, learnt that the Passenger train ticket will have to be exchanged for a Mail ticket and the difference paid before he could travel by the latter. There was no time and he felt an urge, besides, to empty himself. What was he to do? The call of nature was urgent but a ticket had to be bought and the train was due any time. At that moment, he later reported, a hamal came to him, suggested he go to the toilet while he would look after the luggage. Even as he got out, the train steamed in and once again Karnik found himself in a quandary. But the hamal was right there to help him out. "Get into the train first and I'll get you your ticket," he said. And he was true to his word. But by the time Karnik could open his purse to pay the hamal, the latter had disappeared!

Shrikrishna Purshottam Patil of Andheri had gone to Akkalkot via Shirdi. On his return journey he decided to halt at Poona as he fell short of money. He was planning to call on a friend to borrow some cash when a brahmin joined him in his compartment. During the course of conversation Patil mentioned his dilemma whereupon the brahmin told him: "Is that all your problem? Don't worry. You need not disembark. I will fetch you your ticket. You can send me the amount by money order when you reach Bombay." So the brahmin alighted when the train steamed into Poona station and duly bought a ticket and handed it over to Patil. Then he said: "I guess I will go now and get myself a cup of tea!" He left—never again to be seen! It sounds odd, but devotees were frequently helped in similar small ways when such help was least expected. A reluctant ferryman refusing to take a family across a river suddenly makes a volte face when a *fakir* appears out of nowhere and promises to look up the ferry authorities to help the ferryman change his mind. A devotee on a pilgrimage to Girnar faints and has to be revived when a Gosain comes out of the blue with a lota of water and revives the man—and then disappears! When this man, Uddhavesh was on a visit to Shirdi, Baba teasingly asked him: "Didn't I once give you some water to drink?"

Rao Bahadur Moreshwar Pradhan had been to Shirdi and

invited Baba for a special lunch. "Very well, I'll come. Prepare *naivedya* for me," he promised. So the *naivedya* was prepared. The *thalis* were set, beginning with one for Baba. *Puranpolis* were served as was customary. And everyone was waiting for Baba who still had not come. Just then in flew a crow, picked a *puranpoli* from the *thali* set for Baba and just as quickly flew out. Pradhan understood.

On one occasion Baba thrice warned a devotee that the latter's son needed urgent medical attention for an ailment least suspected, through impersonal communication. The warning was ignored the first time. It was repeated. Again it was ignored. But the third warning could not just be brushed aside. A surgeon was summoned who discovered that a mass of puss had formed in the patient's body. It had to be drained and all was well.

Govind Raghunath alias Annasaheb Dabholkar, author of Shri Sai Satcharit once had a dream in which Baba appeared in the garb of a *sanyasi* and promised to come to his home for lunch the next day. Dabholkar acted on the dream seriously. The next day happened to be Holi and Dabholkar invited a few of his relatives and friends for the afternoon meal. He also told his wife to set apart a plate for Baba expecting the latter to arrive as promised in the dream. The *puja* over, *thalis* were laid out as usual for the guests, but there was no sign of Baba! Since the guests could not be kept waiting, Dabholkar reluctantly closed the door and invited the assembled guests to take their food. But even before he could put a morsel in his mouth, there was a knock on the door. Dabholkar heard a voice saying: "Is Raosaheb in?" When Dabholkar opened the door he found two friends of his waiting outside who, however, quickly apologised for intruding at lunch time, but merely said: "Would you mind keeping this for us?" "This" turned out to be an image of Baba!

Both the friends were Muslims. One was Ali Mohammad and another was Ismu Mujavar, *shagird* of Saint Maulana. And how did they chance to get a Baba image? The story was to be recounted to Dabholkar almost nine years after the actual incident took place. Ali Mohammad, it seemed, had purchased the image from a shop out of his great devotion for Baba. One day he fell ill and was being nursed by his brother-in-law. The *murshid* of his brother-in-law was one Abdul Rehman who had no use for any images, not even one of Baba. In his zeal, the brother-in-law had pictures of all the saints that he saw in Ali Mohammad's home removed and thrown into the sea.

In due course, Ali Mohammad recovered and returned to his own home not expecting to see any image but to his immense surprise, even as he opened the front door he noticed Baba's image on the wall opposite! Worried that if his brother-in-law chanced to see it this image too would meet the fate of other pictures, Ali quickly hid Baba's image in his cupboard, but he wanted some one to take charge of it. He thought of Dabholkar and acting on an impulse he brought it to Dabholkar, as it turned out, at a most psychological moment! But Baba had kept *his* word to his devotee. And saved another from embarrass- ment and hurt!

Sai Baba gave Appa Kulkarni an experience of how holy persons strive day and night for their devotees. In 1917, at the fag end of the First World War, government officials were still touring the countryside to recruit soldiers. At that time Kulkarni was transferred to take charge of recruitment. Balasaheb Bhate, a former Mamledar who had retired prematurely from service and settled down in Shirdi had given a photograph of Baba to Kulkarni which he worshipped daily. While he was posted at Thane, Kulkarni felt an intense desire to go to Shirdi for Baba's·darshan but it was impossible for him to get the necessary leave. Baba came to know of this without having to be told. Kulkarni had set off to Bhiwandi to camp there for eight days, but within two days a strange thing happened at Kulkarni's residence in Thane. A fakir who resembled Baba came to his doorstep. The inmates politely asked the fakir whether by any chance he was Sai Baba. "Oh no," said the fakir, "I am not he. But I have come by his order to inquire whether all is well with his family."

Thereupon the fakir asked for *dakshina*. Kulkarni's wife

respectfully offered him a rupee which the fakir accepted. In return he gave her a packet of Sai Baba's *udi* advising her to keep it along with Baba's picture. "May God bless you. I will now have to go. Baba will be waiting for me," he added in parting.

Meanwhile Kulkarni who had planned at Bhiwandi to go further into the interior of the countryside had to cancel his programme as his horse was unwell. He therefore decided to return home to Thane. When, on arrival, he learnt that a fakir resembling Baba had visited his home earlier in the day and that he had missed his *darshan,* he was upset. He was even more upset when he learnt that as *dakshnia* his wife had given the fakir only one rupee. With a heavy heart he went out in search of the fakir. He looked in at the local masjids and *takias* but to no avail. Disappointed, he returned home had his meal and later set out for a walk. Suddenly he saw a man approaching him who looked like the fakir. Kulkarni stopped. The fakir approached him with his arm stretched, and Kulkarni gave him a rupee. He just had three rupees and the fakir wanted more. Kulkarni gave all he had plus another three rupees that his friend had with him. The fakir still wasn't satisfied. He wanted more and Kulkarni agreed to give more if the fakir accompanied him to his home. The fakir agreed. On returning home Kulkarni offered the fakir another three rupees, but to Kulkarni's surprise, the fakir wasn't satisfied. "I have just one ten rupee note with me and no change," Kulkarni said sadly. "Never mind, give it to me!" said the fakir. Kulkarni promptly parted with that. At this point the fakir did a surprising thing. To Kulkarni he returned nine rupees and left without more ado! In his own mind Kulkarni had decided that he would give the fakir ten rupees. It seemed to Kulkarni that Baba had, in his own way, given him an opportunity to fulfil his desire without needlessly depriving him of money. Besides, Kulkarni was sure this way Baba had given him *darshan.*

For his devotee Balkrishna Vishwanath Dev, Mamledar of Dahanu Sai Baba assumed the form of trinity. It so happened that Dev had proposed to invite a couple of nundred brahmins to a feast to observe the concluding ceremony of certain religious rites that his mother was performing. Dev also sent a respectful invitation to Baba enclosing it in a letter to Bapusaheb Jog. Sai Baba told Jog: "I always remember him who thinks of me constantly. I do not require any vehicle for my travels. The moment a devotee calls out to me lovingly my response is instantaneous. So write and tell Dev that I will be coming along with you and a third person."

When Dev received the reply, he was beside himself with joy. It so happened that a month prior to the day fixed by Dev for the proposed feast, a Bengali *goshala* activist sanyasi visited Dahanu and the station master suggested to him that perhaps he might profit by calling on Mamledar Dev. As luck would have it at that very moment Dev happened to drop by at the station and was introduced to the sanyasi. Dev told the sanyasi that perhaps if he could return in another three to four months' time, he could help raise some funds.

Dev then put this behind his mind as he had other things to occupy himself. The day for the feast dawned, in the meanwhile as he was busying himself with the ceremonies he saw to his surprise that the sanyasi had arrived at his doorsteps well ahead of time. Dev was momentarily annoyed as he was not prepared to receive the sanyasi at that point. The sanyasi noted it and said: "Don't worry, I haven't come to talk to you about money. Today I only want to have a meal at your home." "Treat this home as your own," Dev told him. "But I am accompanied by two youngsters," the sanyasi countered.

"No problem," said Dev. "There is time yet for the meals to be served. Tell me where you are putting up and I'll send for you."

The sanyasi replied: "You don't have to send for me. Just tell me when I should come, and we'll be back!"

It was agreed that the sanyasi and the two boys with him should return at 12 noon. So they did and were served and ate heartily indeed. The feast over, the guests, as was the custom, were served with *paan, attar* (perfume) and *gulab pani* (rose water) after which they left. So did the sanyasi and his companions.

After all of them had gone it occured to Dev that the three he had expected, namely Sai Baba, Jog and someone else, had not turned up. Heavy of heart, Dev wrote to Jog saying that he had been deceived. Why had not Baba kept his word?

But even before Jog could read out Dev's letter to Baba, the latter exclaimed: "Ask Dev why he invited me if he could not even recognise me? What a chap! When I present myself before him he is afraid I have come to ask for money. I tell him that I have just come for a meal with two companions which is what I had promised him, and that is what I did. Shouldn't he have known?"

Jog wrote back to Dev telling him precisely what Baba had said. The letter brought tears of joy to Dev's eyes. "It is all Baba's *leela*," he consoled himself.

Baba's care extended even to the children of dead devotees. That was the experience of Shripad Balkrishna alias Baburao Dev. On 31 December 1951, Dev fainted, fell down and sustained an injury and was hospitalised for many days. As a patient in hospital he was visited by his friend Shantaram to whom he casually remarked: "If only I were as fortunate as the daughter of Nanasaheb Chandorkar to whom Baba sent *udi* in 1905!"

Shantaram replied: "Your father was a staunch devotee of Sai Baba and you are a dutiful son. Why won't Baba send you *udi* from Shirdi?"

Next day Shankarrao Lathore, a friend of Dev, called on him at the hospital saying: "You know I was in Shirdi only yesterday. I chanced to tell Vithalrao of your accident and he immediately gave me *udi* and prasad and said they were meant specially for you. Here, take them!" At once Dev was reminded of his casual conversation with Shantaram and he realised that though thirty three years had passed since Baba took his *samadhi* he was always a living force concerned about the well-being of his devotees for ever!

Baba always used to say: "Though the spirit may depart from my earthly tabernacle, know this for certain that my bones will assure you from my *samadhi* and not only I, but my *samadhi* will speak to you. It will communicate with whosoever takes refuge in it." Baba's devotees experience the truth of that remark to this day. Baba told Jog twenty four hours before he took *samadhi:* "I haven't shown you anything. Out of my three and a half *kalas,* I haven't shown you even a fourth thereof. However, people will know me and experience me hereafter." Jog then interpreted it to mean that Baba intended to make his mighty powers felt by his devotees even after his *samadhi.* Later he was to come to know that what Baba was suggesting was that he would become one with OM.

Seth Ratilal Chimanlal, a resident of Ahmedabad, had an amazing experience of Baba's powers. The incident took place on 22 May 1948. Seth Ratilal had boarded the Madras Mail at Adoni at 10 a.m. for Ahmedabad.' He was travelling second class and his co-passengers included Jagdish Munshi, solicitor son of K.M. Munshi and his wife, one Naidu, an Agent of Central Bank and Gopalrao, a well-known cotton merchant and chairman of the Cotton Marketing Committee.

They were a pleasant group and spent their time playing cards and chatting. The Mail was passing through Nizam's territory and reached Gulbarga. Suddenly, without any overt cause, Ratilal became uneasy in his mind. The country was then passing through the trauma of partition and Ratilal was aware that Nizam's Dominion had become a hot bed and centre of intrigue and militant activity. Ratilal was seized with anxiety. He tried to make his companions aware of his fears, but they laughed him off.

Ratilal, however, was not easily put off. He stopped all light-hearted banter and started repeating the name of Sai Baba. Some thirty minutes passed and the train neared Gangapur station. Then it happened.

An armed gang jumped into the train and started looting the passengers in right earnest. At that point all that they could do was to join Ratilal in his *namasmaran.* Out of nowhere it seemed, a burly pathan materialised and stood in front of Ratilal's compartment and no raider dared challenge him! Off went the Razakars who were members of the raiding party and the train limped into Solapur where those who lost their property recorded their complaints. It turned out that of all the compartments, only Ratilal's had been spared by the raiders, but no one knew what happened to the Pathan.

Balkrishna Mankar was employed as the head of a department in Makanji Khatau Cotton Textile Mills and was earning a substantial salary. After his wife expired, he retired from worldly interests and settled down in Shirdi. On Baba's instructions he went off to stay by himself at Machhindragad for doing penance with ten rupees that Baba had given him. Mankar was reluctant to leave Shirdi as he thought he would be deprived of Baba's darshan as well as company but Baba told him that his departure was for his own good.

In Macchindragad Baba gave him *darshan* when Mankar was wide awake and knew that this was no dream. Mankar asked Baba: "Why did you have to send me so far away?" To which Baba replied: "Your mind was restless while you were in Shirdi. I wanted to steady your mind. So I sent you away. It was your belief then that my existence was confined to the three and a half cubits length of my body. Now look carefully for yourself and check that I am as much here with you as I am in Shirdi!"

Mankar bowed before his master.

The prescribed period of his stay at Macchindragad over, Mankar returned to his residence in Bandra, Bombay, via Poona. At Poona he was waiting outside the ticket counter to purchase a ticket when he witnessed an unbelievable happening. An utter stranger, a bare-footed Kunbi peasant with hardly a piece of cloth around his loins and a *kambal* (blanket) thrown across his shoulders was ahead of Mankar in the queue. Mankar noted that the man had bought a ticket to Dadar where, indeed, Mankar had planned to disembark. Noticing Mankar standing behind him, the kunbi casually asked where he might be going and when Mankar said that he was bound up to Dadar, the kunbi said that he too had a ticket upto Dadar but he had suddenly realised that he had some urgent work to finish in Poona and would Mankar use his ticket? "Surely," said Mankar and fumbled into his pocket to pay the kunbi but when he looked up, the kunbi had vanished from sight! He was not to be seen any where, search as he Mankar would. Who could this stranger have been to play the role of the Good Samaritan? Mankar could only guess.

Baba was known to assume various forms to go to the aid of his devotees and even of their children. Once he went to the rescue of a devotee's daughter who was afraid to walk alone at night to her residence, assuming the form of her father. On reaching home the "father" declined to enter the house saying that he had some work to do. All the time her real father was engaged in *parayana* in his own house. Next day, when the daughter berated her father for not accepting her invitation, he realised that it was Baba who had come to his daughter's rescue! May be, he thought, he was also rewarding him for doing *parayana*.

For the concluding ceremony of a vow, Mrs Chandrabai R. Borkar received Baba's *darshan* in the form of a fakir. When Chandrabai was at Pandharpur, she decided to observe *Kokila Vrat* during the month of *Shraavan* (July-August) and went to Kopergaon for that purpose. Every morning and evening without fail, she would do circumambulation at Dattaghat when she had the distinct feeling of having had Baba's *darshan*. Then on Thursday, a young *fakir* arrived at Dattaghat and asked her for alms of *jaggery-bhakri* and garlic chutney! Chandrabai politely told him that she abjured from eating garlic and onion during *shraavan* and that she had come to Dattaghat to hear the koel's notes. "How, then, can I serve you with sweet *bhakri* and onion?" she asked.

But in her mind Chandrabai felt a little unease. Did she say the right thing? So the very next day she went to Shirdi and taking Mrs Jog with her went for Baba's *darshan*. On seeing her Baba said: "Look, I asked her for jaggery bhakri and garlic chutney, but she wouldn't give them to me. Now she has come here!"

Chandrabai felt convinced that by giving her *darshan* and asking for alms, Baba had wanted to perform the concluding ceremony of her vow. She said in a low voice: "I have come here to offer you alms." Mrs Jog who hadn't heard Chandrabai clearly, said: "She has come for your *darshan*". But Baba replied: "She is the sister of my seven births. Wherever I go, she comes in search of me!" But it was also clear that he was there to help a devotee fulfil her vows.

The 'miracles' that Baba performed, often unasked, are mind-boggling. Rao Bahadur S.B. Dhumal, then president of the Nasik Local Board once found that unbeknownest to him, several thousand papers that he could not sign but had to be signed, had indeed been signed overnight, as if by magic. No one had access to them and Dhumal concluded that Baba had come to his rescue in fulfilling an impossible task in record time.

Shantaram Balwant Nachane had a different kind of experience. In 1926, his eight month old son Harihar alias Sainath was playing with other children who were then bursting crackers. A lighted match accidentally fell on Harihar's clothes which quickly caught fire. No one had noticed this. Harihar's mother was busy elsewhere when out of nowhere a fakir appeared before her and said: "See what's going on there!" pointing in the direction where the children were playing. The mother rushed to the spot noticed that her child's clothes were on fire and promptly tore them with great presence of mind. No harm had come to the child itself and Harihar was pronounced safe.

The second wife of Nachane passed away in 1929. For the immersion of her ashes and other obsequies Nachane wished to go to Nasik. Knowing that his devotee was in a confused state of mind, Baba assumed the form of a peon and travelled with Nachane up to Nasik and took enormous trouble for him.

The 'peon' got into Nachane's compartment at Victoria Terminus and was soon engaged in a conversation with Nachane. He introduced himself as one Ganpati Shankar working at the J.J. School of Arts and in no time endeared himself to his new-found friend. The peon said that he had always wanted to go to Nasik and was availing himself of his boss's absence to get leave to fulfil a long-deferred desire. At Nasik the peon was of inestimable help to Nachane, saving him of lot of trouble. The 'peon' parted from Nachane at Nasik promising the latter to visit him at his Andheri residence. However the 'peon' never turned up. Nachane was greatly pleased with all that the 'peon' had done for him and tried to contact him at J.J. School of Arts. But when he called at the School he was told that there was no peon by the name of Ganpati Shankar and certainly nobody was on leave. It was clear to Nachane that it was Baba who had helped him.

2

Throughout these pages mention has been made of the off-white holy ash—*udi*. It is the product of perpetually burning *dhuni* kept in the masjid that was personally applied by Baba to a devotee's forehead as he was due to leave. The word *udi* means 'to go'. Learned men have interpreted it to mean 'going up', ascending on high, soaring into the heaven. Baba's devotees are emphatic that *udi* has miraculous powers. Certainly many cases have been reported of people in pain getting instant relief, of diseases cured and even the dead brought to life.

The most remarkable experience was that of one Pradhan, a resident of Sandhurst Road, Bombay and an employee in the State Revenue Department.

His youngest son had high fever for four days. His pulse became weak and then irregular and then it finally stopped. A doctor had been meanwhile summoned, who examined the boy and pronounced him dead. Pradhan wouldn't believe it and insisted that his son was still alive. In his desperation he applied some *udi* to the child's forehead and holding Baba's photograph before the child's visage, began fervently to pray.

There was nothing that the doctor could do. He tried gently to persuade Pradhan to desist but Pradhan was adamant. Minutes passed. Nothing happened. The doctor gently sought to push Pradhan aside. But Pradhan kept saying: "My Sai Baba is god. He will save my son."

By then some forty five minutes had passed and not a soul in the room moved. Then the miracle happened. The boy suddenly revived, sat up and began to play, as if nothing had happened.

3

Yet another word frequently used is "dakshina." "Dakshina" is an offering. It is based on faith which is belief in God. And it is a well-known saying that a devotee should not go to God or to his *guru* empty-handed.

Those who have attained Perfection are without any desire. They rarely ask for or accept, *dakshina.* In the initial stages Baba also would not accept *dakshina* from any one. If a devotee left something behind at the masjid by way of *dakshina,* Baba would not touch the offering. Invariably some-one would take it away.

Even when he started accepting *dakshina,* he would not accept more than two pice. But in the last ten years of his life there was a sudden spurt in the number of persons visiting him. Then he would accept anything from one pice to five hundred rupees or even a thousand rupees depending upon, one suspects, the paying capacity of his devotee. He observed some strange rules. For example, he would rarely accept a currency note and if one was offered, he would immediately have it converted into coinage. He would never accept *dakshina* after nightfall. Once darkness fell, whatever he had received during the day would be disbursed among the needy. Bade Baba or Fakir Baba as he was known would get anything from Rs 30 to Rs 55, Tatya Patil Rs 15 to Rs 25, Little Amani Rs 2, Jamali Rs 6, Dada Kelkar Rs 5, Bhagi Rs 2, Sundari Rs 2, Bayaji Patil Rs 4, Lakshmibai Rs 4 and the fakirs and other poor people at least Rs 8. He would purchase baskets of fruits when available and have them distributed. Chakranarayan, Christian *fauzdar* of Kopergaon in 1918 has observed in a statement: "He (Sai Baba) was clearly and unmistakeably unattached ... whatever he got, he scatte-red with a liberal hand. When he died, we took possession of his cash; that was only sixteen rupees! Yet he was paying or giving away hundreds of rupees daily. Often we noticed that his receipts were smaller than his disbursements. Wherefrom came the excess for him to pay? We could never make that out. We could only conclude that he had divine powers."

Interestingly again, Sai Baba did not *ask* everyone who came to him for *dakshina.* Nor did he *accept dakshina* from all. Should anyone come to get his *darshan* resolved before hand to give a certain amount and then gave less, Baba would gently remind the devotee of his earlier resolve to the latter's surprise and, no doubt, occasional shame. Should any devotee send *dakshina* through someone else, he too would be reminded of it if it became necessary. If Baba felt that someone had come merely to test him out, no *dakshina* would be asked of him. The wife of one such person who returned home without having given any *dakshina* to Sai Baba saw in a vivid dream her husband's wallet fallen in the lavatory. She narrated the dream to her husband who was so filled with remorse that he sent money to Baba through Money Order. Sai Baba also would not accept *dakshina* from a *sattvic* person who had in the past given *daan* generously to others. Devotees who had vowed to make certain payments to a deity in keeping with a vow and had been remiss would also be told to keep their promise. Baba would seek the exact amount to save the devotees from their plighted word. It would not matter to Baba if a visitor when asked to give *dakshina* declined to do so for whatever reason. His attitude towards the visitor would not change. He would say: "I don't accept anything gratis from anybody. Whatever I receive, I return ten-fold and raise the devotee himself on the path of knowledge."

Sometimes Baba indicated by asking for *dakshina* the raise due to a devotee in the pipeline. Rao Bahadur Sathe who got an increment in his salary of fifty rupees was asked to pay the same amount. Daji Hari Lele and Somnath Deshpande had similar experiences.

In 1917 Gajanan Narvekar was getting high fever. He sent his son to Shirdi with a *dakshina* of five hundred rupees, no small amount in those days. As soon as the *dakshina* was paid, Sai

Baba started shivering and developed high fever. A devotee sitting next to him was visibly upset and asked what the matter was. Baba said: "I have to carry the burden of him whose dakshina I accept!" It was as plain as that. It was not as if by accepting *dakshina* Sai Baba removed the worldly sorrows of his devotees. Often he seemed to accept *dakshina* to stress some moral principle or to suggest the usefulness of some spiritual practice. When Raghuvir Bhaskar Purandare of Perry Road, Bandra, visited Shirdi he was given to prayers and the worship of Vishnu. Baba encouraged him to continue this *upasana*. Whenever he appeared before Baba, the latter would ask him for a dakshina of only two rupees. Once Purandare asked Baba why he asked for only two rupees and not more. Baba told him: "It is not the rupees I want. I want *nishta* (concentrated faith) and *saburi* (patience combined with courage)."

Purandare replied: "But I have already given these."

Baba told him: "Well, keep up your *nishta* and be concerned over fulfilling your promises. Always let truth guide you. Then I will always be with you wherever you are and at all times."

In 1914 when Prof. G.G. Narke stayed with Baba for over thirteen months he was asked several times for a *dakshina* of fifteen rupees. At that time Narke had no money with him as he was unemployed, a fact of which Baba was fully aware of. One day when Narke was all alone with Baba he asked Baba why he asked for a *dakshina* of fifteen rupees when Baba surely knew that he had no money.

Baba told him: "Of course I know about your financial condition. But you are now engaged in reading Yoga Vasishta, aren't you? The part you are now reading is specially important. Get me fifteen rupees out of that!"

What he meant was that what Narke was learning was worth all that money and that when Baba asked for *dakshina* what he meant was that Narke should lodge the lessons he had learnt in his heart where Sai Baba lived as his *antaryami* (inner controller). In 1915, a vaccinator, Triambak Govind Samant, a devotee of Lord Ganesh, came to Shirdi for Baba's *darshan*.

He had only five rupees on him. By way of *dakshina* he gave Baba one rupee, but Baba asked for one more. The poor fellow was most reluctant to give it and a verbal tug-of-war between the two ensued. Baba, however, was determined to get that extra rupee and ultimately Samant yielded. Baba turned the two rupee coins upside down and had a good look at them and then placing his hand on Samant's head, he said: "You have given these two rupees to the one lettered (God). Now you may go. Ganu Mahar will bless you!"

Samant did not quite get what Baba said. He had performed one crore *japa* of the mono-syllabic *mantra* of Shri Ganesh. By his blessing Baba had reminded Samant that he had appeared to him when the latter was twenty one year old in the form of Ganu Mahar and initiated him into the monosyllabic *mantra*. For all that Samant was rather sore at having had to part with an additional rupee that he had not planned to give.

In that mood Samant left for Bombay. When he came to the tonga-stand Samant found out that no tonga was available to go to Kopergaon, the railway station. And since he had no faith in Baba, he was more agitated than ever. But at that moment a tonga came from Rahata. The sole passenger was a Gujarati gentleman who beckoned to Samant to get in. Samant forgot that he did not have sufficient money on his person to pay for the ride. Meanwhile, the gentleman engaged Samant in polite conversation. "I see that you have been to see Sai Baba," he began.

"Yes," said Samant somewhat grumpily.

The gentleman continued: "That's some fakir! You give him one and he asks you for one more!"

That stopped Samant literally in his tracks. It seemed to him that the gentleman was reading his mind. But he kept quiet.

The two reached Kopergaon and the Gujarati gentleman paid the fare for both. He even purchased a ticket for Samant upto Dadar Station. The two travelled together. At Dadar, Samant, out of both courtesy and curiosity, asked the Gujarati gentleman his name and address.

"Oh," said the Gujarati gentlemen, "I am known as Ganu Marwadi. I stay on the upper storey in a chawl behind Masjid station."

Samant noted that down and went his way. Next day he went in search of Ganu Marwadi to pay his debt. But there was no one in the chawl by name Ganu Marwadi. Besides, the entire chawl population was Muslim.

Samant now began to think seriously over the matter. He recollected that when he was twenty one years old, he was going from Triambakeshwar to some other place and had to pass through a forest. As luck would have it he had been captured by some robbers who had threatened to kill him. He remembered praying fervently to Shri Gajanan and hearing a voice call out 'Jai Malhari'. Thereupon the robbers had fled.

On another occasion a similar incident had taken place and when Samant had prayed to Shri Ganesh, he had noticed a man afflicted with black leprosy materialising from nowhere who had told him: "My name is Ganu Mahar." Ganu Mahar had then promised to lead Samant safely out of the jungle on condition that he did not look back. The deal was agreed upon. Samant was asked to move on receiving instructions from Ganu Mahar. The two chatted merrily for a while until suddenly no word came from Ganu. Intrigued, Samant had turned to look back, only to find that Ganu was gone! When Samant realised the similarity of the two names: Ganu Marwadi and Ganu Mahar, it struck him that they were both forms of Sai Baba who had come to his succour at crucial moments. From that moment onward Samant was a confirmed devotee of Sai Baba. He worshipped Baba in the form of Ganapati.

Then there was Hari Sitaram alias Kakasaheb Dikshit who was struggling with the question of Reality, and Illusion. How did one differentiate between the two?

As he was contemplating this ancient question there came to him a man who said he had been sent by Sai Baba to ask for a hundred rupees. Dikshit then had only a rupee on him which he gladly gave to the messenger with a request that the latter convey to Baba his prostrations.

After the messenger left it occurred to Dikshit that Baba surely must have known that he had no more than a rupee on him. Then why did he send word that he wanted a hundred rupees? The only reality was one. Slowly, it began to dawn on Dikshit that he was being given a practical lesson on how to differentiate between Truth and Illusion. The Truth was one. The Illusion, many.

On another occasion Dikshit was reading the second chapter of *Eknathi Bhagwat* along with Balasaheb Bhate and while he was thus engaged there came a message that Sai Baba had asked for a *dakshina* of sixteen and a half rupees, from Dikshit. As on an earlier occasion, Dikshit did not have any money on him, apart from a rupee given him by Baba on Guru Purnima Day. The message had been brought to him by Bapusaheb Buti who had also been instructed by Baba to sit by Dikshit and listen to the reading from *Eknathi Bhagwat*.

Dikshit began to ponder upon the request for sixteen and a half rupee *dakshina,* which was a rather unusual sum to ask. He therefore concluded that somehow that amount had something to do with the reading of that day's part of *Eknathi Bhagwat.*

Buti, meanwhile, sat as directed by Baba to listen to the reading of the *Bhagwat* and in time Dikshit came to the verse '*Kayena vaacha....*'' which was an exposition of what *Bhagwat dharma* meant made by one of the sons of Rishabh Muni. The verse meant: ''Whatever I do through my body, speech, mind, organs, intellect, ego and nature *(prarabdha* - karma at birth) I offer to Narayan who is beyond everything, after pronouncing His Name.''

Dikshit had hardly completed reading Eknath's extensive commentary on the *Bhagwat* when another messenger came from Baba asking Buti to return. This intrigued Dikshit even more. Was there *any* connection between Baba's demand for sixteen and a half rupees and the stanza *kayena vaacha* he had just completed reading? Mentally Dikshit added up the units mentioned in the verse: body 1, speech 1, mind *(manas)* 1, intellect 1, ego 1, organs 10, nature ½. But it all totalled up to 15½. But then, Dikshit told himself, Baba had asked specifically for 16½ rupees. He scrutinised the commentary of Eknath again and found out that though there is no mention of *chitta* (discursive faculty including memory) in the original stanza, in Eknath's commentary there is exposition also on *chitta.* Now that totalled 16½. From this Dikshit understood that Sai Baba's object in asking for 16½ 'rupees' *dakshina* in effect meant that he wanted all those ingredients, *kaaya, vaacha, manas, indriyas* etc to be offered to the Lord.

It also occurred to Dikshit that Sai Baba had asked him to give not 16 but 16½ rupees. What could have been the emphasis on the additional half a rupee, namely Nature? On deep thinking it appeared to Dikshit that even in this Baba's purpose was to focus his attention on one special principle. It was possible to offer whatever actions other organs performed consciously, but Eknath had pointed out that some actions were automatic reflexes of one's nature over which one had no control. Those actions were not of one's own volition but were God-directed. One was only an instrument of God and in that sense one's automatic actions could not be considered as one's own, but only partially one's own. That, thought Dikshit, was the significance of the half rupee.

To the uninitiated in Sai Baba's instructions all this may sound a rationalisation that could be meaningful or plain imaginary. But here we are dealing with a relationship between Baba and a devotee that, at this distance in time, one has better suspend judgment.

Uddhaveshbua alias Shyamdas of Dahanu also had a similar experience of being instructed by Baba through the latter's demand of *dakshina.* Uddhaveshbua had been upset over an accident months ago when he lost his wallet containing lots of money and he had then resolved that unless he had clear instructions from Baba he would not read any *Pothi Purana.* It was a negative resolve—a resolve NOT to do something.

Uddhaveshbua subsequently returned to Shirdi but there were no instructions forthcoming from Baba. Uddhaveshbua returned home, determined not to read *Pothi Purana.* A couple of years passed and during this period there was no occasion for

Uddhaveshbua to go to Shirdi. Once he wrote to Chidambar Keshav Gadgil, Mamledar, who was then at Shirdi seeking Baba's blessings and *udi*. Gadgil duly read out the letter to Baba and asked what reply he should give. "Ask him to come to Shirdi at his earliest," Baba replied. Gadgil wrote as he was told to do and within a week's time Uddhaveshbua was at Shirdi. When Uddhaveshbua went to worship Baba, the latter asked for a *dakshina* of eleven rupees and Uddhaveshbua promptly paid the amount. The next day a similar request came and Uddhaveshbua again paid the sum demanded. This went on for ten days continuously and each day Uddhaveshbua kept paying the amount. On the eleventh day, unable to suppress his curiosity at this behaviour of Baba he asked the latter why he kept asking for eleven rupees.

Uddhaveshbua said: "My ten organs and my mind, I offer to you."
Baba retorted: "They are mine, anyway. Who are you to offer them to me? I have already taken them!"

Then seeing Uddhaveshbua's firm faith in him, Baba said: "Go to Bapusaheb Jog in the afternoon, ask him for eleven rupees and bring him here."

At 3-30 p.m. Uddhaveshbua went to Jog, conveyed to him Baba's message and after listening to the reading of *Eknathi Bhagwat* went to see Sai Baba accompanied by Jog. But Baba would not talk either with Uddhaveshbua or Jog. This went on for three whole days. On the fourth day when Uddhaveshbua went with Jog to Baba, after listening to the reading of *Eknathi Bhagwat,* he found Balasaheb Bhate conversing with the latter. Sai Baba asked Jog: "Well, Bapusaheb, how much did you spend today?"
Jog replied: "Sixty one rupees, Baba."
"How?"
"I gave fifty rupees to Buti and eleven to Uddhaveshbua."
Baba now turned to Uddhaveshbua and asked: "Have you got your eleven?"
"Yes," said Uddhaveshbua.
"No, no!" countered Baba, "you really haven't. Let's see tomorrow. Read the Pothi, too!"

When all the three of them, Jog, Bhate and Uddhaveshbua returned to the Wada, Bhate asked Uddhaveshbua what all the talk was all about. Uddhaveshbua replied saying that though he had said 'yes' to Baba, he hadn't understood the deeper meaning of Sai Baba's statement either and was trying to find out. After some reflection Uddhaveshbua came to the conclusion that Baba's reference to eleven rupees must have reference to his own decision not to read any Pothi unless Baba directed him to do so. Next day at 3-30 p.m. while Uddhaveshbua was engaged in *charan seva* of Sai Baba, the latter asked him: "Have you got your eleven rupees?"

"Are you referring to the reading of Pothi? If so, I understand But which Pothi should I read?" replied Uddhaveshbua.

"Read that Pothi in which there is a dialogue between you (Uddhava) and me!" came the answer.
Uddhaveshbua still did not understand.
He asked: "Shall I read the Bhagavad Gita?"
To which Baba replied: "Read only that in which you and I talk to each other!"

Uddhaveshbua thought that Sai Baba was perhaps asking him to read not the Gita but Jnaneshwari as before. But as soon as this thought entered his mind Baba said: "Go to Bapusaheb (Jog) and get the Pothi."

So Uddhaveshbua took it that Baba was asking him to read *Eknathi Bhagwat.* When Uddhaveshbua went to Jog as directed, Jog was getting ready to read the Pothi. Uddhaveshbua took the Pothi in his hands and went to Sai Baba. Baba opened it at the eleventh chapter and told Uddhaveshbua: "Now read this. Read as it is and try to understand its meaning when you are alone. Go now. Recite my name every day!"

The joy which Uddhaveshbua experienced at that time was indescribable.

Once Ramachandra Atmaram Tarkhad went with his family to Shirdi and gave as *dakshina* the sum he had taken for the purpose. But even then Sai Baba entreated Tarkhad's wife to give him *dakshina*, of six rupees. As she had no money of her own she felt very bad and when she returned to the wada she started crying. When her husband asked her what the matter was, she narrated her predicament to him. Tarkhad explained to her that what Baba wanted was not six silver rupees but the "six enemies" of man—*kaama, krodha, moha, mada, lobha* and *matsarya* (lust, anger, attachment, passion, greed and jealousy)—so she could be pure and desireless.

And he told her: "If you want to test the accuracy of what I have just told you, sit down and tell Sai Baba: "I offer you from the bottom of my heart, man's six enemies *(shadvairi)* and when we go to him later, let us see what he has to say."

Mrs. Tarkhad did as she was told. In the afternoon when the two of them called on Baba he asked her: "Mother, have you brought my rupees?" Mrs. Tarkhad replied: "But I have already given them to you!" Queried Baba: "Have you, really?" And she replied: "Yes, I have." Baba then asked: "And you won't take them back?" Mrs. Tarkhad understood.

CHAPTER 9

"MY LEELA IS INSCRUTABLE"

To know the Eternal, let a man devoted to spiritual life humbly approach a Guru devoted to Brahman and well-versed in the scriptures,

To a disciple who approaches reverently, who is tranquil and self-controlled, the wise teacher gives that knowledge faithfully and without stint, by which is known the truly existing, the changeless Self.

—Mundaka Upanishad
(translated by Swamy Prabhavananda)

Those who themselves have seen the Truth, can be thy teachers of wisdom. Ask from them, bow unto them, be thou unto them a servant.

Bhagawad Gita IV, 34.
(translated by Juan Mascaro)

Let a man devoted to spiritual life, wishing to know the Eternal, surrender to a Guru who is well-versed in the scriptures and devoted to and established in Brahman.

Shrimad Bhagwat
Section XI, Chapter 3, Stanza 21

"My *leela* is inscrutable," Sai Baba would often say. This is literally true. Towards his devotees Sai Baba had imperishable and infinite love and his mode of instruction was born of compassion. Perennially he would be in *sahaj samadhi* and the highest bliss. Because of his omniscience he could understand and know the sorrows and sufferings of his devotees and could ward them off. He never gave a beginner in the quest for spiritual experience, the higher lesson. To each he imparted knowledge according to the capacity of the recipient, to absorb it.

He taught his devotees self-restraint, to live in the world with detachment, to believe in God and love Him, to love one's parents, Guru, holy persons and the poor and the down-trodden. Even dumb creatures were objects of his love. He never lectured to large groups. He had different ways of dealing with different individuals. And he often talked in parables.

His devotees came from all religions. Hindus, Muslims, Christians and Parsis all came to get his *darshan*. Baba himself did not profess any particular religion but confirmed each in his own. He did not wish to found a seat, a *gaddi*, a *peetham* or an ashram and so did not have to trouble himself about appointing a successor.

He allowed those whose end was near or whose worldly responsibilities had been discharged to remain with him or he would encourage them to renounce a life of worldly activities. But in this he was most discriminating. He would strongly dissuade young people wishing to forsake the world from doing so. He also did not favour throwing one's burden on society by begging for alms.

Following are a few instances of how he dealt with different types of devotees:

1. Sakharam Hari alias Bapusaheb Jog along with this wife came for Baba's *darshan* on a Ram Navami Day. Noting that the couple had no progeny and that both were in the evening of their lives, as well as observing great potentialities in Jog, Baba allowed the couple to stay in Shirdi. Sai Baba even gave him *darshan* in the form of Akkalkot Swami and after Megha's death entrusted the duty of worship-*arti* to him. Jog discharged that responsibility diligently and with devotion until Sai Baba's *samadhi*. Jog's life in Shirdi was one of austerity. The Jog couple would get up at 3 am every day, throughout the year and bathe with cold water drawn from the well behind Dikshitwada. Then Jog would attend to his *sandhya*, puja-archa and every alternate day when Sai Baba rested for the night in the *chavadi*, would attend to the morning *arati*.

   After observing his regular morning routine he would go to the masjid at the time of Baba's morning repast. Then he would either accompany Sai Baba to Lendi or recite

Bhagwad Gita at his home until Baba returned. He would help in preparation of *naivedya* of Sai Baba and after the noon *arati* go home with a guest sent by Baba for lunch. In the afternoon, about 3.30 pm he would again call at the masjid, then return and read *Eknathi Bhagwat* until it was time for the evening round of Sai Baba. Many a time Baba would send devotees to Jog when he read *Jnaneshwari* in the morning or *Eknathi Bhagwat* in the afternoon under the pretext of asking for *dakshina* and would direct them to listen to the *parayana*. On the day when Baba planned to spend the night in the *chavadi* Jog would attend to the night *arati* at 9.30 pm. Jog discharged these duties uninterruptedly for years until the day Baba attained *nirvana*.

2. After Balakram Mankar's wife passed away Sai Baba directed him to stay in Shirdi and lead a life of the spirit. He got Mankar to do *tapas* in Shirdi as well as at Matsyendragad and blessed him by giving him *darshan* in Matsyendragad in the waking state. At Baba's suggestion, he would read *Panchadashi*. He died in Shirdi before Baba's *nirvana*.

3. Upasani had come to Sai Baba to get his *darshan*. Baba advised him, much against Upasani's own wish, to stay in Shirdi for four years doing *tapas* but he fled away after three years, it is said much to his detriment.

4. Govind Raghunath alias Annasaheb Dabholkar retired from government service in 1916 on reaching the age of superannuation. A friend of Dabholkar who was also a devotee of Sai Baba requested Baba to give Dabholkar another paid employment to help him meet his family's expenses. "He will certainly get an opportunity to serve but meanwhile let him serve me. A life of happiness is assured for him," Baba said. And Baba added: "To the end of his days he will have everything in abundance. If he devotes himself to me with faith, all his tribulations will end."

5. Sagun Meru Naik came from Hyderabad in the company of a *sowcar* of that state who was a devotee of Sai Baba. At the end of five months' stay in Shirdi when Naik asked Baba for permission to leave Baba clearly told him that he

had not brought Naik from a long distance for nothing. He asked Naik to stay in Shirdi and engage himself in some activity, adding that he would prosper. From that time Naik made his home in Shirdi, setting up a tea stall as well a shop to sell books, agarbattis etc. Naik also interested himself in gardening and tending of cows and was associated with the *samsthan* in rendering service to Sai Baba.

6. If ever there was anyone who was compelled to give up his post in the Police Department and made to tread on the spiritual path, it is Ganpat Dattatreya Sahasrabuddhe alias Das Ganu. Sai Baba did this looking into Das Ganu's intelligence, capacity to compose lyrics on the spot and, of course, his undoubted potential. When Das Ganu paid his first visit in the company of Nanasaheb Chandorkar for Sai Baba's *darshanam* Baba told Nanasaheb: "Tell him (Das Ganu) that composing *lavanis,* participating in *tamashas* and service in the Police Department are to be given up!"

The command was clear and precise. Das Ganu gave up the first two but dilly-dallied about resigning his post in the Police Department. In 1898-99 Kanhya Bhil, a well-known dacoit came to know that his movements were under surveillance by Das Ganu. In turn Kanhya Bhil posed a threat to Das Ganu's life. By surrendering to Shriram, Sai Baba's grace and because of Das Ganu's defence by the Patil who sheltered Kanhya Bhil, Das Ganu escaped by the skin of his teeth. At that time Das Ganu was only a havildar. Once Das Ganu went to a place of pilgrimage on unauthorised leave and standing in the waters of the Godavari with his face in the direction of Shirdi affirmed that if he escaped punishment for the offence of absenting without permission, he would tender his resignation. Fortunately for Das Ganu, a gang of robbers was rounded up at that very place and feigning that he had been there in search of the robbers, Das Ganu avoided punishment.

Das Ganu was aspiring for promotion as Fauzdar and in the process he forgot his pledge solemnly taken. Now he passed his departmental examination for Fauzdar's post and was transferred. The road to his new post passed through Shirdi. Das Ganu wanted to avoid Sai Baba as he did not want to be held down to his pledge. But as fate would have it, while Das Ganu was passing through Shirdi, Sai Baba accosted him. Dismounting from his horse Das Ganu prostrated before Sai Baba who took him to the masjid and said: "Ganu, who was it that had affirmed with waters of Godavari in the hollow of his palms that he would resign?"

Ganu was deeply embarrassed. But he would not say anything.

Baba told him, "So you think you can avoid me? You can't. Better resign from your post or you will have cause to repent."

A few days later Das Ganu was involved in another scrap. An amount of Rs. 32 by way of fine had been realised from a convict in Das Ganu's station to be paid to the Treasury. But in Das Ganu's absence his assistant had pocketed the amount. As the convict was not released, he filed a complaint and an enquiry was ordered. Das Ganu was suspended and there was every possibility of an enhanced punishment. This time, too, Das Ganu resolved that if he were exonerated of the charge, he would give up his job. He was acquitted but this time he kept his word. He resigned from the Police Department.

After he quit service, he made his abode in Nanded, in the Nizam's Dominion and supported himself by performing *kirtanas*. Thanks to Baba's grace he managed to get some land almost for a pittance. He was able to live well on the income from his farm. He did his bit in spreading Baba's fame in Bombay. His *kirtanas* brought him fame and large and admiring crowds. He did not follow the usual practice of circulating the *arati-patra* among those present, at the end of the *kirtan* to collect money. He performed only for the sake of spreading the *bhakti* movement. Das Ganu was a prolific composer and soon became known as a *santkavi* (composer of *padas, kavyas, stotras* and *akhyaanas* on saints) of Marathi language. In his *Arvachin*

Bhatkaleelamrit, chapters 31, 32 and 33 and in *Shri Santakathamrit* chapter 57 are compositions devoted to Sai Baba. Sai Baba sometimes asked his devotees to read these regularly on Thursdays.

7. Abdul of Nanded was destined to serve Sai Baba. Sai Baba appeared in the dream of his murshid Fakir Amiruddin in 1889 and asked him to send Abdul to Shirdi. Abdul came to Shirdi and served Baba until the latter's *mahasamadhi.* Sai Baba himself took care of Abdul as a father would of his son and made him study the Koran.

8. Balasaheb Bhate was a free thinker while at college, an inveterate smoker and a veritable *charvaka* whose creed was "Eat, drink and be Merry for Tomorrow We Die!" He became a mamledar and was an efficient officer much liked by his boss, the Collector who was an Englishman. He was Mamledar at Kopergaon for about five years between 1904 and 1909. Bhate would scoff at his educated friends who met him on their way to Shirdi and describe Sai Baba as a mad man. His friends asked him to see Sai Baba just once and then form his judgement.

In 1909, Bhate camped at Shirdi and met Baba day after day. On the fifth day, Baba covered him with a *gerua* garment. From that day Bhate became a changed man. He did not care for earnings or for his work. To the end of his life he only wished to be at Shirdi, to serve Sai Baba and to live and die in his presence.

Sai Baba made his friend Kakasaheb Dikshit draw up an application for leave for one year and got Bhate to sign it. The Collector, a most understanding man, sanctioned the leave. However, at the end of the year there was no change in Bhate's attitude towards Sai Baba and was granted compassionate pension of about thirty rupees as one afflicted with "religious melancholia."

The day Baba had placed a *gerua* garment on Bhate had become a water-shed in Bhate's life. He had become a changed man. He thereafter made Shirdi his home, attending to his *nitya karma* (daily routine) and reading the

Upanishads for Baba who would often offer comments on what was read to him.

9. Kakasaheb Dikshit once asked Sai Baba in 1912: "Shall I retire from the solicitors' profession and spend the rest of my life in Shirdi?" Why, Baba wanted to know. Dikshit replied that he could not carry on his profession truthfully. Baba told him: "Let others do as they please. But you should stick to the truth. There is no need for you to give up your profession."

    So Dikshit continued as a solicitor while spending as much time as he could at Shirdi. On Baba's suggestion he made it a rule to read *Eknathi Bhagwat* in the morning and *Bhavartha Ramayan* at night and he stuck to this routine till the end of his life.

10. Prof. G. G. Narke who returned from England in 1912 as a qualified geologist and Mining Engineer had no permanent employment for some years and held only temporary prospecting jobs. His mother was understandably anxious about his future. At Sai Baba's instance Narke came to Shirdi and remained without employment for thirteen long months, but could not care less. Some times he had stray fancies that a fakir's life was good for him. In 1914, on a certain day Sai Baba had got ready a number of *kafnis* which he presented to some people. Narke who was watching the distribution of *kafnis* from a distance hoped that one might be conferred on him so that he could wear it on special occasions like *bhajans* in honour of Sai Baba. But Baba stopped distribution even when *kafnis* remained with him. Then he called Narke and placing his hand on his head, stoked it and said: "Do not blame me for not giving you a *kafni*. That fakir (meaning God) has not permitted me to give you one!" Later, Sai Baba saw to it that Narke was settled in Poona as a professor in the Engineering College.

11. The financial condition of Janardan Moreshwar Phanse of Dahanu was not good. He had to face many a calamity and weary of fighting, he started for Rameshwar resolving not to come back to the worldly life. On his way he broke

journey to go to Shirdi and at first sight of Sai Baba he felt that he had met a well-wisher of his of long standing, a feeling which grew on him as he stayed on at Shirdi.

On the eighth day he asked leave of Sai Baba who said: "Go home, instead of to Rameshwar or you may be over-taken by ill-stars."

So Phanse returned home and found that since the day he left his mother had gone on fast, maintaining that if Sai Baba were a true saint he would send her son home. After seven days of fasting she vowed to subsist on a diet of only milk. She gave up her fast when her son indeed returned home.

There is the case of R. A. Tarkhad who went to Shirdi to get away from the rough and tumble of his daily grind and to have peace of mind. However, his first encounter was very unpleasant. As soon as he stepped in Sathewada a gentleman plied him with all manner of questions. "Why have you come to Shirdi? What do you get here? etc" Another gentleman came up to him and said : "Who is a *sthitaprajnya* (man of serene wisdom)? Will you kindly clarify at length."

Tarkhad was very upset, lost his poise and felt he had made a mistake in leaving Bombay and coming all the way to Shirdi. However, concealing his discomfiture, Tarkhad went for Baba's *darshan*. As soon as Tarkhad bowed at the feet of Sai Baba, the latter placed his palm on Tarkhad's head and said to Madhavrao Deshpande: "Why has he come here? Advise him!"

Madhavrao thereupon led Tarkhad away and asked him what the matter was. Tarkhad narrated to him what had happened since he set foot in Shirdi. Madhavrao told him: "That is how Baba sends his message. Even in the midst of turmoil and anxiety, you should direct your mind cons-tantly toward God. Let us return and listen to what Baba has to say."

As they turned back and entered the masjid, addressing

himself to Tarkhad, Baba said: "Brother, keep in mind what Shama (Madhavrao Deshpande) has told you." Tarkhad indeed got the message. He returned to his base and conducted himself with detachment and was able to face life's hardships without a murmur.

Ambdekar, a devotee who was disgusted with life, went to Shirdi determined to commit suicide. He had been out of employment for seven long years and had not found any suitable means of livelihood and he was at the end of his tether. He decided to end his life by jumping into a well. While he was sitting dejectedly opposite Dikshitwada planning to commit suicide Sagun Meru Naik happened to pass by. Without a clue to Ambdekar's state of mind, Sagun wondered whether Ambdekar had ever read the *pothi* of Akkalkot Maharaj. "What is it? Let me see it!" Ambdekar replied, rather off-handedly. Sagun gave it to him. Ambdekar opened it casually and peering at the writing came across the story of how Akkalkot Maharaj had dissuaded a man afflicted by an incurable disease from committing suicide.

The coincidence fascinated Ambdekar and he continued to read the tale and, as he went on reading, his desire to commit suicide receded into the background. Sai Baba had come to his rescue, he felt. He was imbued now with fresh hope. Encouraged by Baba, he acquired proficiency in astrology, found himself in great demand and passed on the message to whoever would listen that every man had to go through life to fulfil his *karma.*

In this matter Baba would encourage each individual to worship one's *ishta devata* as a form of spiritual discipline. He thus persuaded Mrs. R. A. Tarkhad to restart worship of Ganapati with a broken arm, Bhagawantrao Kshirsagar to worship of Vithal, Shantaram Balwant Nachane the worship of the deity at Devpur and Harishchandra Pitale the worship of Akkalkot Swami.

Sometimes Sai Baba would commend a *mantra* that seemed just right for a devotee or approve of a *mantra* with which a devotee was already familiar. At his first meeting with Rao Bahadur M.W. Pradhan he uttered the *mantra Shri Ram Jai Ram Jai Jai Ram,* thus conveying his recognition of the *mantra* that had been given to Pradhan by the family guru. It surely took Pradhan by surprise.

Baba gave Mrs G.S. Khaparde the *mantra* 'Raja Ram' and a variant of the same *mantra* to Ganesan Maharaj. In 1910 when R.A. Tarkhad met Sai Baba for the first time, he was wondering whether he should continue repeating *Shri Ram Jai Ram Jai Jai Ram* which had been given to him as a *mantra.* On seeing him Baba welcomed him lovingly and said: "Come, Ramachandra Maharaj!" implying that Tarkhad should not give up recitation of his *mantra.* Tarkhad got the message.

To Govind Raghunath alias Annasaheb Dabholkar and Radhabai Deshmukh who believed in the devotion to *sadguru,* he commended meditation on and the bhajan of *Sadguru* and the twin lessons of *shraddha* (faith) and *saburi* (patience combined with courage). To M.B. Rege Baba said: "Do not read books but keep me in your heart. If you harmonise head and heart, that is enough!"

To enable devotees to navigate the sea of existence with all its storms, Baba would commend to devotees regular reading of sacred books or *pothis* of saints: to Nanasaheb Nimonkar he suggested *Srimad Bhagwat,* with commentary, to Bapusaheb Jog he suggested *Jnaneshwari* and *Eknathi Bhagwat* and *Geeta Rahasya;* to Uddhavesh bua, Kaka Mahajani and Vaman Narvekar, *Eknathi Bhagwat;* to Dr D.M. Mulky *Jnaneshwari;* to Balakram Mankar *Panchadasi* by Vidyaranya Swami and to Madhavrao Deshpande *Vishnusahasranaama.* To Megha and Bala Shimpi he gave each a *Shiva linga* and to Madhavrao Deshpande a *shaligram* (a black stone in river Gandaki and worshipped as Vishnu) and asked each of them to worship according to rites. Damodar Rasane brought his son Dattatreya to Sai Baba after tonsuring his head to give him his first lesson in writing. Holding Dattatreya's hand, Baba got the boy to write "Hari" on the slate.

How did one get Sai Baba's grace? Baba once answered this

question when Anandrao Patankar came to Shirdi after hearing about the saint's fame.

Patankar told Baba: "I have read many books, studied the Vedas and the Upanishads, but my mind is as restless as ever. I feel that all my reading and study have been wasted. As long as the mind is not steady, how can I realise Brahman? I have come to you in the hope that by your sacred darshan and blessings, I will get my peace of mind."

Baba answered in a parable.

"Listen," he said, "once a merchant came to Shirdi. He was preceded by a horse. The merchant, I noticed, did not want the horse droppings to fall all over the place. He kept collecting them, nine times, in his upper garment. His concetration on the task immediately ahead was notable."

Patankar was mystified. Later he took Dada Kelkar aside and asked him what Baba could have possibly meant. Kelkar who was accustomed to Baba's frequent mystic sayings provided the answer.

"The merchant," explained Kelkar, "is the seeker, the horse is God's grace and the nine droppings refer to the nine-fold path of devotion."

"And what may they be?"

Kelkar continued: "The first is shravan (hearing the attributes, excellencies, or wondrous achievements of, as read or recited), the second, keertan (reciting), the third, smaran (calling to mind and meditating upon the names and perfections of), fourth, Paadasevan (washing, kneading etc of the feet of), fifth archana (outward worship or common service and presenting naivedya), sixth, vandan (adoration), seventh, daasya (service in general), eighth, sakhya (cultivating fellowship) and ninth, aatmanivedan (consecration of one's self unto). Inasmuch as you have come here as a merchant, you should follow the nine-fold path of devotion so that you can attain peace of mind."

Patankar felt that the explanation was sufficient unto itself.

When he went for Baba's *darshan* the next day, Baba asked him: "Well, have you collected the nine nodules of horse's dung?"

Humbly, Patankar replied: "They will be easily collected with your blessings." Baba blessed him.

Often Baba would explain the same principle in allegorical language. "Seetaphal (custard apple)," he would say, "is better than Ramphal (another variety of fruit) for the former is easy to digest while the latter is not." He would therefore commend the principle of *Yade Haq* (servant of God) rather than *Anal Haq* (I am God); *Tuhi, tuhi* (Thou art everything i.e. Thy will be done) rather than *Aham Brahmasmi* (I am the Brahman).

It is said that it is easier for a man who leads the life of a recluse than for a man leading an active, worldly life, to walk on the path of knowledge or devotion. And it is also held that the mere whispering by a guru of a *mantra* into a disciple's ear does not end his responsibilities. Sai Baba would say: "I am not a ear-whispering guru!" Baba watched over his devotees, like a doting parent, correcting them and leading them on the straight and narrow path.

Baba never encouraged gossip nor did he waste words. Once a *yogi* came to Shirdi and was aghast to watch Sai Baba eat his regular meal of a *bhakri* with onions that are with garlic, shunned by *yogis*. Before the yogi could raise the question, Baba guessed what was in his mind and said that one should eat only that which one has the capacity to digest. No food in itself was forbidden to a man.

As for gossip, Sai Baba would say that when a person spoke ill of another, it was he who suffered. Once Mathuradas of Anjanwel, who was heard to indulge in malicious gossip at the home of Sagun Meru Naik was sternly told off. Another was told not to follow the example of a pig that fed on rubbish. Baba could be sharp when he wanted to be. But essentially, his was the message of universal love. "Nobody comes to us," he would say, "without *rinanubandha* (ties of indebtedness in some preceding birth). So never send away anyone who comes to you. A creature shooed away never sets its foot on your threshold."

Among his sayings, here are a few:

Though I am here, and you are beyond the seven seas,
Whatever you do there, I come to know at once.
Wherever you go, I am always with you;
I dwell in your heart, I am within you.
Bow always to me who am in your heart.
Know that I also dwell in the hearts of all creatures—
Whether at your home, doorstep or on the way.
Whether it is an insect, an ant, a fish or a bird,
An animal, a dog or a pig,
In all these I abide for ever
And I pervade everything.
Do not regard yourself as separate from me;
We are one.
Blessed is he who realises this Truth.

Devotees of Sai Baba had his assurance of their security. They
also had an assurance of his love and consideration. At the
masjid a place was usually reserved opposite Baba for
Hardwarbua. Once it so happened that a little girl was
occupying it when Hardwarbua walked in. Somewhat pere-
mptorily he asked her to get up and go elsewhere. It greatly
upset Baba who in turn asked Hardwarbua to leave and take a
seat in the *sabhamandap.* When Hardwarbua returned after a
while, he was told to go back. Baba would not accept an affront
to a child. He wanted the message to sink in.

Baba was also opposed to his devotees borrowing money in
order to come to Shirdi for his *darshan.* One of those who was
warned against it was Lala Lakhmichand who never again
repeated the mistake. For a trivial service Baba would pay
handsomely saying that no service given gratis should be
accepted.

Baba would insist that at a social function no near relation
should be excluded and Rao Bahadur Sathe was ticked off for
not inviting his father-in-law at a function which Baba was to
attend. Baba had no use for drunks and once appeared in a
dream to D.V. Sambhare alias Kolombo who was known for his
addiction to liquor. Baba sat tight on Sambhare's chest and

would not move until the latter promised never again to drink. He stuck to his vow even when his office boss asked him to drink.

Sathe once called at the home of a female devotee more out of curiosity than anything else but was soon enamoured of her. Baba, it is reported, appeared at her door from nowhere which came as a warning to Sathe to beware of his own emotions. He never again called on the lady.

Amusing are some of the incidents recalled by the cognoscente. The proprietor of a printing press had gone to Shirdi and had over eighteen rupees with him which he handed over to Sambhare in secret so that when Sai Baba asked him for *dakshina* he might say truthfully that he had no money on him. When the man accompanied by Sambhare went for Baba's *darshan* the latter asked for a *dakshina* of two rupees. Very truthfully the man said he had no money with him. "In that case," said Baba, "take it from Sambhare and let me have it!"

Baba did not appreciate boasting among his devotees either. Some months after Sambhare had given up drinking Baba did not ask for any *dakshina* at all from him. Sambhare imagined that this was because Baba had come to appreciate his giving up a vicious habit. One evening Sambhare was at the *wada* boasting of having received Baba's grace in the presence of many friends when a call came to him from Baba. When Sambhare rushed to the masjid, the first thing that Baba did was to ask for two rupees as *dakshina*. Sambhare paid it. He also knew that a discreet warning had been issued to him to mend his behaviour.

Radhakrishnaai whom H.S. alias Kakasaheb Dikshit described as the *acharya* of loving devotion lived in Shirdi for many years and served Sai Baba faithfully. Once she happened to insult a person who had come for Sai Baba's *darshan*. Baba reproached her in the presence of many devotees, saying: "Are you aware of the worth of one who ascends the steps of this masjid? Insulting him amounts to insulting me!"

Among persons coming for Sai Baba's *darshan* there were

many who had been devotees for a long time. But there obviously were some who were relatively new to Baba. But Baba would not discriminate between them and expressed his disapproval of anyone who did.

Sai Baba would also restrain his devotees from actions which would only feed their ego, which was an obstacle in their spiritual path. Nanasaheb Nimonkar started with no knowledge of Sanskrit but gradually came to a point where he was an excellent exponent of both the Gita and the Jnaneshwari. Even scholars of Sanskrit would refer to him their doubts. But one day Baba prohibited Nimonkar from expounding both works to put a stop to his growing self-conceit.

The old and the ill, the sick and the starving were all equally welcome to the masjid. When Mrs Tarabai, wife of Sadashiv. Tarkhad was sitting in the masjid there came a leper who was far advanced in his disease. He had little strength left in him and he was filthy. He had difficulty in climbing even the three steps leading to the masjid but managed to move to the *dhuni* and then to Sai Baba and placed his head on Baba's feet. It took so much time for him to take Baba's *darshan* that Mrs Tarkhad could not bear the leper's proximity and wished he would leave soon. Finally he left, holding in his hand a small, dirty parcel.

As he left Mrs Tarkhad felt a great sense of relief but Baba threw one piercing glance at her and sent some one to fetch the leper back. So the poor man returned walking laboriously towards Baba but as he bent low to touch Baba's feet again, Baba picked up the little bundle of dirty cloth and asked the leper: "What do you have in this?"

And then, without waiting for a reply, he opened the bundle to find that it contained some *pedhas*. Baba picked up a piece and offered it to Mrs Tarkhad, singling her out from among many who were assembled in the masjid. Mrs Tarkhad felt a great sense of revulsion but did not have the courage to refuse Baba. So she ate what was offered to her. Baba then took another piece and himself ate it. He then sent away the leper. He gave a similar lesson to Prof. G.G. Narke. In 1916 plague was raging in Shirdi. Sai Baba used to get sweetmeat from a *halwayi* whose plague-stricken corpse was seen lying in his shop. Baba asked Narke to go and get some sweatmeat from the *halwayi's* shop but he was scared to do so. He went to the *halwayi* and told his wife (who was weeping) about Baba's strange request. She pointed to the corpse and asked Narke to take the sweets from the Almirah. Narke picked some sweets all the while fearing that anyone who ate it might catch the infection. But Baba told Narke: "You think you will live if you are away from Shirdi and that you would die if you stay here. That is not so. Whosoever is destined to be struck, will be struck. Whosoever is to die, will die. Whosoever is to be caressed, will be caressed."

Devotees had to keep their promises and if anyone reneged on them, they were reminded of their duties in subtle ways. There lived in Shirdi an old woman Mhalsabai. When Bapurao Shirsathe met her, she blessed him and asked for alms. Shirsathe gave her some money and said he would give her some more when his time came to leave. On the scheduled day of his departure Mhalsabai approached him but he sent her away saying angrily: "Go, get away, how often do I have to pay you?"

He did not think any more of the incident. But then things began to happen. He could not get any vehicle to take him to Kopergaon station. He missed his train. He had to perforce stay overnight at the station. It began to worry him.

When he caught the train the next day he found as his co-passenger another devotee of Sai Baba, Biharilal Vyas. They got to talk. Vyas told Shirsathe: "Do you know, as I started from Shirdi, that mad woman Mhalsabai came and asked me for some money. She was smelling badly. But as soon as I gave her some money she turned back and there came wafting the fragrance of *mogra* and other scented flowers with the breeze! Unbelievable, but true!"

It was then that Shirsathe realised his own arrogance and callousness. Tears came rolling down from his eyes.

Once Damodar Savalaram Rasane invited Sai Baba for a meal but knowing that Baba would not be present personally, requested him that he might send Bala Nevaskar Patil on his behalf. Baba agreed but told Rasane that he should not in any way humiliate Bala because of his low caste. Rasane agreed. He had a sumptuous meal prepared and one plate filled with various items of food was offered to a picture of Baba. Rasane then called out to Bala to come. At that point in walked a black dog and coolly ate from the plate. Rasane waited reverently till the dog finished its meal. Only then were other guests including Bala were served. Rasane was happy.

In May 1915 Shantaram Balwant Nachane went to Shirdi accompanied by his mother-in-law and others. They stayed at a place part of which was occupied by Dada Kelkar, father-in-law of Rao Bahadur Sathe. Dada Kelkar, an orthodox brahmin, abhorred onions; when he found Nachane's mother-in-law slicing onions he offered some harsh remarks which the old lady took to her heart.

A few hours later, Kelkar's grand-daughter started crying saying that her eyes were hurting. Kelkar went to Baba seeking some remedy. Baba said: "Foment the child's eyes with an onion!" "Onion?" Kelkar asked incredulously, "where am I to get one?" Baba, pointing to Nachane's mother-in-law replied: "Ask this mother!" But the lady said she wouldn't give Kelkar any onions and recalled the morning's incident to Baba. "Only if you order me to give him an onion, would I do so. Otherwise not," said the good lady. Baba ordered her to give Kelkar an onion which was duly applied to the child's eye to give her instant relief. Kelkar certainly got his lesson in social behaviour in Shirdi!

Another instance of an ingenious method adopted by Sai Baba was in the case of Govind Raghunath alias Annasaheb Dabholkar, author of Shri Sai-Sat-Charit. A weekly bazaar used to be held in Shirdi. It was a Sunday afternoon. Dabholkar was sitting to Baba's right, kneading his limbs. Suddenly Madhavrao Deshpande spotting some groundnuts in the folds of Dabholkar's coat sleeves couldn't help laughing. When he nudged

Dabholkar some of these groundnuts fell down. How they came to be on the sleeve folds became a topic of fun and speculation. Baba teasingly said: "He has this bad habit of eating by himself without sharing his repast with others! He must have gone to the bazaar by himself just to get the groundnuts to consume in private. Not a good thing to do, is it?"

Dabholkar had not gone to the bazaar and was rather peeved with Baba's remark and he said: "This appears to be one of your leelas! I neither went to the bazaar nor ate any groundnuts. Moreover I never eat anything without sharing whatever I have with others!" Baba who was in a teasing mood so far, suddenly turned serious.

He said: "Of course you share your food with those around you. But how can you give to some one who is not with you? Do you remember me when you are eating? Am I not with you always?"

It was then that Dabholkar realised that eating food is also a sacrificial act and nothing should be eaten without first offering it or remembering God or guru. Another interpretation given to Baba's remark would be that nothing we do is ever hidden from God or guru and that we should therefore be careful and circumspect in our thoughts and deeds.

Once Nanasaheb Chandorkar was confused. While he was sitting with Sai Baba, two Muslim women in *purdah* came for Baba's *darshan*. Being in purdah they were hesitant to come before Baba when he had company. So Chandorkar decided to leave but Baba bade him stay. The women thereafter came forward, removed their veils to take Baba's darshan. One of the two women was old and the other was young and very pretty. Nanasaheb was quite taken with the young girl and wanted to gaze at her but, out of deference to Baba, kept his head down. Sensing his agitation, Baba patted him on the back. After the women took their leave Baba turned to Nanasaheb and asked him: "Do you know why I patted you?"

Nanasaheb replied: "What can remain unknown to you? But how is it that even in your company such thoughts can come in my mind?"

274

"Nana," countered Baba, "you don't have to be agitated. When a faculty performs its natural function there should be no interference. Brahma created this universe and if we don't admire and appreciate it, we would be lacking in aesthetics. Our instincts can be tamed gradually. If our heart is pure, what is there to fear?"

★ The mind is naturally fickle, but do not permit it to be impetuous.
★ Even if the senses are agitated, the body should be restrained.
★ The senses are untrustworthy, so do not hanker after desires.
★ By constant practice (and dispassion) fickle-mindedness will disappear.

Shri Sai Sat-Charit, xlix 170-171

After the intellectual understanding of the Brahman through logical reasoning, the plenary experience will follow sooner or later in the case of the seeker according to his capacity/authority and effort. The plenary experience together with the grace of the Guru lead to plenary bliss. Uddhaveshbua of Dahanu came to Shirdi in 1904 and asked Sai Baba: "When will I get a guru to lead me to liberation?"

Baba told him that he would understand after five years as it was not possible to swallow a whole *bhakri* in one gulp.

At the end of five years Uddhaveshbua had grasped Sai Baba's powers and realized that Baba could lead him on the path of salvation. Baba then directed him to read *Eknathi Bhagwat* regularly.

A rich and avaricious man came to Sai Baba and said: "Please show me the Brahman!" Baba seated him by his side and said to him: "Many people come running to me for worldly pleasures but it is rare to see one like you who seeks Brahman! I will show you not only Brahman but the whole bundle of Brahman!"

So saying, Sai Baba called a boy and said to him: "Go to Nandu grocer and fetch me five rupees. Say Baba needs the money urgently!"

Off the boy ran but returned soon to say that Nandu's house was locked. Then Baba sent the boy to Bala grocer with the same message, but Bala too was not at home. Thereafter Baba sent the boy to one or two other people but none of them was at home at that time. Would Baba have not known this with his inner vision? But this was actually a test of the visitor. He who sought Brahman had with him a bundle of notes worth Rs 250 but he was filled with hesitation and could not bring himself to offer the paltry sum of five rupees as a loan and that too, for a short while!

Watching all this hectic activity, the merchant thought that his original request had been forgotten by Baba. So he said: "Baba, you haven't shown me Brahman yet!" At this point Baba turned to him and said gently: "Don't you see that all the while that was what I was doing?"

What Baba was trying to convey was that unless one surrendered the five *pranaas* (vital airs), five organs, ego, mind and intellect, one could not attain knowledge of Brahman! So Baba told the merchant that he had in his pocket Rs 250, but until he overcame his avariciousness and surrendered his all, Brahman was a far cry.

He added: "My coffers are full. Any one can have his pick, but I have to give according to the capacity of the taker. If you keep this in mind, it will be conducive to your well-being. Sitting in this holy masjid, I never speak an untruth!" Thanking Baba profusely, the merchant left.

Baba was always insistent that everyone should follow the *dharma* prescribed to him by his guru. So, when Swami Vijayanand, a sanyasin, came to Shirdi he was received cordially. A few days later, however, the Swami came seeking Baba's permission to leave as he had received a telegram saying that his mother was ill.

Baba said to him: "If you were so attached to your mother, why did you take *sanyas* in the first place?" Baba refused to give him permission to leave. On the other hand he told the sanyasin: "Let's see. Wait for a few days."

Baba had found through his inner eye that the swami himself had not long to live. So he directed him to go to Lendi and to do *parayana* of *Ram Vijaya*. Thus the Swami passed fourteen days and completed two *parayanas*. As he was about to commence the third *parayana* he was seized with a sudden sickness that left him very weak. He was quickly brought to the *wada* but in a short while he passed away. During his last days Baba had steadied him on the path of the sanyasin's *dharma*.

The devotee and the Lord, the disciple and the guru are one. God or guru bear the blows which fall on the devotee or the disciple. They pass on only such burden that the devotee can bear.

When Dikshit's younger daughter passed away in Shirdi in 1911, he was stricken with grief. Knowing earlier that Dikshit would have to bear the grief of his daughter's loss, Baba had ordered for him a copy of *Bhavaartha Ramayana*. By the time the daughter passed away, the *pothi* arrived. Dikshit took it to Baba who opened it at *Kishkindha kand* which carries a vivid description of the lament of Tara following the killing of Vali and the instruction imparted to her by Rama. Baba asked Dikshit to read it. Dikshit read it with tears in his eyes but it calmed him. It was like a balm applied to a wound.

And so it always was. Baba never failed his devotees in trouble or in doubt. Some years after Nanasaheb Chandorkar had accepted Sai Baba as his sadguru, he was transferred to Pandharpur, but the transfer placed him in a dilemma. Residing in Pandharpur, how could he forego the *darshan* of Lord Vithoba? But could he divide his loyalties between Vithoba and Sai Baba? This bothered Nanasaheb. On his way to Pandharpur Nanasaheb got off at Kopargaon and was on his way to Shirdi when Baba told the devotees sitting around him: "The portals of Pandhari are opened to us. Let us sing His praises with delight." Saying so, he started to sing a bhajan:

I have to go, to go to Pandharpur and stay there
I have to stay, to stay there, for it is the house of my Lord!

Just then Nanasaheb arrived in Shirdi with his family. He prostrated before Sai Baba and requested him to come and stay in Pandharpur. Nanasaheb had not informed about his visit to Shirdi to anyone, nor had he sent a message. So, at his sudden arrival everybody was surprised. His arrival at the masjid coincided with the singing of the particular bhajan referring to Pandhari's doors being open to all and as Nanasaheb heard it, it was music to his ears. Without Baba uttering a word Nanasaheb's dilemma had been resolved.

Interesting, too, is the experience of H.S. alias Kakasaheb Dikshit. Once while going by a rickshaw from Kopergaon to Shirdi, he passed a woman with a basket of guavas on her head. He stopped the tonga and bought the guavas for Sai Baba. The fragrance of the guavas was so tempting that Kakasaheb felt like eating a few himself even before offering them to Baba. It bothered him and he prayed to Baba to take away from him that desire. To his surprise the fragrance of the guavas suddenly ceased and Kakasaheb's desire died down.

While writing a commentary in verse form in Marathi on Ishopanishad, Das Ganu had a telling experience. At one point Das Ganu thought that he would seek Sai Baba's clarification on a doubt that occurred to him. So he called on Baba. But Baba said: "What's your problem? Go to Kaka Dikshit at Vile Parle. His maid servant will resolve your doubt!"

Many present at that occasion thought Baba was merely joking but Das Ganu had such firm faith in Baba that he decided to go to Vile Parle anyway. It was night when he reached Vile Parle and rather than engage Kakasaheb in discussion, Das Ganu decided he would rest for the night and raise his question with Kakasaheb the next morning.

In the morning Das Ganu was still in bed when he heard the sweet voice of a girl singing. He listened to it intently. The thought of the commentary on *Ishopanishad* came to his mind and he wondered what it was this maid servant could teach him. There was nothing much in the song as such. It merely described the loveliness of an orange-coloured sari! When he came out of his bed room he noticed the maid servant washing dishes, but her singing so pleased him that he decided to arrange for an orange-coloured sari to be bought for her that very morning!

Nobody could have been more pleased than this simple maid servant when she received the sari of her song! And she showed it. She wore the sari all day long.

The next morning she was back to work in her old torn sari, but there seemed to be no tinge of sadness still in her voice. She was as chirpy as ever! It was then that the meaning of the beautiful lines in the *Ishopanishad* flashed to his mind:

Ishavasyam idam sarvam, yat kincha jagatyaam jagat...

God permeates the whole universe. Enjoy what is given. The giver and the gift are all filled with the essence that is God.

Thus Sai Baba taught philosophy, devotion, spiritual discipline, morality, conduct in daily life, fellow-feeling for all life without being preachy. It was Saint Tukaram who said that even the ordinary talk of a holy person was in itself instruction. That was also true of Sai Baba.

Once Baba had convincingly shown T.G. Samant that the latter's chosen deity and Baba himself were one and indivisible. Thirty one years after he was no more, Baba could show that he was even in the form of Datta.

In 1949 Gangadhar Laxman Jakhadi of Dadar, Bombay, was a telegraph master at Kalyan Railway Station. At 12 noon as he was going to the canteen for lunch, he saw a sanyasin sitting on a bench. The sanyasin called to him and said: "Take leave for today!"

Curious, Jakhadi took it as a command and sought the Station Master's permission. Ordinarily the Station Master was loth to give in to a request for leave, but this time he granted Jakhadi leave immediately.

Jakhadi then got into a conversation with the sanyasin, who said that he was a devotee of Dattatreya, that he had come to Bombay after a pilgrimage to Mahur, was on his way to Badrinarayan and would Jakhadi please buy him a ticket to Hardwar?

"Do you have any money?" Jakhadi asked the sanyasin.

"Put your hand in my *zoli* and take the money out," replied the sanyasin.

Jakhadi did as he was told to find that the *zoli* contained a lot of rupee coins. "Take all the money," the sanyasin told Jakhadi, but the latter wanted none of it. He merely took Rs 36 for the fare which cost Rs 35 Annas 12 and wanted to return the balance of four annas to the sanyasin.

"Put that four annas back into my *zoli!*" the sanyasin said.

When Jakhadi sought to do so he found that the *zoli* which was only a few minutes ago full of rupees was now empty!

"What happened? Your *zoli* is totally empty!" Jakhadi asked in wonderment.

"Nothing has happened!" the sanyasin answered nonchalantly. "My bank is at Mahur, Gangapur, Shirdi and such other places. When I need money it comes to me. When the need is met, the money returns to its place. What have I got to do with money?"

Then he added: "Sai Baba is an incarnation of Datta, visit Shirdi from time to time and you will not want for anything!"

From that day onwards, Jakhadi began worshipping Sai Baba in the form of Dattatreya. Another Dattatreya and Sai Baba devotee, Subbarao of Guti heard in his sleep in the first week of February 1944, a distinct voice telling him to perform constant *japa* of Datta. Believing that he was being instructed by Sai Baba he decided in his sleep itself to perform the *japa*. But next day, so involved was he in his work that he forgot to keep his promise. Next day Sai Baba gave him *darshan* in an angry mood. On waking up in the morning he received a telegram informing him that his son had been hospitalised with acute asthma. This time he decided to do the *japa* without fail sitting by the side of Baba's photograph. Three days later he received a letter saying that his son's condition had improved and that he had been brought home. Thereupon he performed Datta-*japa* 5,000 times. Subbarao drew benefit from this in yet another way. A government decision to prosecute him for having a revolver stood cancelled.

Dahyabhai Damodardas Mehta, a hardware merchant of Bombay, residing in a chawl near Madhavbaug, started worshipping Sai Baba in 1945. In 1946-47 he was laid down with typhoid. There was a rumour circulating then that the spirit of a carpenter was harassing many people living in the chawl where he was residing. Mehta was frightened and in order to avoid any harm coming to him, he was persuaded by others to wear an amulet round his neck. That did him little good. He developed high fever. He was being treated by a doctor.

One night he felt as if the carpenter's spirit was sitting on his chest. In despair the merchant started calling for Sai Baba whose photograph was close by. At that point he heard a voice emanating from the photograph that said: "Why are you afraid? Here I have been standing since morning with a stick for your protection, but you must throw away that amulet you are wearing!"

And so he did.

His health improved, but not quite. The merchant therefore vowed that if he got well, he would go for Baba's *darshan* and offer a *dakshina* of Rs 101. His recovery began soon after and within a month he had completely recovered.

The merchant deduced from this that no Sai Baba's devotee should fear any incantation or spell, black magic, sorcery or witchcraft.

To a Muslim in Ahmedabad Baba taught that no disrespect should ever be shown to a saint. Ramanlal Mali, a devotee of Sai Baba owned a shop at Bhadra in Ahmedabad. He would burn incense before Baba's picture every day. A Muslim who used to pass Mali's shop used to make fun of Ramanlal. Once when the Muslim was returning home from his work, he saw an *aulia* coming from the opposite direction, making a lot of noise. When the *aulia* came opposite Ramanlal's shop he stopped and said to the Muslim: "What, you make fun of Ramanlal for burning incense before my picture?" Before the Muslim could say anything, the *aulia* disappeared. The Muslim gentleman was quite taken aback and realised the error of his ways.

Mrs Surjabai Kasliwal of Khamgaon in Berar had a dream in which she heard Sai Baba instructing her to do the *japa* of Sai Baba Sai Nath. So, giving up the daily worship of all other gods, she started repeating the *japa* as instructed, On the fourth day, again, in a dream, Sai Baba showed her a *durbar* in which on four similar seats were seated Sai Baba himself, Shri Shantinath, Sri Padmaprabhu and Bhagwan Mahavir.

As Surjabai was about to ask Baba a question, she heard him say: "Look, here are your Shantinath, Padmaprabhu and Mahavirprabhu, ask them!"

On waking up Surjabai pondered on the meaning of the dream and concluded that what Baba wanted her was to continue worshipping her own gods even while showing *bhakti* towards him.

Ratilal Chimanlal Seth of Tarkas Bhavan, Ahmedabad had a different kind of experience. He had offered on a Thursday 1.25 lakh bel leaves to Sai Baba in the form of Shiva. Next day, when Ratilal opened the door of his puja room he found to his surprise and horror that a cobra with raised hood was lying in front of the bel heap. The cobra slowly crept round the pile of leaves and then sat with its hood raised over the photograph of Radha Krishna. Frightened, Ratilal quickly closed the door to the room and decided that he would postpone the ceremony of immersion of the leaves in the river.

Three hours later devotees from far away started coming to have a *darshan* of Sai Baba in the form of Shiva. When Ratilal opened the door of the puja room he discovered to his surprise that the cobra had disappeared. There was no clue as to whence it came and whence it disappeared, but Ratilal was sure that Sai Baba had given him *darshan* in the form of Sheshashayee Bhagwan and that Lord Vishnu Himself was pleased with his devotion and had shown his essential unity with Shiva.

Ratilal could only thank Sai Baba for everything.

2

So much has been written about Sai Baba, but not much about how he spent a day. People came constantly to see him and yet his day was fairly structured and disciplined. He would be seen sitting near his *dhuni* (sacred fire) in the masjid before 5 a.m. That would be the way his day began. He would complete his morning ablutions and sit there by his *dhuni* in silence. He performed no rituals. He never read any book nor did he ever write. His instructions were oral. It is said that he would wave his arms about or point his fingers, making gestures and saying *yade haq.* Visitors were not permitted to go within fifty feet of him. The *sevekaris* (attendants) would carry out their duties of sweeping the floor and replenishing the *dhuni* without a word spoken. The first *sevekari* to arrive was Bhagoji Shinde who would give a massage to Sai Baba, fill his chilim with tobacco, light it and hand it over to Baba for smoking. Sai Baba would have a puff and then give the chilim for him to take a puff. Then Baba would have five or six puffs. At this point a few close devotees would come forward to do *guru-seva.* Their *seva* over, Baba would get up, wash and clean his hands, feet and face delicately with plenty of water. Sai Baba was not known to have a daily bath. He would bathe once in eight or ten days as the spirit moved him, but he was always scrupulously clean.

About 8 a.m. Baba would go to four or five houses in the village for alms. The houses he would visit were those of Bayajabai Kote Patil, Patilbua Gondkar, Appaji Kote, Nandram Savairam and Narayan Teli. Standing in front of the houses he would cry out: *Pori anage chatkur bhakri!* He would collect all the dry *bhakris* in his *zoli* and whatever liquid was given in a tumbler. He would then return to the masjid, eat his *bhakris* and keep whatever was left in a corner of the masjid for anyone who needed food. Birds and beasts were welcome to the repast.

The first sitting would then be held which would last upto 9.30 a.m. Many devotees would come to pay their respects to him. At this sitting he would purchase bananas, guavas and mangoes and distribute them among the devotees.

At 9.30 a.m. he would proceed to the lendi stream accompanied by Abdul and spend an hour there. Baba would sit behind the enclosed *Nanda Deep* from where the lamp was not visible to him. He did not gaze at the lamp. He would collect two pots of water from which he would make offerings to various directions—about the only ritual he observed. Whether he uttered any *mantras* or prayers while doing so is not known.

He would then return from the Lendi and remain in the masjid until 2 p.m. During this time he would hold a second sitting for about an hour when devotees would worship him individually and a congregational worship and *arati* would follow. It would then be time for the afternoon meal or lunch. Sai Baba would preside over the meal with devotees sitting on either side in two rows. The seat to the left of Sai Baba would be reserved for Bade Baba.

He would be alone between 1 p.m. and 2 p.m. It is said that he would sit behind a screen, take out a pouch containing ten to fifteen old coins of various denominations such as one pie, two pies, one anna, two annas, four annas, eight annas and a rupee, and play with them, rubbing his finger tips against their surface. Nobody apparently has heard him utter any *mantra* but he was heard to say: "This is Nana's, this Bapu's, this Kaka's, this Somyas's etc." Should he notice anyone approaching him at this time he would put the coins back in the pouch.

At 2 p.m. Sai Baba would again go to the Lendi and return after three quarters of an hour. He would remain in the masjid between 2.45 p.m. and 5 p.m. The third sitting would be held between 5 p.m. and 6.30 p.m. At 6.30 p.m. he would go out for his evening round for a few minutes, and be back again.

Thus, during the day he would hold three sittings in all, the first between 8.30 a.m. and 9.30 a.m., the second between 10.30 a.m. and 11.30 a.m. and the last between 5 p.m. and 6.30 p.m. During the three sittings he would instruct his devotees. His language was highly cryptic, full of symbology, parable, allegory and metaphor. Often only the individual devotee knew what Baba communicated to him. He preached no sermon, gave no discourses on Vedanta, Upanishads or the Gita. His instruction was mainly in the realm of ethics. He imparted faith in God to those who lacked it, confirmed the faith of those who had it. He would give simple instructions about *nama japa* and other spiritual practices. However if any *yogi* called on him, he would meet him at his own level and communicate with him in appropriate terms. He would counsel devotees to continue with their devotion and he would lead them slowly on the path of self- realization in accordance with their capacity and effort. He would use his supernatural powers to give direct experiences to the devotees who remembered him and fervently prayed to him.

In his early years Baba was said to sleep on a narrow plank about seven to eight feet above ground level, the plank being suspended from the ceiling. But when word went round that he was performing this feat, he apparently gave it up and slept like any normal being, on the floor.

3

The *durbar* of Sai Baba was open to all irrespective of caste, creed, religion or sex. Rich and poor, the good and the wicked all came to him during his sittings. Not even animals were barred. Among those who came to see him or to receive his blessings were lawyers, doctors, teachers, government officials and lay men.

In his early years those who came to see him were mostly holy men. One such was Ramanand Bidkar Maharaj, a disciple of Shri Swami Maharaj of Akkalkot. That was in 1873. Another who visited Baba was Anandnath Maharaj, another prominent disciple of Akkalkot Swami Maharaj. After seeing Baba, Anandnath Maharaj is reported to have said: "Here is a diamond on a dung hill." Anandnath Maharaj is also quoted as having said that anybody who kept away from Baba on the theory that he was mad, besides being a Muslim, was the real loser. Maharaj advised those who wished to attain salvation to approach Baba with humility.

In 1896, a well-known Vaishnavite, Gangagirbaba of Puntambe after meeting Baba is reported to have said that Shirdi was extremely fortunate in acquiring a gem like Sai Baba. Said Gangagirbaba: "This man is no ordinary person. Blessed is the soil of Shirdi on which he has set his foot."

In due course, Sai Baba's fame had reached up to British officials, one of whom, Mr. George Curtis came to Shirdi accompanied by his wife and the Collector of Ahmednagar district one Mr. Maclean.

Baba treated them no better than he would treat anyone else. When one of the Indian officials accompanying the Britishers suggested to Sahasrabuddhe that Baba should cut short his morning routine in order to meet the sahibs he was told that that was impossible. The sahibs had better wait.

Indeed, when Baba was stopped by Mrs. Curtis with a request that she wanted to have a word with him—she had said: 'Aap ke sath kuchh baat karneki hai.' Baba simply told her: "aadha ghanta ther jav" (wait for half an hour). At the end of the half hour when poor Mrs. Curtis again approached him respectfully, she was told this time to wait for one more hour! Unprepared to be told to wait, the burra sahibs left. Mrs. Curtis apparently wanted Baba's blessings to get a child as she was childless. She never got to speak to him. And her wishes went unanswered. However it is recorded that not long afterwards Mr. Curtis himself was promoted vice president of the Governor's Executive Council.

Like high government officials, members of princely families put in their appearance at Shirdi from time to time. In 1904 a lady from the Gaekwar family of Baroda came for Baba's darshan in the company of Sir Bhalchandra Bhatwadekar, a renowned physician of Bombay and a friend of Sir Pherozeshah Mehta. She placed two thalis one filled with rupees and another with guineas, before Baba but Baba returned them without even touching them. The lady thereupon offered some guineas to Mhalsapati who was sitting next to Baba. When Mhalsapati sought Baba's advice, Baba told him: "What do we have to do with guineas? Our poverty is good enough for us!" Mhalsapati oo declined the offer.

In almost all works on Sai Baba—and there are many books written on him—there is hardly any reference to the political ferment of his times. It could not be that Shirdi was too far away from the urban centres to be involved in politics. The Indian National Congress was founded in 1885 when Sai Baba was about 45 years old. He took samadhi in 1918 by which time the Congress had come to be controversial enough to make waves. There were distinguished leaders in Maharashtra but there is only one brief record of one of Maharashtra's great leaders— Lokamanya Bal Gangadhar Tilak—visiting Shirdi. The information has been recorded by Dadasaheb Khaparde.

Ganesh Shrikrishna alias Dadasaheb Khaparde, leader of Berar, was a devotee of Sai Baba. In 1910 he stayed in Shirdi for one whole week from 5th December. Again in 1911, on 6th December he arrived in Shirdi and was detained by Sai Baba for three months. Khaparde's income from legal practice ran into five figures per month. His long stay in Shirdi, in the circumstances, put him to considerable financial loss, but he did not care. And there was a good reason for that. Lokamanya Tilak was serving a sentence in Mandalay Jail in Burma and there was strict police surveillance over the movements of his friends. So Khaparde had a firm conviction that in keeping him in Shirdi, Baba had been undoubtedly wanting to save him from some danger.

On 19 May 1917, Lokamanya Tilak met Sai Baba. Two noted personalities have written conflicting accounts of that meeting. They are Dadasaheb Khaparde and Narasimha Chintaman alias Tayasaheb Kelkar. Khaparde's account is the more feasible. Khaparde maintained a diary. The following is excerpted from his account written on 19 May 1917.

"Sangamner—Shirdi—Yeola: I got up in the morning but so many people gathered that I could not pray. There was a movement to keep us here and not let us go till afternoon and Kelkar appeared to throw his weight on the side of the movement, but most unaccountably I felt angry and insisted upon starting. So, after a *paan-supari* in the house of Mr. Sant, a leading pleader of Sangamner, we started about 8.30 am. We reached Shirdi about 10 am after puncture on the way. We put up in Dixit's Wada. Bapusaheb Bootee, Narayanrao Pandi and the Establishment of Bootee were there. My old friends Madhavrao Deshpande, Balasaheb Bhate, Bapusaheb Jog and others gathered. We went to the masjid and paid our respects to the Sayin Maharaj. I never saw him so much pleased before. He asked for *daxina* as usual and we all paid. Looking at Lokamanya, he said: "People are bad, keep yourself to yourself." I made my bow and he took some rupees from me. Kelkar and Paregaonkar also paid. Madhavrao Deshpande asked permission for us to proceed to Yeola. Sayin Saheb said: "Why do you want to go in the heat to die on the way? Have your food here and then go in the cool of the afternoon." So we stayed, had our food with Madhavrao Deshpande, lay down for a few minutes and then again went to the masjid and found Sayin Maharaj lying down as if sleeping. People gave Lokamanya a *paan-supari* in the *chavdi* there and we returned to the masjid again. Sayin Maharaj was sitting up and gave us *udi* and permission to go. So we started by the motor."

Incidentally, according to Bapusaheb Jog, Sai Baba also told Lokamanya: "You have done a lot for people, but now devote yourself to your own welfare." The Shirdi Diary of Mr. Khaparde is interesting in many ways. Not only does it give one a full picture of what it was to live in Shirdi in those times, but it provides a detailed picture of people who came to see Sai Baba and how he behaved towards them. It is a very human picture of Baba that emerges. Sample entries:

February 9, 1912: I got up as usual, prayed and attended Panchadashi class. During it, we saw Sayin Maharaj go out. After finishing the class, I went to the masjid. Sayin Baba was in a very good mood. The young boy Kishya whom we call Pishya came there as usual. On seeing him Sayin Saheb said that Pishya was a Rohilla in his previous birth, that he was a very good man, that he prayed long and came as a guest to Sayin Saheb's grandfather. The latter had a sister who used to live separate. That Sayin Saheb was a young boy himself then and playfully suggested that the Rohilla should marry her. This was to be and he eventually married her. The Rohilla lived there with his wife for a long time and ultimately went away with her, nobody knew where. He died and Sayin Saheb put him in the womb of his present mother. Pishya, he said, would be very fortunate and the protector of thousands....

Khaparde describes Baba in his many moods. One entry speaks about Baba being "in a very pleased mood and laughed and abused in one and the same breath." It is not clear what Baba was laughing about and why and whom he was abusing. There is a very touching reference to the death of Megha who served Sai Baba very faithfully to the end of his days. Writes Kharpade:

19 January 1912: This was a very sad day. I got up very early and after finishing my prayer discovered that it yet wanted an hour or so to daybreak. So I lay down and was aroused for *Kakad Arti* by Bapusaheb Jog. Dixit kaka told me that Megha died about 4 am. The *Kakad Arti* was done but Sayin Maharaj did not show his face clear and did not appear to open his eyes. He never threw glances spreading grace. After we returned arrangements were made for the cremation of Megha's body. Sayin Baba came just as the body was being brought out and loudly lamented his death. His voice was so touching that it brought tears to every eye. He followed the body up to the bend in the made road near the village and then went his usual way. Megha's body was taken under the Bada tree and consigned to flames there. Sayin Baba could be distinctly heard lamenting his death even at that distance and he was seen waving his hands and swaying as if in *arti* to say goodbye. There was a good supply of dry fuel and flames soon rose very high. Dixit Kaka, myself, Bapusaheb Jog, Upasani, Dada Kelkar and all else were there and praised the lot of Megha that his body was seen and touched by Sayin Baba on the head, heart, shoulders and feet.....I remember how Baba foretold his death three days ago...

Among Baba's rich devotees was Gopalrao Buti (his name has also been spelt as 'Bootee'). He patronised artists who would be eager to pay their respects to Baba by performing before him. One of the artistes was Khansahib Abdul Karim Khan. In 1914 Buti along with some other devotees of Sai Baba was present at the public concert of Khansahib at the residence of Pratap Seth of Amalner. On their invitation Khansahib decided to cancel his tour of Malegaon etc. and go to Shirdi for Sai Baba's *darshan* as Khansahib held Baba in great reverence.

From Amalner Khansahib reached Shirdi with his disciples and camped in the verandah of Kote Patil. They could not have *darshan* of Baba that day until evening. As usual the *bhajan* party gathered in the evening before the masjid. Present among them was Khansahib and his men. One look at Baba and Khansahib was convinced of his saintliness. After the usual enquiries Baba turned to Khansahib and asked him to sing a Marathi bhajan. To the accompaniment of the instruments, Khansahib sang *hechi dana dega deva,* an abhang of Tukaram in *raga Piloo* with such intense devotion that Baba with his eyes closed listened with rapt attention. When the bhajan was over,

Baba opened his eyes and exclaimed: "Ah, how well he sang! Such is his intensity in praying, that one feels like granting his prayer!" Because of Khansahib's performance the night *arati* was delayed, but after it was over, Baba told Khansahib: "Now you will not go away soon. Do not worry about your home. Everything will be well." Kote Patil was asked to look after the guests royally.

Next day a telegram was received by Khansahib from his wife Tahera (Tarabai): "Gulbakavali very sick. Return immediately." (Gulbakavali, Khansahib's daughter, was later to attain fame as Hirabai Badodekar). When the telegram was shown to Baba he told Khansahib not to worry and to call his whole family to Shirdi. Accordingly two disciples of Khansahib were sent to Poona and the family brought to Shirdi. Khansahib's party, including his wife, consisted of about twenty persons all of whom were camping at Kote Patil's. Tahera said to Kote Patil's wife that she would cook for her group. Mrs Patil replied: "Oh no! I have no orders from Sai Baba to permit this. We have been asked to look after you. You tell us what you want and don't want and we will respect your wishes!" Tahera had no option but to acquiesce. On reaching Shirdi Gulbakavali was taken to Sai Baba. Her condition was serious but Baba put *tirth* and *udi* in her mouth. Within 48 hours she had completely recovered. Baba kept Khansahib in Shirdi for ten days and then gave him permission to leave. On the seventh day Tahera pleased Baba by singing *ghalin lotangana vandin charana* in the morning in *raga Bhairavi*.

On the ninth day Baba said to Kote Patil: "Let us have music tonight to the accompaniment of *tanpura*. Call the village folk. Let all hear." On that night a number of people from the village and outside gathered. Pratap Seth of Amalner, Dhanvate of Nagpur, Mrs. Buti and others from Srirampur and Kopergaon also came. Khansahib had acquainted himself with the favourite *bhajans* and *abhangs* of Baba and opened with the composition *aur nahi kachchu kamki main bharose apne Ramki,* in *Darbari Kanada*, then sang Baba's favourite *abhang* of Tukaram *Je ka ranjale ganjale tyasi mhane jo apule* and then

isa tana dhanaki kaun badhai, a *doha* of Kabir in *raga Jogia.*
He concluded with *kaya kaisi royi tajo dijo re prana* in a higher
note in raga Piloo. It was about 2 a.m. when the programme was
over. Sai Baba enjoyed it immensely. He patted Khansahib on
the back, blessed him by placing his hand on the latter's head
and giving him a rupee coin, said: "Don't spend this rupee.
Always keep it in your pocket." He also gave five rupees to
Tahera and told her to keep them in a box. In addition he gave
her a large box of *pedhas.*

Ganpatrao Bodas who never visited holy men and criticized
those who did, was a member of Kirloskar Natak Mandali.
During a halt at Ahmednagar he had a desire to have *darshan*
of Sai Baba. Balasaheb Mirikar, Mamledar of Kopergaon was a
friend of his. On a Sunday he visited Mirikar and next day went
to Shirdi. Going to the masjid he prostrated before Baba and
placed a coconut and dry tobacco before him. Baba asked
Bodas to fill his chilim, enquired about him and asked for
dakshina. Bodas gave a rupee. Baba directed him to have his
meals before leaving and then exclaimed: "What can Baba do
when you quarrel amongst yourselves?" Two days earlier,
Bodas had quarrelled with his colleague Joglekar. So Bodas
realised the power of Baba to know his innermost thought.

Then he proceeded to the dining hall. There some one told him
that he should have emptied his purse when Baba asked for
dakshina. Bodas accepted the advice and decided to act
accordingly at the next opportunity. When he went to take leave
of Baba, he placed his head on Baba's feet who said: "All set
for going?" "I have come to ask for your permission," said
Bodas. Baba gave him leave and again asked for *dakshina.*
This time Bodas gladly emptied his purse before Baba. Baba
then applied *udi* to the latter's forehead and blessed him.

"You have given me *dakshina.* Narayan will amply reward
you," he said.

4

And now we come to the last chapter of Sai Baba's life: his
nirvana. Dasara or Vijaya Dashami has a special significance to
Hindus. It is a day of *simollanghan* i.e. crossing the boundary. It
is the day when kings set out on the campaigns of conquests.
On Tuesday, 15 October 1918, Sai abandoned his physical
frame and merged into Infinity. According to the Hindu
calender, Vijaya Dashmi was over at 12.30 pm on that fateful
day and *Ekadashi* had commenced. At 2.35 pm. Sai Baba
attained *nirvana*. As per the Muslim calender it was the ninth
day and the night thereof was *kattal-ki-rat* (Night of the
Massacre).

Sai Baba had told a devotee of his connections with him in his
past births as far back as seventy two generations. He had
knowledge of the past, the present and the future. As such he
had full knowledge of his departure from the world. It is
therefore no wonder that he planned for the event carefully.

Four months before his end, he called Kasim, the son of Fakir
Bade Baba and entrusted to him an assignment. Giving him
Rs. 250, Sai Baba sent him to Aurangabad to see Fakir
Shamsuddin Mia and arrange for *moulu* or *nat*, (singing of
Mohammad Paigambar's praise), **Qawali** (singing the praises of
awaliyas or holy persons) to the beat of drum and hand
clapping and *nyas* or *langar* (preparing and distributing food).
He also gave Kasim a garland of *sevanthi (rosa glandulifera)*
and directed him to go next to Fakir Banne Mia with it and give
him the message: *"Nou din, nou tarikh, Allah Mia apne dhunia
le jayega. Marji Allahki."* As Kasim was a stranger to
Aurangabad Sai Baba asked Imam Chhota Khan to accompany
Kasim.

They left Shirdi and reached Aurangabad railway station at 3
pm. Fakir Shamsuddin Mia had come to the station. He was
known to Imam Chhota Khan. Shamsuddin Mia asked: "Who
are the guests who have come from Fakir Sai?" Shamsuddin
Mia also repeated Sai Baba's instructions to them word for

word. Then he took them to his place and arranged for everything that very day as wished by Sai Baba.

Next day Kasim and Imam Chhota Khan went to Banne Mia's house. He was standing with one arm upraised in the air. The Arabs around him cautioned the two of them not to approach him lest they were beaten by him. After waiting for one hour, Imam Chhota Khan took courage and put around Banne Mia's neck the garland of *sevanti* flowers given by Sai Baba. Then Banne Mia lowered his upraised arm. Imam Chhota Khan then gave him Sai Baba's message in the latter's own words. Fakir Banne Mia gazed at the sky and tears rolled down his eyes.

Kasim and Imam Chhota Khan, having completed their assignment returned to Shirdi. Four months thereafter Sai Baba passed away.

Fourteen days before his end, Sai Baba made Vaze, a devotee of his, to sit in the masjid for the *parayana* of *Rama Vijaya* and himself sat listening. One round of *parayana* was over in eight days. The second round was completed in three days and nights. Thus eleven days passed. Vaze continued his reading but soon got tired. Sai Baba interrupted it and sent Vaze away.

There were other incidents to indicate Sai Baba's preparations for *nirvana*. Sai Baba appeared in a dream to Bapu Saheb Buti. In the dream Butee was instructed to construct a *wada*. As the *wada* was being got ready Baba directed that when the time came his body should be interred there.

In 1916 Ramachandra Patil of Shirdi became sick. All medical aid proved useless and Patil himself got tired of living. In this state of mind, one midnight, Sai Baba's figure appeared suddenly near the head of Patil's bed. Patil held Sai Baba's feet and asked him when his final release would come. Assuring him Baba said: "You need not have any fear. But Tatya Kote's days are numbered. In 1918, on Vijaya Dashami day Tatya Kote will die. Do not tell him now..."

Ramachandra Patil began to recover and was soon well. Days passed and weeks. Came the month of August 1918. Then August slipped into September. Tatya Kote now fell sick. Baba, too, had bouts of shivering. Kote began to have unbearable pain. At the same time Baba also became enfeebled. The fever subsided after three days but Baba abjured all food and became progressively weak. At that time only Kakasaheb Dikshit was with him. Sai Baba sent him away. But hearing of Baba's worsening condition, he was to return.

For about two years Nanasaheb Nimonkar (Vatandar of Nimon and paternal uncle of Madhavrao Deshpande) had been staying close to Sai Baba and serving him day and night. Also present then in Shirdi were Buti, Jog, Madhavrao Deshpande, Bhate and some others. Though Baba had managed during this time to attend to his personal hygiene unassisted, he had to be helped when he went out for alms. During his evening rounds Buti and Nimonkar would walk with him on either side and sometimes carry him. On 15 October 1918, after noon *arati* Baba sent away Buti, Dikshit and others for their meals. This was slightly unusual because earlier they used to have their meal with Baba at the masjid itself.

As the time for Baba's departure from the earthly scene came those who were with him were Laxmibai Shinde, Bayaji Kote, Bhagoji, Laxman Shimpi, Nimonkar and others. Madhavrao Deshpande was sitting on the masjid steps. Sai Baba took out from his pocket first rupees five and then four and gave nine rupees to Laxmibai. Then, after a time, he said: "I do not feel well here. Take me to the wada."

Sai Baba used to refer to Butee's wada as Dagdi wada or simply wada. Now he said: "Take me to the wada. I would feel better there."

These were his last words.

Sai Baba was sitting as usual, when the end came. His breathing slowed down gradually. Bhagoji noticed it and called out to Nimonkar. Nimonkar put some water in Sai Baba's mouth, but it spilt out.

Nimonkar cried out: "Deva!"

For a brief moment Sai Baba opened his eyes, said: "Ah!" in a weak voice.

It was the end. Leaning against Bayaji Kote who was holding him, Baba passed away. It was 2.35 p.m.

5

A controversy now arose about the disposal of the body. Fakir Bade Baba, the Maulvi and other Muslims said that according to Muslim custom Sai Baba's body should be taken to *kabari-stan* and Hindus should not be allowed to touch the body. But the majority of Baba's devotees were Hindus and many of them said that it was Baba's wish that he should be interred in Buti's wada. Accordingly digging started in the *sanctum sanctorum* of the wada. In the evening the Fauzdar came from Rahata and discussions continued throughout the night.

In the early morning of 16th October, Sai Baba appeared in the dream of Laxman Bhat (Gramjoshi of Shirdi and maternal uncle of Madhavrao Deshpande) and said to him: "Arise immediately. Bapusaheb Jog will not come for the *kakad-arati* today. He thinks I am dead. So you come and worship me!"

Laxman Bhat woke up and rushed to the masjid, ready for *puja*. He removed the cloth covering Sai Baba's face, looked at him with loving devotion and performed the *puja* according to traditional rites. The Maulvi tried to prohibit Laxman Bhat from touching Baba's body but Bhat disregarded him, completed the *puja,* applied tilak to Baba's forehead and placed *paan* and *dakshina* in Baba's closed fists and left.

By then the Mamledar of Kopargaon arrived. Devotees had arrived in large numbers, too, on learning of Baba's passing away. The Mamledar now took the sense of the group. He found that two hundred were in favour of interring the body in Butee's wada while one hundred were opposed to it. That did not end the controversy. The Mamledar stated firmly that unless there was unanimity he would not give permission, in exercise of his power, but refer the matter to the Collector of Ahmednagar.

Kakasaheb made preparations for going to Ahmednagar to

meet the Collector himself. The Muslims were aware that Kakasaheb Dikshit was highly regarded and respected by one and all and commanded great influence in government circles. The outcome of the controversy was therefore in no doubt and would be according to his opinion. As such many felt that there was no use opposing him. So at last the dissenters decided to give conditional consent to the interring of the body in Butee's *wada*. The condition was that just as the Muslims had free access to the *masjid* during the life-time of Sai Baba, they should have the same freedom to visit the *masjid* and the *wada*. To that the Hindu devotees gladly agreed and it was decided unanimously that Sai Baba should be interred in Buti's *wada*, an edifice should be constructed over it and the right of worship should be enjoyed by all devotees irrespective of their caste or religion.

The story about Buti's wada itself is worth telling.

One night while Buti was asleep, he had a strange dream. Madhavrao Deshpande in an adjoining bed had also the same dream. Baba appeared to Buti and directed him to build a *wada* along with a temple. Buti immediately woke up and sat in his bed recollecting his dream. At the same time Madhavrao Deshpande was noticed by Buti to be crying in his sleep. So Butee woke him up to enquire what the matter was.

Madhavrao replied: "Sai Baba came near me and said distinctly: 'Let there be a *wada* with a temple so that I can satisfy the desires of all.'"

As both Butee and Madhavrao had the same dream, they were wonderstruck and prepared themselves for the task. Buti had the resources to construct the *wada*. A plan was drawn up and it received the support of Kakasaheb Dikshit. Next day while the three of them were sitting near Sai Baba, he gave his blessings to the idea.

Madhavrao supervised the construction of the basement, the ground floor and the well. Occasionally Baba would pass by and look at the construction work and make suggestions for improving the appearance of the *wada*. Further construction continued under the supervision of Bapusaheb Jog.

While the construction progressed, Buti felt an urge to build a temple on the ground floor and to instal an idol of Muralidhar in the *sanctum sanctorum*. One day, while Sai Baba was on his usual round, Madhavrao met him at the entrance of the *wada* and conveyed to him Buti's desire. Sai Baba consented gladly and said: "When the temple is built, we shall inhabit it, and ever afterwards live in joy!"

Immediately, a coconut was broken and the foundation laid. The *sanctum sanctorum* and the pedestal for the idol of Muralidhar was then got ready and an order for the idol was placed with a reputed sculptor.

It was about this time that Sai Baba fell ill and his end seemed to draw near. The devotees were distressed and Buti himself was restless. Buti began to wonder whether Baba would live to see the temple, let alone come to stay there as he promised. Of what use was the temple, thought Butee, if Baba was not going to live there?

But Baba was going to "live" there in a different way.

On Wednesday evening, 16 October, Sai Baba's body was ceremoniously taken in procession to Buti's *wada* and placed in the *sanctum sanctorum* where originally, the idol of Muralidhar was to have been installed, and interred. An edifice was also raised over the grave.

Sai Baba had said: *"Ikade Shirdis mas manase mungyavani yetil"* (Here, in Shirdi, my men will come like ants).

To this day, so they do.

SAI BABA HAD NO APOSTLES

Sai Baba built no institution, wrote no tome, initiated no disciple to take over from him. G.G. Narke, Professor of Geology in Poona Engineering College has testified: "A disciple is very different from a devotee. The *guru* is connected by a close and intimate tie with, and has every responsibility for the disciple. He has no such close tie with a devotee and is not bound to bear all his sins and sorrows. Sai Baba had no disciple. The disciple must serve his master to carry out all his wishes strictly and for the better. As Sai said: 'I would tremble to come into the presence of my *guru*'. There was no one prepared to serve him in that way at Shirdi. It seems he once asked 'who dares to call himself my disciple? Who can serve me adequately and satisfactorily'"?[1]

Inspite of this clear and unambiguous testimony of Prof. Narke, some writers on Sai Baba would have us believe that like Jesus Christ or Ramakrishna Paramahansa, Sai Baba of Shirdi had apostles. The chief among such writers is the respected figure of B.V. Narasimha Swami, founder of All India Sai Samaj, Madras, who has given a prominent place among those to Kashinath Govind Upasani, known as Upasani Baba. How and under what circumstances did Narasimha Swami come to hold this view? And is this view based on facts or is it a figment of his imagination? Moreover, is it justified on merits? What is Narasimha Swami's own background?

B.V. Narasimha Swami was born on August 21, 1874 in a respectable family of Brahmins in Coimbatore District (in the old Madras Presidency and now of Tamil Nadu). After graduating in Arts and then Law from Madras University, he joined the Bar and started practice, at Salem from 1895. He soon made his mark as a lawyer. Among his contemporaries at the Bar was C. Rajagopalachari who was later to become India's first Governor General after independence. Narasimha Swami did not confine his activities only to the legal profession but participated in public life and joined the Home Rule League founded by Mrs.

Annie Besant. He was one of the three members of a mission sent to Britain to press India's case for Home Rule. From 1914 to 1920 he served as an elected member of Madras Legislative Council. He was re-elected to the Council in 1920.

In 1921 a tragedy struck his family. His two little children, a boy and a girl, accidentally fell into the well in his compound and were drowned. This was a turning point in his life. He decided to renounce the world, resigned from the Legislative Council, ceased to take part in public life and returned his Vakil's *sanad* to the High Court in 1925. In pursuance of his decision, he left his home in search of a guru. His quest took him first to Tiruvannamalai where Ramana Maharshi had his ashram. He spent three years there and led a life of cloistered seclusion, concentrating all his efforts on the study of Vedanta works and adoption of the necessary consequential steps. There he wrote the first biography of Ramana Maharshi under the title *Self-Realization* which was published in 1931. He also rendered into English with commentary, the original Tamil text of Maharshi's *Upadesha Saram.*

In 1931 Narasimha Swami decided to leave Ramana Maharshi as he felt that he had lost his earlier fervour for *bhakti* in pursuit of Vedanta. This need not have been, for Ramana Maharshi had many devotees for whom he prescribed or advocated *bhakti marga* (the path of devotion), as *atma vichara* or self enquiry did not suit them. The real reason however why Narasimha Swami left Ramana Maharshi was, to put it in his own words, as confided to Narayan Maharaj of Kedgaon: "I have come across many gems, but none of them has satisfied me so far. Each gem I get is very tiny and has dots, cracks or other flaws"? It could be that Ramana Maharshi was not his ordained *sadguru,* but surely this is an unfair criticism or judgement of Ramana Maharshi whose spiritual eminence and real worth was revealed to the wider world outside India by Paul Brunton in his *A Search in Secret India* published in 1935. Unfortunately for Narasimha Swami, after leaving Ramana Maharshi in 1931, he was not destined to discover his *sadguru* Sai Baba until 1936-1937 but came to him after a lot of wandering through the circuitous route of Meher Baba, Upasani Baba, Siddharud Swami and Narayan Maharaj. He spent a considerable part of his intervening five to six years with Upasani Baba whose true nature, it must be said with regret, Narasimha Swami could not fathom.

While in Sakori with Upasani Baba he wrote a biography of his new *guru* in 1934 under the title *Sage of Sakori*. It is an uncritical appreciation of Upasani Baba based on *Upasani Lilaamrit,* a biography of the man dictated by the Baba himself in Marathi and, *ipse dixit* of his devotees. Later on he had some reservations about Upasani Baba to which he has given expression in Chapter 6 of Volume II of *Life of Sai Baba* published in 1956 in which he has devoted a whole chapter of 69 pages to Upasani Baba.

Upasani Baba, it seems on a detailed study of the new version of the book has had a powerful influence on Narasimha Swami to the point that the latter is blind to the defects of the Baba. Thus, in *Sage of Sakori,* Narasimha Swami has certified that Upasani Baba was free from sex cravings and had set an example in *brahmacharya* (celibacy) for his devotees, to emulate. But in his book *Life of Sai Baba,* Vol. II, Narasimha Swami himself states: "He (Upasani Baba) was storing up groups of women to live with him, at first a batch of five and ultimately a batch of twenty five were tacked on to him by ties of marriage" (p.292). "Upasani had later on twenty five wives, a regular harem with a castle and an *antahpuram* in it" (pp 288-89).

Narasimha Swami also makes bold to say in Chapter XVI of *Sage of Sakori* that Sai Baba had obliterated the sense of possession in Upasani Baba and helped the latter to conquer the desire for wealth and possessions (pp 98-104). However, ruefully does Narasimha Swami admit in *Life of Sai Baba* Vol II, through hindsight: "So long as he (Upasani Baba) observed Sai Baba's direction and example of keeping away from women and wealth by his side, his influence and power for good were notably increasing. By about 1927 or 1928 one might see that these reached great heights though signs were not wanting to show that contrary tendencies were beginning to work and undermine the foundations laid by Sai Baba". If these tendencies were visible in 1928, how and why did Narasimha Swami accept uncritically what was told to him by the Baba's disciples? Narasimha Swami goes on to add: "In time these contrary tendencies fully developed and wealth (counted in lakhs and taking the shape of loans, 80 acres of land, massive buildings and hundreds of cattle) was stored up and women were stored up" (p 285).

Further it is not true that "myriads of people" came to know about the worship of Sai Baba through Upasani. If any persons are to be given credit for spreading Sai devotion, the two names which come to mind and which have been mentioned prominently in this connection in *Shri Sai Satcharita* (Ch 15, verses 35-36) are Das Ganu, who spread Sai devotion through his *keertans* and Nanasaheb Chandorkar ("the crown of devotees" as he is referred to by the author of *Shri Sai Satcharita)* who brought eminent people like Hari Sitaram Dikshit, Annasaheb Dabholkar to the *durbar* of Sai. They were to become Sai's staunchest devotees and their services in Sai Baba's cause deserve to be cherished and remembered by all Sai devotees.

Narasimha Swami's lack of knowledge of Marathi also added to his ignorance about Upasani Baba. Thus, without any proof, he states at the beginning of the chapter on Upasani Baba in *Life of Sai Baba:* "Very high praise to him (Upasani Baba) is found in *S.L. Masik* (Sri Sai Leela magazine) and Sai literature written a few years after Baba (Sai Baba) shed his mortal coil. His (Upasani's) very great service to Sai Baba is the fact that through him myriads, if not lakhs of people came to know about the worship of Sai Baba". This does not correspond with known facts. *Shri Sai Leela* ignored all the aberrations and unethical tendencies of Upasani Baba for full five years from its birth in 1923. Only when needled by the charge of sympathising with Upasani Baba did Kakasaheb Mahajani, editor of *Shri Sai Leela* take notice of Upasani Baba's actions in September 1928 in most uncomplimentary terms. (See Annexure)

Narasimha Swami makes much of a stray expression of the author of *Shri Sai Satcharit* (ch.44, 122) that "the best of devotees Upasani" performed the annual *shraddha* of Sai Baba at Varanasi.

It must be mentioned here that the expression "the best of devotees" has been used not only for Upasani but, among others, for Ramachandra Atmaram Tarkhad (ch.9 verse 70), B.V. Deo (ch 40, 20) and others. But the highest praise is reserved for Nanasaheb Chandorkar "the crown of devotees" (ch 15, verse 33), "Sai's best devotee" (ch 50, verse 36), "true *bhakta*" (ch 39, verse 30) and "loving devotee" (ch 33 verse 63), as also "most excellent devotee" (ch 12 verse 50) and "very highly respected" (ch 12, verse 50). Hari Sitaram Dikshit, is referred to not only as "the best of devotees" (ch 23 verse 186), but is called "loving devotee" (ch 45, verse 62) and "pure, intrepid, the great Meru mountain of determination" (ch 23 verse 145). And Megha is referred to as "most excellent devotee" (ch 31 verse 119). Moreover, it is likely that Annasaheb Dabholkar may not have known of Upasani's misdeeds. At about the same time Kakasaheb Mahajani was distancing the Shirdi Sansthan of Sai Baba from the misdeeds of Upasani which he denounced in no uncertain terms. In the circumstances, just one reference to Upasani Baba should not be taken seriously.

Narasimha Swami also mentions in passing what he calls "Divekar agitation against Upasani Baba thus :
"Divekar began his agitation in 1934 and carried on his agitation through *Kirloskar* magazine and court proceedings till 1936. Before it was even half way up the entire tens of thousands (devotees of Upasani Baba) disappeared. It is difficult to find even a thousand people enthusiastic over Upasani Baba. People felt ashamed to say that they had anything to do with Upasani Baba. All that became possible only because of the great aims and standards set up by Sai Baba, of having nothing to do with wealth or women, had been abandoned" (p 287).

It is obvious that Narasimha Swami did not know who this Divekar was. Pandit Mahadev Shastri Divekar, as he was known, in Maharashtra was an erudite scholar, a great religious and social reformer and author of many books in Marathi. Born in a well-to-do and respectable Brahmin family at Ugar Khurd, he had his primary education at Ugar Khurd and Sangli, and his secondary education in Belgaum. After the Bengal partition in 1906 his life took a different turn and he became a disciple of Jog Maharaj the head of Varkari Panth and studied *Jnaneshwari* and *Vicharsagar Mahatmya* under him. Then he went on to study *Vedanta* and *Dharmashastra* under Swami Kevalananda Saraswati (formerly Narayan Shastri Marathe), the founder of the famous Prajna Pathshala at Wai. After completing his studies he taught at Prajna Pathshala from 1916 to 1926 in an honorary capacity.

Founder of many social organizations, including Dharma Nirnaya Mandal of Lonavla, he stood for the right of all Hindus, irrespective of their caste or *varna* to study Vedas, perform *upanayana* ceremony etc. He campaigned against untouchability and advocated the right of re-marriage of widows through his *pravachans* (discourses) and books. He established a body called Buvashahi Vidhvansak Sangh and attacked pretenders and charlatans who claimed or posed to be saints. He was the author of the following books in Marathi:

❊ Dharmashastra Manthan

❊ Nava Hindu Dharma

❊   Gita Pradeep

❊   Arya Samskriti

❊ Hindu Samaj Samartha Kasa Hoil?

❊ Brahmajnana va Bavashai

❊ Majhe Yashaswi Jeevan.

He passed away at Sholapur on August 8, 1971 at the ripe old age of 83. Now it is to the book *Brahmajnana va Buvashahi* that we turn in which there are two chapters of 38 pages which throw a searching light on the life and activities of Upasani Baba. Even a cursory reading of these chapters should make it abundantly clear that Upasani Baba can under no circumstances be described as a saint, much less as an apostle of Sai Baba of Shirdi, let alone the man responsible for spreading Sai Baba's faith.

Swami Shri Sai Sharan Anand once told Vishwas Kher that Sai Baba does not need any intermediaries and he is his own publicist. Devotees may render service to Sai Baba for their own good and spiritual weal but no individual, no matter however big, can possibly entertain the notion that he is an apostle of Sai Baba or attempt to raise any individual to that elevated status.

Sai Baba speaks for himself. He never had any apostle. He does not need one. And Upasani Baba can certainly not be counted as one.

oxoxoxoxo

End Notes

1. Devotees' Experiences of Shri Sai Baba, Part I, p. 34.

2. Swami Saipadananda, "Sri Narasimha Swami" pp 17-36 where a chapter is devoted to "Personal Experience" as narrated by Narasimha Swami.

ANNEXURE - I

The official statement of Shri Laxman Ganesh alias Kakasaheb Mahajani, Editor, Shri Sai Leela and Life Trustee of Shirdi Sansthan of Sai Baba of its Policy and Attitude towards Kashinath Govind Upasani known as Upasanibua - Published in Vol. V, combined issue 6-7-8, p. 617 of Shri Sai Leela - translated from Marathi.

Banoo Terrace, Tardeo,
Bombay, 29 July, 1928

The Editor,
Shri Sai Leela,

Sir,

I am a devotee of Shri Sai Baba and read issues of your magazine carefully. Therefore I am penning the following words for your consideration.

As the Editor, you must be in the habit of reading newspapers and therefore it is not possible that you could not be aware of the controversy regarding the trickery of guru and Shri Upasani episode. Since Khando Upasani made an offering of his daughter to his guru (Upasanibua), leelas of Upasanibua have assumed a character of their own, and the press is agog with excitement, but you would be well-acquainted with Upasani's leelas since a long time. I cannot, however, understand why you have been silent so long, particularly when Sai Baba's name is dragged into it. As a counterblast to 'Shri Sai Leela', the Upasani panth started 'Sai Vak-Sudha' and even then you remained quiet. 'Vak-Sudha' first appeared as a magazine and was later brought out in a book form. Shri Upasani's biography was published in which aspersions were cast on Sai Baba's devotees and yet you did not react. You have reviewed various books from time to time in Shri Sai Leela in course of which you have offered discerning comments. Then how is it that the biography of Upasani has escaped your attention? If your long silence is construed as your being sympathetic to Upasani Panth (and many are already thinking so) whose fault is it? Really speaking, your contact with Upasani is long-standing. He calls himself a disciple of Sai Baba. He has opened an illusive bazaar in the name of Sai Baba three miles from Shirdi and unwary victims have been caught in it. I and my friends feel that if you had exposed this hypocrisy in good time, he (Upasani) would not have proceeded so far as going through the rite of 'offering wife/daughter' to himself. So I earnestly appeal to you to state your position clearly in this connection.

Yours Humbly
Bhagavan Damodar Joshi

Editorial Comments

We have received some more letters of similar kind. Some have asked us to give information about the relationship of Upasani Bua to Shirdi. Hence we are compelled to turn to this subject.

We started Shri Sai Leela magazine with the idea of compiling in one place the experiences of devotees about Sai Maharaj from time to time and publishing literature about Sai Baba and other allied religious topics. We thought it advisable then to remain aloof from criticizing others, 'to expose hypocrisy', and even now are of the same view. There are many sadhus and saints in Hindustan and particularly in Maharashtra. Among them are real satpurush as well as charlatans. If we were to analyse them, Sai Leela will not be able to cope with the task. In objects and substances coming into being in this world or created by God, excepting pure substances like fire, there is a mix of pure and impure objects. And God has endowed only human beings with the intellect of discriminating between pure and impure

306

forms. Animals etc. have not been given this power and that is the basic difference between man and beast. If man does not exercise his intellect, there would be no difference between him and beasts and he would be prone to indulge in beastly acts. If man were to exercise his intellect, he will know who is a *satpurush* and who is an impostor. If intellect is not exercised what will be the result except unrestrained, wild and foolish acts like the 'rite of offering daughter or wife'?

The marks and characteristics of *satpurush* have been described by Samarth Ramdas and Tukaram Maharaj in their works. Eknath Maharaj has expounded with discernment on this subject in his Eknathi Bhagavat. But men who are infatuated with 'false pretensions of guru' will understand this only if they were to refer to these works. Times are such that if a shrewd crafty person pretends to be a *satpurush* there is no dearth of disciples for him. These disciples crowd round him out of blind faith and that crafty guru fully exploits them. With the mere announcement that a certain sadhu has arrived in the town, throngs of men and women rush for his darshan. It had appeared in the press that when this Upasanibua had stayed at Walkeshwar in Bombay, lakhs of people had been for his darshan. But hardly any one out of these would have considered whether he was truly a *satpurush* or some pretender. When the news that a satpurush is in town is passed on by word of mouth (the word is spread of course by Bua's disciples) throngs gather for his darshan. Hardly any one among the darshan-seekers goes with the idea of benefiting spiritually. The large majority visit with such desires as 'may I have a son, may I have wealth, may I succeed in the object of my desire'. The Bua is crafty and seeing the general inclination gives blessings some of which succeed like predictions of an astrologer while some others fail. Those persons in whose cases the blessings have fructified sing praises of the Bua. Those disappointed blame their karma and do not dare to criticize the alleged satpurush. The result thereof favours the Bua. Once the fame of the Bua is established he becomes a *satpurush* for his whole life. There is no dearth of such alleged satpurush in Maharashtra! There is reason to infer from his actions that Upasanibua is an alleged *satpurush* of this kind! Upasanibua resided in Shirdi for some time. Beyond this he has no connection with Shirdi. Sensing the occasion Upasanibua admits to his being a disciple of Sai Baba and some times propounds that Sai Baba is not his guru. Those who have accepted Sai Baba as a controller of their hearts do not go to Upasanibua and much less dance attendance on him.

Shri Joshi writes in his letter that had we exposed the pretensions of Upasanibua in good time, he would not have gone to the extent of carrying out the rite of offering wife/daughter to himself. Shri Joshi is under an illusion. Currently all newspapers have mounted an attack on Upasani Bua and quoting extracts from Sai Vak-Sudha have condemned severely the propositions propounded therein and criticized strongly the rite of offering wife/daughter to him. Yet if Shri Joshi were to go to Sakori, he will find 'Upasani Nagar' teeming with crowds as before. And if his following is increasing even though devotees actually notice there the dominance of young girls in his Ashram, and things like tipri-dance resembling raas-krida etc., it is clear that our writing would not have produced any effect on him. On the contrary, if we had written anything about him, we would have been accused of being jealous of his rise and criticizing him out of spite. This was the only reason why we did not criticize his life. There are many things in his life story after reading which any one can decide what his true worth is. As an example we reproduce an extract therefrom:

'Once on a Thursday, a widow named Janakibai came with puja articles for his (Upasanibua's) darshan. She undressed outside the room, entered in a naked state and worshipped the Maharaj without any misgiving. Seeing this other women censured her but Maharaj refuted them. How can one describe the deep and solemn heart like the sea of this devotee, who worshipped in a naked state among such a gathering without any misgiving?'

(Upasani Charitra, p.270)

There are many such indecent and repulsive things in that life story. There is a mention also of a cobbler having given as an offering his wife to Maharaj. This biography is the first post or stake in the erection of 'Upasani Nagar' established by Upasanibua in Sakori. The foundation of Upasanibua's saintliness was laid by this biography! This life story has been translated in Gujarati and as a result some Gujaratis and Parsis have become his disciples. We have stated above why we have so far ignored this book. However, since our silence has led to misunderstanding among people as Shri Joshi says, we have decided to review this unique book in our next issue!*

'Sai Vak-Sudha' is an independent work of words coming from the mouth of Upasanibua. First, it was a magazine. It came into being as a counterblast to Shri Sai Leela. Later Sai Vak-Sudha was published in a book form. Sai Baba's name is prefixed to this book but except the name, Sai Baba has no other connection with it. Not only this but what is propounded in Vak-Sudha is quite contrary to the eternal, spiritual truths enunciated by Sai Baba to his devotees from time to time. We feel that in order to boost its sales by misleading people this unholy book has been titled as 'Sai Vak-Sudha'.

It will be clearly seen from the above comments that we cannot be having any sympathy for Upasani Panth.

— Editor

This biography was never reviewed in any of the subsequent issues of Sri Sai Leela. Soon Kakasaheb Mahajan ceased to be its editor and his place vas taken by Ramchandra Atmaram alias Babasaheb Tarkhad.

THE HOME COMING OF SAI BABA

Except the Lord build the house, they labour in vain that build it....

Psalm - 127-1

Sai Baba has returned to his home in Pathri after one hundred and fifty years, and is now residing there as the Presiding Deity on the exact spot where he was born. Some time between 1846 and 1850 A.D., a Shukla Yajurvedi Deshastha Brahmin boy of tender eight left his parents in Pathri for good in the company of a sufi fakir in search of the Supreme. He took the path from Pathri to Jalnapur via Manoor (Manvat) and Shailud (Selu). By day he trod over the grass and in the grass he lay himself down at night. He walked step by step. Thus after eight days he reached Paithan-Aurangabad terrain and wandered all over Marathwada, and may be, elsewhere from the age of eight to the age of twenty-five to thirty. The boy was Haribhau Bhusari who came to be known years later as Sai Baba of Shirdi.

In the course of his wanderings Sai Baba is said to have visited Shri Manik Prabhu of Humanabad (1817-1865 A.D.), who is considered to be a Datta-avatar in the Datta Sampradaya. The following account of their meeting appears at p.90 in the biography of Shri Manik Prabhu authored by Nagesh D. Sonde and published by Shri Sansthan. Manik Prabhu, Maniknagar - 585 353, in 1995:

"Historians tell us that when he (Sai Baba) visited Maniknagar, Shri Manik Prabhu was sitting in Darbar. Shri Sai Baba dressed as a Fakir came before Shri Manik Prabhu Maharaj and extending his Lota before him said, 'Prabhuji, fill this cup.' At that time Shri Prabhu's brother Shri Tatya Saheb was sitting nearby having a discussion with some pandits. He was directed by Shri Prabhu to fill the Fakir's Lota, but the Lota would not fill up no matter how much money Tatya Saheb would put in. Shri Tatya Saheb looked at Shri Prabhu in bewilderment. Shri Prabhu with his divine vision was able to recognize the Fakir as a realized soul and put two dry dates and some flowers in the Lota and said smilingly, 'Sai take it'. Miraculously the Lota filled up but the Fakir took only the dry, dates and flowers saying, 'This much is enough for me' and turned the Lota upside down to pour out more money than it could have been filled with. Giving due respects to Shri Manik Maharaj, the Fakir left the place."

It may be mentioned here that Muslims regard Shri Manik Prabhu as an incarnation of Mahaboob Subhani, a Muslim saint which belief they hold even to-day. 'The Manik Prabhu Sampradaya, also reciprocates this faith.' In the festivities at Maniknagar both Hindus and Muslims are said to participate with equal enthusiasm. That is why this Sampradaya is also called Sakalmat Sampradaya of which equality and unity of religious faiths is a tradition, discipline and a basic feature.

Sai Baba once told Hari Sitaram Dikshit that he had begun taking the name of Hari and in the process had seen Him, face to face. He had become Hari Himself as in yore, Shuka, Yajnavalkya, Dattatreya and Kapilmuni had become Hari the same way, as narrated by Eknath, the renowned Saint of Maharashtra (Haripath, Abhang 22, 2).

We do not know much about the fakir who took the boy along with him. For all we know he may have been a mendicant scholar. The time from the day Baba left home to the day he arrived in Shirdi, is shrouded in mystery. However, we do know that he stayed in Aurangabad and instructed a fakir for about twelve years. Some say that his name was Bade Baba alias Fakir Baba alias Fakir Peer Mohammed Yasinmia who came to Shirdi in 1909 and stayed there until Baba's Mahasamadhi in 1918. He passed away at Nagpur in January, 1925. Others say that the name of the fakir whom Baba instructed was Fakir Banne Mia who passed away in 1921. Whatever it may be, Sai Baba came to Shirdi some time between 1868 to 1872 A.D. with Chand Patil of Dhupkhed whose sister was to be married to Hamid, the son of Aminabhai of Shirdi. After, a few days Sai Baba and Chand Patil left for Aurangabad. Two months later, Sai Baba returned alone to Shirdi where he spent the next fifty years of his life.

Now follows the story of "home coming" of Sai Baba to Pathri as personally known to and gathered by Vishwas Kher. When Vishwas Kher and his wife Indira had been to Shirdi in June, 1974 for the darshan of Baba's samadhi, they were in search of a Mahatma who had the rare fortune of coming into close personal contact with Sai Baba and who could testify about his saintliness. While in Shirdi, they heard from K.S. Pathak, the then Court Receiver of Sai Baba Sansthan, the name of Swami Sai Sharan Anand who, regularly visited for years Shirdi in the month of May and stayed in Room No.34 behind the Neem tree near Gurusthan. Vishwas and Indira were in Ahmedabad in November, 1974. They visited Swami Sai Sharan Anand, morning and evening, for a few days at a stretch. Swamiji received them with loving kindness and answered all their queries patiently, frankly, incisively and with insight. They discovered that the individual whom they had met was no ordinary man but a holy person adept in spiritual matters. This contact resulted in total acceptance of Sai Baba of Shirdi as their mentor and spiritual guide (Sadguru) by the Kher couple. They were in continuous contact with Swami Sai Sharan Anand until he breathed his last at Ahmedabad soon after the mid-night of 25th August, 1982. His body was interred in the compound of his Mathi and a Samadhi was constructed by his devotees over his mortal remains at the following address:

14/15 Prakritikunj Society,
New Sharada Mandir Road,
Opposite Shreyas High School,
Ahmedabad - 380 015.

The Kher couple acknowledge their immense debt of gratitude to Swami Sai Sharan Anand for enlightening them about the true nature, mission and powers of Sai Baba.

Then commenced their search for the birth-place of Sai Baba. There was a mystery surrounding the birth, birth-place and family background of Sai Baba. All sources pointed to Pathri as the likely place of his birth. So off were the Khers to Pathri in Marathwada in June, 1975 where they picked up clues casually dropped in conversation, pursued them with zeal, patiently culled the evidence and pieced it together with detachment. All evidence pointed to the Yajurvedi Deshastha Madhyandin Brahmin family of Bhusaris as the one in which Baba chose to take his birth. The story has been narrated briefly on pages 14 to 17 of this book.

In June, 1978 the site of Sai Baba's birth in Pathri was purchased jointly by Kher and Dinkarrao Chaudhari and a committee called "Shri Sai Smarak Samiti, Pathri" was constituted with Dinkarrao Chaudhari, Advocate, Kher's host in Pathri as the General Secretary. Even though Chaudhari had accepted the office of General Secretary, he had made it clear to Kher from the beginning that as the latter had taken the trouble to come all the way from Mumbai for researching into the birth-place of Sai Baba, he (Chaudhari) was being helpful but was then not sufficiently interested or even otherwise in a position to accept any responsibility which would require him to devote time and energy to it. And yet Kher's predicament was that there was no other person of ability and character who could take up the responsibility in Pathri of pursuing the cause of raising a memorial to Sai Baba on his birth-place.

On Kher's advice "the Samiti" applied under the Bombay Public Trusts Act, 1950 to the Assistant Charity Commissioner, Aurangabad on 16th June, 1980 and it was registered as a Public Trust bearing number E-43 (Parabhani) on 31st December, 1980. Then Kher visited Pathri along with his architect Subhash Dali on 20th December, 1980 to enable the latter to prepare a blue print of the shrine to be built on Sai's birth-place. The blue print of the Shrine with the "delivery room spot" marked on it was despatched to the Samiti in March, 1981. There the matter rested and no development worth recording took place for over a decade in this connection.

Come September, 1982. Kher visited Dhupkhed to get at the truth of the story of Sai Baba's coming to Shirdi in the company of Chand Patil. From Kodgaon which is half-way on the road from Aurangabad to Paithan, Dhupkhed is 3 kms. off the main road. On the last but one day of his stay in Aurangabad, Kher was taken by his enterprising and energetic tourist-guide K.K. Jumbade, who also owns a photographic studio of his own near the University campus in Aurangabad, to the heart of the city in Gul Mandi to see the 'beatific smile' on the face of a strange personage with a quizzical look in his eyes. His name was Bulb Baba. It appears that he was so called because earlier used up electric bulbs adorned his peculiar headgear. But why only the headgear, everything else about him also was as peculiar - his attire his footwear, his demeanour etc. Known to be a man of few words, if he spoke at all, he would emerge from anywhere in Gul Mandi and stand before any shop which it was said, would do roaring business on that day. A Mewadi restaurant owner had instructed his staff to honour him whenever "this guest" visited the restaurant and supply his wants.

Bulb Baba struck the Kher couple as an aulia, which impression was confirmed when to the astonishment of the tourist guide and others around, Bulb Baba received the Kher couple most cordially and spoke to them eloquently for forty-five minutes pure Vedanta, interlacing his discourse with quotes from Kabir and may be, his own compositions. He even allowed them to be photographed in his company. Before taking leave of this holy person, Kher dipped his hand in the front pocket of his shirt and found two ten rupee notes which he placed in the saint's hands as his humble tribute which the latter accepted not without pronouncing a benediction! Turning to Indira Kher he said, "A plot of land has been purchased where a shrine costing rupees twenty lakhs is going to be constructed. People from all over the country will throng there for darshan, and your visits to this part of the country will be more frequent and we shall meet." This saintly figure left an indelible impression on the minds of the Kher couple for they can never forget him and his words which are enshrined in their hearts.

The blessing of a saint never goes waste. It fructifies in due course when its time has come. This exactly happened in the case of the Pathri memorial. August, 1991 was a turning point in the story of the Pathri shrine of Sai Baba for it marked the publication of <u>Sai Baba of Shirdi - A Unique Saint</u> by Jaico Publishing House, Mumbai. It gives a complete account of Sai Baba's life and mission. Kher then realized intuitively that the construction of a memorial to Sai at Pathri was no longer to remain a pipe dream but would take shape and form before his very eyes in the next few years. And so it has happened!

All this time Kher's link with Dinkarrao Chaudhari was intact. They corresponded fitfully but Kher remembered to present him with a copy of <u>Sai Baba of Shirdi - A Unique Saint</u> to remind him of his destined mission. Over the years Chaudhari had mellowed and become a devotee of Shirdi Sai Baba. He now agreed to shoulder the responsibility which Kher wanted him to take up. A man of the highest integrity, his ability to take up the responsibility of managing the trust and arranging for proper utilization of funds received, was never in doubt. Kher also interested Sitaram Dhanu, his former colleague on the Board of Management of Sai Baba Sansthan of Shirdi, between 1984 to 1989, in the Pathri project. Dhanu is a long standing earnest devotee of Sai Baba, who is known widely to Sai devotees visiting Shirdi as a person of amiable disposition with superb organizational skills. Kher and Dhanu then jointly planned a visit to Pathri in April, 1993 when they met a local group of 20 to 25 prominent persons.

Already the idea of construction of Sai temple had taken deep roots in the popular psyche of Pathri and it had become a symbol of pride for the local population. Pathri Nagar Parishad passed the plans for Sai's shrine and concreted the road in the alley leading to the site. It also made arrangements at the site to provide adequate water supply for the construction. Things in Pathri now moved fast. Enthusiasm for the Sai temple at Pathri had surged up and at a function held at Sai Baba's birth-place on the festival day of Vijaya Dashami, the day of Sai Baba's Mahasamadhi, dated Thursday, October 13, 1994 bhoomi-pujan was performed by the President of the Pathri Nagar Parishad, Abdullakhan Durrani in the presence of prominent citizens of Pathri. At that ceremony fifteen citizens promised to donate a sum of Rs.10,000/- each. However, only a few of them acted on their word. The digging of the foundation then commenced but the progress was slow.

Enter K.V. Ramani, a businessman engaged in Information Technology in Madras, a philanthropist and a fine specimen of devotee who is the founder of Shirdi Sai Trust which has funded several religious-cum-charitable projects connected with Shirdi Sai Baba. On 20th March, 1995 he received a Circular letter of seventy-one year old T.A. Ram Nathen of Sarangpur, West Bengal from which he gathered that at Sai Baba's birth-place at Pathri, bhoomi-pujan of a proposed memorial to Shirdi Sai had been performed on the auspicious day of 13th October, 1994. T.A. Ram Nathen who passed away on 16th August, 1999 then ran single handedly a one-man enterprise from Sarangpur, which provided news connected with Sai movement free of charge to the innumerable devotees of Sai through out the country.

In the middle of May, 1995, Dinkarrao Chaudhari was standing in a long queue outside the Samadhi Mandir of Sai at Shirdi when he prayed silently to him: 'Baba, why don't you come to your home town Pathri so that we can have your darshan every day?' It seems in retrospect that Baba had decided to grant his wish! Chaudhari found on his return to Pathri an envelope from Kher containing a letter addressed to him by K.V. Ramani, Madras, alongwith a Demand Draft on the State Bank of India, Pathri Branch for the sum of Rs.1,10,000/- towards the proposed shrine of Sai! In his letter Ramani asked for a copy of Trust Deed, a blue-print of the proposed shrine and information such as the total cost of the project, funds collected, balance funds required etc. Kher in his reply to Ramani thanked him for his unsolicited spontaneous donation, placed before him all the facts candidly and also informed him that he had resolved to take active personal interest in the project to ensure transparency, accountability and proper utilization of his donation.

At this stage it appears clear from the events narrated herein after that Sai Baba himself had decided to take the matter in hand and give it a push to make things happen. As Ramana Maharshi has observed : "It is enough for the thoughts of a Jnani to be turned in any direction and the automatic activity begins."

The digging of the foundation now gathered momentum during the course of which two querns, an idol each of Hanuman and Khandoba and articles used in puja, viz. pali and panchpatra made of copper, sahan, pantis and vibhuti like substance similar to the one found at Gangapur were found.

On 16th July, 1995 Kher, Architect Dali and Dhanu visited Pathri. It was their first visit since the digging of foundation and raising of columns had commenced. This visit was not only timely but proved to be purposeful and productive. The presence of Architect Dali facilitated taking decisions on the spot. By then all columns had been erected to a height of 10' and while digging, a basement

316

of 6' x 6' with two arches and a tunnel just below the proposed sanctum sanctorum had been discovered. It was, therefore, decided on the advice and suggestion of Dali to extend the basement to house a Meditation Hall of about the same size as the sabha mandap which could be done at half the cost of a storeyed structure. This decision entailed the alteration of the original plan and preparation of fresh plans for the basement as well as the sabha mandap and the sanctum sanctorum. Dali came up with fresh plans which were matched by receipt of further sums of liberal and substantial instalments of donation in July and November, 1995 from Ramani all on his own, after studying the plans, progress reports and statements of accounts forwarded to him.

A word here about the unassuming Dali won't be out of place. A competent and innovative architect, he combines in himself a thoroughly professional approach and expertise in structural engineering with amazing industry and energy for work. He himself prepared the plans and all working drawings. His plan of sanctum sanctorum designed as a blooming lotus in octagonal shape with a suspended canopy in marble over it, is absolutely original par excellence. No praise is enough for the zest and energy with which he tackled the problems. He visited the marble quarries in Rajasthan to select and make bulk purchases and arranged for masons from Rajasthan to come to Pathri for laying the marble flooring in the sabha mandap and the Meditation Hall with patterns based on geometrical designs in different colours and cladding all columns and rear wall of the sabha mandap and arches linking the columns in marble. He paid regular visits to Pathri once every three weeks to monitor the progress and stayed there for two to three days at a time. And all this he did as a labour of love and not for any monetary gain!

Thus, while the work of constructing the shrine was progressing satisfactorily there was a problem which needed close and urgent attention. It was noticed that at the time of registration of Shri Sai Smarak Samiti, Pathri as a public trust in December, 1980, no trust deed or a constitution or scheme had been filed for carrying on its management or administration. This was a serious lacuna which had to be filled. So on the advice of S.H. Kinikar, a legal expert on public trust law with vast administrative experience thereof, Kher and his two colleagues applied on 20th December, 1995, to the Assistant Charity Commissioner, Parabhani, under Section 50-A of the Bombay Public Trusts Act, 1950 for framing a scheme for the management and administration of the Samiti. Naturally the trustees on record in December, 1980, who were merely paper-trustees and had done nothing since then to further the objects of the trust were joined as opponents.

In April, 1996 when the Assistant Charity Commissioner, Parabhani issued notices to the opponents, the hard core among them resorted to obstructive tactics to thwart the construction of the shrine. And after the hearing of the case on 30th September, 1996 their opposition turned into open hostility, intimidation and threats of violence. It may be mentioned here that, Dinkarrao Chaudhari bore the brunt of their attack stoically and emerged unscathed and with an enhanced reputation. However, this situation forced Kher and his colleagues to suspend the work of construction by which time the laying of the marble flooring in the sabha mandap and the basement had been completed. The Assistant Charity Commissioner gave his judgement on 29th March, 1997 wherein he found all the issues in favour of the Applicants and yet in framing the scheme for the administration of the Samiti, he succumbed to local political pressures on a point or two. To remedy this defect in the scheme, the Applicants approached the District Court Parabhani under Section 72 of the Act. The Opponents also filed their appeal in the District Court.

The Applicants then did not know how long the suspension of construction would last. However, they decided to take some strategic action by building up public opinion against the tactics of the unscrupulous hardcore. Their patience was rewarded after two years when bowing to public pressure, the opponents withdrew their appeal and came to terms. The compromise terms were taken on record by the Parabhani District Court on 13th July, 1998 and the Applicants too then withdrew their proceeding. Thus the legal problem was sorted out so that the construction could now proceed smoothly.

The Board of Trustees comprising seven members constituted under the scheme held its first meeting at Pathri on 9th August

318

1998 and elected Vishwas Kher as its Chairman and Dinkararo Chaudhari as the Managing Trustee. It also decided to proceed with the construction from the point at which it was suspended. It took about four months to organize the resumption of work and primarily with generous contributions funded by Ramani the construction of the Shrine was completed in October, 1999. Particulars about the shrine are given in the annexure hereto.

In between a Shirdi Sai Murti Pranpratishtha Committee was appointed by the trust under the Chairmanship of Dhanu to chalk out the programme for the pranpratistha ceremony and function of Baba's Moorti and the inauguration of Baba's shrine on Vijayadashmi Day i.e. 19th October, 1999. A modest function was planned in view of lack of the infrastructure in Pathri and no formal invitations were printed and issued. The 5 1/2 ft. golden coloured moorti in bronze to be sculpted for which an order had been placed as far back as July, 1995 by Dhanu and Kher with Talim Art Studio, Mumbai, was in the studio, ready for being taken to its destination. The beautiful moorti was carefully loaded into a suitable motor vehicle amidst a small ceremony on 11th October 1999 at Talims Art Studio, and it commenced its journey amidst shouts of joy. The moorti was accompanied by an enthusiastic band of thirty-five Sai devotees in a bus. The carriage party halted for the night at Shirdi where it rained on reaching there, said to be an auspicious sign, and was warmly received by a crowd of Sai devotees. The journey to the destination was resumed on 12th October and when the carriage party arrived at Pathri the same night, it rained there too. A huge crowd waiting there took the carriage with fanfare and bursting of crackers to the site of the shrine after wending its way through the streets of Pathri. It took more than two hours for the procession to reach the site. Next day Sai Baba's moorti was lowered from the carriage and placed in position at the centre of the sanctum sanctorum and was covered with a white cloth.

The rites and ceremonies started on 18th October, 1999 and on 19th October, amidst Vedic Chants by priests, the pranpratishtha of Sai's Moorti was duly completed and was followed by the afternoon arati amidst waving of lights.

At last the long return journey of Sai to his <u>janmabhoomi</u> was complete after one hundred and fifty years!

Thereafter, K.V. Ramani declared the artistically designed and exquisitely executed shrine open by lighting a lamp and Smt. Lakshmi Ramani unveiled the beautiful life-like full-size oil painting of Baba by S.R. Badakere and portraits of Swami Sai Sharan Anand and Bulb Baba on either side. A sensitive and cultured couple who were present at the function observed later that it was an unique and extremely satisfying spiritual experience, the memories of which will always remain with them. They felt that they had come closer to Baba and sensed his presence not only in the temple but also in their home. Many others present also said that their participation in the Pathri temple inauguration was once in a life time opportunity and experience.

Sai's shrine at Pathri is open to all devotees and pilgrims irrespective of caste, creed, religion and sex. May this shrine become an abode of peace and eternal joy to the innumerable Sai devotees spread all over the world.

ANNEXURE — II

Particulars of Sai Baba Shrine, Pathri

Dimensions of the rectangular Temple - 50' x 36' plinth - 4' from the ground level.

Open type design - there are no walls over the parapet but it is adorned by grill so that Sai Baba's golden coloured moorti is visible even from the courtyard outside the temple.

Sabha Mandap - 32' 9" x 32' 9" with a passage of 4' around the sanctum sanctorum for circumambulation.

Marble flooring with patterns based on geometrical designs in different colours.

All columns and rear wall of Sabha Mandap are of pink marble with grains and arches linking the columns are in white marble.

The Sanctum Sanctorum is designed as a blooming lotus in octagonal shape with a suspended canopy in marble and at the centre thereof is the golden coloured moorti of Baba in bronze. The posterior wall of the sanctum sanctorum is built in granite of off-white colour.

A false ceiling is designed with P.O.P. treatment and a moulded border. Spot lighting is also provided over the moorti and the arches.

Halid lighting arrangement is provided in the sabha mandap producing a cool and pleasant effect like the moonshine.

Above the terrace level there is a spire of 36' in height with 2' golden kalash (pinnacle) at the top. The total height of the spire from the ground level is 55'.

In the basement a Dhyan Mandir (Meditation Hall) of 32' 9" x 35' 6" is built with marble flooring.

To give the devotees an idea of the old home, a part of the old foundation is preserved in its natural condition with old arches and connecting passages.

A life size oil painting of Sai Baba is put up with portraits of Swami Sai Sharan Anand and Bulb Baba on either side.

GLOSSARY

Abhang—a particular metrical composition in praise of the Deity in Marathi. Abhangs of Saint Tukaram are famous.

Abhishek—dropping drop by drop holy water, milk etc. over an idol by way of ceremonial ablution.

Agnihotra—the name of an obligatory rite enjoined on three higher caste Hindus.

Akshara—the Immutable

Amaavasya—the day of new moon

Amati—a semi-liquid dish of lentils.

Anaahat—centre or *chakra* for certain functions located at the heart level.

—*dhvani*—harmony of all the sounds in the universe, too profound to be heard by ordinary ears.

Arati—ceremony of waving of lights accompanied by ringing of bells, chanting. It may also be accompanied by sounding of gongs.

Ashrama—a place of spiritual retirement, a hermitage, a place for study and disciplining life.

Ashramas—there are four referable to four stages of life, namely, *brahmacharya* (celibate student), *grihastha* (married householder), *vanaprastha* (retired house holder devoted to intensifying spiritual life) and *sannyasa,* (renunciation of worldly life).

Aulia or avaliya—a holy personage, a sage or saint; one absorbed in contemplation or austere devotion.

Avatar—Lord's descent on earth or incarnation.

Bandobast—Government management of law and order. Fitly arranged or well-ordered condition; order.

Barfi—a sweetmeat—a square or cube of refined sugar baked with flour and clarified butter and dressed up with almond, pistachio etc.

Bhajan—devotional song.

Bhakri—unleavened bread made of any millet.

Bhakti—devotion.

Bharit—baked brinjals or plantains dressed with seasoning.

Bhiksha—alms; money or food given to a mendicant.

Brahman—pure undifferentiated Consciousness. The Supreme Spirit. Ultimate Reality.

Brahmin—the first or the highest of the four *varnas* among the Hindus. Literally, one who knows Brahman.

Chamar—emblem of eminence.

Chaprasi—peon in uniform.

Chatai—matting or a mat of bamboo, date, borassus etc.

Chavadi—village hall.

Chela—disciple.

Chowrie—emblem of eminence.

Dakshina—offerings to holy persons. Money or presents given to Brahmins or young virgins upon occasions.

Darsana—a Hindu philosophical system.

Darshan—sight; vision; the beneficial glow from being in the presence of the great.

Dasas or Dasakootas of Karnatak—a combination of saints (servants of God) of Karnatak.

Deshmukh—an hereditary officer, the head of a *paragana* (district).

Dharma—religion or duty. A comprehensive Sanskrit term embracing the precepts of law, justice, duty and virtue rolled into one.

Dharmashala—a rest house for travellers or pilgrims.

Dhol—large sort of drum.

Dhoti—a long piece of cloth used as a lower garment by men in India.

Dhuni—sacred fire.

Doha—a particular metrical composition in Hindi. Dohas of Saint Kabir are famous.

Durbar—a hall of audience; a levee room, fig. the people assembled.

Durgah—mausoleum of a Muslim saint.

Ekadashi—eleventh day of the waxing or the waning moon.

Fakir—a mohammedan mendicant; fig., person free from worldly encumbrances and cares.

Faujdar—a police official.

Galli—an alley or a lane.

Gandha—mark of sandal paste.

Ganga—the river Ganges, Sai Baba would refer to river Godavari as Ganga.

Gangajal—Ganges water.

Gayatri—a sacred verse from the Vedas, to be recited mentally.

Gayatri Purascharan—performance of recitation of Gayatri and other rites as prescribed by the Hindu scriptures.

Gerua—ochre-coloured.

Ghee—clarified butter.

Ghungaru—jingling bells.

Gopuram—spire.

Goshala—a cowhouse or cowpen.

Gunas—strands or qualities. There are three which may be predicated of all existing things and which intertwined are both the constituents and the changing condition of nature. They are: *sattva* (goodness/harmony/rhythm/light); *rajas* (passion/motion/action/fire) and *tamas* (darkness/inertia/sloth/ignorance).

Gurav—persons either Lingayat or of Gurav caste employed in the service of Shiva temples.

Guru—dispeller of darkness or ignorance. See *Sadguru*.

Haldi Kunkum—*haladi* is turmeric and *kunkum is a powder prepared from turmeric with lemon-juice, alum etc. Kunkum* mark is applied by Hindu married women on the forehead. These two articles are in constant use at the female toilette.

Halal—killing of sheep, fowl etc. according to the form prescribed by Mohammedan law.

Hundi—a bill of exchange.

Ishtadaivat—personal or chosen Deity.

Itihas—the epics and *puranas*.

Jahagir—an assignment by government of lands or revenues. It is military or personal for the maintenance of a body of troops, for the public service, or for the support of an individual or a family.

Japa—mental or oral repetition of mantra. It is midway between static concentration and meditation.

Jnani—the enlightened.

Kafni—a sort of cloak worn by classes of mendicants, covering the whole person but the head and forearms.

Kalpataru—a fabulous tree of Indra's heaven; a tree which yields whatever may be desired.

Karbhari—manager deputy, major domo, minister of state etc.

Karma—an act or deed; action, generally religious action as sacrifice; ablution etc. especially originating in the hope of future recompense and as opposed to speculative religion; also popularly used in the sense of fate accruing as a result of past actions.

Kazi—a Muslim judge who states the precepts of the Koran.

Keertan or **Kirtan**—celebrating the praises of a god with music and singing.

Keertankar or **Kirtankar**—one who performs keertan or kirtan.

Kheer—a dish composed of rice, coconut scrapings, milk, sugar and spices.

Khichri—a boiled mixture of rice and split pulse.

Kokila vrata—an observance among Hindu women throughout that intercalary month which occurs before Ashadha (August-September).

Kshara—the mutable.

Kulkarni—officer of a village under the Patil.

Kund—a pool, a spring of water consecrated to some holy purpose or person.

Lavani—a ballad or song of a particular kind aspecially sung by women.

Lendi—a lump or nodule of the dung (of sheep, goats, horses, camels etc.) A streamlet.

Lila or **Leela**—this universe of change, the manifestation of which can be called a play of God.

Mahasamadhi—the great *Samadhi*—see *Samadhi*.

Mahatma—the great soul.

Mahavakyas—the four great aphoristic dicta which reveal the Supreme Truth, namely, Ayam atma Brahma (Atharva Veda) i.e. Atma who is a *Sakshi* (witness) of your mind is the Brahman; *Tattwam asi* (Sama Veda) i.e. you are That; *Aham Brahmasmi* (Yajur Veda) i.e. I am not the body but the Atma i.e. the Brahman; *Prajnanam Brahma* (Rig Veda) literally, Brahman is pure consciousness. i.e. everything is Sat-Chit-Anand i.e., absolute existence, infinite consciousness and eternal bliss.

Makar—a sign of the Zodiac, viz. Capricorn.

Malang—a dervish of a particular order; it is believed by some that Brahmins who embraced Sufism are called Malang.

Malgujar—a system of land holding (zamindari) in the former C.P. & Berar Province of which Nagpur was the capital.

Mamledar or **Mamlatdar**—the officer in charge of taluka, a sub-division of a district. He is also called Tahasildar in some parts.

Manana—calling to mind and meditating upon the names and perfections.

Mandir—temple.

Manjarpat—a thick coarse cotton cloth originally manufactured in Madrepollam.

Mantra—a mystrical word or sentence; a formula sacred to a deity.

Math or **Mutt**—monastery.

Maya—illusion—the world being an illusion, because seen as something which it is not partly by veiling and partly by ascription. Also used in the sense of Prakriti.

Mogra—a species of Jessamine, Jasminum Zambac.

Moksha—liberation, salvation.

Murshid—guru, holy person.

Nama Smaran—remembrance of the name of the Lord.

Navachandi—a ceremony for propitiation of Devi.

Navaratri—festival during a space of nine days and nights included between the first and the ninth days of the moon of Ashwin (September-October).

Oti—the lap of a woman's sari. *Oti-bharane* is filling with fruits, flowers, rice etc. the lap of a married woman on festive occasion.

Padukas—impressions of the foot-prints in silver, gold, marble etc.

Panchabhautika—composed of the five elements.

Panda—priest at a pilgrimage place.

Panmala—a betel-leaf plantation.

Parayana—regular reading of a religious work to be finished in a prescribed number of days.

Parivrajaka—wanderer, title of a person on the first stage of the path.

Pathshala—a school or academy for the study of Sanskrit and Hindu scriptures.

Pedha—a sweetmeat composed of thickened or condensed milk and sugar.

Pindi—the *Lingam* symbolising Mahadeva.

Pipani—a wind instrument.

Poornima—the day of full moon.

Prakriti—the basic substance or principle of the entire phenomenal or manifest world; the power of Brahman which is the basis of all mind and matter.

Pranam—salutation.

Prasad—consecrated food.

Puja—worship.

Pujari—a priest who worships.

Purdah—veil.

Purusha—the spirit or Brahman when thought of as dwelling within a creature or object is called Atman or *Purusha*.

Punyatithi—death anniversary.

Rajas—see *Gunas*.

Ram Navami—the day of the birth of Ram.

Sabhamandap—a portico or an erection in front of a temple where people assemble.

Sadguru—True Guru or Master who has reached the state of an uninterrupted union with Truth (superconsciousness). *Samadhi* alone reveals the Truth. In *Samadhi* there is the feeling of 'I am' but no 'thoughts'. Sadguru can lead his disciple to the transcendental state of superconsciousness and monitor his progress on the path.

Sadhaka—seeker of the Spirit.

Sadhana—spiritual practice or discipline or endeavour.

Sadhu—a holy person.

Sahitya—materials, implements, tools, apparatus; the means generally (whether of matter or of instrument) required for the production, formation or performance of a thing or an act. The word is also used as meaning literature.

Sakhi—a particular metrical composition in Hindi. Sakhis of Saint Kabir are famous.

Samadhi—temporary or permanent state of spiritual superconsciousness achieved after contemplation (the fulfilment of meditation). The term is also used for the edifice erected over the burial place of a holy person.

Samsar—the cycle of birth and death; the mundane existence, the affairs of life.

Sandhya—repetition of *mantras*, sipping of water etc. to be performed by the first three classes of Hindus at particular periods, viz., sunrise, noon and sunset.

Sansthan or **Samsthan**—a town appointed for the residence and made over for the maintenance of a god, saint etc.

Sannyasa—renunciation of worldly life; the last or fourth stage of the Ashramas—see Ashramas.

Sannyasi—one who has taken *Sannyasa.*

Sastra—Hindu scripture.

Sattva—see *Gunas.*

Shahanai—a wind instrument.

Shira—a sweet dish made from samolina.

Shloka—stanza.

Shraaddha—a funeral ceremony consisting of offerings with water and fire to the gods and manes etc.

Shraddha—faith.

Shruti—Vedas. Knowledge of the Ultimate Reality which can be verified and is universal in character.

Siddhas—the liberated or self-realized soul.

Siddhis—yogic powers.

Smarak—memorial.

Smriti—social and religious code of conduct as delivered originally by Manu and other law-givers to their respective pupils and committed by them, from memory, to writing.

Sowcar—money-lender.

Streedhan—property altogether at the disposal of the wife.

Suttee—a chaste and virtuous wife. Applied especially to the wife who, on being widowed burns herself with the corpse of her deceased husband.

Swadhyaya—perusal of the Vedas or the religious text prescribed for a person.

Swami—a holy personage.

Swayambhu—the self-existent.

Takia—a fakir's stand.

Talati—the stipendiary accountant and registrar of a village.

Tamas—see *Gunas.*

Tamasha—a show, farce.

Tambul or **Vida**—roll of the leaf of Piper betel, with areca-nut, lime, cardamoms etc.

Tapas—religious austerity.

Tehsildar—see *Mamledar.*

Thali—large metal plate.

Tilak—a mark made with coloured earths or unguents upon the forehead; either as an ornament or as a sectarial distinction.

Tirtha—holy water.

Tonga—horse cart.

Tulsi Brindaban—the altar or square erection before the door of a Hindu's house in which the Tulsi is planted. Tulsi is a shrub venerated by the Hindus. Holy basil, Ocymum Sanctum.

Udi—holy ash.

Upasana—observing or keeping an ordinance, a rite, a mantra.

Urs—annual celebration observed at the shrine of a Mohammedan saint.

Vaid or Vaidya—practitioner of *ayurveda,* the ancient Hindu system of medicine.

Vida—see *Tambul.*

Vimana—a chariot of the gods, serving as a conveyance through the skies, self-directed and self-moving.

Wada—a stately or large edifice.

Walpapadi—a sort of bean.

Yade Haq—"I am a servant of God" as opposed to *"Anal Haq"* (I am God).

Yavana—a Mohammedan or an individual of a foreign race generally.

Zoli—a cloth gathered up at the corners.

BIBLIOGRAPHY

ENGLISH WORKS

Arberry A.J., *Sufism,* George, Allen & Unwin Ltd., London, 1963.

Bhagvad Gita, English translátion by Swami Prabhavananda & Christopher Isherwood, New American Library—Mentor Edn. 1954.

Bhagvad Gita, English translation by Juan Mascaro, Penguin Classics.

Cultural Heritage of India, Vol. II, Sri Ramakrishna Centenary Committee, Belur Math, Calcutta.

Das Ganu's *Shri Sainath Stavanmanjari,* English translation by Zarine Taraporevala, Sai Dhun Enterprises, Bombay, 1987.

History and Culture of the Indian People, Vol. VIII, Bharatiya Vidya Bhavan, Bombay.

Isherwood Christopher, *Ramakrishna,* Advaita Ashram, Calcutta, 1985.

Jnaneshvari, English translation by V.G. Pradhan, Introduction by H.M. Lambert, published by UNESCO, through George, Allen & Únwin Ltd, London, 1967.

Kabir's One Hundred Poems, English translation by Rabindra-nath Tagore, Macmillan Co. of India Ltd., 1972.

Kamath M.V., *Philosophy of Death and Dying,* International Himalayan Institute, New York, 1978.

Khaparde G.S., *Shirdi Diary,* Shri Sai Baba Sansthan, Shirdi.

Kher V.B.: Research Papers

— *A Search for the Birth Place of Shri Sai Baba,* Shri Sai Leela, January 1976.

— *The Guru of Shri Sai Baba* I & II, Shrí Sai Leela April & May 1976.

— *Shri Akkalkot Swami Maharaj and Shri Sai Baba,* Shri Sai Leela, July 1976.

— *The Miracle of the Mare* I & II Shri Sai Leela, March & April 1985.

— *How K.J. Bhishma composed 'Shri Sainath Sagunopasana',* Shri Sai Leela, September 1985.

— *The Significance of Shri Sa' Baba's Various Actions,* I & II Shri Sai Leea, October & November 1985.

— *Shri Sai Baba and His Devotee Khushalchand Seth of Rahata,* Shri Sai Leela, July 1987.

— *Sai Baba—The Nature of His functions and Powers,* Shri Sai Leela, August 1987.

— *The Fakir Whom Sai Baba Instructed for Twelve Years,* Shri Sai Leela, January 1990.

— *Sai Baba and Sufis,* Shri Sai Leela, February 1990.
— *Dincharya of Shri Sai Baba,* Shri Sai Leela, March 1990.

Kulkarni V.B., *Princely India and Lapse of British Paramountcy,* Jaico Publishing House, Bombay,1985.

Mahajan V.D., *Ancient India,* S. Chand & Co. (Pvt.) Ltd., New Delhi, VIIth Edn., 1974.

Mehra Parshotam, *A Dictionary of Modern Indian History 1707 — 1947,* Oxford University Press, Bombay.

Mirabai's Devotional Poems, English translation by A.J. Alston, Motilal Banarasidas, Delhi.

Mouni Sadhu, *In Days of Great Peace,* George, Allen & Unwin Ltd., London, 1957
— *Samadhi,* George, Allen & Unwin Ltd., London, 1962.
— *Meditation,* George, Allen & Unwin Ltd., London, 1967.

Narasimha Swami, B.V., *Devotees' Experiences of Shri Sai Baba,* Parts I to III, All India Sai Samaj, Madras, 3rd Edn. 1965-67.
— *Life of Sai Baba,* Vols I to IV, All India Sai Samaj, Madras 3rd Edn. 1980-1985.

— *Shri Sai Baba's Charters and Sayings,* All India Sai Samaj Madras, 1986.

Osborne Arthur, *The Incredible Sai Baba,* Orient Longman, 1973.

Pochhammer Wilhelm Von, *India's Road to Nationhood,* Allied Publishers Pvt. Ltd., New Delhi, 1981.

Pradhan M.W., *Shri Sai Baba of Shirdi,* Shirdi, 7th Edn., 1973.

Ramakrishna's Sayings, Sri Ramakrishna Math, Madras.

Ranade Mahadeo Govind, *Rise of the Maratha Power,* Publications Division, Ministry of Information & Broad casting, New Delhi, 1966.

Ranade R.D., *Pathway to God in Kannada Literature,* Bharatiya Vidya Bhavan, Bombay, 1960.

— *Pathway to God in Marathi* Literature, Bharatiya Vidya Bhavan, Bombay, 1961.

Sahukar Mani, *Sai Baba,* Somaiya Publications Pvt. Ltd., Bombay, 3rd Edn., 1983.

Sai Sharan Anand, Swami, *Shri Sai the Superman,* Shri Sai Baba Sansthan, Shirdi.

Sherwani H.K., Prof. & Dr. P.M. Joshi, *History of Medieval Deccan,* (1295-1724), Vol. I, Government of Andhra Pradesh, Hyderabad.

Shri Sai Leela, English Edition—Official Organ of Shri Sai Baba Sansthan of Shirdi.

Upanishads, English translation by Swami Prabhavananda & Frederick Manchester, Sri Ramakrishna Math, Madras, 2nd Edn., 1983.

MARATHI WORKS

Bhave Vinayak Laxman, *Maharashtra Saraswat* with *Purvani* by S.G. Tulpule, Popular Prakashan, Bombay, 5th Edn., 1963.

Dabholkar Govind Raghunath, *Shri Sai-Satcharita,* Shri Sai Baba Sansthan, Shirdi, 12th Edn., 1982.

Das Ganu Maharaj, *Arvachin Bhakta, Adhyaya* 31-33 *Va Sant Leelamrit, Adhyaya* 57, Shri Sai Baba Sansthan, Shirdi, 8th Edn., 1965.

Dhere Ramachandra Chintaman, *Datta Sampradayacha Itihas,* Nilkanth Prakashan, Pune.

Eknathi Bhagvat, Government of Maharashtra Publication, 1971.

Kher V.B.: *Research Papers*
— *Swami Sai Sharan Anand,* Navashakti dt. 13-6-1976.
— *Saibabanchya Darshanarth Lokamanya Tilak,* Navashakti dt. 30-7-1978.
— *Shri Saibabanche Shirdit Agaman,* Navashakti dt. 1-4-1979.
— *Saibabanchya Durbaras Kahi Namankit Vyaktinchi Bhet,* Prasad Special Sai Baba Issue, August 1979.
— *Shri Saibabache Swechha Niryan*—included in the Marathi translation of *Shri Sai Baba* of Swami Sai Sharan Anand, March, 1982.

Pendse Damodar Shankar, *Jnanadeva ani Namadev,* Continental Prakashan, Pune, 1969.

Sahasrabuddhe P.G., *Maharashtra Sanskriti,* Continental Prakashan, Pune, 1979.

Sai Sharan Anand's *Shri Sai Baba,* Marathi translation by V.B. Kher with six research papers, Dinapushpa Prakashan, Bombay, 1982.

Shri Sai Leela—The main source of information about Sai Baba is of course the monthly Marathi Magazine published by Shri Sai Baba Sansthan of Shirdi. The first issue was published in April 1923 and its first editor was Laxman Ganesh alias Kakasaheb Mahajani. Publication of this magazine was suspended from 1944 to 1947. From 1973 a separate edition of the magazine in English is being published. *Shri Sai-Satcharita* by G.R. Dabholkar was first serialised in this magazine and its publication was completed in 1929.

334

Tendulkar Raghunath and Savitri—*Sainath Bhajanmala*, 3rd Edn., 1954.

Zaver Ramesh, *Jnanadeva Srushti Padel Ka Drishti*, Loksatta dt. 11-11-1990.

GUJARATI WORKS

Mehta Amidas Bhavanidas, *Parabrahma Shri Sadguru Sainath Maharajani Janavajogi Vigato Temaj Chamatkaro*, Bombay, 1918.

Sai Sharan Anand, Swami, *Shri Sai Baba*, 6th Edn., 1966.
— *Shri Sai Leelakhyan*, 1962.
— *Sainathne Sharane*— ıblished posthumously in 1983.

HINDI WORKS

Ranade R.D., Paramartha Sopan, Adhyatma Vidya Mandir, Sangli 1954.

INDEX